# DICTIONARY
## *of* NAVAL
# TERMS

# DICTIONARY
## *of* NAVAL
## TERMS

**DEBORAH W. CUTLER**
**THOMAS J. CUTLER**

**NAVAL INSTITUTE PRESS**
**ANNAPOLIS, MARYLAND**

Naval Institute Press
291 Wood Road
Annapolis, MD 21402

Library of Congress Cataloging-in-Publication Data

Cutler, Deborah W., 1949–
  Dictionary of naval terms / Deborah W. Cutler, Thomas J. Cutler.— 6th ed.
      p. cm. — (Blue and gold professional library series)
  ISBN 1-59114-150-8 (alk. paper)
  1. Naval art and science—Terminology. 2. Navigation—Terminology. I. Cutler, Thomas J., 1947– II.
Title. III. Series.
  V23.C88 2005
  359'.003—dc22

                                                                          2004023835


Printed in the United States of America on acid-free paper ∞
12 11 10 09 08 07 06 05    9 8 7 6 5 4 3 2
First printing

# CONTENTS

In loving memory of Dr. Hugh Welch
Who was always telling me,
"Look it up in the dictionary."

# PREFACE

Every profession has its own argot, a virtual other language by which its practitioners communicate among themselves. One need only watch a medical drama on television to know that doctors and nurses speak in tongues that only they can decipher, and anyone who has ever been to court knows that "legalese" is a language only slightly more understandable than Mandarin Chinese. Despite the frustrations these other languages may cause outsiders, they serve a very useful purpose in allowing professionals to streamline their communications by conveying complex meanings in "shorthand" terminology. They are also a point of pride within their respective professions; few things give a neophyte a sense of belonging more than being able to use the newly acquired language in conversation with more seasoned members or to show off to the uninitiated by speaking the language of the initiated.

Sailors are no different. They use words and phrases like *amidships* and *over the horizon targeting* to communicate concepts important to their profession and to set themselves apart from civilians and other life forms. Some of the terms in the Navy argot are unique to the profession, like *forecastle* and *scuttlebutt*, but others are more common words that also have alternative meanings to Sailors, such as *dead horse* and *tin can*. Some are terms inherited from the Royal Navy, forerunner in many ways to the U.S. Navy, while others are the result of new technologies or are modifications of older words given new meanings in changing times.

This book (and its companion volume, the *Dictionary of Naval Abbreviations*) is written for those newcomers who want—indeed *need*—to be able to understand the language of the naval profession. It is also written for *outsiders* (journalists writing stories about the Navy, Congressional staffers whose principals serve on naval related subcommittees, academics studying naval history, and the like). And, because the Navy has grown so large and so complex, this book is written even for seasoned veterans of the naval profession who, like fluent translators of foreign languages, must still occasionally look up a word.

A certain logic has been employed in the preparation of this book, based on the interests of space and of trying not to insult our readers by stating the obvious. For example, if we use a term in a definition that may be unfamiliar, such as defining *ratline* as "three-strand, tarred hemp used for snaking," we have *not* included "See also snaking." While "snaking" is defined elsewhere in the book, if readers already know what snaking is, there is no need for us to tell them to look up the term; if they do not know what snaking is, they can look it up without being directed to do so. Relevant cross-references that are not intuitively obvious *are* included, however.

Unofficial and slang terms are an important part of the naval vocabulary, so many have been included. Readers who do not know that *ketchup* is a term sometimes used to identify *red lead paint* will be so informed within these pages. Such terms are identified by the qualifier *Inf:* to mark them as "informal." Some of these terms can be rather colorful and readers are warned in advance that if these terms were movies, some would surely receive a "PG" or "R" rating.

Because users of this book may come across old terms as well as new, this revision includes both historic and current terminology. But because terms often come and go, because changes within today's Navy are frequent, and because there is great overlap in the terms used by an organization that is so conscious of its heritage, it is beyond the scope of this work to determine whether a term is still in use or merely once was. It is hoped that such matters will be discernible in context.

Earlier reference was made to the companion book *Dictionary of Naval Abbreviations*. While the *Dictionary of Naval Terms* stands alone as a useful reference tool in "cracking the code" of Navy argot, serious users will do well to avail themselves of (translated *purchase*) the DICNAVAB as well (especially if they don't know what this acronym stands for).

Because the U.S. Navy does so many things, readers will find many subjects treated within these pages (oceanography, logistics, navigation, electronics, strategy, thermodynamics, ballistics, history, naval customs, etc.). We could easily have written a book twice the length of this one on navigational terms alone, but have attempted to cull only the more important terms for this work so that it will serve as a ready reference rather than a ponderous tome good merely for very meticulous researchers and those people in need of a reliable doorstop. This is, of course, a very subjective process and a giant task. No doubt we have failed on occasion, and some readers will discover that we have omitted a term that is important or will find some that might well have been left out in the interests of space. We herewith submit our apologies in advance, but more importantly, we encourage readers to help us make this a better book by sending us their nominations for inclusion in the next edition and suggestions for improvements. Contact *tcutler@usni.org* or *Deborah Cutler, c/o of USNI Dictionaries, 291 Wood Road, Annapolis, MD 21402.*

# DICTIONARY
## *of* NAVAL
## TERMS

# A

**a-** • Preceding certain adjectives and verbs to indicate a condition. Sometimes a hyphen is used, but more often it is dropped by convention. For example: aback, awash, aweigh, etc.

**abaca** • The wild banana plant of the Philippines from which Manila line is made.

**aback** • The wind is on the wrong side of the sail(s), tending to drive the ship astern instead of forward. A square-rigged sailing vessel may be taken aback by an unexpected shift of wind or poor steering.

**abaft** • To the rear of. Closer to the stern. Used instead of "aft of." For example, the mizzen mast can be described as "abaft" the main mast because it is closer to the stern.

**abaft the beam** • A direction between either beam and the stern.

**abandon ship** • To leave the ship in an emergency, such as sinking. Traditionally, ordered by the senior surviving officer.

**abeam** • In approximately the same horizontal plane of the observing ship or aircraft, bearing 90° away from its heading or course. For example, if the wind is abeam, it is coming in directly over the side of the ship.

**able** • Past phonetic word for the letter A; replaced with alfa.

**able seaman** • Merchant and civil service marine rating above an ordinary seaman. Also known as able-bodied seaman, from which the colloquial term AB is derived.

**aboard** • 1. In or upon a ship. 2. On or at any naval activity, such as a naval station. *See also:* close aboard

**abort** • To abandon or quit a mission.

**about** • Significant change of direction of a vessel. Often used with "come." For example, a sailing vessel will come about to change tacks.

**abrasion** • Wearing away of a surface by friction, either by motion while in contact with another part or by mechanical cleaning or resurfacing with abrasive cloth or compound.

**abreast** • By the side of; side by side. *See also:* abeam

**absence indicator** • Pennant flown by a ship to indicate the absence of the commanding officer or embarked flag or staff officer. Also called *absentee pennant. See also:* absentee

**absentee** • Person missing at a muster. Shortened version of absentee pennant.

**absent without leave (AWOL)** • Absent from place of duty without authorization.

**accelerometer** • An instrument used to measure changes in velocity.

**accepting authority** • The officer designated to accept a ship for the government.

**accommodation ladder** • Portable steps from a ship's gangway down to the waterline or a pier alongside; rigged from a davit or crane onboard. Sometimes incorrectly referred to as the gangway. *See also:* bail

**accountability** • The responsibility and obligation imposed by law on military personnel; may apply to equipment (such as being accountable for the safety of a ship) or for actions (such as being accountable for making an attack).

**ace** • Pilot who has shot down five or more enemy aircraft.

**Ace High** • Tropospheric forward-scatter communications system.

**acey-deucy** • Nautical version of the game backgammon. Played on the same board and with the same pieces.

**acknowledge** • Used in communications to notify originator that a message has been received.

**acoustic data analysis center (ADAC)** • Computerized library of data on underwater sound characteristics maintained at the Naval Research and Development Center.

**acoustic mine** • Mine that is detonated by a sound influence, such as that of a ship's propellers.

**acoustic scattering** • Dispersion of sound waves caused by irregular reflection, refraction, etc.

**acoustic torpedo** • Torpedo guided by sound. Active versions emit sounds and home in on their echoes; passive types home in on sound emanations of the target. *See also:* active acoustic torpedo; torpedo

**action addressee** • Addressee on a naval message who is expected to carry out a task. *See also:* addressee; information addressee

**action port (starboard)** • Command to gun and/or missile crews to indicate direction of enemy attack.

**action report** • Detailed report of combat.

**active acoustic torpedo** • Torpedo that emits sound waves and homes in on the sound reflected from a target. *See also:* acoustic torpedo

**active duty** • Full-time service, as distinct from inactive, retired, or reserve duty.

**active sonar** • Equipment that provides information on distant underwater objectives by evaluation of the reflections of its own sound emissions. *See also:* passive sonar

**active USW** • A method of undersea warfare that determines the location and distance of a submarine by measuring the time interval between the transmission of a sound signal and its reflection back to the source.

**activity** • Organizational unit of the Navy established under an officer-in-charge or a commanding officer. Not used in reference to ships or their crews.

**actual track** • The track line actually followed when proceeding from one fixed point on the Earth's surface to another.

**adapter** • Coupling or similar device that permits joining non-matching fittings or those of different size. *See also:* reducer

**addressee** • Activity or individual to whom a naval message is directed for action or information. *See also:* action addressee; information addressee

**adiabatic phenomena** • Changes in material state (volume or pressure) occurring without a gain or loss of heat. Air conditioners work on this principle. [Note: Temperature may change, but total heat contained will not.]

**admeasure** • To measure or ascertain dimensions, size, or capacity of a ship, cask, or similar vessel. The admeasure of a ship is the formal establishment of dimensions upon completion of construction. For merchant ships, the U.S. Coast Guard appoints an admeasurer, whose results constitute the official data upon which fees and licenses are based. In England, Lloyds of London makes the official admeasurements.

**administration** • The management of all phases of naval operations not directly concerned with strategy or tactics.

**administrative board** • A board appointed to render findings based on facts pertaining, or believed to pertain, to a case; to recommend retention in service, separation from service, or suspension of separation.

**administrative command (ADCOM)** • Command without operational function; concerned only with logistics, maintenance, etc.

**administrative control** • Control exercised by a commander whose responsibilities extend to such things as logistics, repair, training, etc., but does not include operational control.

**administrative lead time** • Interval between the start of a procurement action and the actual contracting or ordering.

**administrative separation** • A discharge or release from active duty for administrative reasons, not as a result of a court martial.

**admiral** • The highest ranking officers in the Navy; equivalent to "general" in the Army, Air Force, and Marine Corps. Admirals are also referred to as "flag officers." The current rank structure in the Navy uses "Admiral" without any prefix as the highest rank, "Vice Admiral" as the second highest rank, then Rear Admiral (Upper Half) and Rear Admiral (Lower Half). In the past, "Commodore" and "Commodore Admiral" were used instead of the upper- and lower-half designations. During World War II and in the aftermath, four admirals were promoted to "Fleet Admiral," but it is unlikely that this rank will ever be used again. See also: commodore; flag officer; fleet admiral; rear admiral; vice admiral

**Admiral's March** • Ceremonial music for flag officers and officials of equivalent ranks. The number of ruffles and flourishes preceding this ceremonial tune equals the number of stars authorized for the individual honored.

**admiralty law** • Laws that deal with maritime cases: ships, collisions, etc.

**adrift** • A vessel is said to be adrift when not made fast to a pier, wharf, or the bottom. A Sailor is said to have "gear adrift" if his or her belongings are not where they are supposed to be.

**advance** • 1. Distance gained in the direction of the original course when turning a ship; measured from the point at which the rudder is put over to the point where the ship has steadied on a new heading (to a maximum of 90°). 2. Term used in connection with enlisted promotion; i.e., to be advanced in rate or rank. See also: advancement in rate; transfer

**advanced encryption standard** • Replaced the data encryption standard as the most popular algorithm for encryption.

**advanced gun system (AGS)** • A developing concept that will satisfy requirements for range, accuracy, lethality, and sustained fire. A part of the DD(X) system, it will satisfy USMC requirements for NSFS and is consistent with Army requirements for precision engagement and dominant maneuver warfare. Its attributes include increased volume of fires for forces ashore, greatly increased range and improved lethality, unmanned magazines, and increased sustainability.

**advanced medium-range air-to-air missile (AMRAAM)** • The AIM-120 Advanced Medium-Range, Air-to-Air missile is an all-weather missile with beyond-visual-range capability. In addition to providing an air-to-air capability, AMRAAM also provides air defense support. Serves as a follow-on to the AIM-7 Sparrow missile series. Incorporates active radar in conjunction with an inertial reference unit and microcomputer system, which makes the missile less dependent upon the fire-control system of the aircraft. Once the missile closes in on the target, its active radar guides it to intercept, which enables the pilot to aim and fire several missiles simultaneously at multiple targets and perform evasive maneuvers while the missiles guide themselves to the targets.

**advancement in rate** • Promotion of an enlisted service member to a higher rate.

**advection fog** • Fog formed when warm air passes over cold water.

**Aegis** • A highly automated shipboard combat system that uses specialized computers to integrate various sensors and weapons, enabling the ship to engage multiple aircraft and missile targets simultaneously.

**Aeolus** • Small meteorological sounding rocket.

**aerial mine** • A mine delivered by aircraft. *See also:* mine

**aerodynamics** • The science that deals with the motion of air and the effects of it on bodies in motion within the atmosphere.

**aerographer** • One who works with weather forecasting and related duties. Navy rating is aerographer's mate. Warrant officer advanced from aerographer's mate, whose duties involve weather forecasting.

**aerographer's mate (AG)** • Navy occupational rating trained in meteorology and the use of aerological instruments to monitor such weather characteristics as air pressure, temperature, humidity, wind speed, and wind direction; prepares weather maps and forecasts, analizes atmospheric conditions to determine the best flight levels for aircraft, and measures wind and air density to increase the accuracy of antiaircraft firing, shore bombardment, and delivery of weapons by aircraft.

**aerojet** • *See:* pulse-jet

**affirmative** • Communications term meaning "yes." Conversational term used to mean "yes."

**afloat** • Supported by the water; on the surface. At sea, as in forces afloat.

**aft** • Pertaining to the stern, or toward the stern, of a ship or aircraft. For example, "Move the aircraft further aft to add weight to the stern." According to nautical and naval usage, "aft" is an adverb (let us go aft) and "after" is an adjective (the after cabin). Common usage sometimes permits the use of aft as an adjective as well.

**after** • Meaning further aft, or toward the stern. For example, "the after magazine is closer to the fantail than is the forward one." According to nautical and naval usage, "aft" is an adverb (let us go aft) and "after" is an adjective (the after cabin).

**after body** • 1. That portion of a ship's body aft of the midship section. 2. A detachable portion of a torpedo containing the propulsive and guidance systems, located abaft the energy storage compartment.

**after bow spring** • Mooring line leading aft at an angle from the bow of a ship to the pier alongside; prevents forward motion of the ship. *See also:* spring lines; forward bow spring; after quarter spring; after bow spring

**afterburner** • Part of a jet engine into which fuel is injected and ignited by exhaust to increase thrust for brief periods of time.

**after engine turnup** • That time in the prior-to-launch phase when the pilot has completed his pretaxi checklist.

**aftermost** • Nearest the stern; said of an object or compartment that is on or in a ship.

**afternoon effect** • Thermal gradient caused by the sun's warming of the sea's surface. The effect can cause a reduction in sonar effectiveness.

**afternoon watch** • The watch from 1200–1600 (noon–4 P.M.).

**after quarter spring** • Mooring line leading aft at an angle from the after part of a ship (quarter) to the pier alongside; prevents the ship from moving forward along the pier. *See also:* spring lines; forward quarter spring; after bow spring; forward bow spring

**after truck** • The highest part of the aftermast.

**A-gang** • Auxiliaries division of the engineering department. These Sailors operate and maintain the ship's auxiliary equipment (air conditioning systems, distilling units, air compressors, etc.).

**AGM-65** • *See:* Maverick

**AGM-84** • *See:* Harpoon

**AGM-88** • *See:* HARM missile

**AGM-114** • *See:* Hellfire

**AGM-119** • *See:* Penguin

**agonic line** • A line on a chart that has no magnetic variation; *i.e.,* on which true north is the same as magnetic north.

**aground** • A vessel whose bottom is touching solid ground; not afloat. A condition to be avoided, with some exceptions, *e.g.,* as when a landing craft deliberately goes aground to offload troops and/or supplies.

**ahead** • In front of; forward of the bow.

**ahead-thrown weapon** • Missile projected out ahead of an ASW ship against a submerged submarine, propelled by rocket power or fired from a launcher.

**ahoy** • A distinctly nautical hail to attract attention. Said to once have been the dreaded war cry of the Vikings.

**aide** • Officer assigned as administrative or personal assistant to a flag officer or senior civilian official. Naval aides often wear aiguillettes.

**aids to navigation** • Buoys, markers, lights, bells, fog horns, radio, loran stations, or any similar device to assist navigators.

**aiguillette** • The badge of office of a personal aide to a high-ranking officer or civil official. The aides to the President of the United States wear their aiguillettes on the right shoulder, while aides to all other senior officers and dignitaries wear them on the left shoulder. Dress aiguillettes are extremely ornate, braided loops terminating in two devices which, because of their appearance, are often called pencils. Service aiguillettes are merely simple loops pinned over the shoulder. They distinguish the rank of the officer aides; *e.g.,* four loops for officers of four-star rank and above, three loops for a three-star (vice) admiral, etc. Presidential aides wear aiguillettes of solid gold. Aides to other officers wear blue and gold braid if Navy, red and gold if Marine Corps or Army. One theory of the origin of aiguillettes is that the aide-de-camp of a superior officer carried the rope and pegs for tethering his superiors horse, generally carrying them around his shoulder for convenience. *Inf:* loafers loops; chicken guts.

**aileron** • Movable control surface of an aircraft wing, used to impart rolling motion to the aircraft.

**AIM-9** • *See:* Sidewinder

**AIM-54** • *See:* Phoenix

**AIM-120** • *See:* Advanced Medium-Range, Air-to-Air Missile (AMRAAM)

***Air Almanac*** • A periodical publication of astronomical data, designed primarily for air navigation but often used by surface navigators as well.

**air and naval gunfire liaison company (ANGLICO)** • An organization of Marine Corps and Navy personnel specially qualified for shore control of naval gunfire and close air support.

**air bedding** • An order aboard ship to bring

bedding topside for exposure to the sun and fresh air. The word "air" is used as a verb.

**airborne early warning (AEW)** • The extension of radar detection range by means of airborne search radar and relay equipment to provide early warning.

**airborne stores** • Items intended for carriage internally or externally by aircraft, including racks, launchers, adapters, and detachable pylons. These are items not normally separated from the aircraft in flight, such as tanks, pods, guns, and targets.

**airborne weapon** • All missiles, rockets, bombs, mines, torpedoes, and all similar items intended for carriage by aircraft that are normally separated from the aircraft in flight.

**air boss** • *Inf:* The air officer aboard a carrier who directs aircraft launch and recovery. Informal term for his assistant is mini boss.

**air bunting** • An order to hoist signal flags for drying. "Air" is used as a verb.

**airburst** • A nuclear explosion sufficiently high in the air that the fireball does not significantly interact with the ground or water. This type of burst does not cause significant fallout.

**air capable ship** • All ships from which aircraft can take off, be recovered, or routinely receive and transfer logistic support.

**air cock** • Valve placed at the highest point of engineering equipment, such as boilers, to release trapped air.

**air controller** • One who directs aircraft by radar, radio, electronic pilot, etc. *See also:* air traffic controller

**air-control ship** • A ship assigned responsibility for controlling aircraft in air defense.

**aircraft armament system** • Aircraft arma-ment subsystem that, when interconnected, gives the aircaft its airborne weapons/stores capability.

**aircraft carrier** • Major offensive ship of the fleet, having a flight deck capable of launching and recovering aircraft. Its chief weapon is its aircraft.

**aircraft configuration** • The system and components required to carry or deliver a specific airborne weapon/store.

**aircraft division** • Two sections of aircraft of same type.

**aircraft load plan-A** • A chart used to assign weapons to a particular bomb rack or station for loading.

**aircraft maintenance delayed for parts (AMDP)** • Code to indicate why an aircraft is not operational (due to parts being unavailable).

**aircraft monitor and control** • Functional tests of the aircraft monitor and control system, release system, and jettison system for nuclear weapons.

**aircraft not fully equipped** • Code used to indicate that restrictions are placed on aircraft for lack of equipment.

**aircraft out-of-commission for parts (AOCP)** • Code used to indicate why aircraft is not operational. Implies a longer delay than a delay for parts.

**aircraft squadron** • An administrative grouping of aircraft, usually of same or similar type. Several squadrons can be organized into an air wing.

**aircrew survival equipmentman (PR)** • Navy occupational rating that services vital survival equipment. PRs pack and care for parachutes as well as service, maintain, and repair flight clothing, rubber life-rafts, life-jackets, oxygen-breathing equipment, protective clothing, and air-sea rescue equipment.

**airdale** • *Inf:* Naval aviation personnel. *See also:* brown shoe

**air defense identification zone (ADIZ)** • Airspace above specified area in which ready recognition and control of aircraft are required.

**air defense warning conditions** • Degree of air raid probability: air defense warning red, attack is imminent or taking place; air defense warning yellow, attack probable; air defense warning white, attack is improbable.

**air ejector** • In the steam cycle, a device that uses the suction created by steam flowing through a nozzle to remove air and other noncondensable gases from a condenser or other part of the return-feed system. The purpose is to enable the condenser to maintain a better vacuum thus promoting efficiency of the steam cycle, and to reduce corrosion by reducing oxygen content.

**airfoil** • Surface designed to produce lift from the air through which it passes. Wings and helicopter blades are examples of airfoils.

**airframe** • The structural parts of an airplane that define and influence its shape, strength, and some of its capabilities.

**air group** • In the days of escort or antisubmarine warfare aircraft carriers, the embarked aircraft were organized into an air group. The more numerous aircraft of today's attack carriers are organized into an air wing.

**air intelligence** • Activity formerly known as air combat intelligence. Deals with intelligence aspects of naval air operations.

**air lock** • A double door giving access to and preserving air pressure in a fireroom or similar space under pressure.

**airman (AN)** • 1. An enlisted person in pay-grade E–3 who performs aviation duties. 2. Generic term referring to aviation personnel.

**air officer** • Officer responsible for aviation matters in an aircraft carrier. Heads the air department. *Inf:* Air boss.

**air operations** • The section of the operations department on an aviation-capable ship that is responsible for coordinating all matters pertaining to flight operations.

**air port** • A round window in a ship's side, fitted with a lens frame and a metal cover called a "battle port." Air scoops, screens, and ventilating deadlights are an air port's removable fixtures. Commonly called porthole. *See also:* port; deadlight

**air register** • A device in the casing of a boiler for regulating the amount of air for combustion.

**air scoop** • A device fitted into an air port for catching a breeze.

**air search attack team** • Tactical designation given one or more antisubmarine warfare craft.

**airspeed** • Speed of aircraft through, and relative to, the air; distinct from groundspeed. Indicated airspeed is an uncorrected reading of the airspeed indicator. Calibrated airspeed is the indicated airspeed corrected for instrument errors. True airspeed is corrected for altitude and temperature.

**air support** • *See:* close air support

**air surface zone** • Restricted ocean area for antisubmarine operations.

**Air Systems Command** • Functional command replacing Bureau of Naval Weapons in 1966 Navy Department reorganization. A component of the Naval Material Command.

**air taxi** • Jetborne or hovering flight at very low speed between two points.

**air-to-air weapon** • Carried by naval aircraft

to shoot down enemy aircraft. *See also:* Sparrow; Sidewinder; Phoenix

**air-to-ground weapon** • A weapon fired or launched from an aircraft toward a land target.

**air traffic controller (AC)** • Navy occupational rating that assists in the essential safe, orderly, and speedy flow of air traffic by directing and controlling aircraft under visual (VFR) and instrument (IFR) flight rules; operates field lighting systems, communicates with aircraft, and furnishes pilots with information regarding traffic, navigation, and weather conditions; operates and adjusts ground-controlled approach (GCA) systems; interprets targets on radar screens and plots aircraft positions.

**air transportable sonar** • Sonar equipment designed for aircraft use.

**air transport group** • A task organization of transport aircraft units organized to transport amphibious troops to the objective area, or for logistic support.

**air wing** • The aircraft of an attack aircraft carrier, made up of squadrons. The typical air wing aboard a U.S. Navy aircraft carrier usually contains three FA-18 squadrons, one F-14 squadron, one S-3 squadron, one EA-6B squadron, one E-2C squadron, and one helicopter squadron. *See also:* air group

**Aldis lamp** • A hand-held signal light used in ships and aircraft.

**alee** • In the direction toward which the wind is blowing; downwind.

**alert, dawn or dusk** • Special precautions, normally all hands to battle stations, at time when attack is most likely—prior to first light and at sunset.

**alfa** • Phonetic word for the letter A. Note that the spelling is with an "f" rather than a "ph"; this is to make it compatible with allied foreign navy usage.

**alidade** • A bearing circle aboard ship with a telecopic sight for taking bearings. Usually fitted over a pelorus or gyro compass repeater. A device frequently used by shipboard navigation personnel to sight objects and read either relative azimuth bearing or true azimuth bearing.

**align** • Electronics: to adjust two or more resonant circuits. Gunnery: to adjust guns and their associated fire-control equipment to the same plane of reference, and to line up all aiming devices and bearing transmitters.

**alive** • Alert, as in "look alive!"

**all fast** • Tied or lashed down as necessary.

*All Hands* • A monthly publication about life in the Navy, produced by the Navy, for free distribution to naval personnel.

**all hands** • 1. All personnel aboard ship. 2. Name of a call on a boatswain's pipe; meant to get the attention of the entire crew.

**all hands parade** • A designated assembly place for all hands on board ship. Used for such events as a change-of-command ceremony.

**all night in** • A full night's sleep with no watch.

**allotment** • A portion of an individual's pay, or of an appropriation or fund, regularly assigned to a specified account.

**allowance** • Number of personnel authorized on a peacetime level, reduced from the wartime complement and based on peacetime operations and budgetary considerations. *See also:* complement; manning level

**allowance list** • A listing pf repair parts, equipage, and consumable supplies authorized and required to be on board a ship or in a naval activity.

**allowance parts list (APL)** • A specialized

listing of repair parts required for units having specific equipments/components.

**all-weather air station** • Designated air station to which single-pilot aircraft may be cleared under instrument flight rules (IFR).

**aloft** • Above the decks, on the mast, or in the rigging.

**alongside** • At the side of a ship, pier, or dock; in a parallel position.

**alpha** • *See:* alfa

**altars** • Steps in the side of a graving dock (drydock), extending virtually all the way around the dock. Used to support shores.

**alternating light** • Navigational light showing color or on-off variations. May be flashing, group flashing, occulting, or fixed.

**altimeter** • An instrument that measures in feet, yards, or meters an aircraft's elevation above a given reference plane, such as sea level.

**altitude** • The height of an aircraft above a reference point. True altitude is height above sea level. Absolute altitude is height above ground.

**altocumulus** • A cloud layer (or patches) within the middle level (mean height 6,500–20,000 feet), composed of rather flattened globular masses.

**altostratus** • A sheet of gray or bluish clouds within the middle level (mean height 6,500–20,000 feet).

**ambient** • Surrounding; adjacent to; next to. For example: ambient conditions are physical conditions of the immediate area, such as ambient temperature, ambient humidity, ambient pressure, etc. *See also:* ambient noise.

**ambient noise** • Sound produced in water by sources external to the measuring equipment.

**American Wire Gauge (AWG)** • The standards adopted in the United States for the measurement of wire sizes.

**amidships** • In or toward the middle of a ship as measured fore and aft. Approximately midway between the bow and stern of a vessel. "Rudder amidships" means that the rudder is in line with the ship's centerline.

**ammeter** • Electrical instrument for measuring the flow of current.

**ammo** • *Inf:* Ammunition.

**ammunition ship (AE)** • Logistical vessel whose primary mission is to deliver ammunition to combatants at sea.

**amphibious** • Capable of operating on both land and sea.

**amphibious assault ship (LPH)** • Ship designed to transport and land troops, equipment, and supplies by helicopters.

**amphibious construction battalion (ACB)** • Naval unit organized to provide and operate ship-to-shore fuel systems, construct pontoon causeways, transfer barges and tugs, and to provide salvage and beach improvement capability to a naval beach group.

**amphibious control group** • Personnel, ships, and aircraft designated to control the water-borne ship-to-shore movement in an amphibious operation.

**amphibious force** • Naval force with embarked landing forces that together are trained, organized, and equipped for amphibious operations.

**amphibious lift** • *See:* lift; lift, amphibious

**amphibious operation** • A naval operation in which ships (and possibly aircraft) are used to place an embarked landing force ashore.

**amphibious squadron** • Organization of amphibious assault ships used to transport troops and equipment for an amphibious assault.

**anchor** • Noun: A device used to hold a vessel fast to the bottom, but still afloat. Verb: To make a vessel fast to the bottom by dropping a tethered hook or weight designed for that purpose.

**anchor's aweigh** • Expression used to report that an anchor has just been lifted clear of bottom. The ship now bears the weight of her anchor and is considered to be under way, although not necessarily with way on.

**anchorage** • A place assigned for anchoring vessels.

**anchor at short stay** • Anchor chain at minimum length with anchor still holding.

**anchor ball** • A black, circular shape hoisted to indicate that the ship is anchored.

**anchor buoy** • A small float secured to the anchor by a light line to mark the position of the anchor.

**anchor cable** • Wire, line, or chain running between an anchor and a vessel. Used to tether the vessel when the anchor is in use (on the bottom) and to recover the anchor when the vessel is ready to get under way.

**anchor chain** • Heavy-linked chain that connects an anchor to its vessel. Used to tether the vessel when the anchor is in use (on the bottom) and to recover the anchor when the vessel is ready to get under way.

**anchor detail** • Crewmembers on forecastle assigned to handle the ground tackle.

**anchored** • Made fast to the bottom by an anchor.

**anchor engine** • The driving mechanism for the anchor windlass or its associated cap-stan; normally used to raise the anchor from the bottom; can also be used for a controlled descent of the anchor (vice merely dropping) when circumstances require. Can be located on or below deck in different configurations.

**anchor hawk** • A multipronged device used at the end of an anchor. Larger than a grapnel.

**anchor ice** • Ice that is attached to the sea bottom.

**anchor in sight** • A report made by the anchor detail on the forecastle to the bridge when the anchor itself has been sighted. Followed by "foul anchor" or "clear anchor," depending on whether the anchor has been fouled by debris from the bottom or is clear for hoisting to the housed position.

**anchor is clear** • When the anchor is first clear of the water and there is nothing fouling it or on it.

**anchor is fouled** • The anchor has picked up a cable, debris, rock or coral, or is wrapped in its own chain.

**anchor is shod** • The anchor is covered with mud or bottom.

**anchor lights** • Lights required by Rules of the Road indicating that a vessel is anchored. Also called riding lights. *See also:* riding lights

**anchor man/anchor woman** • Last person of a list or a group. For example, at the Naval Academy, the anchor man (woman) in a class is the last in academic standing and consequently ranks junior to all classmates.

**anchor pool** • A traditional, but unofficial, shipboard lottery in which people buy tickets that show a specific of anchoring time.

**anchor watch** • Crewmember assigned to keep an eye on the anchor chain when the anchor is on the bottom, to watch for signs that the anchor is dragging.

**anemometer** • Instrument for measuring wind speed and/or direction.

**aneroid** • Without fluid or without water. An aneroid barometer uses no fluid.

**angels** • Thousands of feet of aircraft altitude. Cherubs are hundreds.

**angled deck** • The area of an aircraft carrier flight deck that is at an angle to the center line of the ship. This provides separate areas on the flight deck for parking or moving aircraft while others are simultaneously landing or taking off. Much more efficient and far safer than older straight-deck carriers because it allows aircraft to get airborne again after missing the arresting wires rather than crashing into a barrier.

**angle of attack** • The angle at which a body, such as an airfoil or fuselage, meets a flow of air.

**angle on the bow** • Submariner term equivalent to target angle in the surface Navy. Angle between the fore and aft axis of a target and the line of sight, measured from the target's bow to port or starboard through 180°. Estimated angle on the bow is one of the critical observations made through a submarine periscope during an approach to a torpedo firing position.

**annual variation** • A change in Earth's magnetic lines of force, varying in different localities.

**annunciator** • 1. Signal device on a ship's bridge for delivering orders to the engine room. 2. An alerting device used to alert personnel that target designations are pending. *See also:* engine-order telegraph

**anode** • The positively charged electrode of an electrolytic cell.

**anomalous** • Irregular or abnormal.

**antiblackout suit** • Pilot's suit which, when inflated, helps a pilot resist centrifugal force. Also called G-suit and pressure suit.

**anticorrosive paint** • Paint that resists rusting; often applied to hull surfaces.

**anticyclonic** • Any rotational motion in a clockwise manner in the Northern Hemisphere, or a counterclockwise manner in the Southern Hemisphere.

**antifouling paint** • A composition applied over the anticorrosive paint on a ship's bottom to prevent attachment of marine growth.

**anti-icing** • The prevention of ice formation upon an aircraft's surface or engines.

**antirecovery device** • Device incorporated into a mine that causes it to explode if disturbed.

**Antisubmarine Detection Investigation Committee (ASDIC)** • The name of the committee which originally pioneered underwater sound ranging in Britain. As a result, ASDIC became the early name of the British equivalent of sonar.

**antisubmarine warfare (ASW)** • All-inclusive term embracing all techniques used against enemy submarines.

**antisubmarine warfare (ASW) screen** • Formation of ships and aircraft in advance of a Navy force, designed to protect against submarine attack.

**anti-terrorism/force protection** • Refers to measures to enhance unit and personnel security through threat indoctrination, awareness training, and physical security measures.

**antitransmit-receive tube** • A tube that isolates the transmitter from the antenna and receiver.

**Anymouse** • *Inf:* Anonymous. The air safety

magazine *Approach* encourages aviators to share their mishaps or accidents for the purpose of lessons learned by publishing their accounts under the fictitious name *Anymouse*.

**apogee** • The point at which a missile trajectory, or satellite orbit, is farthest from the center of the gravitational field of the controlling body or bodies. *See also:* perigee

**apostles** • Name given to the two large bollards on the main fore deck of a large, square-rigged sailing vessel.

**apparent time** • Time based upon the rotation of the Earth relative to the apparent (true) Sun.

**apparent wind** • The wind as it appears to an observer; the resultant vector of the true wind and the motion of the observing station.

**apprehension** • According to the Uniform Code of Military Justice—clearly informing a person that he/she is being taken into custody. *See also:* restraint

**appropriation** • Government funds provided by Congress for specific purposes. May be continuing or annual. Not the same as authorization. Most defense legislation requires both authorization and appropriation. *See also:* authorization

**apron** • Area of a pier or wharf on which cargo is unloaded. The edge of an airfield, just short of the runway.

**arbor, depth charge** • Device holding a depth charge on its projector. *See also:* K-gun, Y-gun

**arc** • The graduated scale of an instrument for measuring angles, such as a marine sextant.

**arc of visibility** • Portion of the horizon expressed in degrees, through which a navigational light is visible from seaward.

**ardent** • Said of a sailing vessel if her head tends to come up into the wind when sailing close hauled. *See also:* lee helm; weathercocks

**area, forward** • Part of the battle space that is in direct confrontation with or very close proximity to the enemy.

**area, mounting** • Where forces are assembled prior to an amphibious operation.

**area, objective** • In strategic or tactical planning, a geographical area containing a military objective.

**ARIES II** • Four-engine turboprop signals intelligence (SIGINT) reconnaissance aircraft. The EP-3E ARIES II (Airborne Reconnaissance Integrated Electronic System II) is the Navy's only land-based signals intelligence (SIGINT) reconnaissance aircraft. These aircraft are based on the Orion P-3 airframe and provide fleet and theater commanders worldwide with near real-time tactical SIGINT. With sensitive receivers and high-gain dish antennas, the EP-3E exploits a wide range of electronic emissions from deep within targeted territory.

**arm** • 1. To equip a ship or aircraft with weapons. 2. To make a weapon ready to fire or explode. 3. The part of an anchor located between the crown and the fluke. 4. To fill a cavity at the bottom of a sounding lead with soap or tallow to obtain a bottom sample. 5. The upright or nearly upright strength member of a davit.

**armament** • The weapons or weapon systems of a ship.

**armed guard** • Naval gun crews on merchant ships during wartime. Used extensively during World War II.

**Armed Services Vocational Aptitude Battery (ASVAB)** • A test for evaluating the capabilities of enlisted men and women.

**arming** • An operation in which a weapon is changed from a safe condition to a state of readiness for use.

**arming crew** • Sailors who provide weapons and ammunition to carrier aircraft.

**armor** • Protective material used in ships, aircraft, clothing, etc. to counter the effects of explosion, projectiles, shrapnel, etc. Made of various materials depending upon use (steel in ships, Kevlar in personal clothing, etc.).

**armored cruiser** • No longer in service, battle cruisers were bigger than contemporary battleships and carried equivalent firepower, but had little or no armor. *See also:* cruiser, warship

**armored deck** • A deck, below the main deck, that provides added protection to vital spaces.

**armored rope** • Rope with hemp core and a flat wire around each strand; used chiefly in salvage or similar work.

**armor-piercing (AP)** • Ammunition especially designed to penetrate armor.

**armory** • Compartment aboard ship or a building ashore where weapons are stowed and serviced.

**array** • In sonar applications, two or more hydrophones feeding into a common receiver. There may also be antenna arrays for radio or radar.

**arrest** • Restraint of a person by competent authority. Involves relief from military duties.

**arresting cables** • On an aircraft carrier, the cross-deck cables attached to the arresting engine and designed to engage the tailhook of an aircraft to bring it smoothly to a halt.

**arresting gear** • The arrangement of arresting cables, barricade, and below-decks arresting engines designed to stop an aircraft when landing on the deck of a carrier.

**arresting-gear engine** • A complex of cables, pulleys, blocks, and hydraulic resistance cyclinders designed to exert progressive, gradual resistance to the cross-deck cable as it is extended by the momentum of the aircraft landing on the deck.

**arrest in quarters** • Restraint limiting an officer's liberty, imposed as a nonjudicial punishment by a flag or general officer in command.

**Article 15** • The Article of the Uniform Code of Military Justice (UCMJ) that grants the power of a commander to impose nonjudicial punishment.

**Articles for the Government of the Navy** • Rules and regulations for the old Navy. No longer effective, replaced by the Uniform Code of Military Justice. *See also:* Rocks and Shoals

**artificial horizon** • 1. An instrument indicating the attitude of an aircraft by simulating the appearance of a natural horizon with reference to a miniature airplane. 2. A simulated horizon in, or used in conjuction with, a navigation instrument.

**asbestos kit** • Fire-resistant clothing for firefighting. Also called a hot suit, worn by a hot suitman.

**A school** • *See:* class A schools

**A-scope** • A radar display on which slant range is shown as the distance along a horizontal trace. *See also:* planned position indicator (PPI); B-scope

**ashcan** • *Inf:* Depth charge.

**ashore** • On the beach or shore. A Sailor may go ashore on liberty, but if a ship goes ashore, she is aground.

**Aspect** • Short-pulse antisubmarine warfare (ASW) classification device designed for destroyer use but also used in the Sea King helicopter.

**aspect ratio** • The length of any moving surface, measured across the direction of motion, divided by its length in the direction of motion. For a rudder: its depth divided by its width. For an aircraft wing: its span divided by its width. A long thin wing, therefore, has a higher aspect ratio than a short stubby one.

**ASROC system** • Quick reaction, all weather, intermediate range, antisubmarine warfare (ASW) weapon launched from surface ships. The vertical launching system vertical launch ASROC (VLA) version is a rocket propelled, three-stage, antisubmarine warfare (ASW) weapon designed for deployment on CG47-, DDG51-, and DD963-class ships equipped with the MK41 VLS and MK 116 fire control system. The VLA missile provides the fleet with the capability for rapid response, all-weather delivery of an MK 46 torpedo against threat submarines in any direction, at intermediate ranges.

**assault craft** • Landing craft used in amphibious operations.

**assault group** • A subordinate task organization component of an attack force; *e.g.*, an amphibious assault group is composed of assault shipping and supporting naval units designed to transport, protect, land, and initially support a landing force.

**assault shipping** • Amphibious vessels carrying assault troops and equipment for a landing operation.

**assault waves** • Scheduled leading waves of boats and amphibious vehicles for an amphibious landing.

**astern** • Behind a vessel (or formation of vessels); away from a vessel in the direction opposite to her heading. Thus, a fast ship leaves a slower one astern. Someone who falls overboard would be left astern.

**as you were** • Command that means resume former activity or formation.

**at ease, stand at ease** • 1. A command to those at attention in a military formation to assume a more relaxed posture; the right foot remains in place and talking is not permitted. 2. More informal: a command to an assembled group to relax. *See also:* at rest

**athwart** • At right angles to the fore-and-aft centerline of a ship or boat; roughly across a vessel. Sometimes pronounced "thwart-ships."

**athwartships** • Anything that extends from one side of the ship to the other, such as an athwartships passageway.

**athwart the hawse** • Across the stem.

**Atlantic Gulf Stream System** • Major current system flowing offshore near the East Coast of the United States.

**at loggerheads** • A serious difference of opinion. A loggerhead is two iron balls attached by an iron rod, which was heated and used for melting pitch. Sailors sometimes used them as weapons to settle a grudge; *i.e.*, when fighting they were "at loggerheads."

**atmosphere** • The envelope of air surrounding Earth or other celestial body. The atmospheric pressure at sea level is 14.7 psi.

**atmospheric pressure** • The measurable phenomena of pressure exerted as a result of the presence of the gases making up the atmosphere; at sea level it is 14.7 psi.

**atoll** • A ring-shaped coral reef usually found in the Pacific and Indian Oceans, often with low sand islands. The body of water enclosed by the reef is a lagoon.

**atomizer** • Device feeding fuel oil into a boiler as a fine spray. Together with the air register it forms the burner.

**at rest** • A command similar to "at ease" but

less restrictive; right foot remains in place, posture is relaxed, and talking is permitted. *See also:* at ease

**attached** • A person is said to be attached to a command when he or she has been formally ordered to serve in it. *See also:* detached

**attack force** • All ships, troops, and aircraft used in the attack phase of an amphibious assault.

**attack group** • Subordinate task organization component of an attack force; *e.g.,* an amphibious attack group is composed of assault shipping and supporting naval units designed to transport, protect, land, and initially support a landing group.

**attack plane** • Aircraft used primarily to attack ships or land targets rather than other aircraft.

**attack teacher** • Training device for simulation of actual tactics involved in submarine or antisubmarine combat. Originally devised to train submarine commanders in attacking ships. Subsequently a modification was developed for antisubmarine warfare.

**attend the side** • To be on the quarterdeck to formally meet important persons; may involve the use of sideboys and other ceremonial customs. Also called tend the side.

**attention to port, starboard** • Command given to topside personnel when ship is rendering passing honors. Personnel in view of the honored ship are required to come to attention facing the designated side, and salute if ordered.

**attitude** • The position or orientation of an aircraft, in motion or at rest, as determined by the relationship between its axes and some reference lines or planes. "Nose down" would be an example of an aircraft's attitude.

**attrition** • Loss of assets or forces; may be a result of battle or other causes. Refers to students lost in training pipelines due to academic, physical, moral, or self-selected failure.

**augment** • To change from reserve to regular status.

**augmentor** • Device for increasing the efficiency of an air pump in a steam power plant.

**authentication** • Communications security measure designed to prevent fraudulent transmissions.

**authorization** • Congressional permission to carry out a program (generally procurement of ships, aircraft, or weapons) involving expenditure of funds. Actual appropriation of the funds is necessary before they can be spent (or obligated). *See also:* appropriation

**auto cat** • Airplane used to relay radio messages automatically.

**autoignition temperature** • The temperature at which a substance will ignite without the further addition of energy (heat, spark, or flame) from an outside source. Also called ignition temperature.

**automated data processing** • Computer based processing of information and files, and the associated equipment.

**automated weather network (AWN)** • The complex, worldwide collection and distribution network of meteorological data and notices to airmen (NOTAMs) operated by the Air Force for the Department of Defense (DoD).

**automatic pilot** • A device or system that automatically controls the flight of an aircraft or guided missile.

**autonomic fire suppression system** • A damage control system, designed to reduce crew size, that includes an automated firemain break detection and isolation capability, automated boundary cooling and space dewatering systems, and survivable zonal piping with advanced control architecture.

**autumnal equinox** • One of the two points of intersection of the ecliptic and celestial equator, occupied by the sun when its declination is 0°. The point occupied on or about September 23, when the declination changes from north to south, is called the autumnal equinox, September equinox, or first point of Libra, and marks the first day of autumn in the Northern Hemisphere. *See also:* vernal equinox

**auxiliary** • A vessel whose mission is to supply or support the combatant forces. Extra, or secondary, as "auxiliary" engine.

**auxiliary machinery** • Shipboard machinery other than that used for main propulsion. Some examples are anchor engine, evaporators, ice machines, etc.

**auxiliary power unit** • A small turbine engine on an aircraft that provides power when the main engine(s) is not operating.

**auxiliary tanks** • In submarines, variable (ballast) tanks equidistant from bow and stern; built to take full sea pressure and connected into the trimming system. *See also:* ballast tanks; trim; trim tanks

**AV 115/145** • Aviation gas for Navy and Air Force aircraft.

**availability** • Period assigned a ship for accomplishing work at a repair activity. Types of availabilities are restricted, technical, regular overhaul, voyage repairs, and upkeep period.

**availability factor** • Percentage of aircraft that is operational or on the line.

**avast** • Order to stop or cease, as "avast heaving."

**aviation boatswain's mate (AB)** • Navy occupational rating that operates, maintains, and repairs aircraft catapults, arresting gears, barricades, fuel- and lube-oil transfer systems; directs aircraft on the flight deck and in hangar bays before launch and after recovery; uses tow tractors to position planes and operates aircraft support equipment. Service ratings include ABE [launching and recovery equipment]; ABF [fuels]; ABH [aircraft handling].

**aviation electrician's mate (AE)** • Navy occupational rating that maintains, adjusts, and repairs electrical-power generating, converting, and distributing systems, as well as lighting, control, and indicating systems in aircraft. AEs also install and maintain wiring and flight and engine instrument systems, which include automatic flight control, stabilization, aircraft compass, attitude reference, and inertial navigation systems.

**aviation electronics technician (AT)** • Navy occupational rating that performs preventive and corrective maintenance on aviation electronic components supported by conventional and automatic test equipment. ATs repair the electronic components of weapons, communications, radar, navigation, antisubmarine warfare sensors, electronic warfare, data link, fire control, and tactical displays.

**aviation fuel operational sequencing systems** • The set of detailed instructions that cover the operation of shipboard avation fuel systems.

**aviation machinist's mate (AD)** • Navy occupational rating that maintains jet aircraft engines and associated equipment, or engages in any one of several types of aircraft maintenance activities. ADs maintain, service, adjust, and replace aircraft engines and accessories, as well as perform the duties of flight engineers.

**aviation maintenance administrationman (AZ)** • Navy occupational rating that performs clerical, administrative, and managerial duties necessary to keep aircraft-maintenance activities running smoothly. AZs plan, schedule, and coordinate maintenance, including inspections and modifications to aircraft and equipment.

**aviation ordnanceman (AO)** • Navy occupational rating that is responsible for maintaining, repairing, installing, operating, and handling aviation ordnance equipment, such as bombs, rockets, guns, etc. Duties also include the handling, stowing, issuing, and loading of munitions and small arms.

**aviation readiness evaluation** • A biannual evaluation preceding the aviation certification of aviation capable ships.

**aviation ship** • An aircraft carrier.

**aviation storekeeper (AK)** • Navy occupational rating responsible for ensuring that the materials and equipment needed for naval aviation activities are available and in good order; taking inventory, estimating future needs, and making purchases. AKs store and issue flight clothing, aeronautical materials and spare parts, ordnance, and electronic, structural, and engineering equipment. Rating merged with storekeeper (SK) in 2003.

**aviation structural mechanic (AM)** • Navy occupational rating responsible for the maintenance and repair of aircraft parts (wings, fuselage, tail, control surfaces, landing gear, and attending mechanisms); works with metals, alloys, and plastics; maintains and repairs safety equipment and hydraulic systems. Service rating AME works specifically with safety equipment.

**aviation support equipment technician (AS)** • Navy occupational rating responsible for performing intermediate maintenance on "yellow" (aviation accessory) equipment at naval air stations and aboard carriers; maintains gasoline and diesel engines, hydraulic and pneumatic systems, liquid and gaseous oxygen and nitrogen systems, gas-turbine compressor units, and electrical systems.

**aviation warfare systems operator (AW)** • Navy occupational rating that operates airborne radar and electronic equipment used in detecting, locating, and tracking submarines. AWs also operate equipment used in antisurface, mine, and electronic warfare, and play key roles in search-and-rescue and counter-narcotics operations.

**avionics** • Electronics as applied to aviation.

**awash** • So low that water washes over, as in "the ship was so low in the water that her decks were awash."

**away** • Refers to prospective departure from the ship on a mission or errand; *e.g.* "Away the rescue and assistance party." *See also:* square away; where away

**aweigh** • Said of an anchor when clear of the bottom. *See also:* anchor's aweigh

**axis** • 1. Reference line for stationing ships relative to one another; originating at the formation center, it extends out on a specific bearing of some significance (such as most likely direction of attack); examples are a "threat axis" or an "ASW axis." 2. An imaginary line that passes through a body, about which the body rotates or may be assumed to rotate. For example, the horizontal axis, the lateral axis, and the longitudinal axis about which an aircraft moves.

**aye, aye** • A seamanlike response to an order or instruction signifying that the order is heard, is understood, and will be carried out. Differs from "Yes, Sir" (or "Yes, Ma'am") in that the latter is used only to answer a question, but "aye, aye" is used as the response to an order as indicated above. Pronounced "eye."

**azimuth** • Angle measured clockwise between north and the object being sighted; similar to bearing, but more often used to indicate the bearing of a celestial body.

**azimuth circle** • Fitting used on a compass or gyro repeater for measuring bearings or azimuths. Designed primarily for taking celestial sights, it has an adjustable mirror so that the azimuth of an elevated line of sight may be taken, thus differing from a simple bearing circle or alidade (which has a small telescope). *See also:* alidade; bearing circle; pelorus

# B

**Babbitt metal** • Soft, white antifriction alloy of copper, tin, and antimony used for bearing surfaces.

**back** • 1. To reverse engines so that a ship may be stopped or made to go astern, as in the command "all engines back one third." 2. When the wind changes direction counterclockwise (in the Northern Hemisphere), it is said to back. A backing wind in the Northern Hemisphere is usually a sign of worsening weather, while it is a sign of improving weather in the Southern Hemisphere. *See also:* veer

**back and fill** • A sailing maneuver in which the sails alternately catch and then spill the wind to enable the vessel to work up a narrow channel. Sometimes used to describe an engine-powered vessel to indicate using backing power in a confined area.

**background noise** • In radio, it is the unwanted sound resulting from atmospheric conditions and other spurious sources; commonly referred to as static. In sonar, it is the noise that limits echo detection; caused by sea life, sea action, or the system itself.

**backing** • A change in wind direction in a counterclockwise manner in the Northern Hemisphere, or a clockwise direction in the Southern Hemisphere.

**back pressure** • Pressure on the exhaust side of a steam or reciprocating engine.

**backrush** • The flow of water toward the sea after the uprush of incoming waves. Also called backwash.

**backs** • The wind backs when it changes direction counterclockwise. [Note: The direction of the wind is the direction from which it is blowing.] *See also:* veer; haul

**backstay** • 1. Wire or cable supporting a mast in the fore-and-aft direction that tends aft. 2. A piece of standing rigging leading aft. *See also:* stay; forestay; shroud

**back to battery** • Return of a gun to firing position after recoil. *Inf:* Personal recovery from shock, injury, or illness. Sometimes expressed as back in battery.

**back-up alert force** • Part of a ship's internal physical security organization.

**backwash** • Water thrown aft by turning of ship's propeller. The flow of water toward the sea after the uprush of incoming waves. Also called backrush.

**back water** • Command given to oarsmen to reverse usual rowing motion.

**bad conduct discharge (BCD)** • A punitive discharge awarded to an enlisted person for severe infractions of regulations. The only type of discharge that carries greater prejudice is the dishonorable discharge (DD).

**baffle** • Plate used to deflect fluids, gases, or sound waves.

**baffle area** • An area roughly 30° either side of the stern of a ship in which maintenance of a sonar contact is most difficult.

Because of the noise from a ship's own propellers, sonar equipment is frequently designed with a sonar shield directly astern called the baffle area or simply "the baffles" as in "the contact is in the baffles."

**baffles** • *See:* baffle area

**baggywrinkle** • A form of chafing gear; a mat made of many yarns of manila hitched around two lengths of small stuff.

**bail** • 1. To dip water out of a boat. 2. The spreader to which an accommodation ladder topping lift is secured. 3. The handle of a bucket.

**bail out** • To jump or eject from aircraft. The term "punch out" was coined when ejection seats became standard. *Inf:* To rescue one from an administrative predicament.

**bail shackle** • The part of a pelican hook that holds the hook closed over the chain. Also referred to as the link or slip hook link. *Var:* bale.

**baiting** • Tactic designed to lull an enemy, especially a submarine, into a false sense of security and induce it to take action, making it liable to detection or attack.

**baker** • Past phonetic word for the letter B; replaced with bravo.

**balanced rudder** • Rudder in which part of the blade surface is forward of the axis to counterbalance water pressure on the after part.

**balance point** • With reference to an old-fashioned anchor, that point on the shank where the anchor balances. Usually fitted with a pad eye to enable efficient lifting.

**balancing** • In submarines, the maintenance of depth with no way on by riding on top of a density layer. *See also:* hovering

**bale** • *See:* bail shackle

**ball** • *See:* meatball

**ballast** • The weight added to a ship or boat to ensure stability. To pump sea water into empty fuel tanks to increase stability.

**ballast tanks** • Tanks used to surface or submerge a submarine. The name is a misnomer, since they have nothing to do with ballast, which is a function of the trim tanks. Lightly constructed, they have bottoms that are always open to the sea and vents that open quickly to release entrapped air on diving. During submergence, ballast tanks cannot have any air in them; the air bubble will be compressed or expanded as the depth changes, thus altering the submerged trim. Usually blown dry for surface operations, however WWII submarines on surface patrol sometimes reduced their silhouette by leaving ballast tanks partially flooded (called ballasting down, another misuse of terms). Distinguished from variable or trim tanks, which must withstand full submergence pressure because they are closed off from the sea and only partly filled. A few surface ships have ballast tanks for varying trim and buoyancy (amphibious landing ships, for example), but such tanks are relatively simple and never deeply submerged.

**ballistic correction** • 1. Correction in aiming a gun, necessary because of variation in powder temperature, gun erosion, or the motion of the target, wind, or gun itself. 2. A correction in a gyro compass due to a change of course or speed.

**ballistic damping error** • An error introduced in a gyro compass by the accelerating force on the damping fluid when a ship changes course or speed.

**ballistic missile** • A missile that does not rely upon aerodynamic surfaces for lift; in other words, it flies more like a guided bullet. *See also:* cruise missile

**ballistics** • The science of projectile motion. Interior ballistics deals with the inside of a gun; exterior ballistics deals with action of projectiles in flight.

**bamboozle** • To intentionally deceive, usually as a joke. In the old Navy, to deceive a passing vessel as to your ship's nationality. This was a common practice of pirates.

**bank** • 1. Relatively flat subsurface area that is relatively shallow but deep enough for surface navigation. 2. To incline an aircraft about its longitudinal axis. 3. The shore of a river, lake, or harbor.

**bank effect** • Lateral motion of a ship in a narrow channel, where the near bank tends to attract the stern (bank suction) and repel the bow (bank cushion).

**bar** • A long, narrow shoal, or an obstruction to navigation, usually at a harbor entrance.

**barbette** • Armor protecting the rotating part of a ship's turret below the gun house.

**bareboat charter** • Leasing a boat without a crew.

**barge** • 1. Boat for official use of a flag officer. 2. A non-self-propelled cargo carrier in harbors or rivers. Also called a lighter or scow. 3. Used as a verb: "The coal was barged alongside." *See also:* scow

**barkentine** • A three-masted sailing ship with the first mast square-rigged and the second and third fore-and-aft rigged.

**bark or barque** • Usually a three-masted sailing ship with the first two masts square-rigged and the third fore-and-aft rigged. If there are more than three masts, all but the last one are square-rigged.

**barnacles** • Marine crustaceans that attach to and grow on hard objects at or below the surface, particularly on the hulls of ships. A growth of barnacles will have a noticeable effect on a ship's speed.

**barn burner** • An achiever; one who gets things done.

**barograph** • Instrument that provides a continuous record of atmospheric pressure.

**barometer** • Instrument that measures atmospheric pressure.

**barrel** • Measure of volume as used in the petroleum industry, equivalent to 42 U.S. gallons.

**barrette** • A heavily armored cylinder extending downward from a gun turret to the lowest armored deck; provides protection to powder and projectile handling crews.

**barricade** • Prior to the development of the present angled-deck aircraft carriers, propeller-driven aircraft had to be parked on the flight deck forward when other planes were landing on the after portion. Once a plane's landing roll was stopped by the arresting gear, the flight deck crew would quickly detach the tailhook from the gear and roll the aircraft forward to join the other parked planes. Then the barrier or barricade protecting them would be re-erected. Generally, the barricade was a collapsible fence, made of webbing or wire, intended to catch wings or landing gear struts of a plane that failed to engage the regular arresting gear. Small or even heavy damage to a single plane was preferable to lesser damage to several, especially during wartime operations. *See also:* bolter

**barrier combat air patrol (BARCAP)** • One or more divisions of fighter aircraft deployed as a defensive barrier across the most probable direction from which an attack might come.

**barrier ice** • Edge of shelf ice.

**barrier patrol** • Ship or aircraft designated

to detect and possibly take action against passage of enemy ships or aircraft, especially submarines, through a particular ocean area or across a designated barrier line.

**barrier reef** • Offshore reefs separated from land by channels or lagoons.

**basegram** • A message delivered by any suitable means to delivery authorities, such as port directors, who pass them to forces afloat.

**base line, base line extension** • The arc of a great circle passing through two loran stations. The base line is that portion of the line that falls between the two stations; the line extended out beyond the stations is known as the base line extension.

**base loading** • Loading of a ship intended for delivery to a base or a replenishment group. *See also:* combat loading; commercial loading

**base, naval** • *See:* naval base

**base speed** • Resultant speed along a base course when evasive steering or other deviations are superimposed. A ship may speed up or slow down for various reasons, but the base speed will ultimately prevail between two base points.

**basic naval establishment plan (BNEP)** • Outline of the naval establishment for the current year, including force level, deployment of forces, personnel strength, state of training, and degree of readiness, etc.; to be maintained during peacetime, prepared in the Office of the Chief of Naval Operations (OPNAV) for Secretary of the Navy (SECNAV) approval.

**basic test battery** • Series of tests designed to measure intelligence, aptitudes, and potential skills of recruits. Was replaced by a simlar series of tests known as the Armed Services Vocational Aptitude Battery (ASVAB).

**bathyconductograph** • Device used to measure the conductivity of sea water at various depths while a ship is under way.

**bathymetric chart** • One showing depths of water by use of contour lines and color shading. Also called bottom contour chart.

**bathymetry** • Measurement of water conditions such as depth, temperature, salinity, etc.

**bathythermograph (BT)** • Temperature- and depth-sensing device used to obtain water temperatures at various depths while a ship is at anchor or under way.

**battalion landing team (BLT)** • Battalion of troops specially organized for an amphibious landing.

**batten** • 1. Strip of wood or steel used in securing tarpaulins in place over a hatch. 2. A strip of wood or plastic used to stiffen the leech of a sail. 3. Removable wood or steel members used in a ship's holds to keep cargo from shifting. 4. Locking device for aircraft control surfaces.

**batten down** • To cover and fasten down. To close off a hatch or watertight door.

**battery** • 1. Ship's guns of the same caliber or used for the same purpose, *e.g.*, main, secondary, and antiaircraft batteries. 2. In diesel-powered submarines, the main (electrical) storage battery.

**battery control** • Fire control of all gun mounts or turrets of a similar caliber or purpose. Types of control—collective, dispersed, divided, and sector—determine how battery control is exercised.

**battle bill** • List of battle assignments based on ship's armament and ship's complement. *See also:* watch, quarter, and station bill

**battle cruiser** • A lightly armored, high-speed cruiser with the offensive power of a battleship, developed by the British Navy before WWI. *See also:* armored cruiser; cruiser

**battle dress** • Flash and splinter protective clothing worn in battle. When specifically designed battle-dress clothing is not available, the standard uniform can be modified into a battle-dress configuration by tucking trousers into socks, rolling down and buttoning sleeves, completely buttoning shirt, and donning a helmet or other available head gear.

**battle dressing station** • Shipboard first aid station capable of providing medical attention during general quarters.

**battle efficiency award** • A coveted award given to ships and aircraft squadrons whose performance meets exacting standards of combat readiness.

**battle efficiency pennant** • Red pennant with a black ball flown by a ship winning the battle efficiency award. *See also:* meatball

**battle group** • An array of ships, typically (though not necessarily) centered about an aircraft carrier, that is capable of carrying out combat operations.

**battle group inport exercise** • Unit, warfare commander, or group-level exercise designed to enhance participating units' tactical proficiency through the conduct of training scenarios architecture.

**battle lantern** • Battery-powered lantern available for emergency use aboard ship.

**battle lights** • Dim red lights below decks for necessary illumination during darken ship periods. The red spectrum has less of the temporary blinding effect on the retina of the eye than does normal white light; hence, red lighting permits quicker dark adaptation.

**battle line** • Two or more ships formed into a line of battle for the purpose of engaging the enemy in surface gun action. A holdover from days of sailing warships. Today, battle line is a figure of speech that is sometimes used to refer to almost any assembly of fighting ships.

**battle port** • Hinged metal cover for a porthole that protects against battle or weather damage.

**battleship (BB)** • Derived from "line of battle ship" or "ship of the battle line." The battleship, whether of wood or steel, was originally the largest and most powerful man-of-war that could be built. Development of the airplane produced the aircraft carrier, which in World War II replaced the battleship as the primary capital ship of navies. *See also:* armored cruiser; battlecruiser; cruiser; decker; warship

**battle stations** • Crew assignments during battle. *See also:* general quarters; watch, quarter, and station bill

**battle wagon** • *Inf:* Battleship.

**baud** • A measurement unit of electronic data transmission speed.

**Baxter bolt** • Fitting that screws flush into deck, used to fasten down aircraft.

**beach** • 1. As used in amphibious operations, portion of shoreline required for landing one battalion landing team. 2. In oceanography, area extending from shoreline inland to a marked change in physiographic form, or to line of permanent vegetation. 3. To run a ship or boat ashore is to beach it. 4. *Inf:* Shore. A Sailor might say, "I'm going to hit the beach" to mean "I'm going ashore."

**beach capacity** • An estimate, in tons, of the amount of cargo it is possible to unload daily on a strip of beach during an amphibious operation.

**beach dump** • Temporary storage for supplies landed in an amphibious operation.

**beach exit** • Route for movement of material and personnel inland from the beach during an amphibious landing.

**beach gear** • A combination of anchors, purchase blocks, carpenter stoppers, shackles, and wire used to free a stranded ship. The generic term for all equipment intended to be used on the beach during an amphibious landing. Includes all material intended to remain under the command and disposition of the beachmaster, as distinct from that intended for the troops who have been or will be landed.

**beach group, naval** • *See:* naval beach group

**beachhead** • The initial objective of an assault landing. A section of enemy coast used for continuous landing of men and equipment in an amphibious operation. After consolidation of the beachhead, the next move is to break out of same. At this point, the operation takes on the characteristics of regular land warfare, except that until capture of a suitable harbor or port, the beachhead remains the support base.

**beaching gear** • Cradles on wheels used for hauling boats and seaplanes out of the water and onto a ramp or beach.

**beach marker** • Colored panel or other device marking limit of specific landing beaches for assault craft in an amphibious landing.

**beachmaster** • In amphibious operations, the person designated to take charge of logistic activities on the beach after the assault phase of the landing has been concluded.

**beachmaster unit** • Personnel assigned to the beachmaster.

**beach matting** • Steel netting or mesh laid on soft sand to improve traction of vehicles.

**beach party (amphibious)** • Naval shore party that controls boats, surveys channels, and performs other fuctions in supprt of an amphbious landing.

**beacon** • A navigational aid constructed of a stake, pillar, or some other solid support with a distinctive topmark that has been mounted on a shore or shoal. May also be lighted, aerial, radar, radio, radio-marker, radio-range, or infrared.

**beam** • 1. Concentration of energy in a linear direction (as in light beam or laser beam). 2. Extreme width of a ship or boat. In wooden ship construction, the heavy horizontal athwartships timbers, on which the deck planking was laid, were called beams. Because the longest beam spanned the maximum width of a ship, it has become common practice to refer to the maximum width of a vessel as her beam. 3. A transverse frame supporting a deck. 4. A ship heeled over 90° is said to be on her beam ends. 5. Any other ship or object reasonably nearby, in the direction that the beam is normally pointed, is said to be abeam or on the beam.

**beam ends** • A vessel lying on its side is said to be on its beam end. Often used to indicate that a vessel has taken an unusually large roll and was almost on its side.

**beam rider** • Guided missile that follows a radar beam to the target.

**beam-riding guidance** • The missile follows a radar beam to the target. The radar beam is supplied by a source—ship or aircraft—external to the missile. A computer in the missile keeps it centered within the radar beam. Several missiles may ride the beam simultaneously. If the missile wanders outside the beam, it will automatically destroy itself.

**beam width** • Critical characteristic of a

radar transmission governing accuracy of the bearings measured by radar.

**bean jockey** • *See:* messman

**bean rag** • *Inf:* Flag flown in port to indicate that the crew is at mess and that only routine honors should be expected.

**bear** • To be in a certain direction; *e.g.,* the target bears 170°.

**bear a hand** • Hurry up; expedite. Provide assistance, as "bear a hand" with rigging this stage.

**bearing** • The direction of an object from the observer, expressed in three figures from 000° clockwise through 360°. True bearing is measured from true north. Magnetic bearing is measured from magnetic north. Relative bearing is measured from the bow of a ship or aircraft.

**bearing circle** • A ring fitted over a compass or compass repeater with which bearings can be taken by sighting through vanes. If a reflecting device is fitted to facilitate bearings of celestial bodies, it is called an azimuth circle. If a telescope is fitted instead of vanes, it is an alidade.

**bearing drift** • The movement left or right of the bearing to an object in motion, relative to the observer's platform. It is an indication of risk of collision; if a contact has no bearing drift and the range is decreasing, a collision is inevitable unless one or the other (or both) platforms maneuver.

**Beaufort scale** • Descriptive, graduated table of wind velocities. Devised by Admiral Sir Francis Beaufort, R.N.

**becket** • 1. A short length of line with eye-splices at both ends, or with an eyesplice at one end and a stopper knot in the other; used to secure loose items by wrapping (bundling) them together. 2. A short piece of line with its ends spliced together in a circular fashion. 3. The eye at the base of a block, used to attach a line. 4. A rope eye on a cargo net. 5. Shortened form of becket bend.

**becket bend** • A knot used to tie two lines together. Also called a sheet bend.

**beef boat** • *Inf:* Supply ship or cargo ship.

**beep** • To control a drone or pilotless plane. The individual who operates the controls is a beeper.

**beer muster** • *Inf:* Beer party ashore.

**before the mast** • Literally, the position of the crew whose living quarters on board were in the forecastle (the section of a ship forward of the foremast). The term is also used more generally to describe enlisted personnel as compared with officers, in phrases such as "he sailed before the mast."

**belay** • To cancel, as in "Belay the last word." To make fast or secure, as in "Belay the line."

**belaying pin** • A long, round metal rod used for securing lines. Most common use today is in the pin rail of a flag bag for securing signal halyards.

**bell book, engineer's** • *See:* engineer's bell book

**bell bottoms** • A Sailor's uniform trousers that widen at the bottom.

**bellows** • A device used for producing a stream of air.

**bell, ship's** • Used for sounding fog or distress signals, as fire signal, and to denote time. *See also:* ship's bell

**bellyrobber** • *See:* commissaryman

**below** • Downward; below decks; downstairs.

**beltway bandit** • *Inf:* A company, or an

employee of same, located near Washington, D.C., which serves the defense industry.

**bench mark** • A permanently fixed point of known position used for reference in survey or alignment, as in aligning a gun.

**bend** • *See:* knot

**bending shackle** • A U-shaped connecting link that connects the anchor chain to the anchor shackle.

**bend on** • To secure one thing to another, as to bend a flag on to a halyard. To bend on 10 turns means to increase propeller speed by 10 rpm.

**bends** • Affliction caused by formation of nitrogen bubbles in the blood, resulting in paralysis, vertigo, cerebral shock, blindness, etc. Experienced by divers after excessive exposure to pressure or too rapid decompression. Pilots also sometimes experience discomfort from too rapid a change in pressure, which they loosely refer to as "the bends." But because the pressure change is so much less, it cannot compare in severity with the bends experienced by divers.

**benesug** • *Inf:* A good idea. Pronounced "benny sug" (with a hard "g") and derived from the acronym used by the Navy for its "Beneficial Suggestions" program, in which cash awards are given for ideas that lead to cost savings in the Navy

**benthic** • Relating to, or occurring in, the depths of the ocean.

**berg** • *See:* iceberg

**bergy-bit** • Medium-sized piece of glacial ice floating in the sea. Smaller pieces are growlers.

**berm** • A narrow, raised embankment.

**Bermuda Triangle** • An ocean area off the Southeastern United States—popularly called the Bermuda Triangle or sometimes the Devil's Triangle—that has long been known as an area of mysterious happenings, not the least of which are unexplained disasters. No nautical charts show this area under either name, and the U.S. Board of Geographic Names does not officially recognize it. But the apexes of this triangle are generally accepted to be Bermuda, Miami, Fla., and San Juan, Puerto Rico.

**Berne List** • Volume listing international call signs, radio stations, etc., published by International Union of Telecommunications, Geneva, Switzerland.

**Bernoulli's principle** • If a fluid flowing through a tube reaches a constriction, the velocity of fluid flowing through the constriction increases and the pressure decreases.

**berth** • 1. Anchorage or mooring space assigned a vessel. 2. Sleeping place assigned on board ship. 3. A margin in passing something, as a wide berth. 4. To inhabit, as "He is berthing in the forward compartment."

**between the devil and the deep** • In the old Navy, the devil was the longest seam of the ship, running from the bow to the stern. When the devil needed caulking, the Sailor would sit in the boatswain's chair to do it, thus suspended between the devil and the sea.

**between wind and water** • Refers to the part of a ship just at the waterline that is alternately exposed and submerged as the ship heels and rolls. To receive a shot between wind and water is to be hit in a very vulnerable place. Hence, the reference has come to mean the vulnerable part of anything.

**betwixt wind and water** • *See:* between wind and water

**bib** • The portion of a Navy enlisted uniform that hangs from the back of the neck. In the wooden Navy it was the fashion for sailors to have long hair but, it would get blown about by the winds and get stuck in the rigging or machinery. To counteract this, sailors at sea would braid their hair and dip it in the tar used to seal the boards on the ship. When ashore on liberty (as opposed to a longer leave where they would wash the tar out of the hair) they would cut a bib out of sack cloth and tie it around their neck to keep from getting tar on their one good shirt. Thus, the bib eventually became an official part of the enlisted uniform.

**bight** • 1. Loop of rope, line, or chain. 2. An indentation in a coast; a small cove. 3. *Inf:* Caught in a bight is to be entangled in some sort of difficulty.

**bilge** • 1. The inside bottom of a ship or boat. The turn of a bilge refers to the curved plating where a ship's side joins the bottom. A ship is said to be bilged if her bottom has been damaged sufficiently to take on water, as when running aground. But the expression is almost never used to refer to battle damage, even though torpedo damage could technically be so described. To refer to something as bilge or bilge-water is to be contemptuous. 2. *Inf:* To bilge an examination is to receive an unsatisfactory grade. 3. *Inf:* To bilge someone is to fail that person, if one is an instructor or superior; or to get a higher grade if a peer.

**bilge blocks** • Wooden supports under a vessel when she is in drydock.

**bilge diving** • *Inf:* Working in the bilges of a ship.

**bilge keels** • Fins at the turn of the bilge that reduce rolling of a ship.

**bilge pump** • Pump used to clear a vessel's bilge.

**bilge rat** • *Inf:* One who works in the engi-neering spaces of a ship.

**bill** • Assignments, with names, for training, administrative, or emergency activities, *e.g.*, rescue and assistance bill. The end of the arm of an old-fashioned anchor.

**billboard** • The inclined platform near the bow of a ship on which an old-fashioned anchor is stowed, ready to be dropped. *See also:* cat; cat and fish; cathead

**billet** • A specific assignment in a ship or station organization; for example, a ship might have a billet for a ship's doctor.

**billet slip** • Printed form, giving duty and living assignments aboard ship.

**bill of lading** • Shipping document showing the name and address of the shipper and con-signee, and a list of cargo with weights and dimensions.

**bingo** • An order to an aircraft to proceed immediately to a divert field. Bearing, dis-tance, and destination must be provided.

**bingo field** • A landing field or airport that carrier aircraft can use as an alternative land-ing site in the event that the pilot is unable to land aboard the carrier.

**bingo fuel** • The amount of fuel remaining that is sufficient to enable an aircraft to reach its designated bingo field in an emergency.

**binnacle** • The stand or support for a mag-netic compass. Originally spelled "bittacle." In the old Navy, this was a wooden structure mounted in a location convenient to the helmsman. In later years, brass was substi-tuted for wood. Wooden binnacles of various designs were frequently fitted with small cupboard-like compartments for stowage of accoutrements for the watch on deck, such as the log book, candles, or any nonmagnet-ic gear. *See also:* binnacle list

**binnacle list** • A list of personnel excused

from duty because of illness or injury; originally it was placed in the binnacle for the information of the officer of the watch. Although the binnacle list survives with the same meaning, it is no longer placed in the binnacle.

**biologics** • The sounds generated by sea life, when picked up on sonar.

**bioluminescence** • The emission of visible light by living organisms; vessels passing through areas inhabited by such creatures often cause them to glow, which can leave a visible wake at night.

**bird cage** • *Inf:* Air-control officer's station in the island of a carrier.

**bird farm** • *Inf:* Aircraft carrier.

**bitchbox** • *Inf:* An intercom using an amplified sound circuit to communicate between spaces in a ship.

**Bitching Betty** • *Inf:* The cockpit warning system of many aircraft today; usually a female voice.

**bitter end** • The absolute end of a piece of line or cable. The last link of anchor chain in the chain locker.

**bitts** • Pair of short, steel posts or horns on deck or on a pier; used to secure lines. *See also:* bollard; towing bitts

**Black Cats** • Navy and Marine Corps seaplanes that flew and fought effectively during WWII. They were painted black because they usually operated at night.

**black gang** • *Inf:* Personnel of the engineering department of a ship. Now obsolete because the reference was to coal and the coal dust with which old-time engineers had to contend.

**black oil** • Navy standard fuel oil (NSFO), once used extensively by Navy ships. More highly refined than bunker crude.

**black shoe** • *Inf:* A surface warfare officer. The term came to be used when avaitors began wearing green uniforms and brown shoes; avaitors consequently came to be known as brown shoes and surface officers as black shoes. *See also:* brown shoe

**BLADING** • *See:* bill of lading

**blast** • Signal on a ship's whistle; as defined in the Unified Rules of the Road, a "short blast" is defined as 1 second in duration and a "prolonged blast" is 4–6 seconds. A "long blast," once defined as more than 6 seconds in duration, is no longer included in the Unified Rules.

**blind bombing zones** • Air operations area where bombing is permitted without restrictions.

**blind zone** • Electronic-countermeasure term meaning an area where echoes cannot be received.

**blink** • The reflected light from sunlight shining on ice, snow, or white sand.

**blinker gun** • Directional, low-powered, visual-signaling device used aboard ships or submarines for hand-held visual signalling. Also called a blinker tube.

**blinker tube** • *See:* blinker gun

**blinking** • Regular shifting right and left of a loran signal to indicate that the signals are out of synchronization.

**blip** • Visual indication of a target on an electronic indicator screen; for example, an indication of a sonar echo. Also called a pip.

**blister** • Bulge in fuselage or wing of airplane enclosing equipment such as machine guns. A built-in bulge in the hull of a man-of-war to protect against mines, bombs, and torpedoes. Older ships had external blisters added as a postconstruction alteration.

**block** • Device consisting of a pulley encased in a shell, over which a line or wire rope can run freely. *See also:* deadeye; sheave; snatch block

**blockade** • Naval operation barring ships from entering or leaving specific ports or ocean areas.

**block and tackle** • *See:* purchase

**block coefficient** • The ratio of a ship's immersed volume divided by the product of the ship's length, beam, and draft. Serves as a measure of the vessel's fullness.

**blockship** • Ship sunk to block off a channel or harbor entrance.

**bloomers** • *See:* buckler

**blow** • To expel water from a tank with compressed air. *Inf:* A gale or storm.

**blowerman** • Person in fireroom who controls the blowers that force air through boilers for efficient combustion.

**blow tubes** • To inject steam into the fireside of a boiler to remove soot from the tubes.

**Blue Angels** • A team of Navy aviators that performs precision-formation aerobatics for public exhibitions.

**bluejacket** • Navy enlisted person below the rank of CPO (E-7); a Sailor.

**bluenose** • *Inf:* One who has been north of the Arctic Circle by ship or boat.

**Blue Peter** • In Horatio Nelson's day, "Peter" was the phonetic name for the letter P. The signal flag then was the same as now, a blue square with a small white square in the center, and was used for general recall of personnel before getting under way. In later years, the same flag became phonetically known as "Prep," and is currently called "Papa." But the flag itself keeps the symbol-ic name Blue Peter in memory of the days when Nelson would order it hoisted to the foretruck.

**blue shirts** • Personnel who chock and chain aircraft on a carrier's flightdeck; so called because they wear blue shirts for easy identification. *See also:* yellow shirts; red shirts; green shirts; brown shirts; white shirts; purple shirts; grapes

**blue-water ops** • 1. Naval operations at sea; as opposed to "brown" water ops, which occur in rivers or close to the shore. 2. Flight operations conducted when beyond range of a bingo field. At this point it is literally sink or swim for the aircrew; if a successful trap cannot be made, the aircrew will have to eject or bail out.

**bo'sun's pipe** • *See:* boatswain's pipe

**board** • The act of going aboard a vessel. A group of persons meeting for a specific purpose, as an investigative board.

**boarders** • 1. Personnel detailed to go aboard an enemy ship to search, capture, or destroy it. 2. Boarding party in a social sense, as when a group of dignitaries visits a ship.

**boarding call** • An informal visit of courtesy to another ship just arrived made by an officer junior to the commander of the arriving unit and the visiting unit. The purpose is to exchange necessary information. It requires no special ceremonies, other than piping the side. If made by a principal, the call is termed an official call or official visit.

**Board of Inspection and Survey** • Legally constituted group of experienced officers, representing Office of the Chief of Naval Operations (OPNAV), who make periodic inspections of naval ships to evaluate their material and operational readiness.

**board of investigation** • An investigatory

body of one or more persons. No power of subpoena. General term for all such bodies below court of inquiry.

**boat** • A small craft usually capable of being hoisted aboard a ship. Submarines are traditionally called boats, and aircraft carriers are often referred to as boats (usually by the embarked air wing). It is considered a nautical *faux pas* to call a ship a boat.

**boat ahoy** • A call used to hail a boat.

**boat anchor** • A very light anchor with extra large flukes for use in small boats. Generally small and light enough to be handled by hand and stowed in the bottom of the boat or in a locker.

**boat boom** • A spar swung out from a ship's side from which boats can be hauled out or made fast. Permits boats to ride safely alongside a ship at anchor without making contact with the mother ship's hull. Also called a boat spar or riding boom.

**boat box** • First-aid kit for use in a boat.

**boat call** • Flag signal used to establish communication with a boat.

**boat chock** • A deck fitting supporting a boat end that is resting on deck.

**boat cloak** • Cloak worn by naval officers in place of a coat; once a required article of uniform.

**boat deck** • Partial deck above the main deck, usually fitted with boat davits or cranes. Area aboard ship where one or more boats are stored.

**boat falls** • The lines used in hoisting or lowering a boat.

**boat gong** • Signal used to indicate departure of officer's boats and the arrival or departure of various officers.

**boat hails** • Ships at anchor hail approach-ing boats with "Boat ahoy." Responses depend on passengers; *e.g.*, if the commanding officer is on board the boat, the proper response is the name of the ship; if a commissioned officer (other than the captain), response is "Aye, aye"; if enlisted, it is "Hello," etc.

**boat hook** • Wooden staff with a combined hook and pushing surface, usually made of brass at one end; used by members of a boat crew to get ahold of rings, lines, or buoys from the deck of a small craft, or to push away from any object, such as the side of a ship.

**boat markings** • Official words and symbols affixed to ship's boats to indicate their specified use. For example, the captain's gig has the ship's name and an arrow symbol.

**boat oars** • Command given to the crew of a boat that is being rowed, directing them to lay their oars inside the boat alongside the gunwales, blades pointed forward.

**boat painter** • Line attached to the bow or stern of a boat, used to tow it or to secure it. Not to be confused with the sea painter, which is a much longer line used exclusively for towing alongside.

**boat plug** • Threaded drain plug fitting in the bilge of a boat, used to drain the boat when it is hoisted clear of the water.

**boat pool** • Group of boats available for general use at a harbor, port, or base; similar to a motor pool on land.

**boat skids** • *See:* skids, boat

**boat sling** • Rope or chain for hoisting or lowering large boats using a single davit or crane.

**boat station** • Allotted place for each person in a boat crew when a boat is being hoisted or lowered.

**boatswain** • Pronounced "bo-sn." An enlisted Sailor or warrant officer whose major duties are related to deck and boat seamanship.

**boatswain's call** • A tune played on a boatswain's pipe announcing or calling for some standard evolution such as meals for the crew, piping the side, lower away, etc. *See also:* pipe down

**boatswain's chair** • Seat sent aloft or over the side on a line to facilitate repairs or painting. Also used to transfer personnel from one ship to another while the two ships are alongside one another.

**boatswain's locker** • Compartment, usually forward, where deck gear is stowed.

**boatswain's mate (BM)** • Navy occupational rating that trains, directs, and supervises others in marlinespike, deck, and boat seamanship; ensures proper upkeep of the ship's external structure, rigging, deck equipment, and boats; leads working parties; performs seamanship tasks; can be in charge of picketboats, self-propelled barges, tugs, and other yard and district craft; serves in or is in charge of gun crews and damage-control parties; uses and maintains equipment for loading and unloading cargo, ammunition, fuel, and general stores.

**boatswain's pipe** • A small, specially shaped instrument held in the palm of the hand while blowing into it to produce several different high-pitched notes; used to call attention before passing the word, to render honors, to pipe or to issue commands to line handlers, winch operators, etc. Actually a specially shaped whistle (though by tradition never admitted to be such).

**boat waves** • In an amphibious assault landing, the lines of boats proceeding to shore in succession; for example, the first line of boats to arrive on the beach would be the first boat wave.

**bobbing a light** • The process of quickly lowering the height of eye several feet and then raising it again when a navigational light is first sighted, to determine whether or not the observer is at the geographic range of the light.

**body plan** • Line drawing of a ship.

**Boehme equipment** • An archaic, automatic code-sending and code-receiving device.

**bogey** • Unidentified aircraft. Used to describe an image on a radarscope.

**Bogie wire (cable)** • Wire that pulls a bogie car, holding a mine, along the track of a minelayer.

**boiler** • Metal chamber in which steam is generated. Some of its major components are a firebox or furnace, tubes, steam drum, etc.

**boiler central control station** • Centrally located station in a ship that has several firerooms; used for directing the control of all boilers and boiler operating stations.

**boiler emergency station** • Station for a chief watertender from which any fireroom, boiler room, or boiler operating station can be reached.

**boiler full-power capacity** • Total quantity of steam in pounds per hour at the contract-specified pressure and temperature that the boiler can produce.

**boiler pick** • *See:* chipping hammer

**boiler technician (BT)** • A petty officer who operates and maintains boilers and fireroom equipment. When created, it combined two older rates, boilermaker and boilerman.

**bollard** • Steel or iron post on a pier or wharf, used in securing a ship's lines. *See also:* bitts; cleat; dolphin

**bolo** • A line with a padded lead weight or a weighted monkey fist, thrown from ship to ship or from ship to pier in underway replenishments and mooring operations, respectively. Used to pass or bring aboard a larger line.

**bolter** • Describes a jet aircraft missing the arresting gear when attempting to land on a carrier and taking off again for another try.

**bolt rope** • Line sewn around the edge of a sail, tarpualin, or awning to strengthen it.

**bomb farm** • *Inf:* Topside stockpile of bombs used for rearming carrier aircraft.

**bombing, types of** • Glide bombing: attack at angles of 30–55° without brakes or flaps. Dive bombing: high angle attack (60–70°) using dive brakes. Masthead or skip bombing: level flight or shallow glide (under 30°). Horizontal bombing: attack from steady, level flight at high or medium altitude.

**bonding** • The act of providing an electrical connection between two objects; *e.g.*, an aircraft and a refueling truck.

**bone in the teeth** • A visual indication that a vessel is making way. As vessels move through the water, particularly with speed, a bow wave forms that can be seen from some distance. A lookout reporting that a vessel has a "bone in her teeth" indicates that the vessel is moving through the water.

***Booklet of General Plans*** • Set of ship's plans including the list of a ship's dimensions.

**boom** • A horizontal spar, attached with a hinge at one end to a mast or king post, etc. When attached to a mast on a fore-and-aft sailing vessel, the foot of a sail is bent on and the boom is used to efficiently control the sail. Cargo booms are attached to a mast or kingpost with a hinge and fitted with a topping lift at the other end, to serve as a lifting device or derrick. Boat booms are hinged to a ship's side and are rigged out for securing a

ship's boats when the ship is moored or anchored.

**boomer** • *Inf:* A submarine that carries ballistic missiles; an SSBN.

**boom guy** • *See:* lazy jack

**boom hoist** • A whip, or single part of a line, running over a block at the head of a boom and then to the deck where it may be used to handle weights.

**boondocks** • *Inf:* Any remote or isolated place.

**boost** • To supply an aircraft engine with more air or a mixture of fuel and air. Refers to manifold pressure on an engine.

**boot** • *Inf:* Recruit; a newly enlisted Marine or Sailor.

**boot camp** • Recruit training. Term originated during the Spanish-American War, when Sailors wore leggings called boots, which came to mean a Navy (or Marine) recruit. These recruits trained in "boot" camps.

**boot-topping** • Special anticorrosive and antifouling paint applied to the waterline area of a vessel; usually black. Paint applied on hatch coamings where foot scuff marks are likely.

**bore** • The interior of a gun barrel from the after end to the muzzle. The abrupt front of churning water, waves, or series of waves produced as a rising tide proceeds upstream.

**bore sight** • To align the axis of a gun with its sights.

**bottom blow** • Process whereby accumulated sediment is blown out of a boiler's water drum (using a bottom blow valve).

**bottom blow valve** • Valve at the bottom of a boiler's water drum used for blowing out sediment.

**bottom bounce** • Technique that extends a

sonar's effective detection range by bouncing its transmitted sound waves off the ocean bottom.

**bottom contour chart** • *See:* bathymetric chart

**bottom effect** • Sound waves will behave differently in shallower water than in deeper because of the "drag" caused by contact with the bottom (known as bottom effect).

**bottom line** • *See:* lifeline

**bottom loading** • Method of filling tank trucks or tank cars through a leakproof connection at the bottom.

**bottom reverberation** • Reverberation of sound from the sea bottom.

**bounce field** • *Inf:* Simulated carrier deck ashore.

**bouncer line** • In nighttime underwater demolition team (UDT) operations, the point off the enemy beach at which rubber boats are launched.

**boundary layer** • Any object moving in water or any fluid drags along, adjacent to its surface, a relatively thin layer of fluid called a boundary layer. The thickness of the boundary layer is dependent on the viscosity of the fluid.

**bourrelet** • The forward bearing surface of a projectile, machined in a band around its body to provide support for the projectile in the bore. *See also:* rotating band

**bow** • The front or forward part of a ship or boat. Sometimes referred to as the bows, because every ship has both a starboard bow and a port bow.

**bow array** • A sonar arrangement in which the transducer(s) is located in the bow of the ship only. *See also:* conformal array

**Bowditch** • Short name used to refer to the American Practical Navigator, the navigational "bible" originally written by Nathaniel Bowditch in 1802 and updated through numerous editions ever since. Most professional navigators own copies of *Bowditch* and *Dutton's*. *See also: Dutton's*

**bow door** • On landing ships or craft, the bow opens or becomes a ramp to allow troops or vehicles to disembark.

**bower anchor** • An anchor carried on a ship's bow.

**bow hook** • The member of a boat's crew who mans the boat hook forward and handles lines. *See also:* Stern hook

**bow insignia** • Symbolic stars, pennants, or arrows attached to the forward part of the hull of a boat, symbolizing the rank of the officer to whom the boat has been assigned.

**bowline** • A classic knot that forms a loop that will not slip or tighten under tension.

**bow number** • *See:* hull number

**bow painter** • A line attached to the stem of a boat. *See also:* sea painter; boat painter

**bowplane** • A rotatable, horizontal fin located near the bow of a submarine that is used to help the sub dive or rise.

**bowser boat** • Boat used to refuel boats, aircraft, or vehicles.

**bowsprit** • A built-in spar projecting forward and angling up from the bow of a sailing vessel. It extends the head sails and helps support the mast(s) through head stays.

**bow thruster** • *See:* thruster

**box** • In convoy operations, the three rear stations in the commodore's column and in the columns adjacent on either side, are left vacant for air operations when a carrier is stationed in the convoy. This vacant space is known as the box.

**box the compass** • To name all the points of a compass in succession (north, north by east, etc.).

**boys town** • *Inf:* Living space for junior officers.

**brace** • Lines attached to a square-rigger's yards, by which they may be trimmed to the wind. *See also:* splice the main brace

**bracket and halve** • An efficient method of targeting in which a succession of two salvos deliberately straddle the target (one over and one short, or one left and one right). A correction of half the difference in the two shots will cause the shot to fall closer to the target. Continuing this method will eventually hit the target.

**brackish water** • Slightly salty water; specifically, water with a salinity between 0.5 and 17 parts per thousand.

**brash ice** • Relatively small fragments of sea or river ice with a diameter of less than 6 feet.

**brass** • *Inf:* Officers, especially senior ones.

**brassard** • Arm band worn to symbolize some official duty, *e.g.*, a shore patrol brassard.

**brass hat** • *Inf:* An officer in the rank of commander or above. Refers to the gold on senior officers' cap visors.

**bravo** • Phonetic word for the letter B.

**bravo pattern** • The sound-range pattern obtained by bathythermograph readings in water less than 100 fathoms deep. The term relates to bottom effect.

**bravo zulu** • This is a naval signal, conveyed by flaghoist or voice radio, meaning "well done"; it has also passed into the spoken and written vocabulary. "Bravo Zulu" actually comes from the Allied Naval Signal Book (ACP 175 series), an international naval signal code adopted after the North Atlantic Treaty Organization (NATO) was created in 1949. Until then, each navy had used its own signal code and operational manuals. World War II experience had shown that it was difficult, or even impossible, for ships of different navies to operate together unless they could readily communicate, and ACP 175 was designed to remedy this. In the U.S. Navy signal code, used before ACP 175, "well done" was signaled as TVG, or "Tare Victor George" in the U.S. phonetic alphabet of that time. When BZ was first introduced in ACP 175, it was rendered in each navy's particular phonetic alphabet; in the U.S. Navy, BZ was therefore spoken as "Baker Zebra." In the meanwhile, the International Civil Aviation Organization (ICAO) had adopted English as the international air traffic control language. They developed a phonetic alphabet for international aviation use, designed to be as pronounceable as possible by flyers and traffic controllers speaking many different languages. This was the "Alfa, Bravo, Charlie, Delta..." alphabet used today. The Navy adopted this ICAO alphabet in March 1956. It was then that "Baker Zebra" finally became "Bravo Zulu." The signal can be altered to the reverse meaning (*not* well done) by prefixing with a "negat" (for negative).

**bread and water** • Reduced rations with confinement, authorized as a punishment. *Inf:* Cake and wine.

**break** • 1. To unfurl a flag with a quick motion that breaks, or otherwise releases, the light line holding it tightly furled until this moment. Thus, a new commander "breaks" his flag or pennant in a ship. 2. In ship construction, an abrupt change in the fore and aft contour of a ship's main deck; *e.g.*, the break of the deck. *See also:* broken deck

**breakaway** • At the conclusion of an underway replenishment operation, the disconnecting and retrieving of all lines and hoses and the subsequent maneuvers to separate the ships from one another. Breakaways can be routine, carefully observing all safety precautions, or, in the event of an impending attack or the risk of a collision, an emergency breakaway can be ordered, in which case speed takes precedence over safety measures.

**breakaway coupling** • Coupling designed to part easily with a moderate pull.

**breakbulk cargo** • General cargo handled item by item, as distinct from containerized cargo.

**breakdown lights** • Two vertical red lights on foremast that denote "Not under command" (meaning the vessel is broken down). When these same lights are pulsating, it means the vessel has a man overboard and recovery operation under way.

**breaker** • 1. A wave that breaks into foam against the shore. 2. A container for drinking water carried by boats or rafts.

**breaker height** • Vertical distance from the crest of a breaker to the preceding trough.

**breaker line** • The outermost boundary of a breaker area. Also called the surf line.

**breaker, plunging** • A surf wave that builds up rapidly and then crashes forward violently, indicating a rapidly shoaling bottom. *See also:* breaker, spilling

**breaker, spilling** • A surf wave that breaks gradually with the top spilling over forward with little violence, indicating a gradually shoaling bottom. *See also:* breaker, plunging

**break ground** • Come loose from the bottom, as an anchor does when it's hoisted.

**break off** • To carry a line away from the load, let it go, return to the point from which the line is being hauled, take a new hold, and then walk away again. This must obvi-

ously be done by a number of people in order to keep constant pull on the load.

**break out** • 1. Take out of stock or storage, as in "Let's break out some steaks for the evening meal." 2. To prepare for use; for example, one might break out a fire hose in preparation for a damage control drill.

**breasting float** • *See:* camel

**breast line** • A mooring line from ship to pier, perpendicular to the fore-and-aft axis of the ship; prevents lateral movement of the vessel toward or away from the pier. *See also:* spring lines

**breast out** • To temporarily maneuver a ship or boat away from another ship or a pier to which she has previously been alongside, in order to allow another ship to be placed in between. Often done to allow renesting of ships when one arrives or departs.

**breech** • Opposite end from the muzzle of a gun, where rounds are inserted for firing.

**breechblock** • Device that closes the firing chamber of a large gun after loading ammunition. In small arms, the same device is called the bolt.

**breeches buoy** • A device for transferring personnel between ships via highline, or from a stranded ship to the shore. Derived from the early design: a life buoy fitted with a strong canvas bottom with leg holes (looking like a pair of breeches). Thus, if the buoy fell into the water, the passenger would be automatically provided with floatation gear.

**breech mechanism** • Device for closing the breech of a gun; the moving parts that insert the breech block and lock or unlock it.

**breeze** • General term for winds: 22–27 knots (strong breeze), 17–21 knots (fresh breeze), 11–16 knots (moderate), 7–10 knots (gentle), 4–6 knots (light). *See also:* gale;

storm; hurricane

**bridge** • Ship's structure, topside and usually forward, from which the ship is usually controlled (conned) when under way. Modern vessels have control equipment, such as the helm, as part of the bridge equipment. But on older ships these stations were manned in a pilothouse separate from the bridge. Sailing ships were conned from the main deck aft, abaft the aftermost mast; but when huge paddle wheel boxes were added to early steamers, they so interfered with vision that underway OODs stood their watches on the cross-over bridge built between them; hence the origin of the term. The bridge has been the underway conning station ever since.

**bridge deck** • On merchant-type ships, a partial deck above main deck, usually amidships.

**bridge gauge** • A machinery tool or instrument used to determine the drop of a journal in any type of sleeve bearing that is made in halves. It bridges between the two sides of the lower-bearing half, thus the term.

**bridle** • A span of rope, chain, or wire with ends secured and the strain on the midpart, as in towing a ship or pulling an aircraft on a catapult.

**brief** • To instruct people for a specific mission or operation before it is begun. Debriefing means a verbal report after the operation has been completed.

**briefing** • Conference or meeting held to give instruction or provide details on a specific operation.

**brig** • 1. A secure place of confinement aboard a ship at sea. A naval prison or jail. 2. A two-masted, square-rigged sailing ship. Originally an abbreviation for brigantine, but later became a separate type. *See also:* brigantine; hermaphrodite brig

**brigantine** • Sailing vessel with two masts, the foremast square-rigged and the mainmast fore-and-aft rigged. Same as a hermaphrodite brig, except that a square topsail might be carried on the mainmast, well above the normal position for a topsail. *See also:* brig; hermaphrodite brig

**brightwork** • Unpainted brass, chromium, or steel kept clean by polishing. Among small boat enthusiasts, unpainted wood, such as teak.

**bring home** • To move a piece of gear to its proper or stowed position; *e.g.*, a boom being rigged in is brought home.

**broach** • To be thrown broadside to a surf or heavy sea. To get crosswise to the direction of wave travel; particularly dangerous near a beach or shoal water. To break surface partially, either deliberately or accidentally, but not come fully to the surface, as with a submarine. Sometimes called porpoising.

**broad** • Wide, as "broad in the beam."

**broadcast** • A naval term meaning to transmit radio messages to the fleet.

**broad command pennant** • Blue and white pennant flown by an officer—not a flag officer—who commands a major unit of ships or aircraft, such as a division of cruisers or an aircraft wing. *See also:* burgee command pennant

**broad on the bow** • Halfway between dead ahead and abeam.

**broad on the port (starboard) bow** • Said of something having a relative bearing midway between the beam and dead ahead, on the port (starboard) side; 315° (045°) relative.

**broad on the port (starboard) quarter** • Said of something having a relative bearing midway between the beam and dead astern, on the port (starboard) side; 225° (135°) relative.

**broad on the quarter** • *See:* on the quarter

**broadside** • 1. The act of firing all main battery guns to one side at once. 2. Sidewise, as "The current carried the ship broadside toward the beach."

**broken deck** • A weather deck of a ship that is not continuous from bow to stern. Thus, a ship with a raised forecastle would have a broken deck. Different classes of destroyers are frequently referred to as broken deckers or flush deckers. *See also:* break

**broken stowage** • Wasted space in a ship's hold. Small packages are used to fill such hold space.

**broken water** • An area of small waves and eddies in otherwise calm water.

**brow** • Temporary bridge or ramp between the ship and a wharf or pier or another ship moored alongside. Often fitted with wheels at the shore end to allow it to adjust with the changing tide.

**brown shirts** • Plane captains and air wing leading petty officers on an aircraft carrier; so called because they wear brown shirts for easy identification. *See also:* yellow shirts; blue shirts; green shirts; red shirts; white shirts; purple shirts; grapes

**brown shoe** • *Inf:* Aviation officer. The term originated from the fact that before WWII, only aviators and submariners wore khaki and green uniforms, and these uniforms required brown shoes. Surface officers wore only black shoes. The name stuck for aviators. *See also:* black shoe

**brown water ops** • Naval operations in shallow water—such as rivers or areas close to shore.

**B-scope** • Cathode ray indicator that presents a plot of target range versus bearing. *See also:* A-scope; plan position indicator (PPI)

**bubble pulse** • Echo (heard on sonar)

caused by the collapse of the bubble following an underwater explosion.

**bubble sextant** • Sextant that determines the horizontal plane by a leveling bubble instead of the horizon. Less accurate than a regular sextant; hence, it is used only in aircraft or when the horizon is otherwise not usable.

**buccaneer** • A freebooter or pirate. The term is derived from boucan, a grill for roasting meat used by cattle hunters in the West Indies. Because boucaners were essentially poachers with no regard for the true ownership of the cattle they destroyed, in the seventeenth and eighteenth centuries, the term grew to include sea robbers.

**buck** • Small object placed on the wardroom table to mark the place of the officer who is to be served first. The buck is passed around the table so that a different officer is served first with each meal. The object used varies from ship to ship.

**bucket of steam** • Nonexistent item, requested of new personnel aboard ship as a joke.

**Buckeye** • The T-2C Buckeye is a tandem-seat, carrier-capable, all-purpose jet trainer. Used for intermediate and advanced training for Navy and Marine Corps pilots and Naval Flight Officers in training for jet carrier aviation and tactical strike missions. *See also:* Goshawk

**buckler** • 1. Flexible cover attached externally to a turret's front armor plate so that the guns are free to train or elevate, yet water cannot enter the gunport. *Inf:* Bloomer or bloomers. 2. The metal plate over a hawse hole to keep water from passing through it and onto the forecastle deck when the ship plunges into a sea.

**bug** • *See:* speed key

**bug juice** • *Inf:* A substance similar in appearance to Kool-Aid which is served as a beverage aboard USN ships. The color has little bearing on the flavor. Largely composed of ascorbic acid and sometimes used as an all-purpose cleaner/stripper for bulkheads, decks, brass fire nozzles, and pipes.

**bugle** • A horn with limited notes, all controlled by the player's lips, used for military purposes to broadcast a general order to all hands within hearing range, such as taps, reveille, retreat, liberty call, torpedo defense, general quarters. The first bugle calls were said to be written by Joseph Hayden in about 1793, but the bugle has been used for military purposes since antiquity. The first bugles were made from the horns of wild oxen.

**builder's trials** • Trials conducted at sea or at a dock by the builder to prove the readiness of a ship for preliminary acceptance trials.

**builder (BU)** • Navy occupational rating that is like a civilian construction worker. BUs may be skilled carpenters, plasterers, roofers, cement finishers, asphalt workers, masons, painters, bricklayers, sawmill operators, or cabinetmakers. BUs build and repair all types of structures including piers, bridges, towers, underwater installations, schools, offices, houses, and other buildings.

**building ways** • Inclined slides leading into the water upon which a ship is built. When it is time to launch her, the regular supports under the hull are replaced with skids designed to slide down the inclination and support the hull upright until it enters the water. The ways are carefully greased, and at the last moment, just after the christening ceremony, the final holding devices are removed or cut and down she goes.

**bulkhead** • Walls or partitions within a ship, generally referring to those with structural functions such as strength and water tightness.

**bulkheading** • *Inf:* Complaining or grumbling with the intention of being overheard by seniors.

**bulk storage tank** • A fixed tank used to receive, store, and issue fuel for further transportation, storage, handling, or treatment before it reaches an operating tank.

**bull ensign** • The senior ensign aboard.

**bull gear** • Part of a main engine reduction gear. Specifically, the largest, slowest-turning gear in the gear train.

**bullhorn** • Device used to amplify and project one's voice for many to hear; megaphone.

**bullnose** • Closed chock at the apex of a vessel's bow. Has the appearance of a large flared nostril.

**bull rope (line)** • 1. The line taking the greatest weight in cargo handling. 2. The weight-bearing line supporting a topping lift.

**bully beef** • Beef jerky; a staple in the daily menu of the old Navy. Also called salt junk.

**bulwark** • Section of a ship's side continued above the main deck as a protection against heavy weather; extends above the deck like lifelines but is solid in construction.

**bulwork** • A solid, fencelike barrier along the edges of weather decks.

**bumblebee** • Noise-making device for sweeping acoustic mines. *See also:* foxer gear

**bumboat** • A civilian boat selling supplies, provisions, and other articles to the crews of ships. Supposedly derived from "boomboat," signifying a boat permitted to lie at the ships' booms.

**bumwad** • *Inf:* A newspaper or magazine. *Inf:* Toilet paper.

**bungee** • Securing line for the control stick

of an airplane. Part of the parking harness used when an aircraft is on deck.

**bunk** • Any bed used aboard ship or in a barracks; replaced the hammock.

**bunk bottom** • Canvas laced to bunk frame, used instead of springs to support a mattress.

**bunk cover** • Flameproof cover for bedding aboard ship.

**bunker** • 1. Compartment or tank used for stowing fuel. 2. Underground shelter.

**bunker crude** • Unrefined or only slightly refined crude oil burned in steam-powered merchant ships, black in color. The corresponding naval fuel was slightly more highly refined and known as NSFO (Navy standard fuel oil), also jet black.

**bunker gear** • The aluminized protective clothing and boots worn by crash and rescue fire fighters when they respond to alarms.

**bunting** • 1. Cloth from which signal flags are made. 2. The flags themselves, as in the order "Air bunting." 3. Decorative draping.

**buoy** • A floating object, anchored to the bottom, indicating a position on the water, to mark an obstruction or shallow area, or to provide a mooring for a ship.

**buoy tender** • Vessel designed for servicing manmade aids to navigation.

**burdened vessel** • The vessel required to take action to avoid collision under the nautical Rules of the Road. The other vessel is the privileged vessel, which is required to maintain its course and speed. *See also:* privileged vessel; general prudential rule

**bureau number** • Number designation assigned to each aircraft.

**burgee** • A swallow-tailed pennant.

**burgee command pennant** • Red and white

burgee flown by an officer who commands a division of ships, such as submarines or destroyers or a major subdivision of an aircraft wing. Such an officer has the courtesy title of "commodore" while so serving. *See also:* broad command pennant

**burn bag** • Receptacle for classified matter that is to be destroyed.

**burnout** • Point in time or in the missile trajectory when combustion of fuels in the rocket engine is terminated by other than programmed cutoff. *Inf:* Condition of being overworked to the point of lost effectiveness.

**burton** • Small tackle formed by two single-sheave blocks with a hook block in the bight of the running part. Generally used for setting up or tightening rigging, for shifting weights on board, etc. For transferring supplies during replenishment at sea, a burton rig can be set up between ships.

**burton rig** • An underway replenishment rig similar to a yard and stay rig used alongside a pier, except that the yard component is on one ship and the stay component is on the other. *See also:* yard and stay

**bushing** • Metal liner serving as a bearing for a shaft.

**bust** • *Inf:* To fail or make a mistake. *Inf:* To reduce in rate.

**butt** • In the old Navy, a ship's water barrel. *See also:* scuttlebutt

**butt bucket** • *Inf:* Ash tray.

**butterworth** • Method of cleaning and gas-freeing oil tanks by use of seawater under pressure.

**butt kit** • *Inf:* Ash tray.

**bypass** • 1. To divert the flow of gas or liquid. 2. A line that diverts the flow of a liquid or gas.

**by the board** • 1. To go over the side. 2. To be swept away. 3. Forgotten.

**by the wind** • *See:* full and by

**by your leave** • A courteous expression or greeting voiced by a junior who overtakes a senior while walking. The junior holds a salute and says "By your leave, Sir/Ma'am," and the senior responds with "Carry on," while returning the salute. The junior then ends his/her salute as he/she passes the senior and proceeds.

**C-2** • *See:* Greyhound

**C-9** • *See:* Skytrain

**cabin** • Quarters aboard ship for the captain or visiting admiral.

**cable** • 1. Any heavy wire or rope such as towing cable or degaussing cable. 2. An old and little used unit of approximate or estimated length or distance that, after some disagreement, is now generally accepted as being 100 fathoms. *See also:* mariner's measurements

**cablejack** • Device for lifting an anchor chain off the deck to insert a slip hook. Sometimes shortened to jack.

**cable-laid rope** • Three or four plain-laid, three-stranded ropes twisted in a direction opposite to the twists in each rope; used for ropes much exposed to water, such as the anchor cable of old sailing ships.

**cable markings** • Turns of wire and stripes of paint on anchor chain links to show the scope of chain out.

**Cag** • Derived from Commander Air Group,

the informal name given to the commander of an air wing. Originally, the assemblage of aircraft in an aircraft carrier was called an air *group* so its commander got the nickname of "CAG". When air groups became air wings, the nickname remained.

**caisson** • 1. Any temporary structure of wood or metal built to hold back water for repairs or construction. For example, the gate at the entrance to a drydock. 2. Horse-drawn vehicle once used to carry ammunition, now often used to carry coffins at military and state funerals.

**cake and wine** • *Inf:* Bread and water (as punishment).

**caliber** • 1. Diameter of a gun's bore in inches or centimeters, used also to specify the length of the barrel. Thus, a 3-in./50 gun has a bore diameter of 3 inches and a barrel length of 50 times the bore, or 150 inches. A 16-inch, 50-caliber main-battery gun, as fitted in USS *Missouri*, is 5 calibers (80 inches) longer than the 16-in. 45-cal. guns of older battleships and therefore has greater range. 2. Diameter of a rocket head.

**calibrated airspeed** • The indicated airspeed corrected for instrument errors. *See also:* airspeed; indicated airspeed

**calibration** • To check, fix, or correct the graduation of a measuring instrument.

**call** • 1. Formal social visit by an officer and spouse to the home of another. It involves leaving calling cards and was once ridgidly prescribed and carefully followed, including return calls. Now a call is largely passé as a custom. 2. An informal visit of courtesy to another ship just arrived made by an officer junior to the commander of the arriving unit and the visiting unit. The purpose is to exchange necessary information. It requires no special ceremonies, other than piping the side. If made by a principal, the call is termed an official call or official visit. 3. A tune played on a boatswain's pipe, calling for certain prescribed evolutions. *See also:* official visit; boarding call

**call away** • To order a ship's boat or vehicle to be manned and made ready.

**call book** • *See:* morning call book

**call mission** • Type of air support operation in which a specific request is made for an attack against a target.

**call sign** • A group of letters and/or numerals that identifies a station, command, or activity for communications purposes.

**calve** • The process of splitting ice from a glacier to form icebergs.

**camber** • Convex curvature athwartships of the deck of a ship; causes water to run off the deck and over the side.

**camel** • Float used as a fender between two ships or a ship and a pier. Also called a breasting float.

**camel station** • *Inf:* Rendezvous point for ships in the Indian Ocean.

**Canada balsam** • Optical cement, used in binoculars, periscopes, etc.

**can buoy** • Cylindrical, flat-topped buoy. *See also:* nun buoy

**can-do** • *Inf:* Efficient, capable, and willing; *e.g.*, a repair ship might be praised as a can-do ship.

**canister** • 1. A large number of bullets or balls, similar to grape, but made up in a can of the proper diameter to fit the bore of the gun for which it is designed. The can bursts when the gun is fired, resulting in a shotgun effect. 2. An antipersonnel weapon. The same as grape—which was loaded loosely into the cannon—but the canister made it easier to load, gave a more uniform load and, because

it fit the bore of the gun better, was more accurate. In historical accounts of seventeenth, eighteenth, and early nineteenth century action, the phrase "grape and canister" is frequently encountered. *See also:* langrage; dismantling shot; double-shot

**cannibalize** • To remove serviceable parts from one piece of equipment for use in another.

**cannon cocker** • *Inf:* Gunner's mate.

**canopy** • A plexiglass covering over an aircraft cockpit. Canvas or metal cover fitted over part of a boat to provide protection from rain, spray, etc.

**canted deck** • *See:* angled deck

**cap** • The proper term for the top of a mast, except for the highest mast, where it is called a truck.

**capillary waves** • Small waves, less than about 0.5 centimeters in length, with rounded crests and V-shaped troughs, whose characteristics are a function of surface tension.

**capital ship** • Term used to describe the primary or most important ship type in a nation's navy. At one time, the battleship was considered the capital ship of the U.S. Navy; today it is the aircraft carrier.

**caprail** • Rail on the stern of a tug over which a towing cable rides.

**capsize** • To turn over; to upset; as when a boat "turns turtle" (goes keel up).

**capstan** • A vertically-mounted, rotating mechanism used to heave on a line or cable. In sailing days, it was turned manually by wooden bars inserted into the capstan head (also called a drum head) at the top of the mechanism. In more modern versions, a steam or electric engine supplies the power. If a similar mechanism has no connection with an anchor, it is appropriately called a winch rather than a capstan. Generally, if a similar mechanism is mounted horizontally, rather than vertically, it is properly called a windlass. *See also:* windlass

**captain** • 1. A military rank; 0–6 in the sea services and some government services, equivalent to Army colonel. In Army, Marine Corps, and Air Force, however, a captain is an 0–3, equivalent to a Navy lieutenant. 2. The form of address for any commanding officer of a Navy ship, regardless of rank. The senior of a yacht's paid crew is the captain; the owner or any amateur in charge is the skipper. 3. A title by which a ship's master or anyone who has master's papers should be addressed.

**captain's mast** • A hearing held by the commanding officer whereby he or she awards punishment, listens to requests, or commends personnel for meritorious achievements or special service. When used to mete out punishment it is considered nonjudicial.

**captain of the head** • *Inf:* Person responsible for cleaning washrooms and toilets. Known to Marines as the head orderly.

**captain of the port** • The officer (usually Coast Guard) responsible for port security.

**cardinal point** • One of the four principal points of the compass—north, east, south, and west. *See also:* intercardinal points

**careen** • To lay a ship on its side in shallow water or on the beach, generally to work on the hull.

**cargo** • Material carried in ships or aircraft. Classified as dry, bulk, general, heavy lift, deck, dangerous, liquid, refrigerated, etc. May be palletized, breakbulk, or containerized.

**cargo classification** • The division of military cargo by type or function for combat loading (and efficient unloading).

**cargo deadweight** • Cargo deadweight is the total deadweight minus fuel, water, stores, dunnage, and other items required on a voyage; expressed in long tons.

**cargo documentation** • Papers required for a merchant ship to enter or leave a port, including manifest, crew list, stores list, bills of lading, tonnage certificates, and other marine certificates as required.

**cargo hoist** • *See:* cargo whip

**cargo net** • Net made of heavy line used to lift cargo. Also sometimes suspended over the side of a ship to be used for quick embarkation and debarkation of personnel in amphibious operations. *See also:* debarkation net

**cargo papers** • Documents to assist in cargo handling, including bills of lading, manifests, stowage plans, and hatch lists.

**cargo plan** • Plan showing the capacity of each of a ship's holds.

**cargo port** • Opening in a vessel's side through which cargo can be loaded or unloaded.

**cargo rope** • *See:* cargo whip

**cargo whip** • Rope or chain used with a derrick and winch for handling cargo. One end has a heavy hook, the other end is rove through the derrick and taken to the winch. Also called cargo hoist, cargo rope.

**carling** • Short fore-and-aft timber or girder placed under a deck to stiffen it; *e.g.*, under mooring bitts, winches, masts.

**carpenter stopper** • A device used by seamen to hold a length of wire rope in place while also allowing it to be quickly released.

**carriage** • The part of a gun mount that supports the gun itself.

**carrick bend** • Usually seen as a double carrick bend, a much-used knot for bending two different-size lines or hawsers together.

**carrier** • 1. Short for aircraft carrier. 2. Any organization that operates ships for ocean transport. 3. General use of the term as extended to include transporters of freight on land as well.

**carrier air traffic control center** • The center on an aircraft carrier responsible for controlling all carrier air operations except those being controlled by the combat information center.

**carrier controlled Approach (CCA)** • Landing approach to an aircraft carrier during which the pilot is guided in speed, heading, and altitude by a controller aboard the carrier.

**carrier onboard delivery (COD)** • System of delivering support items (such as spare parts and mail) between an underway aircraft carrier and bases ashore. An aircraft that has been designated for this duty is often referred to as "the COD."

**carrier qualification (CARQUAL)** • Training by which pilots are qualified to land aboard aircraft carriers.

**carrier strike group (CSG)** • Formed and disestablished on an as-needed basis, carrier strike groups are built around an aircraft carrier. CSGs provide a wide range of options to the U.S. Government, from simply showing the flag to attacks on airborne, afloat, and ashore targets. Because carriers operate in international waters, their aircraft do not need to secure landing rights on foreign soil. CSGs will typically (though not always) also have two guided missile cruisers (equipped with Tomahawks for long-range strike capability), a guided missile destroyer (used primarily for antiair warfare), a destroyer and frigate (used primarily for antisubmarine warfare), and two attack submarines (in a direct support role seeking out and destroy-

ing hostile surface ships and submarines). A combined ammunition, oiler, and supply ship provides logistic support enabling the Navy's forward presence, on station, ready to respond. The carrier strike group can be employed in a variety of roles to gain and/or maintain sea control.

**carrier task force (CTF)** • Older name for a group of ships centered around one or more aircraft carriers; later changed to "battle group," and still later changed to "strike group."

**Carrier Wave (CW)** • Radio transmission in which intelligence is passed by breaking the signal into discernible entities (dots and dashes). Morse code radio transmissions are transmitted via CW signals.

**carry away** • The act of breaking loose.

**carry on** • An order to resume or continue previous activity. In the days of sail, the officer of the deck kept a weather eye constantly on the slightest change in wind so sails could be reefed or added as necessary to ensure the fastest headway. Whenever a good breeze came along, the order to "carry on" would be given. It meant to hoist every bit of canvas the yards could carry. Through the centuries the term's connotation has changed somewhat.

**carry rudder** • To require constant right or left rudder to offset some external force (such as wind or current) in order to maintain a desired course.

**cartridge** • A complete assembly consisting of an initiator and a pressure-producing propellant in a suitable casing.

**casrep** • *Inf:* Broken; in need of repair. Derived from the acronym CASREP for "casualty report," but used in general conversation to mean something that is not working right.

**cast** • 1. To throw a line, such as heaving a

mooring line over to a pier. 2. Act of heaving a sounding lead into the sea to determine depth of water. 3. To direct the ship's bow in one direction or another when getting under way.

**casting** • The act of turning a ship through 360° without appreciably changing its position; done by alternately backing and going ahead on engines while repeatedly shifting the rudder.

**cast off** • Order given to let go or throw off, mooring lines. *See also:* take in

**casualty board** • A visual display of a ship's compartments and systems; used by damage control personnel to manage emergency repairs.

**casualty control book, engineering** • Maintained by ships to assist in control of engineering damage. Contains machinery readiness bills, examples of casualties, and how to correct or repair them.

**casualty report** • A routine report of any material breakdown. In the short term, necessary for a commander to be aware of the current status of his or her forces; in the long term, permits the accumulation of performance data on specific equipment or systems that can be used to effect improvements or to guide future acquisitions.

**cat** • 1. Short for catapult. 2. Short for cat-o'-nine-tails. 3. To hang an old-fashioned anchor from the cathead with the catfall to its ring, either by hoisting it from the in-sight condition when weighing anchor, or by swinging it from its at-sea stowage with the cat-davit. In preparation for anchoring, the catfall was replaced by an expendable line that was cut on the order, "Let go!"

**cat's-paw** • The ruffled surface of the water that results from a light passing breeze; sometimes called a catskin. A twisting hitch made in the bight of a line forming two eyes (loops) through which the hook of a tackle can be passed.

**catalyst** • A substance that provokes or accelerates chemical reactions without itself being altered.

**cat and fish** • In order to get an anchor aboard in the old sailing navy, the anchor was hoisted using the catdavit to a point where a Sailor could then fish for the padeye located at the balance point of the anchor. This then allowed the anchor to be swung into its stowed position. Later, anchors were stowed on billboards from which they could be dropped directly without first being catted, and the cathead was eliminated entirely.

**catapult** • A device for launching aircraft from a ship's deck.

**catdavit** • A specially designed small davit on the forecastle used for swinging an old-fashioned anchor to its stowed position. In wooden sailing ships it was also used for swinging the anchor from the at-sea stowage to the cathead, in preparation for dropping. Usually in pairs, one on each bow. In iron and steel ships, in which the catheads were eliminated, the catdavits had to have an extremely long overhanding reach, leading to unusual but effective tripod designs. *See also:* cat and fish

**catenary** • The dip in a length of chain or cable because of its own weight. The catenary provides spring or elastic effect in towing, anchoring, or in securing to a buoy.

**catfall** • Part of the anchor gear. A small tackle used to hoist an old-fashioned anchor from the water to the cathead on weighing anchor.

**cathead** • A strong piece of oak projecting over the bows (one on either side) of a vessel, usually with the face of a cat carved on its end. (The reason for this is uncertain.)

Preparing an anchor for sea, or for dropping, involved hanging it from the cathead. The anchor could be let go from this position, or fished and stowed for sea. The cat-davit was used to swing the anchor between the at-sea stowage and the cathead.

**cathode** • The negatively charged electrode of an electrolytic cell.

**cat-o'-nine-tails** • A short piece of rope fashioned into an instrument for flogging. Traditionally, the victim to be punished was required to make his own "cat" by unlaying a portion of a three-strand line, separating each of the strands into three parts, then tarring and braiding the parts into nine "tails." Tradition and pride dictated that the victim make the cat as fearsome as possible by knotting the tails, and even including small nails or other metal objects in the knots. A poorly made or soft cat was considered a mark of the craven. If it did not pass muster, it would be replaced by one that did. *See also:* room to swing a cat

**catskin** • *See:* cat's-paw

**catwalk** • A walkway constructed over or around obstructions on a ship for convenience of the crew; for example, an aircraft carrier has catwalks around and just below the flight deck.

**caulk** • 1. To pack a seam in the planking of a ship. 2. The material used to pack seams so as to prevent leakage or penetration.

**caulking** • Burring or driving up the edges of iron or steel plates along riveted seams to make them watertight. Sealing a gap with a pliable material to make it waterproof or air tight.

**caulk off** • *Inf:* Meaning to sleep or catch a nap. Derived from the days of wooden ships when Sailors sleeping on deck would find their backs marked by stripes of caulking material if the deck was freshly caulked. Often pronounced "cork off."

**caution** • An emphatic notice requiring correct operating or maintenance procedures to prevent damage to equipment.

**cavitation** • Disturbance around revolving propeller blades, struts, etc., caused by collapse of transient-pressure disturbances resulting from flow of water over their surfaces. It increases corrosion, reduces efficiency, and increases the noise detectable on sonar.

**CBR defense** • Chemical, biological, and radiological defense. At various times, this has been known as ABC (atomic, biological, chemical) defense; NBC (nuclear, biological, and chemical) defense.

**ceiling** • 1. The cloud cover which affects flight operations; for example, "flight operations must be canceled today because the ceilng is too low." 2. The minimum height above the ground at which all clouds, at and below that height, cover more than half the sky. 3. A lining or planking inside a ship's hull, including the flooring of a cargo space.

**ceilometer** • Instrument for measuring cloud or ceiling heights.

**celestial equator** • The plane of the equator extended to the celestial sphere. A great circle on the celestial sphere that is, at every point, 90° from the celestial poles.

**celestial meridian** • A great circle on the celestial sphere passing through the north and south celestial poles.

**celestial navigation** • Using the predictability of the Sun, Moon, stars, and certain planets to find locations on the surface of the Earth.

**celestial sphere** • An imaginary sphere of infinite radius concentric with the Earth on which all celestial bodies, except the Earth, are imagined to be projected.

**celsius** • Temperature based upon a scale in which, under standard atmospheric pressure, water freezes at 0° and boils at 100°.

**centerline** • An imaginary line down the middle of the ship from bow to stern.

**center of buoyancy** • The geometric center of gravity of the volume of a ship's displacement taken so that, in computations for metacentric height, the entire buoyant effect of the sea on a ship's hull may be considered as being applied at this single point. Used in combination with center of gravity to calculate location of metacenter.

**center of floatation** • The center of gravity of the waterplane; the point about which a vessel trims.

**center of gravity** • Point in a ship where the sum of all moments of weight is zero. With the ship at rest, the center of gravity and the center of buoyancy are always in a direct vertical line. For surface ships, the center of buoyancy is usually below the center of gravity, and the ship is prevented from capsizing by the additional displacement on the low side during a roll. Thus, the point at which the deck edge enters the water is critical because from here onward increased roll will not produce corresponding increased righting force. In a submerged submarine, center of buoyancy of the submerged hull is always above the center of gravity, and the ship remains upright because of the pendulum effect, which is as important fore and aft as it is athwartships.

**centigrays (cGy)** • A measurement of absorbed radiation equal to 1 rad.

**certificate of registry** • See: registry, certificate of

**CH-46** • See: Sea Knight

**CH-53** • See: Sea Stallion

**chad tape** • A tape with different combinations of perforations representing characters on a keyboard; used in teletype operations.

**chaff** • A radar reflective material used to deceive or counteract unfriendly radar or destructive offensive ordnance.

**chafing gear** • Canvas, line, or other material placed around rigging and mooring lines to prevent wear. See also: baggy wrinkle

**chain bridles** • A special rig used in towing, particularly aircraft.

**chain countermining** • The explosion, either deliberate or accidental, of a series of munitions in close enough proximity to be caused by the adjacent explosions. For example, all of the mines in a channel might be detonated by a single explosion if all the mines are close enough to one another to be detonated by the effects of the others.

**chain grab** • See: wildcat; windlass

**chain hook** • Hand tool for handling anchor chain.

**chain locker** • Compartment where anchor chain is stowed.

**chain of command** • The succession from superiors to subordinates, through which command is exercised; and the succession from subordinate to superior through which requests should go.

**chain pipe** • Heavy steel pipe that leads the anchor chain through the deck to the chain locker.

**chains** • The platform or position in the bow from which the leadsman heaves the lead. In the sailing navy, the masts were braced by standing rigging, much of which was secured to platforms jutting out from the sides of the ship, outboard of her bulwarks. To prevent the pull of the rigging from snapping off the platforms, short sections of chain were led from their outboard edges to points lower on the side of the ship. Leadsmen customarily used these platforms to stand upon when heaving the lead, and hence their nautical designation, the chains, has persisted.

**chain stopper** • Short length of chain fitted with a pelican hook secured to an eyebolt on the forecastle; used for securing anchor and chain in the hoisted (housed) position and for quickly releasing anchor and chain upon anchoring. It also secures the chain after anchoring when the proper scope is out.

**chalk test** • A test of the tightness of a watertight fitting by rubbing chalk on the knife edge. The resultant imprint on the gasket indicates whether or not the knife edge is bearing everywhere against the gasket.

**challenge** • A demand for identification or authentification. Can be that made by a sentry or a demand for a coded signal response made by one ship or unit when encountering another, transmitted by any of a number of means (flashing light, voice radio, etc.).

**chamfer** • To bevel a sharp external edge.

**CHAMPUS system** • Civilian Health and Medical Program of the Uniformed Services. Medical care system for the armed forces; replaced by TRICARE.

**chandelle** • An abrupt climbing turn to nearly a stall in which the momentum of the airplane is used to obtain a steeper climb than its power plant can normally deliver.

**change of command** • An official ceremony marking the changing of a unit's commanding officer, usually attended by invited guests and following traditional protocols.

**channel** • The deeper or marked portion of a harbor or waterway through which ship traffic is directed. A designated frequency or range of frequencies within which a radio transmitter maintains its modulated carrier signal.

**chantey** • A song sung by sailors in rhthym with their work. Also often called a "sea chanty" and pronounced "shanty." Traditionally sung by men walking the capstan around; it became something of a ceremony if they were heaving in the anchor to get under way. If the ship was lucky enough to have a fiddler on board, he might perch on top of the capstan, sawing away on his violin as his shipmates did their best to make him dizzy. *Var:* chanty.

**chanty** • *See:* chantey

**chaplain** • Minister, rabbi, or priest of a recognized religious order, commissioned in the Navy to counsel and serve the spirtual needs of Sailors and Marines.

**charge** • To pressurize a hydraulic or pneumatic system with fluid or air.

**Charlie** • During the Vietnam War, the enemy insurgent forces were known as the "Viet Cong" and several derivative terms emerged, including "VC," "Victor Charlie," and simply "Charlie."

**charlie** • Phonetic word for the letter C.

**Charlie Noble** • Sailors' nautical name for the galley smokepipe. Derived from the British Merchant Service Captain Charlie Noble, who required a high polish on the galley funnel of his ship. His funnel was of copper and its brightness became known in all ports his ship visited. To "shoot Charlie Noble" meant to fire a blank inside the pipe to shake down the soot.

**chart** • Nautical map. Hydrographic charts show depth of water, nature of bottom, and aids to navigation. Aeronautical charts show terrain features and other information for air operations. Charts for U.S. waters are produced by the National Ocean Survey; others by the National Imagery and Mapping Agency.

**chart, bathymetric** • *See:* bathymetric chart

**chart correction card** • A paper record of changes to a nautical chart.

**chart datum** • The geodetic reference used to establish spatial relativity of objects depicted on a chart. "WGS 84" (for World Geodetic Survey 1984) is an example of this type of chart datum. Some potential confusion now exists in that this datum and the one referring to water depths are each very important (especially since the advent of GPS), but they are completely separate references despite their shared names. The plane to which soundings and tide tables on a chart refer (in the United States, usually means low water or mean lower low water).

**charted depth** • The vertical distance from the reference plane to the bottom.

**charthouse** • Compartment on or near the bridge for handling and stowage of navigational equipment. Usually contains a chart table and stowage for charts. Also called chartroom.

**chart overlay** • Transparent sheet to be used with a chart, providing special operational or navigational information such as gunfire support stations, etc.

**chart portfolio** • *See:* portfolio, chart

**chartroom** • *See:* charthouse

**chart scale** • A chart scale is the ratio between a distance on a chart and the corresponding distance represented on the earth.

**chart, sonar** • Chart containing oceanographic data useful in echo ranging under water.

**chase** • The sloping part of the outside of a gun between the muzzle and the slide.

**chaser** • In sailing days of broadside fire—a gun placed so that it could fire ahead (bow chaser) or astern (stern chaser), and thus be used for pursuit or when pursued. *Inf:* Sentry or guard; *i.e.,* brig chaser.

**chatter** • Vibration caused by uneven motion of a machine, possibly resulting in damage to parts. *Inf:* Unnecessary talk on a radio circuit.

**check** • Command to keep a strain on a line, but to ease it out as necessary to prevent parting, as in "Check number-two line." The command to keep a strain even at the risk of parting is "hold," as in "Hold number-three line." *See also:* snub; hold

**checklist** • An individual sequence of procedures designed to ensure that important steps are not omitted when performing a vital task.

**checkman** • Person in fireroom who controls water level in boilers. *See also:* watertender

**check valve** • A valve that permits liquid to flow in one direction only.

**chemical alarm** • Distinctive signal used to warn of an impending gas, nuclear, or biological attack.

**cherry picker** • *See:* crash dolly

**cherubs** • Hundreds of feet of aircraft altitude. Angels are thousands.

**Chester** • By tradition, the name given to the dummy used in man-overboard recovery exercises.

**chevron** • V-shaped mark that denotes rate, located beneath the specialty mark and eagle on a Sailor's rating badge.

**chicken guts** • *Inf:* Aiguilettes *See also:* loafer's loops

**chief learning officer** • The designated and accountable officer charged with ensuring that the central tenets of a learning organization are applied throughout a command or unit.

**Chief of Naval Operations (CNO)** • The senior active duty officer in the Navy.

**chief of staff** • The officer who assists an admiral as second in command, especially in supervising the staff. The senior assistant to a commodore or below is called "chief staff officer" vice "chief of staff."

**chief of the boat** • The senior chief petty officer in a submarine; the commanding officer's right-hand man in the administration of the crew. Equivalent to the command master chief in surface vessels.

**chief petty officer (CPO)** • A naval enlisted person in paygrade E-7. Until 1958, this was the highest rank attainable while still in the enlisted category. For further promotion, one had to look to the warrant grade. Now, however, two superior grades have been established: senior chief petty officer (paygrade E-8), and master chief petty officer (paygrade E-9).

**chief staff officer (CSO)** • The senior assistant to a commodore or equivalent (non-flag officer) who directs the staff in a manner similar to a chief of staff. *See also:* chief of staff

**Chinese landing** • 1. Bringing a boat or ship alongside so that one vessel's bow is aligned with the other's stern. 2. Bringing a ship alongside down-current. 3. Landing an aircraft down-wind.

**Chinese style** • In the old Navy, doing something in reverse of the usual way was doing it "Chinese style."

**chipping hammer** • Small hammer with a sharp peen and face set at right angles to each other; used for chipping and scaling metal surfaces. Also called scaling hammer or boiler pick.

**chips** • *Inf:* Ship's carpenter.

**chit** • *Inf:* Letter, note, voucher, or receipt. Term probably derived from the old East India Company and the Hindu word *chitti*. The word gained wide acceptance in the Far East and was used throughout the British Army and Navy, as well as the U.S. Navy.

**chock** • 1. Metal fitting through which hawsers and lines are passed to redirect their path. May be open or closed. 2. Blocks placed in front and back of wheels to prevent an aircraft or vehicle from rolling. 3. Blocks supporting a boat under repair. *See also:* roller chock

**chock-a-block** • Full; filled to the extreme limit. Two-blocked; fully closed; close up; tight against.

**chockmen** • Men who handle the chocks that are placed around the wheels of an aircraft to prevent it from rolling.

**chop** • Derived from "change of operational control," it is used to indicate the shifting of a ship or unit from one operational commander's control to another. For example, "USS *Wasp* will chop to the Sixth Fleet on 1 December." To chop a message or letter is to initial it, expressing acceptance, approval, support, etc. For example, "Get the captain's chop on this message before transmtting it."

**chopline** • A boundary expressed in longitude and latitude, at which ships change operational control. *See also:* chop

**chopper** • *Inf:* Helicopter.

**chow** • *Inf:* Food. The chow line is the mess line. To chow down means mess call or dinner is served.

**christening a ship** • Ceremony recognizing the official beginning of a ship's life. Usually includes the naming of the vessel by a sponsor and the breaking of a bottle of champagne against the ship's bow as it slides into the water.

**chronometer** • An accurate timepiece, with a nearly constant rate, specially designed for navigational use.

**chuffing** • The characteristic of some rockets to burn intermittently and with an irregular noise.

**church pennant** • A blue and white pennant flown during church service. By tradition, the only flag or pennant that may be flown on the same hoist above the national colors, and then only during services aboard ship. Also flown ashore during church services.

**cigarette deck** • Open deck abaft the bridge of a submarine. Now obsolete because of streamlining. The term developed because it was the only place where personnel were permitted to smoke in the early submarines.

**cigar mess** • A cooperative within the wardroom mess that sold cigars, cigarettes, candy, etc., for the convenience of the members of the mess.

**cipher** • A system in which symbols represent units of plain text of regular length (usually single letters) to conceal the real meaning. The are two basic types: transpositional and substitutional. A transpositional cipher rearranges characters; e.g., the word "anchor" could be become "cnohar" in a transpositional cipher. A substitutional cipher uses other letters or symbols in place of the plain text ones; e.g., the word "anchor" could become "zmxgli" by substitution. Ciphers can be simple or complex, particularly if mechanical or electronic means are employed.

**cipher device** • Hand-operated enciphering and deciphering apparatus.

**cipher machine** • A mechanical or electrical cipher apparatus.

**circuit** • Communication link between two or more points. An assemblage of electronic elements capable of carrying intelligence, signals, or power.

**circular error probable (CEP)** • Estimate of the accuracy of a weapon, used to determine the probable damage to a target. Developed during advent of electronically- or inertially-guided missiles, now applied also to bombing, especially area bombing. Seldom used for gunfire, except shore bombardment.

**circular file** • Inf: Trashcan.

**cirrocumulus** • High clouds (mean lower level above 20,000 feet), composed of small white flakes or very small globular masses.

**cirrostratus** • Thin, whitish, high clouds (mean lower level above 20,000 feet).

**cirrus** • Detached high clouds (mean lower level above 20,000 feet) of delicate and fibrous appearance.

**clamp down** • To sprinkle with water and dry with a moist or dry mop for a light cleaning. Distinguished from swabbing, which uses a wet mop frequently doused and wrung out in buckets of water.

**clap on** • To clap on a rope means to catch hold in order to haul on it. To clap on canvas means to put on more sail.

**class alfa fire** • Fires involving ordinary combustible materials that leave an ash (wood, paper, cloth, etc.). See also: classes of fire

**class A schools** • Service schools where basic technical knowledge required for job performance in a given rating is taught.

**class bravo fire** • Fires involving liquid or semi-liquid substances (gasoline, oil, grease, paint, etc.). See also: classes of fire

**class charlie fire** • An electrical fire. See

*also:* classes of fire

**class delta fire** • A fire involving special materials and firefighting methods, such as when dealing with combustible metals (sodium, magnesium, etc.). *See also:* classes of fire

**class E schools** • This identifies schools designed for professional education leading to an academic degree.

**classes of fire** • Class A (Alfa) fires involve ordinary combustible materials that leave an ash (wood, paper, cloth, etc.). Class B (Bravo) fires involve liquid or semi-liquid substances (gasoline, oil, grease, paint, etc.). Class C (Charlie) fires are electrical. Class D (Delta) fires are special fires not covered by the other classes, such as combustible metals.

**class F schools** • Team training schools conducted in fleet concentration areas, such as Shipboard Firefighting Team Trainer.

**classified information** • Any information the revelation of which must be controlled in the interest of national security.

**classified matter** • Information or material that must be safeguarded in the interest of national security. *See also:* top secret; secret; confidential

**class P schools** • Officer-acquisition schools, designed to provide education and training for midshipmen, officer candidates, and other newly commissioned officers.

**class R schools** • Basic schools that provide initial training after enlistment. Also known as "boot camp" or "recruit training."

**class V schools** • Training that leads to designation as a naval aviator or naval flight officer.

**clear** • 1. To remove stoppages or fouled gear. 2. To remove ammunition from a gun. 3. To pass a point, cape, or other landmark or object. 4. Not enciphered or coded. 5. To approve or obtain approval for. 6. Free for running, not fouled. A mooring line is reported clear of the water, a ship clears her berth, an anchor is reported clear when being hoisted if it is not fouled. *See also:* clear anchor; clear ship

**clearance** • 1. Determination that an individual is eligible to have access to classified information of a specific category. An individual must obtain a security clearance in order to have access to classified information. 2. An aspect of mine countermeasures. 3. Permission for a ship to enter or leave harbor; clearance through quarantine, etc.

**clear anchor** • Report made to commanding officer that the anchor is in sight and is free of any entanglement, particularly its own chain. Opposite of foul anchor. Sometimes expressed as "Anchor is clear."

**clear datum** • If a submarine is detected and subsequently departs the area, it is said to "clear datum."

**clear for running** • Pertaining to a line, ready to run out without fouling.

**clear hawse** • 1. Clear for hoisting the anchor with no problems. 2. No turns in the chains with two anchors down. *See also:* foul hawse

**clear ship** • Prepare a ship for action by removing items such as jackstaffs, stowing paint and other inflammables below, opening ready service ammunition boxes, etc. *See also:* strip ship

**cleat** • An anvil-shaped deck fitting for securing or belaying lines. Consists, essentially, of a pair of projecting horns.

**clew** • In a fore-and-aft sail, the lower corner aft. In a square sail, the two lower corners.

**climatic** • Any element associated with the climate of an area.

**climatology** • The study of the statistical means, frequencies, deviations, and trends of weather elements for an area over a period of time.

**Clinker** • Antisubmarine warfare system for sensing heat from submarine water trails.

**clinometer** • Device for measuring the amount of a vessel's list or how much she is rolling. *See also:* inclinometer

**clip** • *See:* hank

**clipper** • General name for a fast sailing ship. The original Baltimore clippers were heavily canvassed, sharp-ended boats built in the Chesapeake Bay region that developed a reputation for speed, dating from about the beginning of the nineteenth century. The term clipper had its heyday in the mid-nineteenth century with the development of the long, rakish, heavily sparred and canvassed clipper designed for the California trade. Driven by bold speed-demon skippers, these ships set records for the lengthy voyage. This, combined with the sheer beauty of the ships (*e.g., Lightning, Flying Cloud, Sea Witch*), has earned them a place in the romantic history of the days of sail.

**close** • To close means for a ship to go near to; for example, "Close that unknown contact to see if we can identify her."

**close aboard** • 1. Near, as when an enemy shot falls close aboard. 2. When determinng whether honors should be rendered, a ship is considered close aboard when within 600 yards; 400 yards for a boat.

**close air support** • Aircraft action in support of troops; usually so close to own forces as to require detailed integration and coordination.

**close covering group** • Naval vessels formed to protect ships or shore facilities against enemy surface attack.

**close-hauled** • Sailing as close to the wind as practicable; toward the direction from which the wind is blowing.

**closest point of approach** • The position of a contact when it reaches its minimum range to own ship.

**close to the wind** • In sailing terms, being close to the wind is to be sailing in a direction as near as possible to the opposite direction the wind is blowing.

**close up** • Hoisted all the way up; as when signal flags or sails are hoisted up as far as they will go. The act of hoisting a flag to, or in, its highest position. Same as two-blocked.

**clothes stop** • Small cotton lanyard once used for fastening clothes to a line after washing them (nautical equivalent to a laundry clothes pin), or for securing clothes that were rolled up. *See also:* stop

**clothing** • Insulating material wrapped around pipes; covered by lagging.

**Clothing and Small Stores** • A government-operated shop on a base or large ship that stocks standard articles of uniforms and uniform accessories for officers and enlisted personnel.

**cloud** • A visible assemblage of numerous tiny droplets of water or ice crystals formed by condensation of water vapor in the air with the base above the surface of the Earth.

**clove hitch** • A knot often used for fastening a line to a spar or stanchion.

**clump** • *See:* shoe

**clutch** • A form of coupling designed to connect or disconnect a driving or a driven component of a machine or mechanism.

**clutter** • Interference (extraneous signals) on a radar scope tending to obscure real targets. May be due to reflections off of waves, rain, snow, or other sources.

**$CO_2$** • Chemical notation for carbon dioxide; a heavy, colorless gas that will not support combustion. It is used for fighting small fires and in protection systems in motor gasoline and JP-5 spaces aboard ship.

**coach whipping** • *See:* cross pointing

**coaling bag** • Large (4x4 ft.) canvas bag used in transporting material between ships during underway replenishment. Originally designed for use when coaling ship. *See also:* coaling ship

**coaling ship** • Fuel replenishment in the days when naval ships were powered by coal.

**coaming** • Raised framework (edge) around deck or bulkhead openings and cockpits of open boats to prevent entry of water.

**Coast Guard** • A governmental organization charged with various maritime-related duties, including homeland security, drug interdiction, at-sea rescue, enforcing safety-at-sea laws, and customs regulations. It has been under various government departments throughout its history, including the Departments of the Treasury, Transportation, and Homeland Security (as of this writing). In wartime, it can be assigned to the Navy Department, as it was during Word War II.

**Coastie** • *Inf:* A member of the United States Coast Guard.

**Coast Pilot** • Publication designed to augment nautical charts with information that does not easily fit on a chart; provides directions for piloting in inland and coastal waters of the United States and its possessions. Issued by the National Oceanic and Atmospheric Administration.

**cockbill** • With reference to the old-fashioned anchor, it is a-cockbill when hung from the cathead preparatory to being either dropped or fished and secured for sea. Yards are a-cockbill when topped up at an angle to the deck, thus slanted or uneven in appearance. Yards of a square-rigged man-of-war were traditionally cockbilled (tilted as near to vertical as possible) as a sign of mourning analogous to soldiers with rifles reversed, or a horse with boots reversed in the stirrups.

**cockle** • A kink in an inner yarn of rope, forcing the yarn to the surface.

**cockpit** • 1. The pilot's compartment in an aircraft. 2. A well, or sunken place in the deck of a boat, almost always protected with a coaming, for use of the crew or passengers for protection from sea or weather. 3. In the days of fighting sail, the cockpit was a compartment below the waterline where the ship's surgeons would try to cope with battle injuries.

**code** • A form of encryption in which whole words or phrases (vice merely letters) are replaced by others.

**coding delay** • Time interval between transmissions of loran master and slave stations.

**codress** • Message having the address buried in the encrypted text.

**cofferdam** • Void space between compartments of a ship, serving primarily to isolate one space from another, especially to prevent oil or other liquids from getting into a compartment located near a tank. Waterproof wall built around a damaged area of a ship's hull.

**coil down** • To lay out a line in a circle with coils loosely on top of one another. *See also:* flemish down; fake down

**cold cat** • *See:* cold shot

**cold iron** • The condition of an idle engineering plant when all port services are received from an external source such as shore or tender.

**cold-iron watch** • Security patrol in the engineering spaces of a ship whose machinery is not in use or tended. *See also:* cold iron; cold ship

**cold ship** • Ship that is completely dependent upon shore power; having no self-contained propulsion or generation source in use. From steam powered ships without boiler fires lighted, thus having no source of power. Also called dead ship.

**cold shot** • A catapult shot in which insufficient end speed is generated. The aircraft does not have sufficient speed to fly, and usually crashes. May be caused by steam supply problems or other mechanical difficulties.

**collaboration at sea** • An information network distributing intelligence within a battle group or fleet through the use of wireless communication and interactive computing.

**collar** • The metal ring that steadies the base of a mast or supports the upper end of a boom that is stowed upright.

**collateral nature of effects** • Collateral effects are unintentional or incidental, direct or indirect, effects causing injury or damage to persons or objects.

**collier** • Vessel specially designed to carry coal.

**collision bulkhead** • Watertight athwartships bulkhead of a ship, usually near the bow, designed to absorb much of the shock in the event of a collision.

**collision mat** • A mat made of canvas and fiber, designed to be hauled down over a hole in a ship's hull caused by a collision, grounding, or battle damage. *See also:* thrums; hogging line

**colors** • 1. The national ensign (flag); as in "one must always salute the colors when boarding a naval ship during daylight hours." 2. The ceremony of raising the flag at 0800 and lowering it at sunset aboard a ship not under way, or at a shore station.

**column** • Formation of ships, aircraft, or people in single file.

**column open order** • Line of ships in a column having alternate ships staggered a few degrees to the right and left of the guide, with even-numbered ships to the left.

**combat aircrewmen** • Specially qualified aviation enlisted personnel, wearing winged insignia, who comprise the crews of combat aircraft.

**combat air patrol (CAP)** • Fighter aircraft stationed over task force or objective area to provide protection against hostile aircraft.

**combatant ship** • A ship whose main mission is combat.

**combat distinguishing device** • A small metal V worn on various ribbons and medals to indicate the award involved actual combat operations.

**combat information center (CIC)** • The section of a ship or aircraft manned and equipped to collect and collate tactical information.

**combat loading** • The loading of assault troops and equipment for rapid debarkation in predetermined priority during an amphibious assault. *See also:* base loading; commercial loading

**combination lantern** • Light divided into red and green sections; used on a small craft instead of sidelights.

**combined operations** • Operations conducted by forces of two or more allied nations. *See also:* joint operations

**combined publications** • Those designed for use with allied forces. *See also:* joint publications

**combustion chamber** • In a steam torpedo, the chamber in which air, fuel, and water are mixed and ignited to produce steam to power the torpedo turbine. Also called combustion pot. Not to be confused with torch pot.

**combustion pot** • *See:* combustion chamber

**come about** • In sailing, to tack or wear ship; to change direction so that the wind is coming over the opposite side of the vessel.

**comealong** • A fitting, flush with the deck, covering a pad eye or cleat used for securing aircraft, cargo, etc. A seaplane anchor cable clamp.

**come home** • Said of an anchor when it drags toward the ship while heaving in, or of anything as it approaches its normal stowed position.

**comingling** • The mixture of two or more petroleum products resulting from improper handling, particularly in pipeline or tanker operations.

**command** • 1. Order directing a particular action in a specific way; generally executed upon receipt. 2. Authority vested in an individual for the direction, coordination, and control of military forces. 3. Unit, activity, or area under the command of one individual. *See also:* order

**commandant** • Commander of a subordinate command within a larger organization; for example, the Commandant of Midshipmen is subordinate to the Superintendent of the Naval Academy; another example is the Commandant of the Marine Corps, who heads the Marine Corps, which is a subordinate component of the Navy; and because the National War College is a subordinate component of the National Defense University, the college head is called the Commandant.

**command guidance** • After a missile is launched on an intercept course, a computer uses separate radar inputs to track both it and the target, and transmits orders to the missile to change its track as necessary to ensure that it hits the target.

**commanding officer (CO)** • Officer in command of a ship, squadron, aircraft, or naval activity with duties and responsibilities as specified in U.S. Navy Regulations. May be a staff officer in special cases, as the doctor who commands a hospital.

**command master chief** • The senior enlisted person designated to advise the commanding officer on enlisted personnel matters. Similar functions are performed in the submarine force by the chief of the boat.

**commendatory mast** • Ceremony at which the commanding officer commends, congratulates, or decorates members of his command.

**commercial loading** • Loading of a vessel for maximum use of space, rather than for military purposes. *See also:* base loading; combat loading

**commissaryman (CS)** • Petty officer who performs cooking, baking, and butcher duties. *Inf:* Bellyrobber; stew burner.

**commissary store** • Grocery store for military personnel, often located on base. The lower prices at such stores are among the benefits taken into account when military pay scales are established.

**commission** • 1. The document from which a commissioned officer gets rank, status, pay, etc. 2. To put a ship in active service under a commissioned commanding officer, who breaks the commission pennant and sets the watch.

**commissioned officer** • One who derives authority from a commission as granted by the President and confirmed by the Congress

**commission pennant** • Narrow red, white, and blue pennant with seven stars, flown day and night at the main truck of a ship in commission (under command of a commissioned officer). *See also:* distinctive mark

**commodore** • 1. A courtesy title for an officer below rear admiral commanding a squadron, division, or other detachment of two or more ships. 2. A naval rank, not currently in use. When it was used as an official commissioned rank, a commodore was a one-star officer (pay grade O–7), equivalent to brigadier general. Currently, a single star is called a "rear admiral lower half" (and two stars by a rear admiral upper half (pay grade O–8). *See also:* convoy commodore

**communication countermeasures** • Measures—generally highly classified as to technique, intent, and results—designed to detect, locate, interfere with, confuse, or misinform enemy communications or communications equipment. Includes intercept, search, jamming, and other techniques.

**communications satellite** • An orbiting vehicle, either active or passive, that relays signals between communications stations. The U.S. Navy was one of the early pioneers in this technology.

**commutation of quarters** • Old term for a housing rental allowance.

**commuted rations (COMRATS)** • Money paid to an enlisted man or woman when a general mess is not available. *See also:* subsistence allowance

**companionway** • An opening in the deck that gives access to a ladder; includes the ladder.

**company, ship's** • *See:* ship's company

**compartment** • Room or space on board ship; for example, a berthing compartment is a room where enlisted personnel sleep.

**compartment check-off list** • A list of fittings (such as valves, ventilators, internal communications circuits, etc.), with their location and function, that are found in a specific compartment; used for a specific purpose, such as helping damage control parties find these fittings in an emergency.

**compass** • Instrument for determining direction. There are several different types used on naval vessels: magnetic compasses depend on the Earth's magnetic field for their orientation; gyroscopic ones depend upon the tendency of a free-spinning body to align its axis with that of the Earth; magnetic flux-gate compasses combine the features of a magnetic compass with electronic enhancements, thus making it more efficient and practical.

**compass card** • A circular card in a compass that is marked with cardinal points and intercardinal points or with degrees. The compass card appears to rotate as the vessel changes course, but it is the ship that rotates around the card. A lubber's line is marked on the fixed portion of the compass and aligned with the vessel's head, and thus the heading of the ship can be ascertained by reading the direction marked on the compass card that lies at the lubber's line.

**compass compensation** • The process of neutralizing the magnetic effect the degaussing circuits exert on the magnetic compass.

**compass error** • Total difference between compass heading and true heading; composed of an algebraic combination of variation and deviation.

**compass heading** • The direction a ship's head is pointed relative to compass north.

**compass points** • Before compasses were designed to measure direction as finely as 0°–360°, they used the less-precise 32 point system (each point, therefore, covered an arc of 11-1/4°). Each point has a unique name, as follows: North, North by East; North-Northeast; Northeast by North; Northeast; Northeast by East; East Northeast; East by North; East; East by South; and so on.

**compass repeater** • A device that appears to be a compass and functions like one (providing directional readings), but is actually only replicating the readings from an actual compass located elsewhere in the ship.

**compass rose** • Graduated circles printed in several places on a nautical chart to assist in recording bearings and laying courses. The outer circle indicates true direction in degrees; the inner one indicates magnetic direction. Indications of the amount of variation and the amount of annual change are also included.

**compensate** • 1. To adjust water in trim tanks to attain desired buoyancy in a submarine. 2. To flood and void various tanks on a vessel to remove a list. 3. To correct a magnetic compass.

**competitive year** • That on which battle efficiency competition is based. *See also:* Fiscal year

**complement** • Authorized personnel for full combatant manning; designed for full operational effectiveness, considering the inherent capabilities of the unit and the possible requirements of war. *See also:* allowance; manning level

**compressor** • 1. Device or brake, operated by hand, in a chain pipe that governs the movement of the anchor chain. 2. Machine designed to produce air or some other gas under pressure. 3. Component of a gas turbine or jet engine.

**compromise** • Loss of security or potential loss of security resulting from the revelation of classified information to unauthorized individual(s). Includes possible compromise, as when a classified document is lost but it is not known whether it has become available to an enemy.

**computed altitude** • Altitude of the center of a celestial body above the celestial horizon at a given time and place as determined by computation, table, mechanical device, or graphics. In celestial navigation, the computed altitude is compared to the actual sighted altitude to arrive at a line of position.

**concentrate** • To bring units closer together for mutual support, as when ships or aircraft concentrate to make an attack.

**condensate** • Water produced in the cooling system of the steam cycle, from steam that has returned from the turbine or from steam that has returned from various heat exchanges.

**condenser** • Low-pressure, heat-transfer device in which steam is changed back into water by cooling.

**condition 1** • *See:* condition I

**condition 1A** • *See:* condition IA

**condition 1AA** • *See:* condition IAA

**condition 1AS** • *See:* condition IAS

**condition 1E** • *See:* condition IE

**condition 1M** • *See:* condition IM

**condition 2** • *See:* condition II

**condition 3** • *See:* condition III

**condition 4** • *See:* condition IV

**condition 5** • *See:* condition V

**condition 6** • *See:* condition VI

**condition I** • Maximum readiness condition; synonymous with general quarters. May be modified for certain conditions, such as condition 1-AS, in which all antisubmarine watch stations and weapons are manned, but AAW stations are not. Modified conditions are used to minimize crew fatigue, which can be a significant factor over a prolonged period at battle stations. *See also:* readiness conditions

**condition IA** • Shipboard readiness condition in which all necessary hands are on station to conduct amphibious operations. *See also:* readiness conditions

**condition IAA** • Shipboard readiness condition in which all necessary hands are on station to counter an air threat. *See also:* readiness conditions

**condition IAS** • Shipboard readiness condition in which all necessary hands are on station to counter a submarine threat. *See also:* readiness conditions

**condition IE** • Shipboard readiness condition in which full readiness is temporarily relaxed for a brief period (as in a lull in operations) to allow rest and/or distribution of food, etc. *See also:* readiness conditions

**condition IM** • Shipboard readiness condition in which the necessary stations are manned to conduct minesweeping operations. *See also:* readiness conditions

**condition II** • A condition of modified general quarters, in which selected stations are not manned to prevent crew fatigue; generally used only on larger ships. *See also:* readiness conditions

**condition III** • A shipboard condition of readiness commonly associated with wartime steaming where some, but not all, of the ship's weapons and combat systems are kept in a manned and ready status at all times. *See also:* readiness conditions

**condition IV** • A shipboard condition of readiness commonly associated with peacetime steaming. Combat systems are generally unmanned. *See also:* readiness conditions

**condition V** • A shipboard condition of readiness associated with peacetime in-port status. *See also:* readiness conditions

**condition VI** • Shipboard readiness condition used by ships in port where only minimal personnel are required to be on board to maintain minimum security and watch for fire and flooding. *See also:* readiness conditions

**condition xray** • *See:* material conditions

**condition yoke** • *See:* material conditions

**condition zebra** • *See:* material conditions

**conditions of readiness** • *See:* readiness conditions

**conduction** • Transmission of energy through a substance by direct molecular contact.

**cone of silence** • 1. Space directly over radio range station in which signals are not heard, or are greatly reduced in volume. 2. Space directly below a sonar transmitter or receiver where detection of a submarine is not possible.

**coner** • *Inf:* Short for nosecoaner. A crew member on a submarine who does not work in the engineering spaces. A non-nuke.

**confidential** • Classification of information and material that, if disclosed, would be prejudicial to national interests. A lower classification than secret or top secret.

**confinement** • One of the punishments available under the Uniform Code of Military Justice (UCMJ); an offender may be confined in a brig onboard ship if available or in an appropriately configured facility ashore. *See also:* restraint

**conformal array** • A sonar array in which multiple transducers are attached at various locations about the hull, rather than being concentrated in one location. *See also:* bow array

**confusion reflectors** • General term for nonelectronic mechanical devices and materials used in countermeasures against radar. Examples are chaff, gull, kite, and corner reflector.

**Congressional Medal of Honor** • *See:* Medal of Honor

**conn** • Control of ship's movements; the officer in control has the conn. To guide or pilot a ship is spoken of as conning.

**conning tower** • 1. Control station in any armored ship. 2. Control station in a submerged submarine. U.S. WWII submarines were built with conning towers to permit greater periscope-height extension. Most post-WWII submarines have been built without conning towers, and the conning station is an area set aside in the control room.

**Consol** • An electronic navigation system providing a number of rotating equisignal zones that permit determination of bearings from a transmitting station by counting a series of dots and dashes and referring to a table or special chart.

**consolidation** • Transfer of cargo among designated ships (oilers, ammunition ships, etc.) to enable some to return to base and reload while leaving others on station. Most commonly done among oilers.

**constant helm plan** • An evasive maneuver used by a ship that suspects the presence of an enemy submarine in the vicinity. Although the ship appears to be changing course constantly, it will not get very far off its base track. Similar to sinuating.

**construction battalion, naval** • Specially qualified persons organized to do military construction work. The battalion is the basic unit of the Navy's construction force, and it is from the name—construction battalion—that they draw their name: CBs or SeaBees.

Construction battalions may be amphibious (ACB), mobile (MCB), or maintenance unit (CBMU).

**construction electrician (CE)** • Navy occupational rating that is responsible for the power production and electrical work required to build and operate airfields, roads, barracks, hospitals, shops, and warehouses. The work of Navy CEs is like that of civilian construction electricians, powerhouse electricians, telephone and electrical repairmen, substation operators, linemen, and others.

**construction mechanic (CM)** • Navy occupational rating that maintains heavy construction and automotive equipment (buses, dump trucks, bulldozers, rollers, cranes, backhoes, etc.) as well as other construction equipment. CMs service vehicles, gasoline and diesel engines, ignition and fuel systems, transmissions, electrical systems, hydraulic, pneumatic, and steering systems.

**consular shipping advisor** • Naval officer appointed to the staff of a consular authority in a neutral country for naval control of shipping duties.

**contact mine** • *See:* mine

**contact report** • Report of first awareness (visual sighting, radar contact, etc.) of a ship, aicraft, etc. For example, a lookout makes a contact report to the officer of the deck when he or she spots a ship on the horizon.

**containerization** • The shipping of cargo in large containers that can be loaded onto tractor-trailer truck beds or onto trains for further transport.

**continental shelf** • The sea bottom from the shore to a depth of 200 meters. Width varies from nearly 0 to 800 miles. In general, the depth increases very gradually to about 100 fathoms (200 meters), at which point it increases more rapidly and at a steeper slope.

**continental slope** • The sea-bottom slope from the 200-meter line to great depths; varies in degree of slope by 3.5 to 6 percent.

**continuation pay** • Extra pay given to officers as an incentive for them to remain in service.

**continuous fire** • All guns firing independently when loaded; in contrast to salvo fire.

**contour** • A line connecting points of equal elevation or equal depth.

**control differential transmitter (CDX)** • A type of synchro that transmits angular information equal to the algebraic sum or difference of the electrical input supplied to its stator, and the mechanical input supplied to its rotor. The output is an electrical voltage taken from the rotor windings.

**controlled mine** • *See:* mine

**controlled port** • Harbor or anchorage in which entry, departure, berthing, and traffic are controlled by military authorities.

**control room** • Control center of a submarine, containing most of the valves, switches, gauges, and instruments for surfacing and submerging, steering, and general operational control. May include the conning station and torpedo fire-control station.

**control ship** • One that controls and directs the boats in an amphibious assault, usually stationed on the line of departure. Also sometimes called the marker ship.

**control transformer (CT)** • A type of synchro that compares two signals: the electrical signal applied to its stator and the mechanical signal applied to its rotor. The output is an electrical voltage, which is taken from the rotor winding and is used to control a power-amplifying device. The phase and amplitude of the output voltage depends on the angular

position of the rotor with respect to the magnetic field of the stator.

**control transmitter (CX)** • A type of synchro that converts a mechanical input, which is the angular position of its rotor, into an electrical output signal. The output is taken from the stator windings and is used to drive either a control differential transmitter (CDX) or a control transformer (CT).

**control vessel** • The ship that guides and directs the ship-to-shore movement in an amphibious landing. In underway replenishment, this vessel sets the replenishment course and speed, and is usually the guide.

**conventional weapons** • Nonnuclear weapons. This excludes all biological weapons and generally excludes chemical weapons, except for existing smoke, incendiary agents, and agents of riot-control weapons.

**conversion, ship** • Changing a ship's design or characteristics so that there is a major change in its mission or assignment to a different class. *See also:* fram; Service Life Extension Program

**convoy** • A number of merchant ships or naval auxiliaries, or both, traveling together for mutual support and protection, usually escorted by warships and/or aircraft. *See also:* leaver

**convoy commodore** • Officer (naval or merchant) designated to command a convoy. The post is subordinate to the escort commander. *See also:* commodore

**convoy routing** • The assignment of specific ocean paths for convoys to follow; designed for some specific purpose, such as avoiding bad weather or submarine concentration.

**cook-off** • Unwanted explosion of a projectile in a gun barrel due to heat; can occur during prolonged periods of firing that cause the gun's barrel to heat up to the point of danger.

**Copernicus** • The code-name under which the Navy plans to reformulate its command and control structures in response to the realization that information is a weapon. Through Copernicus, warfighters will get the information that they need to make tactical decisions.

**copperplate hand (fist)** • *See:* fist

**coppers** • Large cooking kettles in the galley.

**copy** • To maintain a continuous radio receiver watch, recording all transmissions. *See also:* guard; cover

**co-range lines** • Lines on a map or chart passing through all points having the same tidal range. *See also:* cotidal line

**cordage** • General term for rope and line of all kinds.

**Coriolis force** • Effect of the Earth's rotation on all moving bodies, including air and water masses. The trade winds are deflected from the north and south by this force.

**corner reflector** • Reflector formed of mutually perpendicular surfaces or planes. It increases the radar reflection from any object to which it is attached. Can be used as a confusion reflector to foil an enemy's radar detection capability or as a means of enhancing a craft's radar profile to increase its chances of being "seen" by radar-equipped vessels.

**corpen** • 1. A tactical maneuver when ships put their rudders over sequentially so that they maintain the same *relative* bearings from one another while changing course. Ships "turn" when they maintain the same *true* bearings to one another, while a corpen maintains the same *relative* bearings to one another. For example, ships traveling in a column would maintain the same order and therefore the same relative bearings after a 180° change of course if they used a corpen

maneuver, whereas the order of the ships in the column would be reversed (giving them different relative bearings to one another while maintaining the same true bearings) if they used a turn maneuver to change course 180°. 2. A signal flag used to signal corpen maneuvers. *See also:* turn

**corpsman** • Short for hospital corpsman; an enlisted medical technician; medic.

**corvette** • A small combatant patrol vessel, smaller than a frigate.

**cotidal line** • A line on a chart connecting points at which high water occurs at the same time.

**counter** • *See:* counter stern

**counter-battery fire** • Gunfire from a ship directed at enemy artillery ashore.

**counterbattery fire** • Fire delivered against active enemy weapons or fire control stations or both.

**counter current** • A secondary ocean current or eddy adjacent to and setting in a direction opposite to the main current, as on both sides of the Gulf Stream.

**counter flood** • To take water into a ship's tanks or compartments to reduce list or inclination by bow or stern by compensation. Must be done with care, for total buoyancy is also reduced.

**countermeasures** • A form of warfare carried on to eliminate or reduce the threat from or effectiveness of enemy equipment or practices. For example, electronic jamming can be employed as a counter measure against radar.

**countermining** • The detonation, either accidental or deliberate, of munitions caused by nearby explosions.

**countermining distance** • The limiting distance between mines that will avoid chain-countermining. Recommended minimum spacing for each type of mine is prescribed from statistical results of experiments. Also called countermining radius.

**countermining radius** • *See:* countermining distance

**counter stern** • Overhang at the stern of a ship. A ship with a cruiser stern has no counter. In other words, on a ship with a counter stern, the main deck extends farther aft than the point at which the stern enters the water; on ships with cruiser sterns, the main deck is even with that part of the stern that enters the water.

**country** • Definite area of a ship, such as admirals' country, officers' country, CPO country, Never used without a modifier.

**coupling** • Metal fitting at the ends of a fire hose or fuel hose to permit attachment to another length or fitting.

**course** • The intended direction of travel. Often designated as true, magnetic, compass, or grid; *e.g.*, "Steer course 000° pgc (per gyro compass)."

**course over the ground** • The direction of the path over the ground actually followed by a vessel. The preferred term is "track."

**court-martial order** • A published order announcing the results of a court-martial trial.

**court of inquiry** • Three or more officers convened for purposes of investigation. Convening authority must be an officer with general court-martial authority. Has subpoena power and designated witnesses may have counsel. *See also:* board of investigation

**court of military appeals** • The highest appellate court, established under the Uniform Code of Military Justice (UCMJ), to review the records of certain trials by court-martial.

**courts-martial** • The types are summary (lowest), special, and general (highest). *See also:* summary court-martial; special court-martial; general court-martial

**covenant leadership** • Leadership method in which leaders and followers make commitments to each other. The followers promise to serve and the leaders in return promise to commit themselves to mission accomplishment, to the good of the institution, and to the personal and professional growth and well-being of their shipmates. Leaders further promise respect, clear direction, meaningful work, and the tools and training to do that work, as well as recognition for a job well done.

**cover** • 1. The proper nautical term for a uniform hat or cap. 2. To maintain a continuous radio receiver watch with the transmitter calibrated and available. 3. Command to don hats or caps. *See also:* copy; guard

**covering fire** • Gunfire delivered to protect or cover certain operations, such as minesweeping.

**covert** • In intelligence work: secret, clandestine. Opposite of overt.

**cow's tail** • Frayed end of a rope or line; also called a fag or fag end. *See also:* Irish pennant

**cowl** • Bell-shaped air funnel or scoop, projecting above the deck or deckhouse of a vessel; used for ventilation.

**cowling** • Removable aircraft covering, as on a cockpit or engine.

**coxcombing** • Fancy knot work of coils of line worked around a tiller handle, stanchion, etc. *See also:* sennit; square knotting; MacNamara's lace

**coxswain** • Enlisted person in charge of a small boat; pronounced "cox-un."

**crab** • To move sidewise through the water (or air, in the case of an aircraft). To catch a crab in rowing is to inadvertently strike the water on the recovery stroke.

**crack** • Unnavigable break in sea ice caused by tide, temperature changes, current, or wind.

**crackerjack** • *Inf:* The traditional enlisted Sailor's uniform.

**cradle** • A stowage rest for a ship's boat, or any large object secured on deck. *See also:* saddle

**crash and dash** • *Inf:* Touch and go landing.

**crash dolly** • *Inf:* Wheeled device for moving crashed aircraft on a carrier flight deck. With the increased size and weight of aircraft, a wheeled crane is now generally used. Flight deck personnel have any number of names for it, such as Tilly the Toiler, cherry picker, etc.

**creeping attack** • Coordinated antisubmarine warfare (ASW) attack using noiseless approach with all target information furnished by an assisting ship. The attacking ship does not echo range. The submarine cannot hear the assisting ship echo ranging at a distance and is unaware of the quiet approach of the other until the carefully placed depth charge(s) go off.

**crew** • The people who operate a ship, boat, aircraft, turret, gun, missile, etc. Refers to the sport of competitive rowing.

**crib** • Rigid structure of timber, rock, concrete, and heavy wire used to close a harbor entrance, or serve as a bridge support or temporary breakwater, etc.

**critical** • Said of a reactor when the number of neutrons produced by fission is enough to continue the reaction. Associated terms are criticality and critical positions of control rods. *See also:* self-sustaining

**critical velocity** • The speed at which a current can scour the bottom enough to main-

tain required channel depth.

**critique** • Critical review of an operation or exercise held in the form of a conference.

**Cromwell current** • Subsurface current of the Pacific that flows west to east under the north equatorial current.

**cross-decking** • The practice of sending personnel from one ship to another to facilitate training.

**cross-deck pendant** • A heavy, abrasion-resistant section of an arresting cable; positioned on a carrier flight deck so that aircraft tail hooks will engage it.

**crossing the line** • Crossing the equator. Seafaring tradition calls for a special ceremony when a vessel crosses the line, during which those who have crossed before (called "shellbacks") initiate those who have not (called "pollywogs") into "Neptune's realm."

**crossing the T** • Classic tactic in a surface engagement wherein one battle line crosses and concentrates its fire upon the van, or leading units, of the other. Can also apply to an action between only two ships when one presents its broadside to the other's bow or stern, thereby having a distinct firing advantage.

**cross pointing** • Line, canvas, or leather braided around stanchions for decoration and protection. Also called coach whipping.

**crosspointing** • Line or strips of canvas or leather braided about a rail or stanchion as decoration and protection. Tapering a rope's end by cutting away the inner yarns and braiding the outer ones.

**cross signal** • In the nautical rules of the road, the illegal practice of answering a ship's whistle signal of two blasts with one blast, or vice versa.

**crosstree** • Wooden or steel spreader with a slot at each end, at right angles to the mast, over which the masthead shrouds are passed in fore-and-aft-rigged sailing vessels.

**crow** • *Inf:* The eagle on a petty officer's rating badge.

**crow's nest** • Lookout station aloft, generally on the foremast. The crow (the bird, not the rating badge) was an essential part of the early sailor's navigation equipment. These land-lubbing fowl were carried on board to help the navigator determine where the closest land lay when the weather prevented sighting the shore visually. In the case of poor visibility, a crow was released and the navigator plotted a course that corresponded with the bird's because it invariably headed toward land. The crow's nest was situated high in the mainmast where the lookout stood watch. Often he shared this lofty perch with a crow or two since the crows' cages were kept there; hence the crow's nest.

**crown** • The rounded part of an anchor below the shank. A knot in the end of a line made by interlacing the strands.

**crud** • In nuclear reactor operations, an old, informal term that has been legitimatized to a degree. It refers to the black radioactive coating that precipitates from the pure water of the primary loop during the production of power.

**crud burst** • Occasional temporary peaks of radioactivity in the primary loop have been theoretically ascribed to a piece of crud that, breaking loose from the inner surface on which it was originally deposited, lodges on or near one of the radioactivity sensors. According to reactor operating instructions, a rise in radioactivity beyond a specific point requires shutdown of the reactor, regardless of the suspected cause. Thus, a crud burst can give rise to an erroneous suspicion of a serious reactor casualty. *See also:* crud

**cruise** • 1. A voyage of some duration and usually for some specific purpose, such as a shakedown cruise. 2. *Inf:* Tour of sea duty. 3. *Inf:* A period of enlistment. *See also:* deployment

**cruise missile** • A guided missile that flies aerodynamically (similar to an aircraft) rather than ballistically to reach its target. *See also:* ballistic missile

**cruiser** • A type of warship, originally designed to be less armored and armed than a battleship; usually smaller and faster, thus cheaper to build and operate. Suitable for any naval duty except combat against battleships. Currently, cruisers are almost exclusively employed as antiair warfare (AAW) escorts for aircraft carriers. Cruisers were once named after cities, but in more recent times that tradition has been abandoned. Today's cruisers are often named for famous battles, such as Leyte Gulf. *See also:* heavy cruiser; armored cruiser; battle cruiser; warship

**cruiser stern** • A stern so shaped that it does not overhang the water, usually with a nearly perpendicular drop to the waterline after which it is cut away radically to provide for the rudder and screw(s). Differs from a counter stern, which is cut away before it enters the water. The rudder post, or operating shaft, cannot be seen in a ship with a cruiser stern, whereas it can be seen under a counter. The cruiser stern is so named because it resembles the stern of a man-of-war. *See also:* counter

**crush depth** • The depth at which the pressure hull of a submarine will collapse.

**cryptanalysis** • The process whereby an adversary's encrypted message traffic is "broken" back to plain text by analysis procedures other than having the enemy's cryptographic key.

**cryptoboard** • Group of personnel specifically designated for encrypting and decrypting messages.

**cryptocenter** • A secure area aboard ship used by the cryptoboard when encrypting or decrypting messages.

**cryptochannel** • Crypto aids, indicators, and instructions that comprise a basic unit in cryptographic communications.

**cryptogram** • A communication in visible, secret writing.

**cryptographer** • One who encrypts or decrypts messages.

**cryptographic key** • That which allows encrypted messages to be read. Can be electronic, mechanical, or a simple systematized correlation of characters.

**cryptography** • The science of rendering plain text into unintelligible text and vice versa for security purposes. Types include codes and ciphers.

**cryptologic technician (CT)** • Navy occupational rating that works with various coding and cryptographic systems. Depending on their special career area, CTs control access to classified material, translate foreign-language transmissions, operate radio direction-finding equipment, employ electronic countermeasures, and install, service, and repair special electronic and electromechanical equipment. CTs require special security clearances. (Service ratings: CTA [administrative]; CTI [interpretive]; CTM [maintenance]; CTO [communications]; CTR [collection]; CTT [technical].)

**C school** • *See:* class B schools

**culinary specialist (CS)** • Navy occupational rating that operates and manages Navy dining facilities and bachelor enlisted quarters. CSs are cooks and bakers in Navy dining facilities ashore and afloat; ordering, inspecting, and stowing food. They maintain food service and preparation spaces and equipment, and keep records of transactions and budgets for the food service in living quarters ashore. Formerly called "mess management specialists."

**cumshaw** • *Inf:* Something procured without official payment. Used as to indicate unauthorized work done, or equipment given to a ship or station without official sanction, as in "that test set is a cumshaw item," or "see if you can cumshaw a spanner wrench from that ship moored alongside." Comes from the beggars of Amoy, China, who said "*kam sia,*" meaning grateful thanks.

**cumshaw artist** • One who is adept at cumshaw. *See also:* cumshaw

**cumulonimbus** • A massive cloud with great vertical development, the summits of which rise in the form of mountains or towers, the upper parts often spreading out in the form of an anvil.

**cumulus** • A dense cloud with vertical development, having a horizontal base and dome-shaped upper surface, exhibiting protuberances.

**cup of joe** • *Inf:* Cup of coffee. Two explanations as to the origin of the term exist. One says it is derived from the old term for coffee, "jamoke." The other attributes it to the ruling by Secretary of the Navy Josephus Daniels, outlawing alcoholic beverages on Navy ships; this meant the strongest drink available was coffee and was named for the Secretary.

**current** • Water flowing in essentially a horizontal motion. In navigation, the deduced horizontal motion (measured as set and drift) that accounts for the difference between a dead-reckoning position and a fix at the same time.

**current direction** • The compass heading toward which water moves. Differs from wind direction, which is the compass heading from which it comes.

**current, ocean** • Continuous movement of the sea, sometimes caused by prevailing winds, as well as large constant forces, such as the rotation of the Earth or the apparent rotation of the Sun and Moon. Examples: the Gulf Stream, the Cromwell Current, the Kurishiro (Japanese Current). *See also:* inshore currents; offshore currents; rip current (tide)

**current pattern secondary** • Water movement that varies from the prevailing current pattern.

**current ship's maintenance project (CSMP)** • Record of repairs, alterations, etc.

**current standing-wave ratio (ISWR)** • The ratio of maximum to minimum current along a transmission line.

*Current Tables* • National Ocean Survey (formerly Coast and Geodectic Survey) publications giving data on tidal currents for various localities throughout the world. *See also:* Tide Tables

**current, tidal** • Currents along the coast caused by the rise and fall of the tides. Water movement associated with the rising tide is the flood current; that associated with the falling tide is the ebb current. Between flood and ebb currents is a period of no current, called slack water, which corresponds to the stand between flood and ebb tides.

**cusp** • Sand deposited by wave action in the form of points or bars projecting seaward along a beach.

**custodian** • Officer responsible to his commanding officer for custody, handling, and safeguarding of classified publications.

**customs of the service** • Unwritten naval practices having the force of usage and tradition. An example is the removal of caps or hats by officers entering a compartment

where the crew is eating.

**cut** • Landing signal officer's (LSO's) signal to a pilot to close the throttle, allowing the aircraft to settle aboard the carrier.

**cut and run** • *Inf:* To leave quickly, from the practice of cutting a ship's moorings in a hasty departure.

**cutlass** • A short, curved-blade weapon with a large hand guard, designed for cut-and-thrust combat. Issued to enlisted men for battle and maintained in ship's armories until the beginning of World War II. Officially declared obsolete in 1949.

**cut of his jib** • The nationality of early sailing ships was frequently determined by the shape or cut of their jib sails. Use of the phrase as applied to a sailor originally referred to his nose, which, like the jib, is the first feature of its wearer to come into view. Ultimately, it was extended to describe a person's general appearance.

**cutter** • 1. A type of rig used on sailing vessels, having a single mast located farther aft than that of a sloop. The original Revenue Service vessels used this rig and hence were called cutters. Today the term is applied to all Coast Guard ships above 65 feet in length. 2. A type of square-sterned pulling boat.

**cutwater** • The forward-most portion of the bow, which cuts the water as she moves ahead.

**cyberdep** • A method for recruiters and recruit training center division commanders using computers to interface with delayed entry personnel prior to their entering recruit training centers for training.

**cybrarian** • Person who maintains software inventories.

**cyclone** • Violent storm characterized by high winds working in a circular pattern over a large geographic area. In the western Pacific, it is called a typhoon; in the Atlantic, a hurricane. *See also:* hurricane; typhoon

**cyclonic** • Any rotational movement in a counterclockwise manner in the Northern Hemisphere, or a clockwise manner in the Southern Hemisphere.

# D

**damage control** • Measures to preserve and re-establish shipboard watertight integrity, stability, maneuverability, and offensive power of a vessel; to control her list and trim; to make rapid repairs of matériel; to limit the spread of and provide adequate protection from fire and or flooding; to limit the spread of, remove the contamination by, and provide adequate protection from toxic agents; to care for wounded personnel.

**damage control bills** • Written procedures for operating the various systems of a ship (such as a ship's drainage system) in order to provide efficient damage control.

**damage control book** • Contains material information in the form of texts, tables, and plates concerning facilities and characteristics of a vessel, showing and explaining complicated piping and wiring systems, among other things; used to carry out efficient damage control evolutions.

**damage control central (DCC)** • Compartment located in as protected a position as practicable, from which measures for damage control and preservation of the ship's fighting capability are directed.

**damage controlman (DC)** • Navy occupational rating that performs the work neces-

sary for damage control, ship stability, firefighting, and chemical, biological, and radiological (CBR) warfare defense. DCs instruct personnel in damage control and CBR defense, and repair damage-control equipment and systems.

**damping** • Reduction of oscillation by any means.

**dan buoy** • Temporary marker buoy used during minesweeping and other operations to indicate boundaries of swept path, swept area, known hazards, etc.

**Danforth anchor** • An anchor with particularly deep flukes that pivot around a stock located at the bottom of the anchor. This design has the advantages of allowing the flukes to rotate around a stock (thereby increasing the biting effect) and of being stowed with the convenience of a stockless anchor.

**danger angle** • A limiting angle (maximum or minimum) between two fixed objects on shore (a horizontal danger angle), or between the top and bottom of a fixed object of known height (a vertical danger angle), which may be used to insure safe passage clear of an outlying shoal or other danger to navigation.

**danger area** • *See:* restricted area

**danger bearing** • Limited bearing of a fixed object on shore that may be used to ensure safe passage clear of an outlying shoal or other danger. In other words, a mariner will stay clear of danger by remaining on one side of a danger but will stand into danger by being on the other side of the bearing.

**danger signal** • Signal used by vessels in compliance with the Nautical Rules of the Road; five or more rapid short blasts of a ship's whistle to indicate a possible collision or other emergency.

**dan layers** • Vessels assigned the duty of laying dan buoys during mine warfare or other operations.

**dark adaptation** • Becoming visually accustomed to darkness in order to achieve good night vision; because it takes the human eye some time to adjust to different light conditions, an adequate amount of time must be allowed for proper dark adaption before going on watch or manning an aircraft in low light conditions. This is achieved by shielding the eyes from exposure to light. Also, red and blue light does not have the same deleterious effect on night vision as does common white light.

**darken ship** • Blackening out all lights visible from outside the ship.

**data communications** • Electronic or electrical transfer of data from one place to another and the translation necessary to make it understandable at its destination.

**data encryption standard** • The formerly popular algorithm for encrypting data. Now replaced by the advanced encryption standard (AES).

**date-time group (DTG)** • Six numerals and a letter indicating date (first two digits), time (four digits), and time zone description (letter) of the origin of a message. For example, 071311Z would be 1311 (1:11 PM) on the seventh day of the month in the Zulu (Greenwich) time zone. Normally assigned by the communications watch officer or signal officer.

**datum and datum time** • An antisubmarine warfare (ASW) term: the last-known position of a submarine is the datum; its time at that point is the datum time. If a ship is torpedoed and no additional information is available, the position and time of torpedoing are used as datum and datum time.

**datum plane** • Same as chart datum.

**davit(s)** • A fixed or movable crane that projects over the side of a ship or over a hatchway for hoisting heavy objects. Usually used in pairs when handling boats, one at each end. Some of the tragic losses of life during nautical disasters, such as the *Titanic* sinking, were traceable to lifeboat davits that could not be handled properly under the existing circumstances (heavy list, overloaded boats, panicky passengers, etc.), with the result that many improved styles have been developed by which a boat can be readily swung inboard or outboard, and even launched automatically using only the force of gravity.

**Davy Jones** • The traditional mythological spirit inhabiting the sea; usually considered evil. The sea bottom is sometimes referred to as Davy Jones's locker.

**dawn alert** • *See:* alert, dawn or dusk

**dawn and dusk combat air patrol (DAD-CAP)** • Special applications of night combat air patrol that fill the gap during dawn or dusk between the use of combat air patrol and night combat air patrol; an extension of the use of night fighters over a target area.

**day's duty** • A tour of duty or a watch lasting 24 hours.

**day's work** • 1. Account of courses and distances run from noon to noon. 2. Twenty-four hours of navigating a ship; once a periodic requirement for junior officers.

**day and night distress signal** • Hand-held smoke and flare projector.

**day beacon** • Unlighted structure that serves as a daytime aid to navigation. *See also:* daymark

**daymark** • The shape or signals displayed by a vessel to indicate a special purpose, such as fishing, laying cable, and dredging. The identifying characteristics of a day beacon.

**dayshape** • *See:* shape

**D-Day** • Term used to designate day on which an operation (such as an amphibious landing) commences. D + 7 means 7 days after D-day and D - 3 means three days before D-day. Because the term was used in conjunction with Operation Overlord (the cross-channel invasion of Nazi-held Europe by Allied Forces on 6 June 1944), that day is often referred to as "D-Day."

**DD(X)** • The DD(X) program is a concept under development by the U.S. Navy for a centerpiece of a "Family of Ships" that will operate within the construct of the Surface Combatant Navy to deliver a vast range of warfighting capabilities, maximizing and revolutionizing the combat capability of the Fleet. The advanced design all composite superstructure will include a nuclear overpressure resistance capability, will resist the effects of externally and internally bursting conventional (blast, fragmentation) warheads, will include electromagnetic compatibility (EMC) and electromagnetic protection (EMP) technology, and will have reduced radar cross section and infrared signatures. The ships will also have integrated multifunction masts, integrated power systems (to include electric drive), and a weapons system that will include a peripheral vertical launch system and an advanced gun system capable of delivering surface volume fires.

**deactivate** • 1. To close down a unit; for example, to shut down an aircraft squadron that is no longer needed. 2. To lay a ship up for possible future use; crew is removed, ship is sealed up, anticorrosion measures are taken, etc. *Inf:* Put into mothballs.

**dead ahead** • Directly ahead; bearing 000° relative.

**dead astern** • Directly aft; bearing 180° relative.

**deadeyes** • Circular blocks of wood with three holes and a groove for a rope or an iron strap around them. With pairs of deadeyes, rigging can be set taut by lanyards.

**deadhead** • 1. Log floating on end and mostly submerged. Also called a sleeper because of potential damage to passing boats or ships. 2. A heavy post on a pier to which lines are secured.

**dead horse** • *Inf:* An advance in pay.

**dead in the water** • Said of a vessel that has stopped and has no way on, but is not moored or anchored, nor is in any way fast to the ground or a pier, etc.

**deadlight** • 1. A hinged metal cover for an air port; a battle port. A ventilating deadlight is such a cover, fitted with light-obscuring baffles to permit ventilation without the escape of light. 2. A heavy glass set flush with the deck for admitting light below.

**dead load** • A wheeled vehicle used instead of an aircraft during catapult testing.

**deadman** • Timber or similar object buried in ice or the ground to secure guys, tackles, or ship's lines. If in ice, can also be called ice anchor. Synonym for Irish pennant.

**deadman control** • A device that controls the primary pressure/flow valve in a refueling system. The valve opens only when an operator applies pressure to the handle, trigger, etc. If pressure is removed, the valve closes and fuel flow stops.

**dead reckoning (DR)** • Method of navigation using direction and amount of progress from the last well-determined position.

**dead-reckoning tracer (DRT)** • Plotting machine that takes inputs directly from the gyrocompass and speed log, allowing users to record the ship's track and that of other vessels (input from radar or sonar) on sheets of tracing paper in a true (rather than relative) configuration.

**deadrise** • Vertical distance between a vessel's keel and the turn of the bilge.

**dead ship** • A ship without power; also called a cold ship.

**dead space** • Area within maximum range of weapon, radar, radio, or observer that cannot be covered because of obstacles or inherent limitations.

**deadweight** • Total deadweight refers to the carrying capacity of a ship; cargo deadweight is the total deadweight minus fuel, water, stores, dunnage, and other items required on a voyage; expressed in long tons.

**deadweight tonnage** • The difference between a ship's loaded and light displacement.

**deadwood** • Solid strength-member in a sailing vessel between the keel and sternpost aft; or between the stem and keel forward, where the hull lines narrow down to such an extent that there is insufficient space for the usual framing.

**de-arming** • An operation in which a weapon is changed from a state of readiness for initiation to a safe condition.

**deballasting** • The process by which seawater is emptied from tanks to protect the ship from underwater damage and to increase its stability. *See also:* ballast; ballast tanks

**debarkation net** • Large rope-type net used as a ladder on a ship's side for troops embarking or disembarking. Similar to cargo net.

**debarkation station** • Where personnel on a ship assemble to debark into boats.

**debrief** • A verbal report delivered after an operation has been completed.

**Decca** • Medium-frequency, continuous-wave radio navigation system. For precise positioning within range of transmitters.

**decipher** • To convert an enciphered message into plain text by means of a cipher system.

**deck** • 1. A horizontal surface on a ship upon which one can walk; the approximate equivalent of a floor in a building. The uppermost complete deck (extending from stem to stern) is the main deck. Complete decks below it are numbered from the top down: second deck, third deck, etc. Partial decks between complete decks are called half decks; those below the lowest complete deck are platform decks, or flats. Partial decks above the main deck, if they extend to the sides of the ship, are called, according to location, the forecastle deck, middle deck, or poop deck. Those that do not extend to the side are superstructure decks. Weather decks are those exposed to the weather. In aircraft carriers the topmost deck is the flight deck, and the next one below is the hangar deck. Partial decks above the hangar deck are called gallery decks. Decks often get their names from construction, as armored flight deck, protective deck, splinter deck; or from employment, as boat deck, gundeck, berth deck. 2. The officer of the deck's watch is called the deck, as in the expression, ". . . has the deck," meaning he or she has charge of all deck functions and, if under way, is supervising all maneuvers of the ship. *See also:* flat(s)

**deck ape** • *Inf:* Deck hand; person assigned to seaman duties aboard ship.

**decker** • Describes the size and offensive power of a sailing man-of-war. A three-decker carried guns (as many as 120) on three gundecks as well as on the upper or weather deck. History records only one four-decker, the *Santissima Trinidad* of Spain, sunk at Trafalgar. Ships rated as two-deckers and above were considered fit to "lie in the line of battle," thus "ships of the line," later "battleships." HMS *Victory* is a three-decker, preserved in Portsmouth, England. USS *Constitution*, a powerful frigate, might have been called a one-decker had such a term been in use. Since her spar deck (weather deck) carried a full battery of guns, however, she was technically a double-banked frigate. USS *Independence*, razed from a marginal two-decker, became a very successful double-banked frigate.

**deck gang** • *Inf:* Persons attached to a ship's deck department.

**deck hand** • A crew member who works topside, on deck; usually a seaman. *Inf:* Swab jockey; deck ape.

**deckhead** • An infrequently used term to describe the inner, bottom surface of a deck as seen from below; same as the ceiling (as the word is used ashore) of a compartment; same as overhead.

**deckhouse** • Topside ship's structure resembling a small house in construction.

**deck load** • Gear or cargo stowed topside on the weather deck.

**deck log** • Official day-to-day record of a ship in commission and thus a legal document when signed; record of ship maneuvers (such as courses and speeds) and status (such as moored or under way), among other things. Distinct from the engineering log.

**deck pads** • Nonskid plates or mats secured to the deck where traffic is heavy.

**deck plane** • Standard fire-control reference plane on a ship; because a ship's weapons systems must operate on a moving ship and there are no fixed reference planes as on land (the horizon is unreliable), the deck plane is used a solid reference.

**deck plates** • Metal decking components. Also called floor plates. *Inf:* The point of view of the common Sailor, as in "Down on the

deck plates everyone is wondering when the ship will get under way."

**deck seamanship** • Maintenance and operation of topside gear such as anchors, cargo rigs, mooring lines, underway replenishment gear, etc.

**deck status light** • A three-colored light (red, amber, and green) controlled from the Pri-Fly. The light displays the status of the ship to support flight operations.

**declassify** • Remove security classification from information. The process includes notifying holders of the information.

**declination** • A heavenly body's angular distance north or south of the celestial equator. Used as a coordinate with Greenwich hour angle (GHA) to identify positions of celestial bodies; the celestial equivalent of latitude in the terrestrial system.

**decode** • To translate code into text by means of a code book or some other means. Loosely used as synonym for decipher.

**decompression sickness** • Diving injury caused by a gas such as nitrogen or helium forming bubbles in the bloodstream during a too-rapid ascent. Commonly called "the bends."

**decontaminate** • To free from the harmful residue of chemical, biological, or radiological attack. For example, a shipboard water washdown system is used to decontaminate a ship that has been attacked with CBR weapons. The contamination is washed overboard.

**decoration** • A medal or ribbon awarded for exceptional courage, skill, or performance.

**decrypt** • To convert a cryptographic message into plain (readable) text by a reversal of the encryption process (not by cryptanalysis). Same as decipher. *See also:* decode

**deenergize** • To remove from operation

electrically.

**deep** • 1. An ocean bottom depression of great depth, usually more than 6,000 meters. 2. A report by a leadsman to indicate depth: for example, "By the deep six." *See also:* lead-line; deep six

**deep air support** • Air action against enemy forces at such a distance from friendly forces that less care in targeting is required than in a mission where friendly fire might be a problem. *See also:* close air support

**deep creep attack** • Surprise depth charge attack for use against a submarine deeply submerged and using slow speeds. Effective only when surprise can be achieved. *See also:* creeping attack

**Deep Freeze** • The Navy's research expedition to the Antarctic.

**deeps** • *See:* lead line

**deep scattering layer** • Ocean layers that scatter sound or echo it vertically. Thought to be of biological origin, they range in depth from 150 to 200 fathoms during the day and migrate to or near the surface at night.

**deep sea lead** • *See:* sounding machine

**deep-sea lead** • A heavier lead than a hand lead, used to sound (measure depth) in water over 30 fathoms. Also called dipsey lead. Now largely replaced by echo sounder.

**deep six** • *Inf:* Throwing an object away or overboard.

**deep-submergence rescue vehicle (DSRV)** • Small submarine, able to be carried piggyback on a large submarine or transported by air to a disaster scene, then submerge, find a sunken submarine, and make a watertight joint with the submarine's escape trunk. Development of the DSRV was made necessary by the far-ranging, deep-diving, high-speed nuclear submarines for which the standard rescue chamber was inadequate.

**deep tanks** • Compartments strengthened to carry water or liquid cargo.

**deepwater waves** • Surface and wind waves having a wave length less than half the water's depth.

**Defense Mapping Agency** • Earlier name for the government agency that produces navigational charts and publications. Superceded by the National Imagery and Mapping Agency (NIMA) and subsequently superceded again by the National Geospatial-Intelligence Agency (NGA).

**defense switched network (DSN)** • An upgrade and name change to the automatic voice network (AUTOVON), a military telephone system.

**defilade fire** • Technique (using elevated fire) to deliver ordnance on shore targets located behind some terrain feature.

**deflection** • Lateral angular correction applied to target bearing to obtain hits in naval gunnery.

**degaussing** • Reducing the magnetic field of a ship by wrapping the ship fore and aft permanently with wire that may be energized to neutralize it, thus protecting against magnetic mines and torpedoes. *See also:* deperming; flashing

**degree** • A unit of circular measure equal to $1/360^{th}$ of a circle.

**delegating** • Entrusting to someone else.

**delivery groups** • Four-letter pronounceable groups assigned to individual activities and commands to be used in the transmission and delivery of messages.

**delta** • 1. The alluvial sand deposit, usually roughly triangular, near the mouth of a river. 2. Phonetic word for the letter D. 3. The triangular shape of a supersonic aircraft wing.

**demonstration group** • Component of a force organized to conduct deceptive operations involving a feint.

**demurrage** • Cost incurred when a merchant ship is delayed while loading or discharging cargo.

**density layer** • A stratum of water of lower temperature or greater salinity than that above. Has significant effect on sonar performance, and may be large enough that a submarine at neutral buoyancy can ride it (maintain depth with no effort of her own).

**dental technician (DT)** • Navy occupational rating that assists dentists. DTs have a variety of "chairside," laboratory, and administrative duties. Some are qualified in dental prosthetics (making and fitting artificial teeth), dental X-ray techniques, clinical laboratory procedures, pharmacy and chemistry, or maintenance and repair of dental equipment.

**Department of Defense (DOD)** • Branch of the U.S. government that includes the offices of the Secretary of Defense and the Departments of the Army, Navy, and Air Force.

**Department of the Navy (DON)** • The executive part of the naval establishment; includes the headquarters of the U.S. Marine Corps, the entire operating forces of the U.S. Navy and U.S. Marine Corps, all reserve components, all field activities, forces, bases, installations, activities, and functions under the control of the Secretary of the Navy. *See also:* Navy Department

**departure** • The technical point at which a ship leaves an anchorage or harbor. Thus, a typical entry in the ship's log might read: "With Brenton Reef Lightship bearing 070° true, distance two miles, took departure for Portsmouth, England, on course 135° true

and per p.g.c. (gyro compass), speed 15."

**departure buoy** • *See:* sea buoy

**departure report** • Prepared by a repair activity on completion of a ship's overhaul, listing work undertaken, percentage completed, items deferred with reasons for the deferrals, and a summary of the cost.

**deperming** • Reduction of permanent magnetism by energizing coils temporarily placed vertically around a ship. The purpose is protection against magnetic mines and torpedoes. *See also:* degaussing; flashing

**deploy** • Generally, to send ships or squadrons abroad for duty. Specifically, to change from a cruising or approach formation to a formation of ships for battle or amphibious assult.

**deployment** • A cruise in foreign waters. Assignment or positioning of forces to accomplish a mission.

**deployment bag** • Part of parachute gear that keeps the canopy deflated until shroud lines are completely paid out.

**depressurize** • To remove air or hydraulic fluid from a system.

**depth** • *See:* depth of water

**depth bomb** • Explosive dropped from aircraft to damage or destroy submarines. Depth bombs are dropped from aircraft, depth charges from ships. The difference is that aircraft weapons must have a predictable trajectory in air and hence require a standard bomb shape. *See also:* depth charge

**depth charge** • Antisubmarine warfare explosive dropped from ships. *Inf:* Ashcan. *See also:* depth bomb

**depth finder (sounder)** • *See:* echo sounder

**depth of water** • The vertical distance from

the surface of the water to the bottom.

**depth-sounding sonar** • A direct-reading device for determining the depth of water in fathoms or other units by reflecting sonic or ultrasonic waves from the ocean bottom.

**derelict** • Abandoned vessel at sea, still afloat.

**dereliction in the performance of duties** • Willfully or negligently failing to perform assigned duties, or performing them in a culpably inefficient manner.

**derrick** • A boom and tackle used for hoisting heavy objects. Named after Thomas Derrick, a hangman of Queen Elizabeth's time who devised a portable hangman's tree.

**deserter** • Person absent from his or her command, without authority, whose apparent purpose is to stay away. Absence over 30 days is presumptive, but not full legal proof, of desertion.

**desig** • Name of one of the signal flags used by the Navy; when preceding a hoist of other flags, it indicates that the ones following are to be read literally, rather than as code groups.

**designator** • A 4-digit code number describing an officer's qualifications and specialties. Example: an 1100 officer is an unrestricted line officer with no special qualifications, whereas an officer designated as an 1110 is a surface warfare officer. *See also:* file number; signal number

**design class** • Ships that are originally built from the same plans and intended to be identical. Change orders issued over time may eventually make them dissimilar in some respects.

**despedida** • Occasionally used term for a farewell party for a person or group of people leaving a station or command.

**destroyer** • Originally torpedo boat destroyer; ship type designed as an answer to the small torpedo boats that came with the advent of the torpedo. A small, high speed, lightly armed and unarmored jack-of-all-trades. There are various configurations for special employment, also illustrating the design changes necessitated by constantly developing technology. The type has grown enormously in size while retaining the name destroyer. Torpedo boats were only about 100 tons, the first destroyers twice that size. By WWI, destroyers were 1,000 tons, torpedo boats had disappeared, and destroyers had taken on their functions. Since WWII, destroyers have grown to more than 10,000 tons. *Inf:* Can; tincan.

**destroyer escort (DE)** • As developed during WWII, an ocean escort intended principally for convoy of merchant ships but with some destroyer characteristics. Since WWII, the type has undergone some design and mission changes and is now known as a frigate. A small, ocean-going, multipurpose ship of about 4,000 tons, single screw, moderate speed, with some AAW and ASW capability.

**destroyer tender (AD)** • A ship specially designed to tend to the needs of destroyers; equipped with maintenance shops, repair parts, etc., specifically associated with the equipment found on destroyers.

**destruction fire** • Slow, deliberate, accurate gunfire to destroy a target ashore.

**destructor** • An explosive or other device for intentionally destroying classified equipment, a missile, aircraft, or their components because of safety considerations or to prevent compromise.

**detachable link** • In an anchor chain, a connecting link that can be taken apart and then reassembled. Differs from a shackle in that it is the same size and shape as the other links and can go around the capstan and through the hawspipe like any link.

**detached** • Term used when personnel are ordered away from present duty; personnel are considered attached to a ship or station when formerly ordered to serve in that command; therefore they are detached when ordered elsewhere.

**detachment** • Temporary smaller unit formed from other naval forces. For example, a helicopter squadron might form a detachment of two helicopters and the associated personnel to work off a destroyer.

**detail** • A group of individuals assigned to a particular duty; for example, several seaman might be assigned to a cleanup detail and instructed to remove all trash from around a barracks. To assign persons to a particular duty; for example, to detail several petty officers to maintain security around a barracks.

**detailer** • An individual in the Bureau of Naval Personnel who makes personnel assignments.

**detailing, personnel** • Assignment of personnel to fill requirements of billets.

**detent** • Mine release gear on a minelayer.

**deviation** • Magnetic compass error due to the magnetic properties of the ship. Expressed in degrees east or west.

**deviation table** • List of compass errors due to deviation for representative headings through 360°, posted near each magnetic compass.

**devil's claw** • Device used to hold an anchor chain. *See also:* compressor

**Devil's Triangle** • *See:* Bermuda Triangle

**dew point** • The temperature to which air must be cooled at constant pressure and constant water vapor content to reach saturation.

**diagram (beach, boat, landing, etc.)** • Graphic representation of beach limits, boat assignments, landing order, etc., in amphibious operations.

**Dial-X** • Internal communication system for Polaris submarine.

**diaphone** • Fixed fog signal used as an aid to navigation.

**dicing** • High-speed, low-altitude, low-oblique aircraft photo operations.

**diesel fuel marine** • A fuel oil.

**diffuse** • To spread widely, scatter.

**dike** • An embankment or wall, usually of earth or concrete, surrounding a storage tank to impound the tank's contents in case of a leak or spill.

**Dilbert** • *Inf:* Person who dopes off, acts stupidly. Dilbert was born during WWII as the nonhero of an effective series of instruction books and cartoons for naval aviators.

**dinette** • *Inf:* The mess hall in a submarine.

**dinghy** • Small (less than 20 feet), handy, square-sterned pulling boat. May be rigged for oars or sail.

**dip** • 1. A correction of observed sextant altitude, needed because of the curvature of the Earth. 2. To lower the national colors part way and then raise them as a form of salute. The procedure is for the merchantman to dip first and hold his flag "at the dip," (*i.e.*, about one-third of the way down) until after the warship has dipped in answer and then two-blocked. Warships render another form of passing honors but do not dip to each other. This custom originated in the days of sail, when merchant ships were required to lower sails to permit an approaching warship to inspect them. Today it is a courtesy only.

**dip, magnetic** • The inclination to the horizontal of a magnetic compass needle caused by the Earth's magnetic field.

**dipping sonar** • Sonar equipment used by helicopters and hydrofoils.

**dipping the ensign** • Lowering the national colors as a form of salute between ships at sea. *See also:* dip

**dipsey lead** • *See:* deep-sea lead; sounding machine

**dipsy** • *See:* deep-sea lead; sounding machine

**dip the eye** • To arrange the loops (eyes) of two mooring lines on the same bollard so that either line may be removed without moving the other. Accomplished by passing the eye of one line up through that of the other and then around the bollard.

**direct fire** • Gunfire delivered using the target itself as the point of aim for the guns or director. *See also:* indirect fire

**direction of relative movement** • The direction of motion relative to a reference point, itself usually in motion.

**directive** • 1. Military communication in which policy is established or a specific action is ordered. 2. Plan issued with a view to placing it in effect when so directed, or in the event that a stated contingency arises. 3. Any communication that initiates or governs action, conduct, or procedure. *See also:* Navy Directives System

**disbursing clerk (DK)** • Navy occupational rating that maintains the financial records of Navy personnel. DKs prepare payrolls, determine transportation entitlements, compute travel allowances, and process claims for reimbursement of travel expenses. DKs also process vouchers for receiving and spending public money and make sure accounting data are accurate. They maintain fiscal records and prepare financial reports and returns.

**disbursing officer** • Officer who keeps pay records and pays salary allowances and claims.

**discharge** • Process of separating enlisted men and women from the service. May be honorable, general, undesirable, bad conduct, or dishonorable.

**disciplinary barracks** • An activity to receive, confine, classify, segregate, and provide work, drill, and training for courts-martial prisoners.

**dishonorable discharge** • The most severe punitive discharge; reserved for those warrant officers (W-1) and enlisted members who should be separated under conditions of dishonor, having been convicted of serious offenses. It may be awarded only by a general court-martial (GCM).

**dismantling shot** • Projectile fired from a smoothbore cannon during the seventeenth, eighteenth, and early nineteenth centuries, intended to destroy the rigging of an enemy ship. Usually consisted of heavy iron bars or cannon balls chained together. *See also:* grape; canister; double-shot; langrage

**dismissal** • A court-martial punishment of separation from the service with dishonor. Only officers, commissioned warrant officers, cadets, and midshipmen may receive a dismissal; it can only be awarded by a general court-martial (GCM). It is considered the equivalent of a dishonarable discharge.

**dispatch (despatch)** • Former term for message.

**dispensary** • A medical facility offering services less elaborate than those of a hospital.

**displacement** • The weight of water displaced by a vessel. *See also:* tonnage

**disposition** • Prescribed arrangement of the single ships or major subdivisions of a fleet, for a specific purpose, such as cruising, approach, maintaining contact, or battle.

Prescribed arrangement of all the tactical units composing a flight or group of aircraft.

**distance learning** • The use of technology to apply numerous methods of instruction at disparate locations, on demand, 24 hours per day.

**distance line** • A marked line used between ships during underway replensihment operations to assist in maintaining correct distance apart.

**distance measurements** • *See:* mariners' distance measurements

**distance (tactical)** • Distance between foremasts of adjacent ships or cockpits of adjacent aircraft.

**distinctive mark** • Flag or pennant flown aloft to indicate that a ship is in commission and to indicate the status of the senior officer aboard. It may be a commission pennant, broad or burgee command pennant, personal starred flag of a flag officer, or the Red Cross flag.

**district, naval** • Geograpical area in which all naval activities except those of the operating forces come under the control of a flag officer, the commandant. Currently, no longer used, except for the Washington DC naval district.

**ditching** • Controlled landing of a disabled aircraft on water.

**ditty bag (box)** • Small canvas bag or a box used by Sailors and Marines to stow odds and ends of their personal gear. Ditty bag (or box) was originally called ditto bag because it contained at least two of everything—two needles, two spools of thread, two buttons, etc. With the passing of years, the 'ditto' was dropped in favor of ditty and remains so today.

**diurnal** • Having a period of, occuring in, or related to, a day.

**diurnal inequality** • Pertaining to tides, the difference in the height or the time of the two high waters or the two low waters each day. Pertaining to tidal currents, the difference in the velocity of either of the two flood or ebb currents each day.

**divert** • An order for an aircraft to proceed and land a specified field. This is a non-emergency situation.

**dividers** • A hand instrument consisting in its simplest form of two pointed legs joined by a pivot; used principally for measuring distances or coordinates by transferring the spread of the legs to a distance scale. Similar to a drawing compass except both legs have points rather than one having a pencil lead.

**diving bell** • Specialized object that can withstand the pressures and other hazardous conditions of deep submergance to allow humans to descend into the ocean's depths; used as a submarine rescue chamber.

**diving planes** • Surfaces used to control vertical motion of a submarine underwater. Can be located on the bow and on the stern; or on the sail, in which case, they are called sail planes.

**division** • The basic administrative unit into which personnel are organized aboard ship, in aircraft squadrons, or at shore activities. Several divisions form a department. A tactical subdivision of a squadron of ships or aircraft.

**division book** • Before computers, the division officer's record of names, watch, quarter, station assignments, and other pertinent data. Some data was also kept in the form of division personnel cards.

**division officer** • Junior officer assigned by the commanding officer to head a division.

**Division Officer's Guide** • Long-time standard reference and text book used by junior officers in the Navy who are (or are aspiring to be) division officers.

**division parade** • 1. Occurs when a division falls in for muster or inspection. 2. Can also refer to the space on deck assigned for activities such as muster or inspection. *See also:* foul-weather parade

**division police petty officer** • Petty officer detailed by division officer to assist the chief master-at-arms.

**dixie cup** • *Inf:* The traditional white uniform hat of enlisted personnel.

**dock** • Basin either permanently filled with water (wet dock) or capable of being filled and drained (drydock or graving dock).

**docking keel** • Keel-like projection between the main keel and the turn of the bilge; used to support the ship on blocks in drydock.

**docking plan** • Plan for drydocking a ship; includes a carefully detailed drawing showing details of a ship's bottom that is used for arranging the support blocks in the drydock in order to leave access for sonar domes, hull openings, etc.

**docking report** • Report that gives the reason(s) for drydocking, the ship's condition, and what work was performed while docked.

**dockmaster** • Person in charge of drydocking (or undocking) a ship.

**dock trials** • Test of a ship's operating equipment, including engines, while alongside the pier or other docking facility, performed prior to sea trials and after construction or overhaul. Part of a builder's trials for new construction. *See also:* fast cruise

**dodger** • Canvas, wood, or metal windshield on an exposed bridge or conning station.

**dog** • 1. Small metal fitting used to close doors, ports, and hatches. 2. A four-hour watch split into two watches creates two dog watches. 3. To split a watch with a shipmate is to dog it. 4. Past phonetic word for the letter D; replaced with delta.

**dog down** • Tighten dogs or clamps on a port, hatch, or door to ensure watertight integrity.

**dog tag** • *Inf:* Metal identification plate worn on a chain around the neck. In arduous conditions, this form of identification has a better chance of remaining intact than does a paper or plastic I.D.

**dog watch** • One of the 2-hour watches, 1600–1800 (4–6 PM) or 1800–2000 (6–8 PM). A "cur" tailed watch, designed to facilitate messing or the evening meal.

**doldrums** • 1. Areas on both sides of the equator where light breezes and calms persist. 2. A person is said to be in the doldrums if his or her personal affairs stagnate rather than progress.

**dolly** • 1. A low platform with wheels used for transporting or shifting heavy objects. 2. A large cablejack mounted on wheels, used on aircraft carriers. Now largely replaced by mobile cranes, known usually as cherry pickers. *See also:* crash dolly

**dolphin** • A cluster or clump of piles used for mooring. A single pile or a bollard on a pier is sometimes called a dolphin.

**Don't Tread on Me flag** • A flag designed during the American Revolution to symbolize the colonists' defiance to the British Crown (referring to the trampling of rights); believed to be flown on one or more naval vessels during that struggle. Flown on U.S. naval vessels, in place of the Union Jack, during the Bicentennial celebration and again during the war on terrorism. Also authorized to be flown by the oldest ship in the Navy.

**donkey engine** • Small auxiliary engine used for lifting, etc.

**door** • A device that closes a vertical opening between compartments. A light-weight partition not intended to provide watertight integrity might have a simple joiner door; a watertight bulkhead would have a watertight door of equal strength. For damage control, some watertight doors are electrically or hydraulically operated from a central control station (damage control central). A hatch is a similar device in a deck allowing vertical access.

**dope** • *See:* the dope

**doper** • *Inf:* Drug-smuggling vessel.

**Doppler** • Apparent change in pitch (frequency) of sound or radio wave caused by relative movement between the source and hearing agent; can be used to determine if a detected object is approaching or moving away.

**Doppler effect** • The change in frequency of radar or sonar caused by a target's motion toward or away from the detector can be used to determine target motion. *See also:* doppler

**Doppler radar** • A radar system that differentiates moving targets from fixed ones by evaluating the change in frrequency of the reflected waves caused by the motion fo the target,

**Doppler shift** • Apparent change in pitch (frequency) of sound or radio wave caused by relative movement between the source and hearing agent.

**dory** • Small, flat-bottomed boat that is rowed, used chiefly by fishermen. Easily nested in large numbers because of removable thwarts and sloping sides, dories were the work boats of the famous Grand Banks fishing schooners.

**dosimeter** • An instrument used to measure personal cumulative exposure to radiation. Carried by persons working on or around nuclear machinery, its direct reading can give the individual an immediate evaluation of how much radiation he/she has been exposed to. *See also:* film badge

**double** • A ship is said to double a projecting point of land when she sails around it.

**double-banked** • Boat with two persons on a thwart, or two on an oar.

**double-banked frigate** • In days of sail, a frigate was a three-masted, square-rigged man-of-war carrying guns on her gun deck, her raised forecastle, and her poop. The forecastle and poop decks were connected by gangways along either side for convenient access, but the gangways were not heavy enough to support guns. In the development of ship design, large frigates were built with especially heavy gangways, until the combination of forecastle—gangway—poop deck became a single weather deck above the gun deck, known as the spar deck, and guns were mounted along its entire length. Such a frigate was called a double-banked frigate. HMS *Serapis*, captured by John Paul Jones, was such a ship, as is USS *Constitution*.

**double bottoms** • For strength and survivability, vessels are often built with two bottoms, in a hull-within-a-hull arrangement. These double bottoms can be sectioned off by watertight bulkheads to create separate compartments capable of stowage and/or ballasting.

**double-ended** • 1. A boat with similar ends (such as a whaleboat) is sometimes called double-ended. 2. Ships equipped with missile launchers mounted both forward and aft.

**double hooking** • Process used when

switching a boat or other load from one ship's crane to another.

**double luff** • *See:* purchase

**double-shot** • The custom of loading two cannon balls into a single cannon with a single explosive charge, during seventeenth, eighteenth, and early nineteenth centuries. While the practice made the shot potentially more lethal, it also reduced the range and accuracy, making it effective only at short ranges. *See also:* grape; canister; dismantling shot; langrage

**double up** • To double mooring lines for added mooring strength. One of the concluding procedures when securing a ship to a pier. *See also:* single up

**down by the head (stern)** • Lower in the water than normal at the forward (after) end of the ship.

**downgrade** • To lower a security classification previously assigned.

**downhaul** • Any line, wire, or tackle that applies a downward pull. *See also:* outhaul; inhaul

**downloading** • An operation that removes airborne weapons and stores from an aircraft.

**down time** • The time equipment is out of commission because of failures of parts, power, or other factors.

**downwind** • The direction towards which the wind is blowing; with the wind.

**down with the helm** • Order to put the helm a-lee; *i.e.,* down to leeward. The rudder goes opposite to the helm or tiller, turns to the weather side, and the ship's head comes to the wind. Used as a maneuver in tacking. Also down helm.

**dowse (douse)** • 1. To lower quickly, as a sail. 2. To extinguish a light or a flame. 3. To

wet down or immerse in water.

**draft** • 1. Depth of a ship beneath the waterline, measured vertically to the keel. 2. A group of new personnel assigned to a command.

**drafting machine** • Mechanical parallel ruler used in navigational piloting and plotting.

**draft marks** • Numeral figures on a vessel's hull, used to indicate how much of the ship is beneath the water.

**drag** • 1. Forces opposing direction of motion due to skin friction, profile, and other components. 2. To pull the anchor along the bottom as a result of high winds or current. 3. The amount that a ship is down by the stern. 4. *Inf:* At the U.S. Naval Academy, a midshipman's date or escort.

**Dreadnought** • A class of battleship that took its name from the first of the type, HMS *Dreadnought*, built in 1906 with extraordinary speed and in great secrecy. At one stroke, she rendered all older battleships obsolete. Sometimes used generically as a synonym for battleship.

**dredging** • Dragging an anchor along the bottom at short stay to steady a ship's head in narrow channels or when going alongside a pier. To deepen a harbor or channel.

**dressing lines** • Lines used in dressing ship.

**dressing ship** • Displaying national colors at all mastheads, as well as the flagstaff, for special occasions. *See also:* full dressing ship

**dress (right or left)** • When in ranks, a command to form a straight line, guiding from the directed side.

**drift** • 1. Speed of current in knots. 2. The lateral motion of a rotating projectile largely due to gyroscopic action. 3. The displacement, because of wind, of an aircraft's track from its true heading. 4. The amount of anchor chain on deck for working purposes when mooring. *See also:* leeway; set

**drift angle** • Horizontal angle between the fore-and-aft axis of an aircraft and its path relative to the ground.

**drift ice** • Ice that has drifted from its point of origin.

**drift lead** • Lead weight dropped over the side with the line slack or leading aft. Indicates whether the ship is dragging her anchor.

**driftmeter** • Device in an aircraft used to observe drift. Also called drift sight.

**drift sight** • Device in an aircraft used to observe drift. Also called a driftmeter.

**drill** • Training exercise in which actual operation is simulated, such as a general quarters drill.

**drogue** • Device used to slow rate of movement; *e.g.,* a drogue parachute on an aerial mine. *See also:* sea anchor

**drone** • Remotely controlled, unmanned aircraft.

**dropping safe** • Releasing an airborne weapon in a safe or unarmed condition so that it will not function upon impact.

**drum** • A capstan-head mounted with the axis horizontally, usually as an adjunct to an ordinary windlass or capstan, used for assistance in hauling lines.

**drum head** • *See:* capstan

**drum hooks** • A sling containing a pair of moveable hooks; used for hoisting a drum, cask, or barrel.

**drum, steam** • Large cylindrical shell at the top of a boiler in which the steam collects.

**drum, water** • Cylindrical tank at the bottom of a boiler; also called mud drum.

**drydock** • A watertight basin that allows examination and work on the bottom of a ship.

**dry pipe** • Perforated pipe at the highest point in a steam drum to collect the steam.

**dry run** • Rehearsal in which all motions are gone through except the critical one.

**dual band radar** • An advanced radar system with improved performance in adverse environments and reduced maintenance requirements that includes increased detection of stealthy targets in sea-land clutter and better periscope detection, among many other improvements.

**duct** • A layer in the atmosphere that readily traps electromagnetic energy permitting extended transmission ranges.

**dud** • Explosive ammunition that has failed to function.

**dulcimer** • Gong-like musical device used to formally announce dinner.

**dump** • 1. A storage place where military supplies are temporarily stored. 2. Temporary stock of supplies.

**dungarees** • Blue cotton work clothes; older term used to describe working clothes for enlisted Sailors.

**dunking sonar** • Another term for a dipping sonar.

**dunnage** • 1. Any material used to separate layers of cargo, create space for cargo ventilation, or insulate cargo against chafing. Usually refers, however, to cheap wood boarding used for these purposes. 2. A Sailor's personal gear.

**duplex circuit** • One that permits radio communication in both directions at the same time.

**duplex pressure proportioner** • Firefighting device aboard ship that mixes foam and water in correct proportions.

**Dutch courage** • The courage obtained from drink. Comes from the custom initiated by the famous Dutch Admirals Tromp and deRuyter of giving their crews a liberal libation before battle with the English.

**Dutchman** • *Inf:* A spacer piece in piping or duct aboard ship used to replace a piece of equipment, such as the heating element in a ventilation duct.

*Dutton's* • Navigational reference and text book originally written by Benjamin Dutton in 1926 and updated through many revisions since. The title has been modified several times over the years (original title was *Navigation and Nautical Astronomy*) but today is known as *Dutton's Nautical Navigation*. Most professional navigators own copies of both *Dutton's* and *Bowditch*. *See also: Bowditch*

*Dutton's Nautical Navigation* • *See: Dutton's*

**duty** • Requirement to remain on board ship (or station) after working hours in a work or watch status to deal with contingencies that may arise. Can be used as a noun, as in "I have the duty tonight," or as an adjective, as in "duty section" or "duty engineer," etc.

**dye marker** • Brightly colored chemical that spreads when released in water; used to temporarily mark a spot on the surface of the water.

**dynamometer** • A device used to measure mechanical force.

# E

**E-1–9** • *See:* enlisted paygrades

**E-6** • *See:* Mercury

**EA-6** • *See:* Prowler

**eagle screams, the** • *Inf:* Payday.

**ear banger** • *Inf:* One who is overanxious to please.

**earthing** • *See:* ground

**ease** • 1. To do something slowly, as ease away from the pier or ease the strain on a line. 2. Relax the strain.

**ease her** • Reduce the amount of rudder the ship is carrying. Generally, an order given as the ship approaches the desired course.

**ease off** • To ease a line; slacken it when taut.

**easy** • Past phonetic word for the letter E; replaced with echo.

**E award** • Shorthand name for the battle efficiency E, awarded to ships who excel in selected exercises in gunnery, communications, etc. Ships earning the E paint it on their superstructure and the crew wears a corresponding ribbon on their dress uniforms.

**ebb** • Tidal current moving away from land or down a tidal stream.

**ebb current** • Current caused by the decreasing height of tide, generally set seaward.

**ebb tide** • *See:* tide

**echo** • Phonetic word for the letter E.

**echo sounder** • Instrument for determining depth of water by measuring time for a generated sound emission to reach the bottom and return as an echo. Also called depth sounder or depth finder. *See also:* fathometer

**economizer** • Heat transfer device on a boiler that uses the heat of the stack gases to preheat the feed water. *See also:* feed heater

**eddy** • Circular motion caused by water passing obstructions or by action of adjacent currents flowing in opposite directions. Sometimes a synonym for countercurrent.

**editor-message text format** • The Automatic Digital Network (AUTODIN) message formatting software endorsed by the Navy.

**eductor** • Pump used to empty flooded spaces.

**egg** • Escape capsule used in certain specialized highspeed aircraft.

**eight-o'clock reports** • Reports received by the executive officer shortly before 2000 (8 PM) from the heads of departments. The executive officer, in turn, makes eight o'clock reports to the commanding officer. Sometimes called the twenty-hundred reports.

**ejection seat** • Device that expels the pilot safely from a high-speed aircraft in the event of an emergency.

**Eldridge method** • A method of mooring with two anchors in which one anchor's chain is dipped through the other's hawsepipe before either anchor is let go.

**eLearning** • 24/7 access for Sailors to course-work, lectures, demonstrations, and interactive education.

**electrician's mate (EM)** • Navy occupational rating that operates and repairs a ship's or station's electrical powerplant and electrical equipment. EMs also maintain and repair power and lighting circuits, distribution switchboards, generators, motors, and other electrical equipment.

**electrohydraulic steering** • A system having a motor-driven, hydraulic pump that creates the force needed to position the ship's rudder.

**electromagnetic** • Having both magnetic and electric properties.

**electromagnetic spectrum** • The total range of the various radiation frequencies and corresponding wavelengths.

**electromagnetic vulnerability** • Those characteristics of an electronic system that allow degradation as a result of electromagnetic environmental effects.

**electronic counter-counter measures (ECCM)** • A form of active electronic warfare (EW) in which measures are taken to prevent the enemy from successfully employing electronic countermeasures (jamming, deception, etc.). *See also:* electronic counter measures; electronic support measures

**electronic countermeasures (ECM)** • A form of active electronic warfare (EW) in which enemy electronic equipment is adversely affected. ECM is an active form of EW (in which enemy emissions are jammed, distorted, or mislead), whereas ESM is passive (involving only the gathering of emissions information for intelligence purposes). Measures taken to prevent the enemy from successfully employing ECM are known as electronic counter-counter measures (ECCM).

**electronic navigation** • Navigation using such electronic devices as loran, GPS, etc.

**electronics technician (ET)** • Navy occupational rating responsible for electronic equipment used to send and receive messages, detect enemy planes and ships, and determine target distance. ETs maintain, repair, calibrate, tune, and adjust all electronic equipment used for communications, detection and tracking, recognition and identification, navigation, and electronic countermeasures.

**electronic support measures** • Radar surveillance conducted in passive mode designed to intercept hostile radar emissions.

**electronic support measures (ESM)** • A form of active electronic warfare (EW) in which enemy electronic emissions are detected and analyzed for intelligence purposes. ESM is passive in nature while ECM is an active form of EW (in which enemy emissions are jammed, distorted, or mislead). Measures taken to prevent the enemy from successfully employing ECM are known as electronic counter-counter measures (ECCM).

**electronic warfare (EW)** • Those aspects of warfare in which the electronic spectrum is used to detect, mislead, counter, etc. enemy capabilities. Includes passive and active measures. *See also:* electronic support measures; electronic countermeasures; electronic counter-countermeasures

**elevator** • A control surface, usually hinged to a horizontal stabilizer, that is used to control the aircraft about its lateral axis. On aircraft carriers, elevators are used to move aircraft between the flight deck and the hanger deck.

**El Nino** • A complex and, as yet, little understood oceanic phenomenon mainly in the Pacific, but with widespread weather effects, such as an increase in the frequency of hurricanes in the Atlantic. It involves an interruption of Pacific trade winds with marked changes in ocean currents. This includes a temporary shift of the Peru Current, which interrupts upwellings vital to coastal fishing off South America. Called El Nino (the Christ child) because it usually occurs at Christmastime.

**Elokomin rig** • Arrangement of tackle and hoses for fueling a ship under way from another ship alongside. Named for the oiler USS *Elokomin*, which originated it.

**embark** • To go aboard a ship or aircraft.

**embarkation officers** • Landing force officers who advise naval unit commanders on combat loading and act in liaison with troop officers. Formerly called transport quartermasters.

**embayed** • A sailing ship is embayed when

the wind is blowing right into a bay so that she cannot weather either side of the mouth of the bay to get out.

**emerald shellback** • *Inf:* One who crosses the equator, at the Greenwich Meridian, by ship.

**emergency breakaway** • *See:* breakaway

**emergency drill** • A rehearsal of the action to be taken by ship's crew in an emergency, such as fire or flooding.

**emergency ratings** • Special ratings created during wartime or national emergency.

**emergency speed** • The maximum speed of a vessel with all safety considerations ignored in the face of some emergency. Under normal conditions, a vessel would not operate its machinery beyond certain specified safe limits (steam pressures, lubricating oil temperatures, etc.), but in an emergency situation, those limits could be ignored in order to maximize speed.

**emergency surgeable** • After a strike group ends its maintenance phase, and once it has completed basic phase work-ups, it is deemed emergency surgeable. Normally, it is the three-month window after leaving the shipyard.

**empennage** • The tail section of an aircraft, including the stabilizing and control surfaces.

**encapsulated torpedo** • A torpedo that is included in a deep water mine and released for attack when the mine is properly stimulated.

**encipher** • To convert plain text into unintelligible language by a cipher system, usually letter by letter. Encipher, encode, and encrypt are often used synonymously. *See also:* encrypt; encode

**encode** • To convert plain text into unintelligible language, usually word by word. Often acomplished using a code book. Encipher, encode, and encrypt are often used synonymously. *See also:* encrypt; encipher

**encrypt** • To convert plain text into unintelligible form by means of a cryptosystem. Encipher, encode, and encrypt are often used synonymously. *See also:* encode; encipher

**end for end** • To reverse something, as end for end the boat falls, which means to shift ends to spread the wear evenly throughout the falls or line.

**endorsement** • Something, such as a signature, voucher, or written elaboration that approves or validates.

**energize** • To put into operation electrically.

**enfilade** • Technique for delivering ordnance to a target whose long axis is parallel to the line of fire; for example, along the long axis of a trench.

**engagement stars** • Stars embroidered on battle streamers and/or worn on campaign ribbons to denote specific battles, campaigns, or operations.

**engineer's bell book** • Official record of the engine orders received in the engine room(s) from the bridge.

**engineering aide (EA)** • Navy occupational rating that provides construction engineers with the information needed to develop final construction plans. EAs conduct surveys for roads, airfields, buildings, waterfront structures, pipelines, ditches, and drainage systems. They perform soil tests, prepare topographic and hydrographic maps; and surveys for sewers, water lines, drainage systems, and underwater excavations.

**Engineering Duty Officer (EDO)** • Officer of the restricted line specializing in engineering duties afloat and ashore. An AEDO specializes in aeronautical engineering, an OEDO in ordnance engineering.

**engineering log** • Daily record of important

events and certain data concerning the machinery of a ship.

**engineering officer of the watch (EOOW)** • Officer on duty in the engineering spaces.

**engineering operational casualty control** • Standard procedures to control anticipated casualties.

**engineering spaces** • *See:* machinery spaces

**engineman (EN)** • Navy occupational rating responsible for the proper operation and maintenance of internal-combustion engines (both diesel or gasoline), refrigeration, air-conditioning, and distilling-plant engines and compressors.

**engine orders** • Formalized commands given to prompt the appropriate response from the engineering spaces in order to attain the speed desired. For example, a conning officer wishing to make top speed would give the engine order "All engines ahead flank."

**engine-order telegraph** • Device on the ship's bridge and duplicated in the engine room(s) and firerooms(s) for giving and acknowledging orders to the engines. Also called annunciator.

**engine order telegraph (EOT)** • A device on the ship's bridge to give engine orders to the engine room. Also called annunciator.

**enlisted man or woman** • Navy personnel below the grade of warrant officer; designated by paygrades E-1 through E-9.

**enlisted paygrades** • Standardized levels of military pay for enlisted personnel in the armed forces. Specific paygrades in the Navy correlate to rates as follows: E-1 is seaman [or fireman, airman, constructionman, hospitalman, dentalman] recruit; E-2 is seaman [or fireman, airman, constructionman, hospitalman, dentalman] apprentice; E-3 is seaman [or fireman, airman, constructionman, hospitalman, dentalman]; E-4 is petty officer third class; E-5 is petty officer second class; E-6 is petty officer first class; E-7 is chief petty officer; E-8 is senior chief petty officer; E-9 is master chief petty officer. *See also:* paygrade; officer paygrades

**ensign** • 1. The most junior commissioned officer in the Navy and Coast Guard; designated by paygrade O-1. 2. The national flag flown by a warship from the gaff under way, flagstaff in port.

**entrance** • The part of a ship's hull from the stem aft to where it reaches its full beam. High-speed ships require extremely fine entrances.

**EP-3** • *See:* Aries II

**equator** • The primary great circle of Earth, or a similar body, perpendicular to the polar axis.

**equatorial tides** • Tides occurring approximately every two weeks when the moon is over the equator.

**equinoctial** • Pertaining to the climate or regions on or near the equator.

**equipage** • General term used to indicate material of a nonconsumable nature that is necessary to be aboard for a ship to perform its mission properly; usually carefully accounted for by a system of signed receipts.

**equipment operator (EO)** • Navy occupational rating that works with heavy machinery such as bulldozers, power shovels, pile drivers, rollers, and graders. EOs use this machinery to dig ditches and excavate for building foundations, break up old concrete or asphalt paving and pour new paving, loosen soil and grade it, dig out tree trunks and rocks, remove debris from construction sites, raise girders, and move and set in place other pieces of equipment or materials needed for a job.

**equisignal** • Term used primarily in connection with radio navigation; pertains to two or more signals of equal intensity.

**equivalent full-power hours (EFPH)** • A standard for indicating the amount of nuclear energy consumed. Naval reactors are rated in terms of the number of hours of full-power energy built into them, which is a direct measure of the amount of nuclear fuel. A half hour at full power is the same as one hour at half power, although distances run and speeds attained vary as the cube law. Thus, a 2,000-hour reactor that has logged 1,000 EFPH is half expended.

**equivalent service rounds (ESR)** • A standard for indicating gun erosion. All rounds fired, including reduced charges, are recorded in terms of service rounds and when a specified number is reached, depending upon the gun type, caliber, etc., the gun barrel must be replaced.

**erosion** • A gradual wearing away, such as a gully that is eroded by water.

**erratic** • Operating in an unusual manner that may result in possible breakdown or failure.

**escape hatch** • A small hatch installed to permit escape from a compartment when ordinary means of egress are blocked. Developed to a high degree in modern submarines, which have escape trunks fitted to receive a rescue chamber or a deep-submergence rescue vehicle, an additional hatch for unassisted escape, and numerous such specialized operating mechanisms and devices.

**escape trunk** • A narrow passage in a vessel designed to allow emergency egress from a compartment. *See also:* escape hatch

**escort** • 1. Combatant ships protecting a convoy or task force. 2. Aircraft assigned to accompany other aircraft for protection. 3. A person who accompanies a visitor in a classified area. 4. A person who accompanies a body to a burial place.

**escort commodore** • The officer in charge of a group of ships assigned to provide protection to a convoy or other assemblage of ships.

**escort vessel** • Old name for destroyer escort (now frigate). Now used to designate any warship escorting another ship or ships.

**estimated position (EP)** • The navigational position determined from estimates rather than from known data.

**evaporator** • Device aboard ship for making freshwater from seawater.

**evaps** • Short for evaporators.

**evasive steering** • Ship tactics used to confuse a would-be attacker (such as a stalking submarine); includes zigzagging, sinuating, etc.

**evening watch** • *See:* first watch

**even keel** • Floating evenly and level without list or uneven trim.

**even strain** • To exert power evenly and steadily to avoid parting a line. *Inf:* Relax.

**evolution** • A semi-informal term used to describe an event or series of events; for example, shiphandling practice can be described as a training evolution.

**executive officer (XO)** • The second in command of a ship, station, aircraft squadron, etc. *Inf:* Exec; XO.

**exercise** • A simulation or drill. Can be grand in scale, such as a multiship amphibious exercise, or smaller in nature such a small arms firing exercise for the gunner's mates. Can also be used as a verb, as in "Exercise the guns at dawn."

**exercise head** • A specialized head on a weapon (such as a missile or torpedo), generally carrying telemetering equipment instead of a warhead.

**exhaust trunks** • *See:* uptakes

**expansion joint** • A joint that allows expansion, contraction, or flexing in a pipe, ship's decks, or superstructure.

**expeditionary strike force (ESF)** • A combination of carrier strike groups (CVSGs) and expeditioary strike groups (ESGs) that work together should the need arise.

**expeditionary strike group (ESG)** • A bulked-up version of the former three-ship amphibious ready group. The ESG consists of one amphibious assault ship, one dock landing ship, one amphibious transport dock, one embarked Marine expeditionary unit, three surface combatants, one submarine, and shore-based aircraft.

**expendable bathythermograph** • Refers to the probe that is dropped in the water and not recovered. *See also:* bathythermograph

**explosimeter** • Device used to test for the presense of a concentration of gases and vapors in the air.

**explosive ordnance disposal unit** • Personnel with special training and equipment to render explosive ordnance safe and supervise the safe removal of all forms of ordnance.

**exposure suit** • Special clothing designed to help resist exposure to cold water. Used by aviators, fishermen, yachtsmen. Also called survival clothing.

**extender** • Device holding detonator of a mine or depth charge in safe position.

**extra duty** • Additional work assigned as punishment, autorized by the Uniform Code of Military Justice.

**extra military instruction** • Extra tasks assigned to one exhibiting behavioral or performance deficiencies, for the purpose of correction.

**extremely high frequencies (EHF)** • One of the designations of the frequency spectrum; covers the range 30,000–300,000 MHz (30–300 GHz).

**eye** • A fixed loop in a line.

**eyebrow** • Curved metal ridge over an air port designed to shed water.

**eyes of the ship** • The forward-most portion of the weather deck—as far forward as a person can stand—where fog lookouts are customarily stationed. Most ships of the old Navy had figureheads on their bows, and the term is supposed to refer either to their eyes or to those of the fog lookouts.

**eye splice** • A loop in the end of a line created by bending the line back on itself and splicing (interweaving) the strands of rope firmly together. Made for attaching the line to a hook or other similar device without chafing.

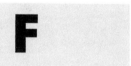

**4Rs** • *See:* Four Rs

**F-14** • *See:* Tomcat

**F/A-18** • *See:* Hornet; Super Hornet

**face curtain** • A sheet of heavy fabric that is installed above an ejection seat. It is pulled down to trigger the ejection seat and protect the pilot and crew against wind blast.

**facsimile** • 1. The transmission of photographs or other material by wire or radio. The U.S. Navy had limited facsimile capability long before "FAX" machines became a ubiqui-

tous part of life. 2. An exact copy.

**fag end** • The extreme end of a rope; more specifically, when it has become frayed or untwisted. *See also:* cow's tail

**fahrenheit temperature** • Temperature based upon a scale in which, under standard atmospheric pressure, water freezes at 32° and boils at 212°.

**fairing** • A part or structure that has a smooth, streamlined outline; used to cover a nonstreamlined object. For example, a non-aerodynamic projection on the side of an aircraft's fuselage would be covered by a specially designed fairing to improve the aerodynamic flow.

**fairlead** • 1. A fitting, such as a block, that provides a low-friction passage for a line or cable. 2. An unhampered route for a line or cable.

**fairway** • The navigable part of a body of water.

**fake down** • To lay out a line in long, flat bights, the whole being much longer than wide, in such form that when needed it will pay out freely without bights or kinks. A coiled or flemished line cannot do this unless the coil of the line is able to turn, as on a reel. *See also:* coil down; flemish

**fall** • 1. The rope and blocks that make up a tackle; *e.g.*, a boat fall. 2. In a tackle, specifically that portion of the rope that is between the two blocks. Counting the falls in a tackle yields a usable estimate of the mechanical advantage provided by that tackle. *See also:* purchase

**fall in** • Command to form ranks. The command to disband is "fall out."

**falling glass** • Lowering atmospheric pressure as registered by the barometer; normally a sign of approaching foul weather.

**fall off** • Said of a ship or the bow of a ship when it drifts away from a desired position or direction.

**fall of shot** • The point of impact of naval gunfire. Location of the fall of shot (point of impact) is important for corrections to the aim. *See also:* gun director

**fall out** • *See:* fall in

**fancy work** • Decorative knots and pieces of canvas, used particularly in gigs and barges, as adornment on rails, etc. *See also:* MacNamara's lace

**fantail** • The aftermost deck area topside in a ship.

**farewell buoy** • *See:* sea buoy

**farm** • Open stowage area, as in a "bomb farm," where ordnance is stowed.

**fast** • Snugly secured; for example, said of a line when it is fastened securely. *See also:* fast cruise

**fast automatic shuttle transfer (FAST) system** • Replenishment system designed to speed the transfer of ordnance and supplies between ships at sea through specialized equipment aboard the supply ship.

**fast cruise** • Trials conducted while the ship is fast to a pier or at anchor, with only the ship's crew aboard. The purpose is to train personnel in all operations of the ship's equipment and to check out its proper operation in as many ways as practicable while simulating underway condtions as closely as possible.

**fast ice** • *See:* landfast ice

**fathom** • Measure of length, used for measuring the depth of water, equal to 6 feet. Originated from a seaman holding a length of line along his outstretched arms.

**Fathometer** • Trademarked electronic device

that measures depth by measuring the time used by sound waves to reflect off the bottom. *See also:* echo sounder

**feather** • 1. To change the pitch of a variable-pitch aircraft propeller to reduce air resistance when not in use for propulsion. 2. To turn the blade of an oar horizontally at the finish of a stroke to reduce resistance of air or water. 3. The spray formed by the periscope of a submerged submarine moving through the water at moderate to high speed. 4. The bow (stern) spray of a high-speed ship.

**feather merchant** • An uncomplimentary term of mild scorn applied to those new to the service.

**feedback** • Evaluative or corrective information about an action or process after it has commenced.

**feed heater** • Heat transfer device used to heat feed water before it goes to the boiler. *See also:* economizer

**feedwater** • Water that is preheated and/or purified before it enters a boiler. *See also:* feed heater

**feint** • A phony operation intended to deceive the enemy.

**fender** • A device of canvas, wood, line, cork, rubber, etc., slung over the side of a ship in position to absorb the shock of contact between ships or between a ship and a pier.

**fend off** • To push away from a pier or another ship when coming alongside in order to prevent damage or chafing.

**fetch** • The distance a wind blows over the sea surface without interference; a factor in the buildup of waves.

**fiber rope** • General term for cordage made of vegetable fibers such as hemp, manila flax, cotton, or sisal; in contrast to synthetic fibers like Dacron and nylon.

**fid** • Sharply pointed, round spike-shaped wooden tool used to separate the strands of a line for splicing. *See also:* marlinespike

**fiddle bridge** • Collapsible supports under the arresting gear on an aircraft carrier's deck.

**fiddle rack (boards)** • Wooden device set on a table at sea in rough weather to hold table gear in place.

**fiddley** • Wide opening immediately above a fireroom, through which ventilators are led. *Var.* fidley.

**fiddley hatch** • Framework around the opening of a deck hatch leading below decks.

**fidley deck** • Raised platform over the engine and boiler rooms, particularly around the stack.

**fidley grating** • Steel gratings fitted over boiler room hatches.

**field change** • Necessary parts and instructions to make an authorized post-factory modification to machinery, ordnance, or electronic equipment.

**field day** • A particular day devoted to general cleaning, usually in preparation for inspection.

**field ice** • Ice formed by freezing of the ocean surface. Also called sea ice.

**field-strip** • To disassemble the major groups of a piece of ordnance for routine cleaning and oiling; opposed to detailed stripping, which may be done only by authorized technicians.

**fife rail** • A wooden or metal rail near the base of a mast, bored with holes to receive belaying pins; seen today on Navy ships on flag bags.

**fighter director** • A fighter direction ship or aircraft is one specially equipped for that purpose. It is controlled by personnel outside the ship or aircraft who are called fighter directors.

**fighter sweep** • Offensive mission executed by fighter aircraft to destroy enemy aircraft or installations.

**figure-8 fake** • Method of coiling rope over an elevated railing in which the turns form a series of overlapping figure-eights, advancing about one or two diameters of the rope for each turn; usually done over the lifelines.

**file** • A line of persons standing in formation, one behind the other. A typical military formation consists of both ranks and files; those in ranks are standing next to each other, those in files are standing one behind the other. Personnel lining up to receive innoculations would be in a single file.

**file number** • Old term for the record identification number of naval officers, assigned at time of commissioning and retained permanently; also called a service number. File numbers are no longer used and have been replaced by social security numbers.

**film badge** • A small piece of unexposed film, arranged in a badge pinned to clothing and worn by personnel working in a nuclear environment to measure their cumulative exposure to radiation. Periodically changed and evaluated in the nucleonics laboratory of the activity. It gives a more accurate measure of cumulative radiation exposure than does a simple dosimeter.

**final diameter** • Diameter of a circle made by a ship completing a 360° turn with constant rudder angle. *See also:* tactical diameter

**final power amplifier (FPA)** • The final stage of amplification in a transmitter.

**fire and rescue party** • *See also:* rescue and

assistance party

**firebox** • The section of a ship's boiler where fuel oil combustion takes place.

**fire classes** • *See:* classes of fire

**fire classification** • *See:* classes of fire

**fire control** • System by which the ship's armament is directed. Roughly defined as "aiming." Accomplished by such things as fire control radars, optical directors, etc.

**fire controlman (FC)** • Navy occupational rating that maintains the control mechanisms used in weapons systems on combat ships. Complex electronic, electrical, and hydraulic equipment is required to ensure the accuracy of guided-missile and surface gunfire-control systems. FCs are responsible for the operation, routine care, and repair of this equipment, including radars, computers, weapons-direction equipment, target-designation systems, gyroscopes, and range finders.

**fire control technician (FT)** • Navy occupational rating that maintains advanced electronic equipment used in weapons systems. Complex electronic, electrical, and mechanical equipment is required to ensure the accuracy of guided-missile systems and underwater weapons. FTs are responsible for the operation, routine care, and repair of this equipment.

**fire-control tower** • Either a separate structure or a part of the conning tower containing fire control equipment in warships.

**fire for effect** • Order given when ranging salvos are on target and maximum damage to the enemy is desired.

**fire main** • The saltwater line that provides fire-fighting water and flushing water throughout the ship.

**fireman (FN)** • Enlisted person (paygrade E-3) who works in the engineering spaces.

**fire mission** • An assignment in shore bombardment to fire on a specific target.

**fire party** • Personnel aboard ship in the duty section organized to fight fires.

**fire room** • Compartment containing boilers and related equipment.

**firesides** • In an oil- or coal-fired boiler, fire outside the boiler tubes imparts heat to the feed water inside the tubes, giving rise to the two terms, firesides (outside the tubes) and watersides (inside the tubes).

**fire support area** • Specific area assigned a ship for gunfire during an amphibious operation.

**fire support ship, inshore (IFS)** • Shallow-draft, rocket-firing ship for fire support duty close to the beach during amphibious assault.

**fire wall** • A bulkhead separating two compartments within an aircraft, providing protection for personnel from dangerous engine components.

**firing lock** • The mechanism in the breech of a gun that contains the firing pin.

**firing-stop mechanism** • Device that prevents a gun from firing into its own ship's structure.

**first call** • A bugle call sounded five minutes before quarters, colors, or tattoo.

**first dog watch** • The watch from 1600–1800 (4–6 P.M.). *See also:* dog watch

**first-in, first-out (FIFO)** • A logical method of stowing supplies so that the oldest stock is issued first.

**first lieutenant** • Officer responsible for the upkeep and cleanliness of the ship, boats, ground tackle, and deck seamanship in general. Archaic term for a ship's second in command.

**first light** • The beginning of morning nautical twilight; *i.e.*, when the center of the morning sun is 12° below the horizon.

**first watch** • The watch from 2000–2400 (8 P.M. –midnight). Also known as the evening watch.

**fiscal year** • The year as defined for monetary purposes. Different from the calendar which inconveniently ends during a holiday season. When originally used in the Navy, it ran from 1 July to 30 June but later was modified to run from 1 October to 30 September.

**fish** • 1. A tapered batten of hard, strong wood bound to a spar to strengthen it. 2. Streamlined weight on the end of an aircraft's trailing, suspended antenna. 3. In the old Navy, to fish an anchor was to engage the hook of the catfall in the pad eye of the balance point, an operation resembling fishing. 4. *Inf:* Torpedo.

**fishhook** • The small, sharp broken strands that project from a wire line or hawser after much use or heavy strain. Indicative of progressive failure. Can cause injury if handled without protective gloves.

**fist** • A continuous wave (CW) radio operator's key or sending hand. A slow or rusty operator was said to have a glass fist. An expert had a copperplate hand or fist.

**fitness report** • Periodic evaluation of an officer's performance of duty and worth to the service, signed by his or her commanding officer.

**fitting** • Generic term for any part or piece of machinery or installed equipment that is used to effect a connection between components.

**fitting out** • Preparing a ship for commissioning and active service by placing on board the material authorized by the allowance list.

**fix** • A navigational position determined

from terrestrial, electronic, or astronomic data.

**flag bag** • The place where the ship's signal flags are kept. The term "bag" is archaic; modern flag bags are usually specially designed metal containers.

**flag bridge** • In a ship designed for service as flagship, a separate bridge for the use of a flag officer and staff. Usually on a different level from the ship's navigating bridge and distinctly separate from it.

**flaghoist** • Method of communicating between ships by using flags run up on signal halyards.

**flag lieutenant** • Personal aide to a flag officer.

**flag officer** • Officer of rank above captain, authorized to fly a personal flag. Equivalent to a general officer. *See also:* admiral

**flag plot** • An enclosed tactical and navigational center used by a flag officer and his or her staff in exercising tactical command of ships and aircraft.

**flag secretary** • Personal aide to a flag officer who directs the paperwork of the staff.

**flagship** • The ship from which an admiral or other unit commander exercises command.

**flagstaff** • Vertical spar at the stern of a naval ship from which the national ensign is displayed when the ship is anchored or moored.

**flagstaff insignia** • Distinguishing devices fitted to the top of flagstaffs to indicate the rank of the officers or important civil officials associated with the boat, headquarters, etc. where the flag is located. Specific devices correlate as follows: A spread eagle represents an official whose authorized gun salute is 19 or more guns (service secretaries, the Chief of Naval Operations, Commandant of the Marine Corps, etc.); a halberd represents a flag or general officer and certain civil officials (assistant service secretaries, consul generals, etc.); a ball represents an officer of the grade of captain or various civil officials (first secretary of a legation); a star represents an officer of the grade of commander or equivalent; and a flat truck represents an officer below the grade of commander or civilian equivalent. The head of the eagle and the cutting edge of the halberd must face forward and the points of the star must be aligned fore-and-aft.

**flake out** • *Inf:* To lie down, take a nap, or "take an even strain on all parts."

**flameout** • In-flight jet aircraft casualty; the engine shuts down.

**flame safety lamp** • Special lamp designed to test the oxygen content of the air in a compartment.

**flammable liquid** • A liquid having a flash-point below 100° Fahrenheit.

**flammable material** • A material that is capable of burning.

**flank speed** • Maximum speed for a ship.

**flap** • 1. Pyrotechnic device used to attract attention or illuminate an area. 2. The tendency of a blade to rise with high-lift demands as it tries to screw itself upward into the air. 3. *Inf:* Chaotic crisis.

**flapper valve** • A valve, usually large, closed by swinging a hinged plate onto its seat, seated firmly by pressure above the plate or disc. Lends itself to quick closing, remote operation, and automatic action if water instead of air comes down the pipe. Disaster to USS *Squalus* in 1939 established the requirement for such valves in the hull air-induction system of submarines.

**flare** • 1. The outward curve, away from the centerline, of the sides of a boat or ship above the waterline; reverse of tumble home. Flare causes the sides of a ship's bows to be concave, thus forcing the water away and simultaneously reducing the depth to which the bow plunges. 2. A light-producing pyrotechnic used for illumination, to attract attention, or act as a marker.

**flareback** • An unwanted ejection of flame and hot gas from the breech of a gun. In a ship propelled by steam, flareback is the backfire of flame and hot gases into a ship's fire room from the firebox.

**flash** • The highest precedence assigned to a naval message, indicating that it is of the greatest urgency. *See also:* precedence

**flash burn** • The burn from the flash of a bomb or projectile, countered on board ship by flashproof clothing (battle dress).

**flashing** • Reducing the amount of permanent magnetism in a ship by placing temporary energizing coils horizontally around the ship. *See also:* degaussing; deperming

**flashing light** • 1. Communication using a code transmitted by blinker or signal searchlight. 2. A navigational aid whose period of light is less than the period of darkness. Occulting lights are on more than they are off, while flashing lights are off more than they are on. *See also:* occulting light

**flashless charge** • Gunpowder charge for large-caliber guns that reduces the flash of detonation; suitable for night actions.

**flash plate** • A metal plate on the forecastle, on which the anchor chain rests. It is so called because of the sparks created when the anchor is let go.

**flash point** • The lowest temperature at which a fuel will vaporize and form a combustible air-vapor mixture.

**flashproof clothing** • Protective clothing

specially designed to resist the effects of flash burns caused by detonations of explosives. Sometimes called battle dress.

**flat hat** • Blue cap formerly worn by enlisted men in winter months. Similar in shape to the officer's cap, but without the visor.

**flat-hat** • *Inf:* A low flying and stunting aircraft.

**flat(s)** • Plating or gratings installed only to provide working or walking surfaces. Should not be confused with decks, although sections of a flat could resemble a deck.

**flattop** • *Inf:* Aircraft carrier.

**flaw** • Sudden gust of wind.

**fleet** • Generic term applied to a group of ships operating together to accomplish a common mission. A formal organization of ships, aircraft, Marine forces, and shore-based fleet activities, all under a commander who exercises operational and administrative control.

**fleet admiral** • Rank above admiral. Also known less formally as five-star admiral because of the rank device worn. Not currently in use.

**fleet air wing** • A group of patrol squadrons, land- and carrier-based, with tenders and supporting fleet air support squadron.

**fleet ballistic missile (FBM)** • Shipborne ballistic missile designed to be carried on deterrent patrols by nuclear submarines. Types of U.S. FBMs are Polaris, Poseidon, and Trident missiles.

**fleet ballistic missile submarine (SSBN)** • Nuclear-powered submarine designed to deliver ballistic missile attacks against assigned targets from either a submerged or surfaced condition. *Inf:* Boomer.

**fleet in being** • A naval force that acts as a factor of strength because of its existence. A classic example is Germany's High Seas Fleet during WWI, which only fought one major battle with the Royal Navy; but because it existed, the British had to keep their fleet nearby, ready to respond should the Germans sortie.

**Fleet Marine Force (FMF)** • A balanced force of combined arms comprising land, air, and service elements of the U.S. Marine Corps. A Fleet Marine Force is an integral part of a U.S. Fleet and has the status of a type command.

**fleet response plan** • A plan that allows the Navy to surge six carrier strike groups to a trouble spot, followed quickly by two more.

**fleet up** • To advance in position or importance, usually within the same unit. For example, if the executive officer of a particular ship had to permanently leave the ship because of a medical condition, the operations officer might fleet up to become the executive officer.

**flemish** • To coil down a line on deck in a flat, tight, circular arrangement. Useful for appearance only, because the line will kink when taken up or used. *See also:* fake down; coil down

**flight** • A specified group of aircraft generally engaged in a common mission.

**flight clearance** • Formal permission to make a flight.

**flight deck** • A ship's deck from which flight operations are conducted. On an aircraft carrier, the flight deck is the uppermost full-length deck; on other ships it is a partial weather deck area.

**flight gear** • Clothing and equipment worn by aviators.

**flight leader** • Pilot in tactical command of a group of aircraft assigned to perform a specific mission.

**flight line** • Relating to an airfield: A line along which planes are parked prior to take-off. Prescribed path of aircraft taking photographs or making other observations.

**flight log** • Naval aviator's record of flight time.

**flight pay** • Extra pay earned by aviation personnel. *Inf:* Flight skins.

**flight plan** • Specified information filed either orally or in writing with air traffic control, relative to the intended flight of an aircraft.

**flight quarters** • Manning of all stations for flight operations aboard ship.

**flight surgeon** • Medical officer specially qualified for duty with an aviation unit.

**Flinders Bar** • Iron rod or bundled rods inserted vertically into the binnacle of a magnetic compass; compensates for the vertical component of the Earth's magnetic field and its resultant deviation. Named for Matthew Flinders, the British navigator who discovered the need for it.

**floater net** • Net made up of floats connected by line; used to supplement life rafts and lifeboats.

**floating drydock** • Movable dock floating in water; ships are floated into it when the dock is down (*i.e.*, partially submerged). Then the dock is raised by pumping the ballast tanks, lifting the dock and the enclosed ship to facilitiate repairs to the underwater body of the ship.

**floating dump** • Supply of critical items held on landing craft for quick delivery ashore to assault troops during amphibious operations. Also called offshore dump.

**floating reserve** • Amphibious troops kept aboard ship after the assault begins, in case they are needed.

**floes** • Large, flat pieces of ice broken loose from a sheet of ice that originally formed in the sea.

**flogging** • A form of punishment in the old Navy that involved whipping an offender. *See also:* cat-o'-nine-tails

**flood currents** • Currents caused by an increase in the height of tide.

**flood tide** • Tide rising or flowing toward land. *See also:* ebb tide; tide

**floor** • Wide structural beams arranged in a supportive web inside a ship's bottom.

**floor plates** • *See:* deck plates

**Florida current** • Water flowing north into the Atlantic Ocean from the Caribbean Sea through the Straits of Florida and off the East Coast of the United States from Florida to Cape Hatteras, where it becomes the Gulf Stream. Part of the Gulf Stream system.

**flotilla** • Administrative or tactical organization consisting of two or more squadrons of ships together with a flagship or tender or both.

**flotsam** • Floating wreckage or trash. The terms "flotsam" and "jetsam" are actually legal terms originating in marine law. Flotsam is the accidental floating debris resulting from a ship sinking or damaged in a manner that causes it to leave debris floating in the ocean; not that which sinks to the bottom. Jetsam is debris resulting from the deliberate jettisoning of materials into the sea, as when cargo is thrown overboard from a ship in danger of sinking.

**flounder plate** • A triangular steel plate with reinforced eyes at each corner, used to join chain bridles in towing.

**flukes** • Roughly triangular plates on the ends of an anchor's arms; designed to dig into the bottom when the anchor is dropped which helps to secure the vessel.

**flush-deck destroyer** • *See:* flushdecker

**flush-decker** • 1. Ship whose weather deck extends unbroken the length of the ship. 2. Nickname applied to several classes of destroyers that served in the early years of the twentieth century.

**fly** • 1. The edge of a flag that runs perpendicular to its staff. Usually (with rectangular flags) the long dimension or length of a flag. 2. The outboard end of a flag, away from the halyard. *See also:* hoist

**flycatcher operations** • Defense against enemy small craft in an amphibious objective area.

**flying boat** • Type of seaplane that can float on its hull in the water.

**flying bridge** • Topmost bridge of a ship, usually above the navigating bridge or conning tower; generally open and exposed to the weather.

*Flying Dutchman* • A nautical superstition that claims there is a ghost ship sailing the seven seas. Superstition has it that any mariner who sees the *Flying Dutchman* will die within the day. The tale of the *Flying Dutchman* trying to round the Cape of Good Hope against strong winds and never succeeding, then trying to make Cape Horn and failing there too, has been the most famous of maritime ghost stories for more 300 years. The cursed spectral ship sailing back and forth on its endless voyage, its ancient white-haired crew crying for help while hauling at her sail, inspired Samuel Taylor Coleridge to write his classic "The Rime of the Ancient Mariner," to name but one famous literary work. The real *Flying Dutchman* is supposed to have set sail in 1660.

**flying jib** • In sailing ships that carry more than a single jib, the outer one, farthest forward, is the flying jib.

**flying moor** • In a flying moor, the ship drops the downstream anchor first as she approaches her anchorage, pays out the chain as she steers for the spot to drop the upstream anchor, then veers the upstream chain and heaves in on the first until centered. *See also:* moor

**fly over** • A display of aircraft in the air for ceremonial or publicity purposes. Roughly equivalent to a parade in the air. *See also:* Blue Angles

**foam blanket** • A dense layer of foam applied to a burning or susceptible surface to smother flames or prevent ignition.

**fod** • Objects that if not removed from a flight operations area might cause damage to an aircraft engine if sucked in, or injury to personnel if blown into an eye, etc. Comes from the acronym "FOD" which means "foreign object damage."

**FOD walkdown** • Activity aboard aviation ships where personnel line up and walk the flight deck from end to end, picking up any object that might damage an engine if sucked in or, if picked up by jet blast, might cause an injury to personnel. The "human broom" picking up any and every small item on the flight deck. Term comes from the acronym for "foreign object damage" that has come to mean the objects themselves, as in "she picked up a large piece of FOD on the flight deck."

**fog** • A visible assemblage of numerous tiny droplets of water or ice crystals formed by condensation of water vapor in the air with the base at the surface of Earth.

**fog buoy** • *See:* towing spar

**fogey** • *See:* fogy

**fog lookouts** • Special lookouts stationed in periods of low visibility. Generally sent to the eyes of the ship, because in the thick fog they might well be the first to see or hear another ship or object when danger of collision might exist. Lookouts may also be effectively sent aloft when the fog is dense but close to the surface of the water.

**fog nozzle** • Firehose fitting that forces water into a very fine spray or fog.

**fogy** • *Inf:* Increase in pay because of length of service.

**foot line** • The bottom-most lifeline. *See also:* lifeline

**foot (of a sail)** • The bottom edge.

**foot rope** • The rope attached to the underside of a yard on which Sailors stood while loosing or furling sail; now obsolete except for the few remaining square-rigged sailing ships.

**force** • 1. A body of troops, ships, or aircraft, or combination thereof; major subdivision of a fleet. Part of a task force. 2. A measure of wind intensity, as force 4. 3. The action of one body on another, tending to change the state of motion of the body acted upon; usually expressed in pounds. *See also:* task organization

**forced draft** • Air under pressure supplied to the burners in a ship's boilers; machinery used to deliver this air is called a forced draft blower.

**forced draft blower** • *See:* forced draft

**FORCEnet** • Part of the Seapower 21 concept; pertains to the combination of Navy and Marines Corps information networks with those of other services, so they can share data. *See also:* Sea Strike; Sea Shield; Sea Basing; Sea Trial; Sea Warrior; Sea Enterprise; Seapower 21

**force tabs** • With reference to war plans, the statement of time-phased deployments of major combat units by major commands and geographic areas.

**fore and aft** • Lengthwise dimension or direction parallel to a vessel's centerline, as in "form a line fore and aft from the forward magazine to the after one so that we can shift ammunition." Opposite of athwartships, which is across a vessel.

**fore-and-aft cap** • *See:* garrison cap

**fore-and-aft sail** • A sail designed to have a leading edge (luff) and a trailing edge (leech), cut in a triangular or a quadrilateral shape, but neither square nor rectangular. Designed to be fitted to fore-and-aft-tending booms instead of athwartship-tending yards.

**forebody** • Ship's hull forward of amidships.

**forecastle** • Forward section of weather deck. Pronounced "folk-sul." Vicinity of the ground tackle.

**forecastle deck** • Partial deck over the main deck at the bow.

**forefoot** • Part of the keel that curves up to meet the stem, or where the stem joins the keel of a ship.

**fore leech** • The luff of a fore-and-aft sail. *See also:* leech

**foremast** • On a vessel with two or more masts, the forward-most mast. If the second mast is much smaller (as in a yawl or ketch) than the first, then the first is called the mainmast and the second the mizzenmast.

**forenoon watch** • The watch from 0800–1200 (8 A.M. –noon).

**forestay** • Wire or cable supporting a mast in the fore-and-aft direction that tends forward. *See also:* stay; backstay; shroud

**foretop** • Top of the foremast. Heavy structure supported by a foremast; houses fire control equipment. Rare in modern warship design.

**foretruck** • The highest point of the forward mast.

**forfeiture of pay** • A type of punishment awarded at a court-martial or for nonjudicial punishment, depriving the accused of all or part of his or her pay.

**formation** • 1. Any ordered arrangement of two or more ships or aircraft proceeding together. 2. A formal arrangement of troops.

**forward** • Toward the bow, as in "Mount 51 is forward of Mount 52."

**forward area** • *See:* area, forward

**forward bow spring** • Mooring line in the bow area of the ship that leads forward from the ship to the pier or wharf; prevents the ship from moving aft along the pier. *See also:* spring line; after bow spring; forward quarter spring

**forward-deployed naval forces** • Ships and staffs permanently homeported in overseas locations.

**forward-firing weapons** • Weapons—such as missiles, rockets, and guns—that are propelled in a forward direction.

**forward-looking infrared** • A sensor system that uses heat (infrared emanations) as its targeting source.

**forward quarter spring** • Mooring line in the after area of the ship that leads forward from the ship to the pier or wharf; prevents the ship from moving aft along the pier. *See also:* after bow spring; after quarter spring; forward bow spring; spring lines

**foul** • 1. To entangle, confuse, or obstruct. Examples are: an anchor can be fouled if it is entangled in its own cable; a missile firing range is fouled if a recreational craft strays into it. 2. Jammed or entangled; not clear for running. 3. Covered with barnacles, as a "fouled bottom." 4. To collide with.

**foul anchor** • An anchor entangled in its chain or cable, or for any other reason, is not clear for hoisting all the way up.

**foul deck** • A flight deck that is obstructed such that it cannot be landed upon.

**fouled runway** • Runway is not ready for operations.

**foul ground** • Shallow sea area marked by rocks, reefs, shoals, wrecks, etc.

**foul hawse** • To have an obstruction or potential obstruction in the hawse pipe (or hawse hole) that prevents normal heaving in. *See also:* hawse

**fouling** • The attachment of various marine organisms (such as barnacles) to underwater portions of the ship (hull, rudders, etc.); a problem for vessels because it causes drag and thereby speed reduction.

**foul lines** • Painted lines on the flight deck which delineate an area which must be kept clear for flight operations to proceed safely.

**foul weather** • Rainy or stormy weather.

**foul-weather parade** • Occurs when a division forms up inside a ship (hangar, etc.), rather than out on deck, to conduct quarters, inspections, etc. *See also:* division parade

**founder** • To sink as a result of the hull flooding. A ship that strikes a rock and subsequently sinks is said to have foundered; a ship that sinks as a result of explosion would not be said to have foundered. Sometimes the word "flounder" is incorrectly used to mean "founder."

**four-in-hand** • The act of preventing a tackle from overhauling by gripping in both hands the parts of the fall between the blocks.

**four-0 (4.0)** • Perfect; 100%.

**four piper** • A ship with four stacks. Some cruisers were referred to as four pipers, but the term found general and affectionate use in relation to the very large group of WWI flush-deck destroyers that were the backbone of the U.S. Navy's destroyer force during the between-the-wars years. The fifty destroyers transferred to England during WWII, before U.S. entry, were this type. Although nearly all appeared identical to anyone but those who knew them, to a destroyerman of that time they exhibited many fascinating differences.

**four-point moor** • Using four anchors to allow a vessel to maintain its position accurately, or to shift its position by heaving in or slacking off during diving operations. The four anchors are placed as close to 90° relative to one another as possible—in other words, at four equal intervals relative to the vessel.

**Four Rs** • Recruiting, Readiness, Retention, and Respect

**fox** • Past phonetic word for the letter F; replaced by foxtrot.

**foxer gear (FXR)** • Noise-making device towed astern to foil acoustic torpedoes.

**foxtail** • 1. Short-handled brush for sweeping small areas; a dust-pan brush. 2. Short line attached to a jackstay.

**foxtrot** • Phonetic word for the letter F.

**fram** • Originally an acronym for "fleet rehabilitation and modernization" program; has come to mean a virtual rebuilding of the entire ship with particular attention to adding new and innovative capabilities not in her original design or configuration, yet not changing her basic designation. Not a conversion that would, presumably, alter the fundamental employment or purpose of the vessel. Usually applied to destroyers, for whom the fram program was first created. *See also:* Service Life Extension Program (SLEP)

**frames** • Athwartships strength members of a ship's hull, numbered from forward aft and used as reference points to locate fittings, division parades, etc.; analogous to ribs.

**frap** • 1. To wrap with line or cover with canvas or some other material; done for protection. For example, frapping a mooring line along areas where it might rub against a pier provides rubbing protection to the line. 2. To bind lines together to increase tension or strength. 3. To bind for protection; for example, wrapping lines around a furled sail to keep it from flappng in the wind. 4. *Inf:* At the Naval Academy, to be put on report.

**frapping gear** • Line, canvas, or other materials used to frap.

**frapping lines** • Lines passed around the forward and after boat falls to steady the boat in a seaway as it is being hoisted or lowered.

**free** • To clear or untangle, as in "Free that line."

**freeboard** • Vertical distance from the weather deck to the waterline.

**freebooter** • *See:* buccaneer

**freeing port** • A deck-level opening in the ship or in a bulwark to permit water to escape.

**free surface (effect)** • The surface exposed when liquid in a partially filled ship's compartment or tank is free to move from side to side as the ship rolls. Because the liquid goes to the low side, a large free surface is always dangerous to stability. The only way to eliminate the free surface effect is to completely fill or empty the compartment.

**freeze point** • The temperature at which wax crystals form in fuels.

**freezing** • Cessation of motion between two contacting surfaces due to a lack of lubrication.

**frequency** • In electronics, the rate at which a cycle is repeated. Originally expressed in terms of "cycles per second" (or kilocycles, megacycles, etc.), the term "hertz" has replaced "cycle per second," as in "kilohertz" (kHz), megahertz (MHz), etc., to honor physicist Heinrich Hertz.

**frequency shift keying (FSK)** • Frequency modulation somewhat similar to continuous-wave (CW) keying in amplitude modulation (AM) transmitters. The carrier is shifted between two differing frequencies by opening and closing a key.

**fresh air snipe** • *Inf:* Engineering ratings who spend part of their time in areas outside the engineering spaces. Includes ratings such as interior communications electrician and electrician's mate.

**freshen the nip** • 1. To shift a line to equalize the wear. 2. To set up again.

**freshwater king** • Person in charge of the ship's evaporators and water supply.

**Fresnel lens** • A specially designed multi-prismed lens, invented by Augustin Fresnel (pronounced Fray-nell) in 1822 used extensively in lighthouses. Much more effective at collecting and directing light rays, it produces a beam five times more powerful than the old reflector system used before its invention.

**friendly fire** • Accidental htting of freindly forces when attempting to deliver fires on the enemy.

**frigate** • In modern navies, the frigate is smaller and usually slower than a destroyer, designed primarily for escort duties but can be used for other purposes. For a time, the U.S. Navy was alone in using the designation frigate for its large destroyers (destroyer leaders) in recognition of the place the early frigates held in our history, but it has now reverted to the common practice of all other navies, using the term for smaller vessels (formerly called destroyer escorts and ocean escorts). In the days of sail, a full-rigged ship, mounting guns on a single gundeck and on the forecastle and poop deck (sometimes on a spar deck as well, depending on the construction of the ship); fast and maneuverable, smaller than a ship of the line. The British Navy used frigates as adjuncts to their battle fleet, for scouting, signaling, etc. The U.S. Navy designed and used them for inependent duty as ocean raiders, able to defeat anything fast enough to catch them.

**frock** • When a person has been selected for promotion, but the promotion has not yet gone into effect, he or she might be frocked; *i.e.* to assume the uniform and title, but not yet receive the pay, of the new rank.

**frogmen** • *Inf:* Underwater demolition team (UDT) personnel.

**front** • The transition zone between two air masses of different density. Since temperature is the most important regulator of atmospheric density, a front almost invariably separates air masses of different temperature.

**frontal system** • Simply a system of fronts as they appear on a surface analysis or prognosis chart.

**fuel trunk** • Topside connection in surface ships through which fuel is taken aboard.

**full and by** • Said of a sailing vessel when she is sailing as close to the wind as possible.

**full and down** • Said of a ship when all spaces are full of cargo and the ship is down to the maximum specified draft and drag.

**full dressing ship** • For special occasions, displaying national ensigns at all mastheads as well as the flagstaff, and rigging a rainbow of signal flags from bow to stern over the mastheads.

**full rigged ship** • A sailing ship with all possible sails set.

**full sea bag** • Complete outfit of uniforms and related gear. *Inf:* Relating to a person's mental abilities, as in "He's not packing a full sea bag."

**full speed** • 1. A prescribed speed that is greater than standard speed but less than flank speed. 2. Highest sustainable speed. Flank speed is faster, but cannot be sustained because of the strain on the engineering plant.

**funnel** • Ship's smokestack; stack.

**furl** • To make up in a bundle, as in "furl the sail."

**fuselage** • Body of an airplane.

**fuse pendant** • A wire or line safety link designed to part before the whole rig is carried away.

**fuze** • Mechanical, electrical, electronic, or magnetic device for detonating the explosive charge of a weapon.

**fuze (projectile)** • The detonating portion of a gun projectile; may be one of several different designs: auxiliary detonating, base detonating, mechanical time, point detonating, or proximity fuze. *See also:* projectile

# G

**gaff** • Small spar on the aftermost mast of a naval ship, from which the national ensign is displayed while under way. The upper spar of a four-sided fore and aft sail, such as a spanker. In days of sail, the national ensign flew from the spanker gaff.

**gale** • Strong wind, usually described as moderate gale (41–47 knots); or whole gale (48–55 knots). *See also:* breeze; storm; hurricane

**gallery deck** • Partial deck between the flight deck and the hangar deck of an aircraft carrier.

**galley** • 1. A shipboard kitchen. 2. A low vessel propelled by oars, once common among Mediterranean and Baltic navies.

**galling** • Tearing away of a metal surface by friction.

**galvanize** • To coat iron or steel with rust-resistant zinc.

**galvanometer** • An electrical instrument for measuring small currents.

**gangplank** • Temporary bridge from the ship to a pier, or to another ship alongside. Brow is the more correct term. *See also:* brow

**gangway** • 1. An order to stand aside or stand clear. 2. An opening in the rail or bulwarks of a ship to permit access on board. 3. Walkway for leaving and boarding ship. 4. Get out of the way.

**gantline** • Line passing through a single block aloft. A single block whip, or tackle, at the top of a mast or stack; for sending gear aloft.

**garbage scow** • A simple craft found in a harbor or port area that makes the rounds to vessels in port to receive their trash and garbage. *Inf:* A ship that is not well maintained; a dirty ship.

**garble** • An error that makes a message incorrect or unintelligible.

**garboard strake** • A continuous line of shell plating or planking running along either side of the keel.

**garrison cap** • A soft, wedge-shaped, visorless military cap that folds flat. Common to all the U.S. Armed Services, it is often called an "overseas cap" or "fore-and-aft cap" in the Navy. Grade insignia is worn on the left side of the cap.

**gasket** • 1. Strip of sealing material placed between adjoining parts (usually metal) to prevent the passage of fluid (liquid or gas). An excellent example is the rubber gasket around watertight doors that seals against the so-called "knife edge" of the door and prevents air and/or water from passing through once the door is closed. 2. A small line or strip of canvas used to secure a sail to a boom or gaff.

**gas-turbine system technician (GS)** • Navy occupational rating that operates, repairs, and maintains gas-turbine engines; main propulsion machinery (including gears, shafting, and controllable-pitch propellers); assigned auxiliary equipment; propulsion-control systems; electrical and electronic circuitry up to printed circuit modules; and alarm and warning circuitry. GSs perform administrative tasks related to gas-turbine propulsion-system operation and maintenance.

**gate vessel** • Vessel used to open and close a gate opening in antisubmarine nets protecting a harbor or narrow passage.

**gator** • 1. *Inf:* Amphibious vessel; short for alligator (an amphibious animal). 2. *Inf:* Slang term for the ship's navigator. *See also:* gator freighter

**gator freighter** • *Inf:* Amphibious warfare cargo ship. *See also:* gator

**gauge glass** • Device for indicating the water level in a tank or boiler.

**gedunk** • Snacks. The place where Sailors can purchase snacks.

**general alarm** • The signal for manning battle stations. Nowadays given by an electrical Klaxon over a ship's general announcing sys-

tem. In days past, various other means—such as bugle calls, fife and drum, or a loud boatswain's pipe—were used.

**general announcing system** • System of loudspeakers throughout a ship or station over which the word may be passed to all hands. Public address or PA system. Generally known in the Navy as a 1MC.

**General Classification Test (GCT)** • A test for scoring basic capabilities of enlisted personnel. This test was replaced in the 1960s by the Armed Services Vocational Aptitude Battery (ASVAB).

**general court-martial** • The highest trial court within the military judicial system, (the others being summary and special). A general court-martial is the most serious level of military courts. It consists of a military judge, trial counsel, defense counsel, and at least five court members. An enlisted accused may request a court composed of at least one-third enlisted personnel. Unless the case is one in which the death sentence could be adjudged, an officer or enlisted accused may also request trial by judge alone. In a general court-martial, the maximum punishment is that established for each offense under the Manual for Courts-Martial, and may include death (for certain offenses), confinement for life, a dishonorable or bad-conduct discharge for enlisted personnel, a dismissal for officers, or a number of other lesser forms of punishment. A pretrial investigation under Article 32, UCMJ, must be conducted before a case may be referred to a general court-martial, unless waived by the accused.

**general discharge** • An administrative discharge given to military personnel who do not qualify for an honorable discharge.

**general mess** • *See:* mess

**general officer** • Brigadier general and above.

An officer of the Army, Air Force, or Marine Corps whose rank insignia is one or more stars. Equivalent to Navy and Coast Guard flag officer. General officers and flag officers are authorized to fly personal flags of appropriate design and color, leading to the term "flag officer" used by the sea services.

**general orders** • Numbered directives of a general nature and wide application issued by the Navy Department and signed by the Secretary of the Navy.

**general prudential rule** • The general caveat within the Rule of the Road that permits a privileged vessel to maneuver to avoid collision or other hazard when in extremis. "In obeying and construing these rules due regard shall be had for all dangers of navigation and collision and to any special circumstance which may render a departure from these rules necessary to avoid immediate danger."

**General Purpose Electronic Test Equipment (GPETE)** • Test equipment that has the capability, without modification, to generate, modify, or measure a range of electronic functions required to test several equipments or systems of basically different designs.

**general quarters** • 1. Stations for battle. 2. The condition of full readiness for battle. 3. To sound general quarters is to give the signal, or the general alarm, that will bring all hands to their battle stations as quickly as they can get there.

**general rating** • *See:* rating

**geographical position** • In celestial navigation, that point on Earth at which a given celestial body is in the zenith at a specified time. Any position on the Earth defined by means of its geograpical coordinates.

**Geographic Reference (GEOREF)** • Worldwide grid system used to facilitate reporting and plotting of ships and aircraft.

**George** • *Inf:* Junior ensign on board.

**george** • Past phonetic word for the letter G; replaced with golf. *See also:* George

**Gibson girl** • Portable radio for sending distress signals; once carried on life rafts.

**GI can** • Trash can.

**gig** • 1. Ship's boat designated for the use of the commanding officer of a ship. 2. Ship's boat assigned for the use of a chief of staff. 3. Ship's boat assigned for the use of a squadron or division commander not of flag rank.

**Giligan hitch** • *Inf:* Any unseamanlike or unorthodox knot, hitch, or bend.

**gimbals** • A pair of rings, one within the other, with their axes ar right angles. Usually they support a compass or gyro repeater, in which case their purpose is to keep it horizontal despite motion of the ship. Any gyroscope requires a set of gimbals to give it the requisite three degrees of freedom; *i.e.*, freedom to move its axis in any direction. Almost always used in pairs, hence referred to in the plural.

**gipsy** • *See:* gypsy

**give way** • An order to begin pulling oars together.

**glacon** • A fragment of sea ice ranging in size from brash to medium floe.

**gland** • A seal designed to prevent leakage of water, steam, or oil along a movable shaft, such as propeller shafts, submarine periscopes, or turbine rotors.

**gland steam** • Steam introduced into a shaft gland packing to prevent air leakage into, and steam leakage out of, a turbine.

**glass** • Barometer. Telescope or long glass.

**glass fist** • *See:* fist

**glide bomb** • A winged missile, unpowered.

**gnomonic projection** • A map or chart projection in which points on the surface of a sphere or spheroid, such as Earth, are conceived by radials from the center to a tangent plane. One useful attribute to these projections is that great circle lines appear as straight lines, unlike the more common Mercator projection on which rhumb lines appear as straight lines and great circles as curves.

**go adrift** • To break loose.

**gob** • *Inf:* An enlisted man.

**godown** • *Inf:* Warehouse or storehouse along the waterfront, especially in the Orient.

**goldbrick** • *Inf:* A loafer, or to loaf.

**Golden Dragon** • *Inf:* One who crosses the 180th meridian, or the International Date Line, by ship. *See also:* Golden Shellback

**golden rivet** • *Inf:* The mythical last rivet which completes a ship.

**Golden Shellback** • *Inf:* One who crosses the equator at the International Date Line by ship. *See also:* Golden Dragon

**gold lace** • Officer's gold braid used to denote rank, etc.; once actually made of gold, now usually synthetic.

**golf** • Phonetic word for the letter G.

**gonzo station** • The rendezvous point for aircraft carrier battle groups off the Straits of Hormuz in the Persian Gulf.

**gooseneck** • The pivot fitting at the base of a boom or gaff, so named because of its shape.

**Goshawk** • The T-45A Goshawk aircraft, the Navy version of the British Aerospace Hawk aircraft, is used for intermediate and advanced portions of the Navy/Marine Corps

pilot training program for jet carrier aviation and tactical strike missions. The T-45A has replaced the T-2 Buckeye trainer and the TA-4 trainer with an integrated training system that includes the T-45A Goshawk aircraft, operations and instrument fighter simulators, academics, and training integration system. There are two versions of T-45 aircraft currently in operational use, the T-45A and T-45C derivatives. The T-45A, which became operational in 1991, contains an analog design cockpit, while the new T-45C (began delivery in December 1997) is built around a new digital "glass cockpit" design.

**go-to-hell hat** • *Inf:* Overseas or garrison cap.

**gouge** • *Inf:* A prepared solution to a problem or examination. *Inf:* To cheat.

**grab rope** • 1. A safety line secured along a boat boom, hung knotted from the span wire between boat davits. 2. Any line fastened to a lifeboat or life raft. Also called a life line.

**grade** • Graduations in authority and pay among petty officers and officers. Similar to rank. *See also:* rate; rating; rank

**Grandpa Pettibone** • A cartoon character appearing in *Approach*, a naval aviation safety magazine, to illustrate aviation safety topics. *See also:* Anymouse; Dilbert

**granny knot** • A false (bungled) square knot; unsymmetrical. To be avoided because it slips, and if jammed tightly, cannot readily be cast loose.

**grape** • 1. Small iron balls used for antipersonnel ammunition in the days of sail. 2. *Inf:* The refueling personnel aboard an aircraft carrier, so called because they wear purple jerseys for easy identification. *See also:* canister; purple shirt; langrage

**grapnel** • Small, four-armed anchor used mainly to recover objects in the water. Boarding parties use them to hook onto another vessel or a dock. Smaller than a hawk. Also called a grappling iron.

**grappling iron** • *See:* grapnel

**graticule** • The network of lines (usually representing parallels and meridians) on a map, chart, or plotting sheet.

**grating** • 1. Metal or wooden lattice work used to cover hatches while still providing ventilation below. 2. Wooden or metal lattice work used to raise the feet of watchstanders above the deck to keep them dry.

**graving dock** • Basin with a gate or caisson sealing the entrance, in which ships can be built or dry-docked. Same as drydock.

**great circle** • The intersection of the Earth's surface and a plane through the Earth's center. The shortest route between two points on the surface of the Earth.

**greens** • 1. Term used by aviation personnel for their green working uniform. 2. Term used by Seabees for their green utility uniform. 3. A pre-WWII uniform worn by both aviators and submariners. Heavy woolen material, green in color with black buttons, black stripes on the sleeves, khaki shirt, black tie, and no shoulder boards. The warm weather version was similarly cut, cotton khaki.

**green shirts** • Member of the catapult or arresting gear crew on an aircraft carrier; so called because they wear green shirts for easy identification. *See also:* yellow shirts; blue shirts; red shirts; brown shirts; white shirts; purple shirts; grapes

**Greenwich hour angle (GHA)** • Angular distance west of the Greenwich celestial meridian. In conjunction with declination, identifies position of celestial bodies for navigation. *See also:* declination

**Greenwich Mean Time** • The mean (average) solar time as measured from the meridian of Greenwich. Has been superceded by Universal Time.

**Greenwich Meridian** • The meridian through Greenwich, England, near London; the reference meridian for measuring longitude and time. Also called the prime meridian. Longitude 0°. Exactly halfway around the world from the International Date Line.

**Greyhound** • A high wing, twin-engine monoplane cargo aircraft, designed to land on aircraft carriers. The C-2A Greyhound provides critical logistics support to carrier strike groups. Its primary mission is the transport of high-priority cargo, mail, and passengers between carriers and shore bases. The interior arrangement of the cabin can readily accommodate cargo, passengers, and litter patients. Priority cargo, such as jet engines, can be transported from shore to ship in a matter of hours. A cargo cage system, or transport stand, provides restraint for loads during launches and landings. The large aft cargo ramp (door) and a powered winch allow straight-in, rear cargo loading and unloading for fast turnaround. The C-2A's in-flight open-ramp capability allows supplies and personnel to be airdropped. Operational versatility is also provided by the onboard Auxiliary Power Unit that provides unassisted engine-starting capability in remote areas.

**grid, JAN** • Joint Army-Navy grid system covering the entire Earth, adopted to afford secure means of referring to geographical positions.

**grid navigation** • Navigation using grid directions. Often used in polar navigation, with grid coordinates on the chart replacing latitude and longitude.

**grid variation** • In grid navigation, the difference between grid north and magnetic north. Also called grivation in aerial navigation.

**grinder** • Paved area at a shore activity, used for drill and parades.

**gripe** • Device for securing a boat at its davits or in its cradle.

**grivation** • *See:* grid variation

**grog** • In the old British Navy, it was a mixture of rum and water invented by Admiral Vernon, whose affectionate nickname was Old Grog. *Inf:* Any alcoholic drink, but particularly rum.

**grommet** • Reinforced hole in a sail or awning. The round metal or fiber stiffener in a flat hat or officer's cap.

**groove** • Prescribed flight path of an aircraft making a perfect approach for a carrier landing. The pilot is said to be "in the groove."

**grooves** • Lands and grooves in a gun make up the spiraled rifling that imparts spin to the projectiles for ballistic stability; the lands are the raised portion of the rifling and the grooves are the recessed tracks between.

**ground** • 1. To run a ship ashore; to strike the bottom. Usually a result of ignorance, violence, or accident. As a special case, certain amphibious vessels are designed for deliberate grounding, to put combat troops ashore. 2. The act of providing an electrical connection between an object; *e.g.,* an aircraft and the ground.

**ground-controlled approach (GCA)** • Aircraft approach to landing during which the pilot is guided in altitude, speed, and heading by advice from an air traffic controller.

**Ground-Controlled Intercept (GCI)** • Technique by which a pilot is guided to intercept a target by provision of speeds, headings, and altitudes from a controller.

**grounded plug** • A three-pronged electrical plug used to ground portable tools to the ship's structure. It is a safety device that must always be checked before portable electrical tools are used.

**ground effects machine (GEM)** • A vehicle designed to move across the Earth's surface while actually suspended above the surface on a cushion of air. When this principal is applied to a seagoing craft, it is called a surface effect ship (SES).

**groundpounder** • 1. *Inf:* Marine or soldier. 2. *Inf:* Administrative officer; nonflyer.

**ground resonance** • A condition of geometric imbalance in helicopters; caused by offset dynamic forces when the helicopter makes improper contact with the deck. If allowed to continue, destruction of the helicopter is imminent.

**ground speed** • Aircraft speed relative to the surface of the Earth (ground). *See also:* airspeed

**ground swell** • The sea swell encountered as a result of distant or past storms.

**ground tackle** • General term for all anchoring equipment aboard ship.

**ground wave** • That portion of a radio wave in proximity to, and affected by, the ground; somewhat refracted by the lower atmosphere and diffracted by the surface of Earth. *See also:* sky wave

**ground waves** • Radio waves that travel along the surface of the Earth. *See also:* sky waves

**ground zero (GZ)** • The detonation point of a weapon; usually nuclear.

**group** • 1. Several ships or aircraft, normally a subdivision of a force, assigned together for a specific purpose. 2. The words or collections of letters in a cipher or code message are known as groups. *See also:* task organization

**group flashing light** • Navigational aid showing groups of two or more flashes at regular intervals. Flashing lights are off more than they are on, occulting lights are on more than they are off.

**group grope** • *Inf:* Full deck launch of a carrier air group for a specific mission.

**group occulting light** • Navigational aid showing two or more eclipses at regular intervals, the eclipses being shorter than the flashes. Flashing lights are off more than they are on, occulting lights are on more than they are off.

**group-rate marks** • Short diagonal stripes worn on the upper part of the left sleeve by nonrated personnel: white for seamen, red for firemen, green for airmen, light blue for constructionmen.

**growler** • Small piece of floating ice with only a few feet showing above the surface. Usually a remnant or fragment of an iceberg. A serious hazard to navigation because of the difficulty of seeing it visually or detecting it on radar. *See also:* bergy-bit

**G-suit** • Special clothing for aviators that prevents blackouts during high "G" (gravitational) effects; actually squeezes the legs to prevent blood from pooling there, thus keeping an adequate flow to the brain.

**guard** • Usually refers to radio guard. In a group of ships, one maintains a continuous radio receiver watch on applicable frequencies or radio schedules, so that other ships can secure their radio watch. Medical guard (doctor available); mail guard (receives and sends ashore U.S. mail), etc.

**guard mail** • Mail delivery system established in an internal network of colocated or nearby activities. Ships anchored near one another will often establish a guard mail

delivery system.

**guard of the day** • That part of the ship's Marine guard on duty for the day, kept in readiness for a call to the quarterdeck.

**guardship** • A ship maintaining a prescribed communication watch on certain radio frequencies, or performing common duties for a group of several ships in port together. A ship ordered to maintain a readiness to get under way immediately.

**gudgeons** • Metal loops or rings on the hull of a boat into which the pintles of the rudder fit.

**guess-warp, guestwarp, geswarp** • 1. Rope rove through a thimble on a boat boom for the convenience of boats making fast alongside. Usually terminated in an eye splice for simplicity in securing. 2. A rope run along a ship's side as a grab line, guy rope, or additional towline to steady a boat towed astern. 3. A hauling line run by a boat to a buoy, wharf, dolphin, bollard, etc., for warping (moving) purposes.

**guide** • Vessel designated in a formation or disposition as the one for others to keep station on.

**guided missile cruiser** • A cruiser armed with one or more types of guided missiles as part of the main armament.

**guided missile destroyer** • A destroyer armed with one or more types of guided missiles as part of the main armament.

**guided missile frigate** • A frigate armed with one or more types of guided missiles as part of the main armament.

**guided weapon** • A weapon that has no propulsion but does have guidance control capability.

**guidon** • Identification pennant used as a reference for a marching unit.

**Gulf Stream** • *See:* Gulf Stream system

**Gulf Stream system** • Part of a large North Atlantic clockwise circulation of warm water. Originates near the equator as the North Equatorial Current, forms the Antilles and Florida Currents, and is known as the Gulf Stream north of Cape Hatteras as it moves north-northeast off the coast of the United States. It becomes the North Atlantic Current off the Grand Banks as it continues northeast toward Iceland, the British Isles, and Scandinavia. The Current also flows east toward the coast of Europe and then south, and eventually west, toward the Caribbean along the equator to complete the circle. Also called Gulf Stream.

**gull** • A form of radar confusion reflector.

**gun** • A gun is an elongated tube, closed at one end and open at the other (in modern times with rifling in the bore) that is used to direct a projectile that has been propelled out the open end by an explosive charge in the closed end.

**gunar** • A gun system that uses radar as part of the fire control system. Originally an acronym, similar to radar.

**gunboat** • A small, moderate-speed, vessel armed with guns and generally used for general patrol and escort duties. In the old Navy, a barge or minimally capable craft whose primary purpose was to mount as many guns as possible.

**gun captain** • Petty officer in charge of gun crew.

**gundeck** • 1. A covered deck mounting guns broadside. 2. *Inf:* To fake or falsify something, such as a report. 3. *Inf:* To pretend to be drunk.

**gun director** • Optical- or radar-controlled system used to aim guns.

**gun elevation** • Vertical angle of the axis of the bore of a gun above the horizontal plane.

**gun house** • Visible part of a turret extending above the barbette. An enclosed gun mount is sometimes called a gun house.

**gun layers** • Those who lay the gun on the target (aim); thus the pointer and trainer.

**gun mount** • An assembly consisting of one or more guns and the associated equipment needed for proper operation: elevating and training mechanisms, recoil and counter-recoil equipment, armor and/or shielding, etc.

**gunner** • Warrant officer who has advanced normally from aviation ordnanceman, fire-control technician, or gunner's mate.

**gunner's mate (GM)** • Navy occupational rating that operates, maintains, and repairs all gunnery equipment, guided-missile launching systems, rocket launchers, guns, gun mounts, turrets, projectors, and associated equipment. GMs also make detailed casualty analyses and repairs of electrical, electronic, hydraulic, and mechanical systems. They test and inspect ammunition and missiles and the related components, as well as train and supervise personnel in the handling and stowage of ammunition, missiles, and assigned ordnance equipment.

**gunnery officer** • Officer in charge of a ship's (or squadron's) gunnery department. *See also:* weapons officer

**gunport** • Aperture in the front armor plate of a turret, through which a gun projects. In wooden ships the gunports were along the broadside.

**gun salute** • Blank shots fired in honor of a dignitary or in celebration. The national salute is 21 guns, fired for a chief of state. Lesser dignitaries rate progressively fewer guns, according to rank. The number, in any case, is always odd.

**gun tackle** • *See:* purchase

**guntub** • The cylindrical splinter protection around a deck gun aboard ship.

**gunwale** • Upper edge of a boat's side. Pronounced "gun-ul."

**guppy** • A WWII fleet submarine that has been streamlined, given a more powerful battery, and fitted with a snorkel.

**gust** • A brief, rapid increase in wind speed.

**guy** • Line used to steady or support a spar or boom. Also called a vang.

**guyot** • A flat-topped mountain in the sea, or tablemount. *See also:* seamount

**gybe** • *See:* jibe

**gypsey** • *See:* gypsy

**gypsy** • Cylindrical device at the end of the shaft of a winch or windlass on which the turns of a line are taken for heaving. Sometimes called a gypsy head. *See also:* warping head; capstan; drum

**gypsy head** • *See:* gypsy

**gyro angle** • In torpedo firing, angle between axis of own ship and final torpedo track, measured clockwise from own bow.

**gyro compass** • A compass having one or more gyroscopes properly torqued to indicate true north; pgc means per gyro compass, and is nearly the same as true direction because gyro error is normally very small. *See also:* standard compass

**gyro error** • The angle between true north and north as indicated by a gyro compass.

**gyropilot** • Automatic steering device connected to a gyrocompass; designed to hold a ship on its course without a helmsman. Also called iron mike and iron quartermaster.

**gyro repeater** • An instrument containing a compass card driven by a remotely located gyro compass. Short for gyro compass repeater. Used for steering, taking bearings, azimuths, etc.

**gyroscope** • A mechanical device containing a spinning mass mounted in concentric gimbals so that it can assume (and/or maintain) any position in space.

**H-3** • *See:* Sea King

**hack chronometer** • Spare or comparison chronometer. Not the principal one on which a ship's navigation is based. It is the chronometer the navigator takes with him to compare with that of another ship, an observatory ashore, etc.

**hack, under** • *Inf:* Punishment for officers, involving restriction to their quarters. Formal term is "suspension from duty," "confined to quarters."

**hail** • To address or call to a nearby ship or boat. *See also:* ahoy; boat hails

**halberd** • Ax-like device fixed to the top of a flagstaff to indicate that the individual represented by the flag is a flag or general officer. *See also:* flagstaff insignia

**half-breadth plan** • Engineering drawing of a ship showing the outlines of horizontal sections of the hull from the main deck to the keel.

**half deck** • A partial deck between complete decks. Does not extend the full length of the ship as does a complete deck. *See also:* deck; gallery deck

**half hitch** • A knot used for securing a line

to a post; formed by turning the bitter end around the standing part and then passing it through the bight. *See also:* knot

**half-mast** • To fly a flag halfway up the mast, as a sign of mourning. Also called half-staff.

**half-staff** • *See:* half-mast

**half switch** • Batteries in parallel, and the motor(s) in series, in a diesel submarine; resulting in minimum speed.

**halliard** • *See:* halyard

**halyard** • The line used to hoist a flag, pennant, or sail. Also halliard.

**hammerbox** • Noise-making device for sweeping acoustic mines.

**hammock** • An old-fashioned, traditional sailor's bed, made of heavy canvas and swung from a pair of hooks on the underside of the deck above; *i.e.*, swung from the overhead.

**hammock ladder** • Nonexistent item (like a "bucket of steam") often requested of new personnel aboard ship.

**hand** • Member of the ship's crew. All hands means every person on board.

**hand billy** • Small, portable water pump.

**hand lead** • Weight and line used in taking soundings—measuring the depth of the water—by hand.

**hand-over-hand** • Expresses the idea of one hand after the other, as when a line is hauled in rapidly or when a person climbs a line without using the legs and feet.

**hand salute** • *See:* salute, hand

**handsomely** • Carefully, deliberately, smartly.

**hangar deck** • Deck, below the flight deck of a carrier, where aircraft are parked and serviced.

**hangar queen** • *Inf:* Aircraft that is not fly-able because of maintenance problems and is therefore kept on the hangar deck out of the way of the operational aircraft; often cannibalized as a source of spare parts for functioning aircraft.

**hangfire** • The delayed detonation of an explosive charge in a gun. Usually caused by the overheating of the gun barrel. *See also:* misfire

**hank** • A metal or plastic ring, shackle, or hook, often with a spring-loaded closure (a piston, plunger, or snap) for securing the luff of a headsail to its stay. Sometimes called a clip, snaphook, or piston hank. Loops of small line used for seizing, whipping, etc.

**happy hour** • Period of entertainment aboard ship, including refreshments. The name has been adopted to signify a period at a bar or club ashore when prices are reduced.

**harassing fire** • Sporadic shore bombardment gunfire to prevent the enemy from resting, regrouping, or moving.

**harbormaster** • Officer in charge of piloting, berthing, and traffic in a harbor; also responsible for navigational aids and hydrographic information.

**hard** • 1. Section of a beach especially prepared with a hard surface for amphibious operations. 2. Full or extreme, as in the command "Hard right rudder." *See also:* hard over

**hard over** • Condition of a rudder that has been turned to the maximum possible rudder angle.

**HARM Missile** • The AGM-88 High-Speed Antiradiation Missile (HARM) is an air-to-surface tactical missile designed to seek out and destroy enemy radar-equipped air defense systems. The AGM-88 can detect, attack, and destroy a target with minimum aircrew input. The proportional guidance system that homes in on enemy radar emissions has a fixed antenna and seeker head in the missile's nose. A smokeless, solid-propellant, dual-thrust rocket motor propels the missile.

**Harpoon** • A conventional warhead missile designed for shipboard launch against surface targets. Modifications may be fired from a submerged submarine or an aircraft. Designated A/U/RGM-84, the Harpoon is an all-weather, over-the-horizon, antiship missile system with active radar guidance, low-level cruise trajectory, and sea-skim or pop-up maneuvers in the terminal mode.

**Harrison cargo gear** • Cargo handling system using traveling overhead cranes instead of booms and winches.

**hash mark** • *Inf:* Stripe worn on left forearm by enlisted Sailors to indicate a minimum of four years service; therefore, a Sailor with seven years service would wear one hash mark, but one with eight years service would have two hash marks, etc.

**hatch** • In a strict sense, this term refers to the watertight covering over a hatchway (which is the access opening in the deck of a ship, providing vertical access). Often used to describe the opening rather than just the cover. Not to be confused with a door, which provides horizontal access through bulkheads and other vertical surfaces. *See also:* hatchway

**hatch beam** • Steel support for a cargo hatch cover.

**hatch boom** • Cargo boom positioned over a cargo hatch.

**hatch coaming** • Raised framework around a hatch on which the hatch cover rests; prevents water from pouring down an open hatch.

**hatch cover** • Wooden or steel cover for a hatch.

**hatch hood** • Canvas cover rigged over an open hatch to keep out rain, spray, and wind.

**hatch list** • List and location of all cargo loaded through a particular hatch.

**hatchway** • Same as hatch, but with emphasis on the opening rather than the cover. *See also:* hatch

**haul** • 1. To pull or drag. 2. The wind hauls when it changes in direction with the sun; *i.e.,* clockwise in northern latitudes. The opposite of haul is "back." 3. When a ship changes course so that her head lies nearer to the wind than before, she is said to haul up or bear up. *See also:* veer

**haul down** • When using signal flags as a means of conveying orders, a command is executed (order is given) when the signal is hauled down. In other words, an order communicated by flaghoist is executed at the moment the flaghoist is hauled down (dropped to the deck).

**hauling part** • That part of a tackle to which power is applied, in contrast to a standing part.

**haul off** • 1. Haul to the wind, or haul your wind, means to sail closer to the wind, usually when the ship has been sailing free. One hauls off to windward and bears off, or falls off, to leeward. 2. Changing a vessel's course to keep clear of another vessel. *See also:* fall off

**haul out** • 1. When a ship moves out of a formation, it is said to haul out. 2. To make fast to a boat boom.

**hawk, anchor** • *See:* anchor hawk

**hawse** • The area at the bow of a ship where the anchor(s) is stowed. The distance between the ship's head and her anchor, as it lies on the bottom.

**hawse buckler** • Metal cover over a hawsehole to prevent water from entering.

**hawseholes** • Opening in a vessel's hull where the anchor cable passes through.

**hawsepipe** • Heavy casting through which the anchor chain runs from the deck down and forward through the ship's bow plating. *See also:* hawseholes

**hawser** • Any line over five inches in diameter. Smaller vessels sometimes refer to the anchor cable as a hawser, even though its size may be less than five inches.

**hazardous material (HAZMAT)** • Material that, due to its quantity, concentration, physical, chemical, or infectious characteristics, may pose a substantial hazard to human health or the environment when released or spilled.

**hazardous waste (HW)** • Any hazardous material—liquid, solid, or gaseous—which is no longer usable for its original intended purpose or which has been contaminated by a foreign substance.

**head** • Toilet and/or washroom. Derived from the days of sail when the toilet facility for the crew was forward on either side of the bowsprit. The upper corner of a triangular sail.

**header box** • An extension of the salt water compensating line that is open to the sea and equalizes fuel tank pressure in a submerged submarine.

**heading** • 1. The direction in which a ship or aircraft is pointed. 2. That part of a message preceding the text; contains such information as the identities of the sender and intended receivers, precedence, etc.

**head line** • Mooring line that is made fast forward of the ship's pivot point.

**headroom** • Clearance between the decks.

**head sails** • Those sails set forward of the mast(s), such as jibs, spinnakers, etc.

**headstay** • A supporting line extending from the top of the forward mast down to the bow or bowsprit. *See also:* forestay

**headway** • Forward movement of a vessel through the water; opposite of sternway.

**heart** • Center strand of fiber or wire rope.

**heave** • 1. To throw, as in heaving a line. 2. To pull, as heave in. The nautical past tense is hove. 3. To come into sight; *e.g.,* as soon as she heaves into sight, or when she heaves over the horizon.

**heave around** • To activate a windlass to which a line or chain is attached. To turn to; work hard

**heave away** • An order to start heaving on a capstan or windlass, or directly on a line.

**heave in** • To haul in, as when retrieving a mooring line.

**heave out** • Rise and shine; get out of bed.

**heave out and trice up** • In the old Navy, an announcement given at reveille to persons sleeping in hammocks. It meant, "Get up and lash up your hammocks." It continues in use in the modern Navy as a matter of tradition, despite the lack of hammocks.

**heave right up** • The order to heave the anchor all the way up, without stopping at short stay.

**heave short** • To heave around on the anchor chain until the anchor is at short stay, or just short of breaking ground.

**heave to** • To stop a ship; make her dead in the water. In the case of heavy weather, a ship may heave to in order to take the most comfortable and safest heading; she is, in this case, considered to be hove to, even though making considerable way through the water, from the actions of wind and sea.

**heaving** • 1. The vertical displacement, or

up-and-down movement, of a ship in a sea-way; as distinguished from pitching, which is essentially a rotation about an athwartships axis. Heave generally refers to an upward movement, bodily, of the entire ship, but is sometimes applied only to bow or stern in a less specific sense; *e.g.*, her heaving bows. 2. Throwing. For example, a heaving line is thrown from ship to ship or ship to pier. *See also:* pitch; roll; surge; sway; yaw

**heaving line** • Relatively light line with a weighted end that is thrown across to a ship or pier when coming alongside; it acts as a messenger for a mooring line. The weight is called a "monkey fist."

**heaving link** • *See:* heaving line

**heavy cruiser** • This term has lost its original meaning, since none are now in commission. During WWII it was useful to distinguish cruisers carrying 8-inch guns (heavy) from those with 6-inch (light cruisers). Size and displacement were not factors; only the armament. Heavy cruisers were designated CA, while light cruisers were CL. *See also:* cruiser

**heavy weather** • Stormy weather with rough seas.

**hedgehog** • An antisubmarine warfare (ASW) ahead-thrown weapon; a mortar-type projector mount that fired a contact-fuzed projectile. Hedgehogs were fired ahead of a ship as she approached the known or estimated position of a submerged submarine. They were fired in elliptical patterns to increase the chance of one or more scoring a hit, thus causing all to explode. *See also:* mousetrap

**heel** • 1. The temporary inclination or leaning of a vessel to port or starboard, caused by wind and sea or inertia, as when a ship heels in a high-speed turn. Not to be confused with rolling. 2. The lower end of a mast. *See also:* list; roll

**heel and toe** • Period of duty (watch), alternating with an equal period of rest. *See also:* watch and watch

**height of eye** • The height an observer is above the surface of the sea when making an observation. The higher the individual is, the greater the distance to the horizon. For example, an individual on the bridge of an aircraft carrier will be able to see an approaching vessel at a significantly greater distance than an individual on the bridge of a destroyer will, because the latter's bridge is not as high (has a lower height of eye).

**Hellfire** • Air-to-ground, laser guided, subsonic missile with significant antitank capacity. It can also be used as an air-to-air weapon against helicopters or slow-moving fixed-wing aircraft. The air-to-ground (AGM)-114 provides precision striking power against tanks, structures, bunkers and helicopters. Capable of defeating any known tank in the world today, it can be guided to the target either from inside the aircraft or by lasers outside the aircraft.

**helm** • In simplest terms, it is a vessel's steering wheel. Orders to the helm use "right" and "left" (never "starboard" and "port") to indicate the direction of the rudder.

**helmsman** • Steersman; one who steers a ship or boat.

**her** • *See:* she

**Herald equipment** • Sonar and listening devices used in harbor defense.

**hermaphrodite brig** • Two-masted sailing vessel with the foremast square-rigged and the mainmast fore-and-aft-rigged. *See also:* brig; brigantine

**hertz (Hz)** • A unit of frequency equivalent to one cycle per second; named for German physicist Heinrich Hertz *See also:* frequency

**HH-1** • *See:* Iroquois

**high** • An area of high pressure, referring to a higher atmospheric pressure in the horizontal plane, such as a surface isobaric chart.

**higher high water (HHW)** • The higher of the two high waters during any tidal day.

**higher low water (HLW)** • The higher of the two low waters of any tidal day.

**highline** • A line rigged between two ships under way, for transferring stores and/or personnel. The simplest transfer rig. Stores and personnel are transferred on a wheeled trolley riding on the highline and hauled back and forth between the ships.

**highlining** • Exchange of material or personnel between ships under way, using the highline with associated trolleys and skids.

**high water** • The maximum height of water resulting from tidal and weather conditions.

**high water stand** • Interval of time at high water (before it begins to recede) when tidal level does not vary appreciably. *See also:* low water stand

**hitch** • 1. A knot whose loops hold together in use, particularly under strain, yet remain easily separable when the strain is removed. 2. Method of securing a line to a hook ring or spar; *e.g.,* clove hitch. 3. *Inf:* Term of enlistment. *See also:* knot

**hit the deck** • 1. Get up; rise and shine. 2. An order given to assume the push-up position. 3. Drop to the prone position, as when under fire. 4. Sometimes used with other words, such as "Hit the deck running," meaning to get to work quickly.

**hit the rack** • *Inf:* To turn in; go to bed.

**hit the silk** • *Inf:* Make a parachute jump.

**hockle** • A kink in a wire or a line.

**hogging** • Distortion of a ship's hull caused by waves in a seaway, which results in the bow and stern being lower than the amidships section; opposite of sagging.

**hogging line** • Line passed under the keel and secured on the opposite side of the ship. Used for pulling gear, such as a collision mat or patch, under a ship's bottom.

**hogging strap** • A line rigged to keep a towline close to the caprail or fantail of a tug.

**HogsHead** • Bollard

**hoist** • 1. A display of signal flags at a yardarm. 2. To lift. 3. The vertical portion (edge) of a flag that lies alongside its staff. *See also:* fly

**hoist away** • Go right on hoisting until stopped by another order.

**hoist in** • Bring a boat (or some other object) aboard ship from the water.

**hoisting eye (ring) (rod)** • Fittings in a boat to which the boat falls are attached for hoisting. Also called hoisting ring or hoisting rod.

**hoisting pad** • Metal plates supporting a pad eye or ring by which a boat is hoisted.

**hoist out** • To lower a boat, or some other object, from a ship down to the water.

**hold** • 1. Compartment in a ship, below the main deck, used for stowing cargo. 2. A command to a line handler that means to take sufficient turns around the cleat or bitts to prevent any more line from running out. *See also:* check; snub

**holdback** • Catapult fitting for holding back an airplane until it is time for launching.

**hold captain** • In amphibious operations, a person who supervises the loading and unloading of a ship's hold.

**holding bulkhead** • The innermost of a series of bulkheads that form the tanks and voids of the torpedo protection system.

**holding ground** • The bottom in an anchorage. Usually described as good or bad, depending on the ability to hold an anchor.

**holiday** • Unscrubbed or unpainted section of a deck or bulkhead. Any space left blank or unfinished through inadvertence.

**holiday routine** • Period aboard ship involving no work or drills.

**Hollywood shower** • *Inf:* An excessively long shower. *See also:* Navy shower

**holystone** • Small stone used with sand and water to scrub wooden decks.

**homeplate** • *Inf:* The aircraft carrier from which a pilot normally flies.

**home port** • Seaport from which a ship bases; the families of crew members normally live near or in the home port in order to maximize the time they can be together. Applies to the home base for an air squadron or other naval units.

**homesteading** • *Inf:* Describes the practice of remaining in the same port or area for a long period of time; for example, a person serving three back-to-back tours in the San Diego area would be said to be homesteading.

**homeward bound pennant** • A pennant flown by ships returning to the United States after an extended period away. Traditionally very long (1 foot of length for each day away). After arrival it was cut up and passed out to the crew for memorabilia.

**homing guidance** • In this type of guidance, the missile picks up and homes in on some kind of emission from the target; for example, radar emissions from the target, the heat given off by the target's engines, etc.

**honey barge** • *Inf:* Garbage scow.

**honors and ceremonies** • Collective term: official guards, bands, salutes, and other activities that honor the colors, celebrate a holiday, or greet a distinguished guest or officer.

**hood** • 1. Canvas cover; *e.g.,* hatch hood, periscope hood. 2. A light shield made of metal, rubber, etc. For example, a radar repeater might have a hood to prevent excess light from making it difficult to see the scope.

**hook** • *Inf:* Anchor.

**hooker control** • A watch station that assists the landing signal officer during night carrier landings.

**hookmen** • Personnel who disengage the aircraft's arresting gear hook (tailhook) from the arresting cable on the flight deck. They wear green jerseys and helmets.

**hook on** • To attach boat falls to the pad eyes at the bow and stern of a boat, then hoist it clear of the water.

**horned scully** • Underwater beach obstacle designed to tear holes in boats.

**Hornet** • All-weather fighter and attack aircraft. The single-seat F/A-18 Hornet is the nation's first strike-fighter. It was designed for traditional strike applications, such as interdiction and close-air support, without compromising its fighter capabilities. With its excellent fighter and self-defense capabilities, the F/A-18 increased strike mission survivability and supplemented the F-14 Tomcat in fleet-air defense.

**horns** • 1. Horizontal arms of a cleat. 2. Projecting arms of a stage to which rigging lines are secured. 3. Fragile tubes sticking out of a mine that cause the mine to explode when they are crushed.

**horse latitudes** • Sea areas on outer margins of trade winds, around 30° north and south latitude, where prevailing winds are light and variable.

**horsepower** • A unit of power equal to the power necessary to raise 33,000 pounds one foot in 1 minute.

**hospital corpsman (HM)** • Navy occupational rating that assists medical professionals in providing health care to service people and their families. HMs act as pharmacists, medical technicians, food-service personnel, nurses' aides, medical or dental assistants, battlefield medics, x-ray technicians, and more. Their work falls into several categories: first aid and minor surgery, patient transport, patient care, prescriptions and laboratory work, food-service inspection, and clerical duties. Once called pharmacist's mates.

**hospital ship (AH)** • An unarmed ship, marked in accordance with the Geneva Convention, staffed and equipped to provide full medical and surgical facilities.

**hot caseman** • Person who disposes of the ejected cases from a gun. Also called hot shellman.

**hotel** • Phonetic word for the letter H.

**hot poppa** • *Inf:* Hot suitman.

**hot pump** • To refuel a carrier aircraft without stopping the engine.

**hot refueling** • Aircraft refueling with one or more of the aircraft's engines operating.

**hot shellman** • *See:* hot caseman

**hot, straight, and normal** • In submarines, a report from the sonar operator that torpedoes just fired are running hot (proper ignition of the engine has occurred), straight (steering properly), and normal (no unusual noises are being emitted, which might indicate a malfunction). Originally used to report

the performance of steam torpedoes in WWII.

**hot suitman** • Person trained to rescue crews from burning aircraft. He or she wears a specially designed protective suit.

**hot switch** • To exchange pilots in an aircraft with the engine(s) running.

**house** • To stow or secure in a safe place, as to house the anchor.

**housing chain stopper** • A device fitted with a screw turnbuckle and a pelican hook to keep the anchor chain from moving in or out of the hawse. *See also:* stopper

**housing line** • The middle one of the three lifelines around the perimeter of a ship. From top, they are lifeline, housing line, and foot line. When an awning is housed, gutters to carry off the rain are formed by bringing alternate lashings down to the housing line.

**hove** • Nautical past tense and participle of heave.

**hovering** • 1. In helicopters, to maintain altitude over a fixed point. 2. In submarines, the maintaining of a constant depth with no movement forward or back. *See also:* balancing

**hove taut** • Pulled tight.

**how** • Past phonetic word for the letter H; replaced by hotel.

**hug** • To keep close. For example, a vessel hugs the shore.

**hulk** • A worn-out vessel, stripped of all useful gear.

**hull** • The body or central shell of a vessel.

**hull down** • Said of a ship visible over the horizon by her upper works alone. If the hull is fully visible, ship may be described as hull up.

**hull maintenance technician (HT)** • Navy occupational rating that is responsible for maintaining ships' hulls, fittings, piping systems, and machinery. HTs install and maintain shipboard and shore-based plumbing and piping systems. They also look after a vessel's safety and survival equipment and perform many tasks related to damage control.

**hull report** • A report submitted to a vessel's commanding officer by a division officer after the latter has inspected his or her assigned spaces to ascertain the condition of decks, bulkheads, fittings, etc.

**hull up** • Said of a ship that is fully visible over the horizon. If the ship is visible over the horizon by her upper works alone, she may be described as hull down.

**human performance** • Integration of learning methods and social action within the context of organizational values, missions, and culture.

**hummock** • An irregular ridge on sea ice.

**hung weapon** • An airborne weapon that cannot be fired or dropped because of a malfunction.

**hunky-dori** • *Inf:* OK; fine. The term was coined from a street named Honki-Dori in Yokohama. As the inhabitants of this street catered to the pleasures of Sailors, the street's name became synonymous for anything that is enjoyable or satisfactory.

**hunter-killer force (HUK)** • A naval force consisting of an ASW carrier, associated aircraft, and escorts.

**hunting** • Self-perpetuating oscillation caused by an electronic component searching for a desired quantity, as in a servosystem. *See also:* mine countermeasures

**hurricane** • Destructive cyclonic storm with winds of more than 65 knots. In the Western Pacfic it is called a typhoon, a cyclone in the Eastern Pacific. *See also:* breeze; gale; storm; cyclone; typhoon

**hydraulic fluid** • Fluid with constant vis-

cosity and temperature characteristics for use in hydraulic systems.

**hydraulics** • The branch of mechanics that deals with the action or use of fluids forced through tubes and orifices under pressure to operate various mechanics.

**hydro-flap** • Planing surface swung down beneath the fuselage of land aircraft to assist in emergency water landings.

**hydrofoil** • A surface craft designed to "fly" in water. By use of submerged foils (similar in design to wings), the hull is lifted from the water much as an aircraft is lifted from the ground. The consequent reduction in hull drag permits greater speed.

**hydrography** • The science of determining the condition of navigable waters; underwater geography.

**hydrophone** • An underwater microphone.

**hydrostatic pressure** • Pressure at a given water depth due to water mass above, normally measured in pounds per square inch.

**hydrostatic test** • A test used to detect leaks in closed systems (such as steam piping) by inserting water under pressure.

**hyperbolic navigation system** • A method of radio navigation, such as Loran, in which pulses transmitted by two ground stations are received by an aircraft or ship.

**hypothermia** • An abnormally low body temperature.

**ice anchor** • 1. Timber, or deadman, buried in ice, to which ship's lines are secured. 2. A one-fluked anchor that can be used to hold a vessel's position in ice.

**iceberg** • A very large floating piece of ice, generally hazardous to vessels if it enters sea lanes; comes from a Scandinavian term for "mountain."

**iceblink** • White glare in the sky produced by reflection from ice.

**icebreaker (AGB)** • A specially designed U.S. Coast Guard vessel with a spoon-shaped bow, protected propellers, and powerful engines for operations in heavy ice.

**ice concentration** • The percentage of ice cover, usually expressed in tenths, in a given area of water.

**ice fields** • Large, drifting ice pieces, offshore. A form of pack ice.

**identification, friend or foe (IFF)** • An electronic system built into radar systems to permit the exchange of identification information; allows operators to distinguish friends from enemies. *Inf:* Parrot.

**identification tag** • Metal tag worn by all personnel when directed, recording their name, file or service number, blood type, and religious affiliation (optional). *Inf:* dog tag.

**idler** • A crewmember who does not stand regular watches.

**ignition compression** • The heat generated by compression in an internal combustion engine that ignites the fuel, as in a diesel engine.

**ignition temperature** • The minimum temperature required to initiate self-sustained combustion, independent of any heating or heated element. *See also:* autoignition temperature

**illuminate** • The targeting of an object with radar, especially for weapons guidance purposes. Differs from "paint," in that painting is generally used to denote detection and tracking; illumination is generally for targeting and/or guidance of weapons.

**illuminating fire** • Firing of illumination rounds to silhouette the enemy and/or provide illumination for naval operations or troop operations ashore.

**illustrator-draftsman (DM)** • Navy occupational rating that prepares mechanical drawings, blueprints, charts, and illustrations needed for construction projects and other naval activities. DMs may specialize in structural drafting, electrical drafting, graphic arts mechanics, and/or illustrating.

**imagery** • In meteorology, a picture of the Earth and its atmosphere reconstructed by converting the data stream received from a satellite into consecutive lines of picture elements.

**immediate** • A category of precedence reserved for messages relating to situations that gravely affect the security of national or allied forces or populace, and that require immediate delivery. Higher precedence than priority and routine, but lower than flash. Also called operational immediate. *See also:* precedence

**impulse charge** • Propellant designed to start a self-propelled missile, such as a torpedo, on its way.

**inactivate** • To lay a ship up for possible future use; crew is removed, ship is sealed up, anti-corrosion measures are taken, etc. *Inf:* Put into mothballs.

**inboard** • 1. Toward the centerline of a ship. 2. When two or more vessels are nested together alongside a pier, the vessel closer to the pier is inboard of the one (or ones) further away. *See also:* outboard

**inboard lifelines** • Temporary lifelines erected inboard of the permanent lifelines during heavy weather. Many smaller vessels, such as destroyers, are provided with regular sets of these lines and the stanchions to support them.

**in bows** • An order to bow oarsmen to bring their oars into the boat and to prepare to come alongside a vessel or dock.

**inchop** • To cross a boundary (chopline) into an area requiring a change of operational control; for example, "USS *Oriole* will inchop to the Sixth Fleet on 30 August." *See also:* chop; outchop; chopline

**inclination diagram** • Polar-coordinate graph used to record roller path data when aligning gun batteries aboard ship.

**inclining experiment** • Computation of the metacentric height of a ship by use of weights to cause a list. The result is a measure of the stability of the vessel.

**inclinometer** • 1. Instrument for measuring inclination from the horizontal, as in the lines of force of the Earth's magnetic field. 2. An instrument for measuring an aircraft's inclination of its longitudinal axis. 3. Sometimes used (incorrectly) as a synonym for clinometer.

**index correction** • Correction to sextant altitude in celestial navigation to allow for the index and horizon mirrors not being precisely parallel.

**index error** • The inherent error in sextant readings resulting from the index and horizon mirrors not being precisely parallel. Compensated for in celestial navigational solutions by the "index correction."

**india** • Phonetic word for the letter I.

**indicated airspeed** • Indicated airspeed is an uncorrected reading of the airspeed indicator, as opposed to true airspeed, which is corrected for altitude and temperature. *See also:* airspeed

**indicator** • In cryptography, an element within the text that provides a guide to decryption.

**indirect fire** • Aiming guns by laying them on a point of aim that is not the actual target, but instead bringing them on target by artifical range and deflection corrections. Used when the real target cannot be seen by the gun layer(s).

**Individual Ready Reserve (IRR)** • The Ready Reserve is composed of the Selected Reserve (SELRES) and the Individual Ready Reserve (IRR). Members assigned to full time support positions who serve on extended Active Duty for Special Work (ADSW) or Active Duty for Training (ADT), or who drill for pay are in the SELRES. Members not assigned to a pay billet are in the IRR.

**inertial guidance** • Computer system designed to guide a missile, aircraft, or ship independent of outside information, using the inertial properties of gyroscopes.

**inertial navigation system** • System designed to guide a ship by a device independent of outside information, using the inertial properties of gyroscopes.

**inertia reel** • Device for automatically restraining a pilot's shoulder harness when a force of two or three Gs is applied. Automobile seat belts also use this technology.

**influence mine** • A mine that is actuated by some effect (magnetic, acoustic, etc.), caused by a target in the vicinity.

**information addressee** • Addressee on a naval message who is not expected to carry out any specific action(s); provided for information purposes only *See also:* addressee; action addressee

**information systems technician (IT)** • Navy occupational rating that is responsible for the Navy's vital command, control, communications, computer and intelligence systems and equipment. ITs use state-of-the-art multimedia technology such as fiber optics, digital microwaves, and satellites on a global basis, and work with telecommunications equipment, computers, and associated peripheral devices. The old radioman rating was absorbed into this rating.

**infrared (IR)** • The portion of the electromagnetic spectrum with wavelengths just slightly longer than visible light energy—thermal energy. With special infrared equipment, infrared waves can be detected thereby providing an extra "visibility" capability for detection or homing.

**in hack** • *Inf:* A nonjudicial punishment of restriction to specified limits; for example, a commanding officer might restrict a junior officer to his or her stateroom as a punishment for frequent lateness in relieving the watch.

**inhaul** • Any line used to haul in (bring the object toward). Opposite is outhaul.

**inhaul line** • Line used to haul the trolley back to the delivering ship during highline transfer.

**inhibitors** • Chemical compounds that reduce the rates of chemical reactions.

**injector** • Device using a jet of steam to force water into a boiler.

**inland rules** • Rules of the nautical road that are applicable in most inland U.S. waters.

**Inland Rules of the Road** • The Inland Navigation Rules (in accordance with the Inland Navigational Rules Act) govern the conduct of vessels in the inland waters of the United States. The U.S. equivalent to the International Rules of the Road.

**inland waters** • Those areas, shown on most coastal and harbor charts, where the Inland Rules of the Road apply. If not specifically determined by local ordinance, they are defined as waters inland of a line roughly parallel to the coast, drawn through the outermost aid to navigation (buoy, lighthouse, etc.). Not to be confused with territorial waters.

**inlet** • A narrow strip of sea extending into the land.

**innage** • Depth of liquid in a tank measured from the liquid's surface to the bottom of the tank.

**inner bottom** • Innermost bottom of the two in a double-bottomed ship.

**in ordinary** • *See:* ordinary, in

**in-port watch** • Watch set when a ship is in port; as opposed to the underway watch.

**inshore** • Toward land. If already ashore, inshore means further away from the sea.

**inshore currents** • The motion of water inside the surf zone; includes longshore and rip currents.

**insignia** • A badge or emblem of authority or honor.

**inspection** • There can be many types, ranging from a careful and critical examination of personnel, material, and record keeping, to the ceremonial inspection of an honor guard at a spit-and-polish formation.

**instantaneous automatic gain control (IAGC)** • A circuit that can vary the gain of the radar receiver with each input pulse to maintain a nearly constant output of peak amplitude, thereby providing a relative consistency of image.

**in step** • Said of a towing vessel and its tow when both meet and ride over the seas at the same time. In other words, each will be at same relative position (on the crests, in the troughs, etc.) on different waves at the same time.

**instruction** • Serially numbered directive issued by commanders ashore and afloat. May contain policies, procedures, orders, doctrine, and information of a continuing or permanent nature. A component of the Navy Directives System.

**instrument landing system** • Radio and radar system enabling aircraft to land in low visibility.

**integrated circuit** • A circuit in which many elements are fabricated and interconnected by a single process (into a single chip), as opposed to nonintegrated circuits in which the transistors, diodes, resistors, and other components are fabricated separately and then assembled.

**integrated tumblehome** • A modern hull design that reduces radar cross section making a ship less detectable by enemy radar systems.

**integrate power system (IPS)** • A modern propulsion system that uses electric drive to reduce acoustic noise, lower operating and support costs, and provide greater flexibility in ship design.

**intelligence specialist (IS)** • Navy occupational rating involved in collecting and interpreting intelligence data. An IS analyzes photographs and prepares charts, maps, and reports that describe, in detail, the strategic situation all over the world.

**intended track** • A track line representing the intended path of travel of a ship from one fixed point to another relative to the surface of the earth.

**intercardinal points** • Those points between the four cardinal points (north, south, east, west) of the compass; intercardinal points are designated as northeast, southeast, etc.

**intercom** • Ship's voice intercommunication system. Also informally called "squawk box."

**interdiction** • Destruction of supply lines (roads, bridges, railroads, tunnels, supply dumps, etc.), to prevent the support of enemy front lines.

**interdiction fire** • Intermittent gunfire on roads, road junctions, railroads, airfields, etc., to prevent enemy use.

**interior communications** • All telephones, call bells, alarms, and other forms of communications used to exchange information within the ship.

**interior communications electrician (IC)** • Navy occupational rating that operates and repairs electronic devices used in a ship's interior communications systems—television systems, public-address systems, electronic megaphones, and other announcing equipment—as well as gyrocompass systems.

**interlock** • Safety switch that cuts off electricity when compartment doors or access covers, or panels on an electrical device are opened.

**International Civil Aviation Organization** • The International Civil Aviation Organization (ICAO) adopted English as the international air traffic control language. They also developed a phonetic alphabet for international aviation use, designed to be as pronounceable as possible by flyers and traffic controllers speaking many different languages. This was subsequently adopted by the Allied Navies and is the "Alfa, Bravo, Charlie Delta..." alphabet used today. The Navy adopted this ICAO alphabet in March 1956.

**International Ice Patrol** • A patrol operated in accordance with an international agreement for the prevention of disasters caused by collisions of vessels with ice. The American contribution to this patrol is the responsibility of the U.S. Coast Guard.

**International Low Water (ILW)** • Reference plane below mean sea level, calculated by multiplying half the range between mean lower low water and mean higher high water by 1.5.

**International Maritime Organization (IMO)** • An organization that provides the machinery for cooperation among nations in the field of governmental regulation and practices relating to technical matters of all kinds affecting shipping. Also encourages and facilitates the general adoption of the highest practicable standards in matters concerning maritime safety, efficiency of navigation and prevention and control of marine pollution from ships. The organization is also empowered to deal with administrative and legal matters related to these purposes. The original name was the "Inter-Governmental Maritime Consultative Organization," or IMCO, but the name was changed in 1982 to IMO.

**International Rules** • Rules of the nautical road made effective by agreement of the major maritime powers for use on high seas and most inland waters of the world except the United States.

**International Rules of the Road** • Officially known as The International Regulations for Preventing Collisions at Sea (abbreviated as ColRegs). Rules of the nautical road made effective by agreement of the major maritime powers for use on the high seas and most inland waterways of the world. They are binding on public and private ships of all signatory powers when on the high seas (international waters), and they apply on the inland waters of all such countries unless superseded by duly enacted special rules (as in the United States, where the Inland Rules take precedence). *See also:* Inland Rules of the Road

**interpolation** • The process of finding a value between two known values on a chart or graph.

**interrogating radar** • A radar feature that sends a special signal designed to trigger a response from a target; used as an aid in discerning whether a target is a friendly or an enemy.

**interrogative** • In any naval message, means: "Question"; "I do not understand"; "meaning not clear"; etc.

**interrupted quick-flashing light** • A navigation light showing quick flashes for several seconds followed by a period of darkness.

**intertidal zone** • The zone between mean high water and mean low water.

**intervalometer** • Device for measuring depth charge interval, used to lay a barrage or pattern. An electrical or electro-mechanical device that controls the release or firing of airborne weapons/stores at a specified interval or sequence.

**Intruder** • Name assigned to the A-6 aircraft; an all-weather, low-altitude, carrier-based, two-seater attack aircraft. Primary mission is close-air-support missions and attacks on land bases and ships under any weather conditions.

**inversion** • With respect to temperature in the undersea environment, an inversion indicates an increase in temperature with increased depth (since the norm is for temperature to decline with increased depth). With respect to temperature in the atmosphere, an increase in temperature with height is considered an inversion, since normally temperature decreases with height in the atmosphere.

**ionosphere** • A layer of ionized air above the Earth that reflects some radio transmissions.

**Iriquois** • A utility helicopter, the HH-1N Iroquois is primarily used for search and rescue, command and control, and maritime special operations missions.

**Irish pennant** • Loose, untidy end of line left adrift. Also called a deadman or cow's tail. A loose thread on a uniform.

**irons** • 1. Unable to maneuver. A sailing ship caught with the wind coming from ahead or in any direction in such a way that she cannot cast to either side is said to be "in irons." 2. Handcuffs and leg irons.

**island** • Structure above the flight deck of an aircraft carrier containing command and flag bridges, the primary flight control station (pri-fly), radars, antiaircraft weapons, and more.

**isobar** • A line on a chart connecting points of equal atmospheric pressure.

**isobars** • Lines connecting points having the same atmospheric pressure reduced to a common datum, usually sea level.

**isobath** • A line on a map or chart that connects all points having the same depth below the surface of the ocean.

**isotherm** • Line connecting points of equal temperature.

**isothermal** • Having an equal temperature throughout.

**isothermal layer** • A layer of water throughout which a constant temperature exists.

**isotherm follower** • Device used to study the movement of subsurface layers of sea water.

**iswas** • *Inf:* Any crude or improvised measuring or calculating device used to determine a change of position.

**item** • Past phonetic word for the letter I; replaced by india.

# J

**jack** • 1. Short for union jack; a blue, white-starred flag flown at the bow jackstaff of a vessel at anchor. 2. To jack over the engines is to turn them over. *See also:* cablejack

**jackass** • 1. Cover over a hawsepipe to keep water from flowing through. 2. A cover over the entrance to the pipe leading to the chain locker; designed to keep water out of the chain locker. *See also:* buckler

**jack box** • Receptacle into which sound-powered telephone plugs or jacks are fitted.

**jack-of-the-dust** • Person in charge of the provision issue room.

**jackstaff** • Flagpole at the bow of a ship from which the union jack is traditionally flown when the ship is not under way. [Note: During the war on terrorism, the union jack has been replaced by the "Don't Tread on Me" flag.]

**jackstay** • Wire or line rigged for a special purpose, such as hanging seabags.

**Jack-tar** • Sailor. *See also:* tar

**Jacob's ladder** • Flexible, portable ladder with rungs attached to rope or wire sides; can be flung over the side for temporary use or suspended from a boat boom. *See also:* sea ladder

**jamoke** • *Inf:* Old naval term for coffee, derived from jamocha.

**Japan Current** • Western Pacific counterpart of the Atlantic Gulf Stream System; flows north along the coast of Japan. Also called the Kurosiwo or Kuroshio.

**jarhead** • *Inf:* Marine.

**JDAM bomb** • The Joint Direct Attack Munition (JDAM) is a guidance kit that converts existing, unguided bombs into precision-guided "smart" munitions. The tail section contains an inertial navigational system (INS) and a global positioning system (GPS). JDAM improves the accuracy of unguided bombs in any weather condition. It can be launched from every fighter or fighter-attack aircraft in the Navy's inventory.

**jeep carrier** • *Inf:* Small aircraft carrier built in great numbers during WWII; officially known as escort carriers (CVE).

**Jeheemy** • Salvage rig used to rescue swamped or stranded boats during an amphibious landing. Invented by Commodore Byron McCandless.

**jet assisted take-off (JATO)** • An auxiliary rocket device temporarily attached to an aircraft needing extra thrust for a takeoff under unusual conditions, such as a short runway.

**jetsam** • Material thrown overboard. The terms "flotsam" and "jetsam" are actually legal terms originating in marine law. Flotsam is the accidental floating debris resulting from a ship sinking or somehow damaged in a manner that causes it to leave debris floating in the ocean (not that which sinks to the bottom). Jetsam is the debris resulting from the deliberate jettisoning of materials into the sea, as when cargo is thrown overboard from a ship that is in danger of sinking.

**jet stream** • Relatively narrow wind currents of high velocity (100–300 knots) at 30,000–60,000 feet altitude. Generally from west to east, but meandering. The jet streams have a significant effect on world weather (storms), and are associated with air turbulence.

**jettison** • 1. To throw overboard. 2. A voluntary sacrifice of cargo designed to reduce weight when a ship is in distress. 3. Release of an airborne weapon or store by an emer-

gency or secondary release system.

**jetty** • Any solid structure, such as a breakwater, that extends into the water for the purpose of forming a harbor or protecting channels or shoreline from erosion.

**Jew's harp** • Ring or shackle at the upper end of the shank of an anchor to which anchor chain is secured. Any harp-shaped shackle.

**jewelry** • Gear used to fasten together sections of a pontoon causeway.

**Jezebel** • AN/SSQ-38 passive sonobuoy, used for locating targets.

**jib** • A triangular fore-and-aft sail set forward of the foremast. In square-rigged ships it balanced the spanker and assisted the helmsman in maintaining a steady course. The flying jib is a sail set forward of the regular jib, almost always, found in ships with bowsprits. Large ships might carry as many as three or four jibs and have their own private nomenclature for them.

**jibboom** • A separate spar that extends the bowsprit.

**jibe** • The shifting of a fore-and-aft sail from one side to the other by allowing the wind to cross the vessel's stern; the opposite of tacking, where the wind crosses the vessel's bow. Can be done on purpose or by accident. In the case of the latter, it can be dangerous, particularly when a large boom is involved. Even under the most controlled conditions, the weight of canvas and booms, which can slam from one side of the ship to the other with tremendous velocity, can be very dangerous to rigging and personnel. A controlled jibe is also called wearing. An alternative spelling is "gybe."

**jig** • Past phonetic word for the letter J; replaced by juliett.

**jigger** • *See:* jiggermast

**jiggermast** • 1. Fourth mast aft in a four-masted ship; often shortened to simply jigger. Some two-masted vessels, such as yawls, also call their aftermost mast a jigger instead of a mizzenmast. 2. Any small mast on a sailing vessel, but especially the mizzenmast on a yawl. *See also:* sail nomenclature

**Jimmy legs** • *Inf:* Guard or master-at-arms.

**job order** • A written directive used by a repair facility to order a specific job to be completed in response to a formal request previously submitted by a ship to the repair facility.

**joe pot** • *Inf:* Coffee pot. *Inf:* Short for jamoke, which was once the naval term for coffee.

**joiner door** • Conventional nonwatertight door aboard ship.

**joint** • Involving elements of more than one of the armed services; such as the Joint Chiefs of Staff and joint operations. *See also:* combined operations

**Joint Army-Navy grid** • *See:* grid, JAN

**joint command** • A command composed of forces from more than one service.

**joint exercises** • Exercises in which two or more of the armed services take part. *See also:* combined operations

**Joint Long-Range Strategic Study (JLRSS)** • Broad appraisal to assist in the development of guidance based on military strategies and concepts for the future. Provides general guidance for military research and engineering objectives. JLRSS is pronounced "jellers." Updated annually.

**joint operations** • Operations involving more than one service of a nation. *See also:* combined operations

**joint publications** • Publications for use by more than one of a nation's services. *See also:* combined publications

**Joint Standoff Weapon (JSOW)** • The Joint Standoff Weapon (JSOW) is a key program that replaces five types of air-to-ground weapons currently in the Navy's inventory. It is a joint Navy-Air Force program, with the Navy as the lead service. It provides a family of precision-guided weapons enabling defended target engagement from increased standoff distances (15 to 65 nautical miles) enhancing aircraft survivability. It was designed with reduced observability to enhance operational effectiveness against current and future surface-to-air threats. JSOW is capable in adverse weather conditions and allows for the engagement of multiple targets from a single aircraft launch position. The JSOW family employs a common weapon body for all variants. The AGM-154A variant carries BLU-97 combined-effect bomblets for use against area targets and is combat proven against targets in Iraq and Yugoslavia. AGM-154B is designed for use against light-to-medium armored targets and carries a payload of 6 BLU-108 Sensor Fused Weapon (SFW) sub-munitions. A third variant, the AGM-154C incorporates an uncooled, terminal-guidance infrared seeker and the Broach multistage warhead. The AGM-154C provides the warfighter with precision accuracy against targets vulnerable to blast fragmentation and penetration.

**Joint Strategic Capabilities Plan (JSCP)** • Annual translation of national objectives into terms of military objectives, which become directives for conduct of military operations during the life of the plan. JSCP pronounced "jay-scap." Updated annually.

**joint strike fighter** • Fighter aircraft designed for use by more than one service.

**Joint Tactical Radio System (JTRS)** • A DoD

initiative designed to provide a flexible approach to meet diverse warfighter communications needs through software-programmable radio technology. Service requirements are "clustered" so that similar requirements can be met with a single acquisition effort. The lead service for each acquisition effort serves as the cluster manager. The goal is real-time communications—through voice, data, and video—among U.S. military and allied warfighters.

**Jolly Roger** • Skull-and-crossbones flag traditionally associated with pirates. Traditionally flown during crossing-the-line ceremonies.

**journal** • The part of a shaft, pin, or rotating piece fitted into and working in a bearing.

**journalist (JO)** • Navy occupational rating that serves as the Navy's information specialists. JOs write press releases, news stories, features, and articles for Navy newspapers, bulletins, and magazines. They perform a variety of public-relations jobs. Some write scripts and announcements for radio and TV; others are photographers or radio and television broadcasters and producers. The photo work of JOs ranges from administrative and clerical tasks to film processing.

**JP–4** • *See:* JP fuel

**JP–5** • *See:* JP Fuel

**JP fuel** • Jet propulsion fuel; used by those naval aircraft and surface ships with gas turbine propulsion. Different grades are designated JP-4, JP-5, etc.

**jubilee pipe patch** • Damage-control patch for piping; resembles an elongated hose clamp under which a sheet of packing is laid.

**Judge Advocate General (JAG)** • The senior legal officer in the Navy.

**Julie** • A type of sonobuoy (AN/SSQ-23) that releases charges to explode at predetermined depths to provide echo-ranging information.

**juliett** • Phonetic word for the letter J.

**jumbo boom** • Heavy-lift boom aboard ship.

**jumper** • 1. Traditional Sailor's blue or white pullover uniform shirt. 2. Connecting pipe, hose, or wire for emergency use aboard ship that bypasses the normal flow.

**jumping the line** • The practice of a tug going ahead with full power and a slack hawser to give a powerful jerk using her momentum. Sometimes used to move a stranded ship.

**jump ship** • 1. *Inf:* Leaving ship without authority or permission; going AWOL or UA. 2. *Inf:* To be transferred to another command. *See also:* over the hill

**junior officer** • Technically, lieutenant commanders and below. In actual practice, usually only ensign, lieutenant junior grade, and lieutenant are considered junior officers.

**jurisdiction** • The limits or territory within which authority can be exercised.

**jury rig** • Any temporary or makeshift device, rig, or piece of equipment, such as a jury rudder, jury mast, etc. Many a ship has been saved by a clever jury rig.

# K

**kamikaze** • A member of a Japanese air attack corps in World War II; assigned to make a suicidal crash on a target, such as a ship. The actual translation is "divine wind."

**kapok** • Natural, silky, light, waterproof

fibers that clothe the seeds of the tropical ceiba tree. Used for stuffing life jackets.

**Karry Krane** • Mobile, crash-handling crane for small aircraft carriers.

**kedge** • To carry out an anchor in a small boat some distance from the parent ship or craft, drop the anchor, then haul the ship or craft up to the anchor; can be repeated many times to move a ship that has been becalmed or broken down.

**kedging** • *See:* kedge

**keel** • Central, longitudinal beam or timber of a vessel from which the frames rise. The keel is considered the backbone of the vessel and the frames analogous to ribs.

**keel block** • One of a series of blocks along a dry-dock bed; used to support the keel of a vessel in dry dock.

**keel depth** • For a surface ship, the distance of the keel below the waterline. For a submarine, the operating depth. Some foreign navies use the depth of water over the deck as the measure of submerged depth.

**keelhaul** • *Inf:* To reprimand severely. It is derived from the ancient punishment of hauling a man from one side of the ship to the other under the bottom by means of ropes passed under the keel. Keelhauling was never practiced by the U.S. Navy.

**keelson** • Originally a timber or steel fabrication bolted on top of a keel to strength it. Now any structural member used to strengthen the hull or support a heavy weight.

**keel stop** • Marker on a boat's keel that indicates its proper fore-and-aft placement for lowering into the chocks.

**keeping ship** • Observing the routine of a ship when not engaged in exercises or operations.

**keep the sea** • 1. Refers to staying at sea

and remaining effective under all conditions. 2. A term of praise, admiration, professional regard.

**kelp** • The largest known seaweed (algae), which grows on rock or stone bottom; may be as long as 600 feet with fronds 4 feet wide.

**Kenter shackle** • Patented anchor chain link that disassembles on removal of a pin. Now replaced by connecting shackles of a later design. *See also:* detachable link

**ketch** • A small sailing ship, fore-and-aft rigged, fitted with a tall mainmast and a much shorter mizzenmast, stepped in front of the rudder post. In appearance, the ketch is similar to a yawl, but the yawl has its aftermost mast stepped behind the rudder.

**ketchup** • *Inf:* Red lead paint.

**keying interval** • The elapsed time between successive rings on echo-ranging sonar.

**K-gun** • A split version of the Y-gun, the K-gun could be mounted on the sides of the superstructure, firing one depth charge outboard. *See also:* Y-gun

**kick** • Swirl in the wake of a ship caused by rudder action when making a turn. Same as knuckle. Used as a reference by ships turning in column, one astern of the other.

**kick plate** • 1. Bright metal plate, to absorb scuff marks on the vertical parts (steps) of a ladder. 2. Dark stripe near the deck of a light-painted bulkhead. 3. Protective plate near the base of a door.

**kid** • *See:* kit

**kilo** • Phonetic word for the letter K.

**kilohertz (kHz)** • 1,000 hertz or cycles per second.

**kiloton** • A mulitplication factor for nuclear weapon yields. Each kiloton is equal to the explosive force of 1,000 tons of trinitro toluene (TNT) explosive.

**king** • Past phonetic word for the letter K; replaced by kilo.

**king posts** • Sturdy vertical posts supporting the cargo booms of cargo ships. Often erected in pairs. The centerline pillars in a cargo ship's hold.

**kink** • A twist that disturbs the lay of line or wire.

**kit** • Small container, such as a mess kit or spit kit (spittoon). Sometimes called a kid.

**kite** • 1. A light sail used in a light breeze, in addition to the working sails. 2. A type of radar reflector designed to provide false readings to the interrogating radar.

**Klaxon** • Trademark name for an electrical horn or warning system.

**knee knocker** • *Inf:* The raised coaming at the bottom of a doorway aboard ship; designed to reduce the size of the hole in a structural bulkhead and to inhibit the flow of water, but famous for bruising Sailor's knees and shins.

**knife edge** • The rim of a door frame, hatch, or post that meets the gasket for a watertight fit.

**knock** • The tendency for gasoline to burn too rapidly, causing engine noise and loss of power.

**knocked down** • Said of a vessel that has been pushed over onto her side, usually because of sustained high winds, but sometimes for other reasons (shifting of cargo, flooding, etc.). Also sometimes referred to as laid down.

**knock off** • Quit working.

**knot** • 1. Although the term knot has roughly the same meaning as it does in civilian life (that is a means of fastening lines together or to another object), some nautical practi-

tioners observe a distinction among knots, hitches, and bends. Strictly speaking, a knot is formed when two lines are joined together in a permanent fashion; hitches and bends are generally less permanent and are formed by attaching a line to another object (such as a post). 2. Unit of speed equaling 1 nautical mile (6,080 feet) per hour. "Knots per hour" is a redundant (and therefore incorrect) usage.

**knowledge management** • Process of building and managing a base of information, advice and know-how. Includes applying quality control to the knowledge base.

**Kort nozzle** • A cylindrical steel casing fitted around the propellers of certain vessels to increase efficiency.

**Kuroshio** • *See:* Japan Current

**Kurosiwo** • *See:* Japan Current

**label plate** • The plate in a boat that contains, among other data, the maximum number of personnel the boat should carry under good weather conditions.

**labor** • A ship is said to labor when she moves with difficulty in a rough sea, putting heavy strain on her hull and equipment.

**Labrador Current** • A cold-water current flowing south along the coast of Labrador; the principal carrier of icebergs that menace the sea lanes of the North Atlantic. Upon meeting the Gulf Stream, it turns east and then northeast.

**labyrinth packing** • Rows of metallic strips or fins that minimize steam leakage along the shaft of a turbine.

**lacing** • Line that secures canvas by passing through the eyelets or grommets in the canvas.

**ladder** • 1. Nautical term for stairs. 2. A manual method of range-finding, using a succession of salvos fired at deliberate differences in range to establish hitting gun range.

**ladder screen** • Canvas or metal sheet secured on the underside of a ladder.

**lag** • The tendency of rotor blades to resist acceleration.

**lagging** • The insulation around pipes aboard ship. *See also:* lagging of the tides

**lagging of the tides** • Occurs when the tides caused by the sun come shortly after those caused by the moon, resulting in later tides than usual. *See also:* priming of the tides

**lagoon** • Body of water adjacent to land and communicating with the sea that has been created by the encirclement of a reef (usually coral).

**laid down** • A vessel is said to be laid down when her keel has been laid as an early stage of her construction. *See also:* knocked down

**land breeze** • Breeze coming off the land in the evening. After sunset, the land cools faster than the sea and thus it cools the adjacent air, which then flows to displace the warmer sea air.

**landfall** • The first sighting of land at the end of a voyage.

**landfast ice** • Ice of any type that is attached to the shore, beached, or stranded in shallow water. Sometimes shortened to fast ice.

**land ice** • Any ice floating on the sea that broke from a glacier.

**landing craft** • A naval craft designed for conveying troops and equipment from a ship to a land destination for an amphibious assault.

**landing gear** • The components of an aircraft (including wheels, floats, or skis) that support and provide mobility for the aircraft on land, water, or other surfaces.

**landing party** • A portion of a ship's crew detailed to go ashore in an organized unit for a military operation.

**landing ship** • An assualt ship designed for long sea voyages and rapid unloading onto a beach; LST, for example.

**landing signal officer (LSO)** • Officer who directs pilots in landing on an aircraft carrier.

**landlubber** • Seaman's term of derision for one who has never been to sea, or who has never learned seamanlike ways. Someone who exhibits these unseamanlike characteristics might be described as lubberly.

**lands** • Lands and grooves in a gun make up the spiral rifling that imparts spin to the projectiles for ballistic stability; the lands are the raised portion of the rifling, the grooves are the recessed tracks between.

**lang lay** • With respect to cordage, the lay in the strands and the lay in the rope are in the same direction.

**langrage** • Shot once used in naval warfare for tearing sails and rigging; consisted of bolts, nails, and other miscellaneous pieces of iron, glass, etc.; sometimes enclosed in a canister. *See also:* canister; grape; dismantling shot

**lanyard** • A strong piece of cord fastening something, or used to pull something, such as a firing lanyard. A relatively small line, rove between two deadeyes, forming a sort of tackle for setting up the shrouds of a sailing ship and keeping them at the proper stretch

**lapping head** • Abrasive device for removing copper fouling from the bore of a gun.

**lapse rate** • The decrease of an atmospheric variable wih height; the variable being temperature unless otherwise specified.

**larboard** • *See:* port and starboard

**laser** • A device that converts light of mixed frequencies to discrete, visible, radiation.

**lash** • To secure with line or wire by wrapping and tying with seamanlike knots in the case of line, or with an approved hitch in the case of wire.

**lashing** • Line, wire, or chain used to bind or fasten an article.

**lash-up** • An uncomplimentary term applied to a rig, device, or system to mean it is in disorder.

**lateen sail** • A fore-and-aft sail triangular in shape (or nearly so, with one very short side), still used in the Near East. It is slung from a lateen yard, a very long, drooping spar, sometimes fashioned from two sticks lashed together, which crosses a relatively low mast at an angle of about 45°, the low end being about one-third the length of the upper. Also once used on the mizzenmast of square-riggers until replaced by the spanker late in the eighteenth century. Believed to have been derived from the word "Latin" to describe these sails which were prevalent in the Mediterranean Sea (sometimes called the Roman Lake).

**latitude** • The measure of angular distance in degrees, minutes, and seconds of arc, from 0° to 90° north or south of the equator. Arcs (or circles) connecting points of equal latitude are called "parallels" because they are parallel to the equator.

**launch** • To float a ship on completion of building. Traditionally done by sliding down the building ways, although many ships, expecially big ones, are now launched by floating them out of the drydock in which they were built. An open powerboat.

**launcher** • Device for holding and firing a rocket, guided missile, or a projectile such as a depth charge.

**law officer** • Officer member of a court-martial who is a qualfied lawyer. A member of the Judge Advocate General (JAG) Corps.

**lay** • 1. The direction of the twist of strands of a rope. 2. Expresses "to move oneself." For example, if given the command "Lay to the quarterdeck," an individual should go to the quarterdeck.

**lay before the mast** • To assemble or fall in, usually to make reports. Reference is to ancient custom when crew members stood forward of the mizzenmast facing officers who stood on the quarterdeck, which is aft of the quarterdeck.

**layer depth** • The thickness of the mixed layer nearest to surface of the sea; the depth to the top of the thermocline. A term much used in antisubmarine warfare.

**lazaret** • 1. Storage compartment in the stern of a ship or boat. 2. An isolation hospital for people from quarantine vessels who have contagious diseases.

**lazy guy** • *See:* midship guy

**lazy jack** • A bridle of light line from the topping lift or mast of a sailboat to each side of the boom, between which the sail is contained when hoisting or lowering. Also called a boom guy. A line used to retrieve a towing hawser.

**lead** • 1. Short for hand lead or sounding lead, a device for measuring depth of water. Pronounced "led." 2. The tendency of rotor blades to remain in motion during deceleration. Pronounced "leed." 3. Narrow passage in pack ice through which a ship can navigate. Pronounced "leed."

**leadership** • The art and science of causing people to do what is required to accomplish a task or mission. Generally characterized as consisting of responsibility and authority. Good leadership is characterized as not only accomplishing tasks but doing so in a manner that preserves the dignity of the subordinates involved and minimizes any potential negative effects that may be part of a difficult task. Good leaders will find ways to cause individuals to carry out an assignment willingly rather than out of fear of reprisal.

**leading edge** • The forward edge of an airfoil that normally meets the air first.

**leading petty officer (LPO)** • The petty officer who assists the chief and/or officer in charge of a division, work center, or some other organizational subdivision.

**lead line** • Specially designed weight on the end of a long line, used for taking soundings. Also called a hand lead. Pronounced "led." The lead weight sometimes has a dished-in bottom for arming with tallow to obtain a bottom sample. Fathoms are indicated by bits of leather and cloth, called marks, at 2, 3, 5, 7, 10, 13, 15, 17, 20, and 25 fathoms. Depths between marks are estimated by eye and called deeps.

**leadsman** • Individual who takes soundings (measures depth of water) from a slowly moving ship by swinging the lead line forward, letting it go, and feeling the bottom; noting depth by seeing how much line is out, then reporting it by calling out "By the mark two" or "By the deep six," etc. Pronounced "ledsman."

**lead time** • The length of time before something must be completed. For example, an operation can be better planned before actual execution if enough lead time is provided.

**lead yard** • Shipyard that builds the first ship in a design class. It furnishes specified services to follow-on yards that build additional ships of the same class. Pronounced "leed."

**league** • Unit of distance. Approximately three nautical miles, or 3,041 fathoms. Rarely used now. *See also:* mariners' distance measurements

**learning continuum** • A structured approach to education and training, defined by the Navy as an integrative approach to the Sailor's career and personal development that blends covenant leadership, organizational valuation of education, the Navy Learning Model, and a Sailor-centric structural focus.

**learning organization** • As defined by the Navy, a structured product of the organizational learning process. Characterized by adaptability, flexibility, and a valuation of member/client participation in all processes.

**leatherneck** • *Inf:* A U.S. Marine. Referring to the leather neckband that was formerly part of the Marine uniform. Often capitalized.

**leave** • Authorized vacation or absence from duty other than liberty, which is generally of shorter duration. Leave carries with it permission to travel beyond the allowed radius of liberty. The term "shore leave," as a subsitute for liberty, is rarely used anymore. *See also:* liberty

**leaver** • A section of a convoy that breaks off from the main convoy to proceed separately to its own prearranged terminal port. When detached, the leaver section becomes a leaver convoy. If it is a single ship, it is referred to simply as a leaver.

**leave rations** • Cash payment in lieu of rations in kind while on leave, for enlisted personnel.

**lee** • 1. The direction toward which the wind

is blowing, or the opposite direction from which the wind is blowing. 2. An area sheltered from the wind; downwind.

**leech** • 1. The after edge of a fore-and-aft sail. 2. Either vertical edge of a square sail.

**lee helm** • Short for lee helmsman.

**lee helmsman** • The watchstander assigned to take control of the helm in the event that the helmsman becomes incapacitated. The lee helm also usually controls the speed of the ship by working the engine order telegraph in response to orders by the conning officer. Formerly referred to the helmsman who stood on the lee side of the wheel.

**lee shore** • A shore that is leeward of the ship.

**leeward** • Side of the ship opposite the direction from which the wind is blowing. (Pronounced loo-urd.) *See also:* lee

**leeway** • 1. The drift of an object, with the wind, on the water's surface. 2. The sideward motion of a ship due to wind and current. 3. The difference between a ship's heading (course steered) and a ship's track (course made good); sometimes called drift.

**left-handed** • Counterclockwise. Extended to mean not the right way or backwards.

**left-laid** • *See:* right-laid

**legalman (LN)** • Navy occupational rating that serves as aides to Navy lawyers. LNs work in Navy legal offices performing administrative and clerical tasks necessary to processing claims, conducting court and administrative hearings, and maintaining records, documents, and legal-reference libraries. They give advice on tax returns, voter-registration regulations, procedures, and immigration and customs regulations governing Social Security and veterans' benefits, and perform many duties related to courts-martial and nonjudicial hearings.

**level** • Shipboard floors above the main deck. Numbered 0-1, 0-2, 0-3.

**liberty** • Permission to be absent from a ship or station for a short time.

**lie off** • To heave to at some distance from shore.

**life buoy** • Buoyant device, often fitted with a light and smoke maker, for throwing to someone in the water. Also called life ring.

**life float** • Same as life raft.

**lifeguard** • Aircraft and ships detailed to prepositioned stations in order to be ready to recover personnel who fall overboard or who are in aircraft which crash into the sea.

**lifeguard submarine** • One stationed to rescue downed airmen; often used in areas where surface vessels cannot operate.

**life jacket** • Life-saving floatation device worn like a jacket. Also called a life vest. *Inf:* Mae West.

**lifeline** • 1. The lines along the outboard edges of a ship's weather decks to prevent personnel from falling overboard; more precisely, the top line is the lifeline, the middle line is the housing line, and the bottom line is the footline. 2. Any line used to assist personnel, as when entering a smoke-filled compartment. 3. Knotted lines secured to a line spanning the distance between lifeboat davits and hanging down into the boat; held onto by the boat's crew when hoisting and lowering for safety purposes. 4. Any line attached to a lifeboat or life raft to assist people in the water. Also called a grab rope.

**life preserver** • Device to keep an individual afloat. May be a jacket, ring, knapsack, belt, yoke, or vest.

**lifer** • *Inf:* One who has declared his or her intention to make the service a career; also one who is suspected of such intentions.

**life raft** • A specially designed floatation craft, carried by a larger vessel, to be used as a lifesaving device in the event that the vessel sinks. Can be as simple as a metallic tube covered with cork and naval canvas, or more complex, as in modern life rafts which are usually made of rubber and are automatically released and inflated when submerged.

**life ring** • *See:* life buoy

**lift** • Specified quantity of cargo requiring transportation. To transport cargo or personnel.

**lift, amphibious (or assault)** • Total capacity of assault shipping used in an amphibious operation.

**lift off** • To take off or leave the deck in a controlled condition of flight.

**light characteristics** • The sequence and length of light and dark periods, and the color or colors, by which it is identified.

**light cruiser** • No longer used. During WWII, it was useful to distinguish cruisers carrying 8-inch guns (heavy) from those with 6-inch guns (light cruisers). Size and displacement were not factors, only the armament. Heavy cruisers were designated CA, while light cruisers were CL. *See also:* cruiser

**lightening hole** • Hole cut in a steel plate in order to lighten it without sacrificing much strength.

**lighten ship** • To make a ship lighter by removing weight.

**lighter** • Barge-like vessel used to load or unload ships.

**lighter-than-air (LTA)** • Blimps, dirigibles, and other devices whose lifting capability depends on being inflated with a gas of less specific gravity than air.

**lighthouse** • A distinctive structure exhibiting a major light, designed to serve as an aid to navigation.

***Light List*** • Publication (series) describing aids to navigation that are maintained by the U.S. Coast Guard. *See also:* Lists of Lights

**light lock** • A double-door system, similar to an air-lock, used to permit access to spaces from which light cannot be allowed to show. Another system involves a switch on the door to cut off interior lighting unless the door is shut. A third is a simple maze with the surfaces painted dull black, which permits passage but allows no escape of light.

**light off** • Start; literally to start a fire in, as in "Light off a boiler." *Inf:* To start an engine, controversy, investigation, etc.

**light period** • The length of time in seconds required to complete one cycle of the identifying characteristics of an aid to navigation.

**light ship** • The act of dispensing with blackout precautions.

**lightship** • An anchored, manned, floating navigational light, in the form of a ship, with the advantage of being able to go to harbor for upkeep. Now rare, being replaced by unmanned buoys or structures.

**light water** • *See:* Purple-K Powder

**lignum vitae** • Very dense wood used in propeller shaft bearings.

**lima** • Phonetic word for the letter L.

**limb** • In celestial navigation, the upper or lower edge of the sun or moon as sighted against the horizon. When using the upper edge of the body, it is known as the upper limb, and when using the lower edge it is the lower limb.

**limber hole** • Fore-and-aft hole through the frames in a boat's bilges, permitting water to flow through toward the bilge pump suction point.

**limited duty officer (LDO)** • A formerly enlisted person who has earned a commission; generally limited to responsibilites related to his or her rating/specialty.

**limpet mines** • Explosives attached to the hull of a ship by enemy swimmers.

**line** • 1. Rope (fiber or wire) that has been put to some specific use. 2. A formation in which ships or personnel are formed on a guide. 3. General term sometimes used for the equator, as in "crossing the line." *See also:* rope

**lineal number** • When officers are commissioned, they receive a unique lineal number which decides seniority. Even those commissioned at the same moment will receive different lineal numbers, based upon class standing. The lower the lineal number, the more senior the officer.

**line chief** • Person in charge of the area where aircraft are fueled, armed, etc.

**line drawing** • A representation of the ship's form in three separate planes; similar to a blueprint. The longitudinal is known as the sheer plan. The transverse section is the body plan, and the horizontal is the half-breadth plan.

**line echo wave pattern (LEWP)** • A radar feature, normally an indicator of severe weather.

**line of departure** • In amphibious assault, the line from which the scheduled boat waves leave, on signal, for the beach.

**line officer** • Officer eligible for command of a line unit. Line units are ships, aircraft squadrons, seal teams, etc. The term is derived from the days when ships formed in a battle line to engage in combat.

**line of sight** • Straight line, used to describe radio frequency transmissions that do not follow the curvature of the Earth.

**line service** • Fueling, arming, engine warm-up, and minor adjustments of aircraft.

**lines per minute** • A setting used for HF radio weather fascimile transmissions.

**line squall** • A violent windstorm occurring along a weather front.

**line-throwing gun** • A gun specially rigged for throwing a line from one ship to another or from a ship to a pier. The projectile carries a light line, which is used to pull a messenger across.

**liquid crystal diode (LCD)** • A gray or black display of numbers or shapes, commonly used in electronics.

**list** • A semi-permanent inclination of a ship to one side; different from heel and roll, which are momentary inclinations. A ship rolling back and forth would not be listing, unless the middle of the roll were not at the even-keel position; *i.e.*, a ship with a 10° port list might roll between 0° and 20° port. Implies a less than optimum condition.

**listening sweep** • Sonar search conducted without sound emanation; passive use of sonar.

*List of Lights* • Publication listing aids to navigation in foreign ports. *See also: Light List*

**lithographer (LI)** • Navy occupational rating that runs Navy print shops and is responsible for producing printed material used in naval activities. LIs print service magazines, newspapers and bulletins, training materials, and official policy manuals. They operate printing presses, do layout and design, and collate and bind printed pages. The usual specialties are cameraman, pressman, and binderyman.

**littoral** • The coastal zone including the

beach to the coastal waters.

**littoral combat ship (LCS)** • The Littoral Combat Ship (LCS) will take advantage of the newest generation hull form and tailored, modularized combat systems package designs which will enable the LCS to defeat enemy littoral defenses including mines, fast swarming small boats, and submarines, ultimately ensuring maritime access in any environment.

**littoral warfare** • The ability to mass overwhelming joint and allied military force and deliver it ashore to influence, deter, contain, or defeat an aggressor. Expeditionary maneuver forces, surface fires, air wings, mine warfare forces and special operations forces provide the joint task force with the ability to conduct military operations anywhere in the world within several hundred miles of the sea. Supporting coalition naval forces provide anti-submarine, antisurface, and anti-air capability. The littoral area of control extends from the open ocean to the shore, and to those inland areas that can be attacked, supported and defended directly from the sea.

**Liverpool bridle** • A towline harness designed to permit a tug to maintain control over its heading in all kinds of weather.

**lizard** • A short length of rope used for some specific purpose. The line hanging down from a boat boom for securing boats is an example. *See also:* traveling lizard

**load** • 1. Command to put ammunition into the gun. 2. A single round of ammunition. 3. To stow supplies in a boat, vehicle, ship, or aircraft. 4. To "lose the load" is to lose all electrical power in the ship.

**loading** • Operations that install airborne weapons and stores on or in an aircraft; may include fusing bombs and stray voltage checks.

**loading, base** • *See:* base loading

**loading, combat** • *See:* combat loading

**loading, commercial** • *See:* commercial loading

**loading machine** • Dummy gun used to train gun crews in loading.

**loading, rail** • During an amphibious landing, the loading of boats at the rail of the ship (that is, while the boats are still on board) instead of after they are waterborne.

**load line marking** • An indication of draft (load) limits, displayed by international agreement on all merchant ships as well as on some naval vessels. *See also:* Plimsoll mark

**load list** • Items carried in a ship of the mobile support force, which supports the fleet under way.

**loafer's loops** • *Inf:* Aiguillettes.

**local apparent noon (LAN)** • The instant that the center of the sun is exactly over the upper branch of the meridian of the observer; *i.e.*, the highest altitude to which the sun will climb on that day, relative to the observer.

**local hour angle** • In celestial navigation, the angular distance west of the local celestial meridian; the arc of the celestial equator or the angle at the celestial pole between the upper branch of the local celestial meridian and the hour circle of a point on the celestial sphere, measured westward from the local celestial meridian through 360°.

**lock** • Compartment in a canal that can be filled or pumped out in order to raise or lower vessels to different levels.

**lodgement area** • The area, resulting from a consolidation of several beachheads, that is the base for subsequent operations inland.

**log** • 1. Device for measuring a ship's speed and distance traveled through the water. 2.

To record something is to log it. 3. Short for logbook. *See also:* taffrail log; pitometer log

**log book** • A chronological record of events, such as an engineering watch log or a deck log.

**log, deck** • *See:* deck log

**loggerhead** • Iron balls on a long handle, used for melting pitch in deck and hull seams to make them more watertight.

**logistics** • The science of planning and carrying out the movement and maintenance of military forces.

**log room** • The engineer's office aboard ship.

**loll** • A ship having a list that makes her unstable is said to loll or have a loll.

**long blast** • *See:* blast

**longeron** • A fore-and-aft structural member of an airplane fuselage.

**longevity pay** • The increase over base pay that is computed on years of service. *See also:* fogy

**long glass** • Nautical telescope. A medium-powered (up to 16x) monocular telescope used on ships, especially for spotting signals. The long glass is the traditional symbol of authority on board ship, and some ships still provide the OOD in port with a ceremonial one to carry about while standing watch.

**longitude** • Measure of angular distance in degrees, minutes, and seconds east or west of the prime meridian at Greenwich.

**longitudinal** • The lengthwise dimension; for example, the longitudinal axis of an aircraft runs lengthwise from the nose to the tail.

**longitudinal frames** • Frames of a ship that run fore and aft. Most ships are built with transverse framing; that is, frames perpendicular to the keel. Certain types, however, are built with frames parallel to the keel. Generally, these are tankers whose fluid cargoes can accept greater flexing of the hull. *See also:* frames

**longitudinal wave** • A wave in which particles of the transmitting medium are displaced perpendicularly to the wave itself; *e.g.,* sound waves in air or water.

**long-range active detection (LORAD) system** • A shipboard active long-range sonar system.

**longshore currents** • Currents within the surf zone that parallel the shoreline and are caused by waves breaking at an angle to the shoreline.

**longshoreman** • Laborer who loads and unloads marine cargo; generally the same as stevedore.

**long ton** • A unit of weight used in maritime situations equal to 2,240 pounds (1.016 metric tons or 1,016.05 kilograms). A ton is only 2,000 pounds, whereas the long ton is 240 pounds heavier.

**look alive** • To be alert, move quickly.

**lookout** • Crew member stationed as a visual watch; can be specified as air, horizon, surface, fog, etc.

**loom** • 1. The shine of a light that can be seen even though the light is below the horizon. 2. The rounded part of an oar from blade to handle.

**loran** • An electronic navigational system by which hyperbolic lines of position are determined by measuring the difference in the time of reception of synchronized pulse signals from two fixed transmitters. Derived from the acronym for "long-range navigation."

**lose the load** • *Inf:* To lose electrical power.

**love** • Past phonetic word for the letter L; replaced by lima.

**low** • An area of low pressure in the horizontal plane, referring to the isobars on a surface chart.

**lower away** • Lower right on down. For example, to lower away a boat from the davit heads down into the water.

**lower high water (LHW)** • The lower of the two high waters of any tidal day.

**lower low water** • The lower of the two low waters of any tidal day.

**lowest normal tides** • Reference plane lower than mean sea level by half the maximum tidal range, without consideration of wind or barometric pressure influences.

**low frequencies (LF)** • One of the designations of the radio frequency spectrum; covers the range 30–300 kHz.

**low water stand** • Interval of time at low water (before it begins to rise again) when the level of water does not vary appreciably. *See also:* high water stand

**lubber's line** • Reference mark on a compass or radar scope corresponding to the ship's head.

**lubberly** • Unseamanlike; clumsy. A lubber is an unseamanlike person. *See also:* landlubber

**lube oil** • Common term for lubricating oil; used to reduce friction and cool machinery.

**lucky bag** • 1. Traditional name for a space or container for stowage of articles found adrift. Unclaimed articles aboard ship are periodically sold at auction from the lucky bag, with the money made going to the ship's recreation fund. A Sailor losing something might be lucky enough to find it in the lucky bag and reclaim it. 2. Title of the yearbook for the midshipmen at the Naval Academy.

**luff** • 1. To head into the wind so that the upwind edge of the sail ripples with wind passing on the back side. 2. The leading edge of a fore-and-aft sail. *See also:* leech

**luff on luff** • Combined purchases consisting of a luff tackle with another luff tackle clapped on its hauling part. *See also:* purchase

**luff tackle** • *See:* purchase

**lug sail** • A small boat rig, a four-sided sail whose head (top) is supported by a yard or spar fastened obliquely to the mast.

**lunar time** • Time based upon the rotation of Earth relative to the Moon.

**Lyle gun** • Gun used in lifesaving to throw a lifeline to a ship in distress. Also called a line-throwing gun.

**M970** • Semi-trailer, tank, 5,000-gallon fuel dispensing, with underwing and overwing aircraft refueling nozzles.

**Mach** • A measurement of sonic speed under standard atmospheric conditions. Mach 1.0 is approximately 766 miles per hour.

**machinery index** • Comprehensive listing of all machinery and related equiment, other than electronic, installed on board.

**machinery repairman (MR)** • Navy occupational rating that is skilled as a machine-tool operator. MRs make replacement parts and repair or overhaul a ship engine's auxiliary equipment, such as evaporators, air compressors, and pumps. They repair deck equipment, including winches and hoists, condensers, and heat-exchange devices. Shipboard MRs frequently operate main propulsion machinery in addition to performing machine-shop and repair duties.

**machinery spaces** • The part of a ship containing propulsion and auxiliary machinery, and under the cognizance of the engineering officer. Also called engineering spaces.

**machinery trials** • Tests of main propulsion machinery of a ship. May be builder's, acceptance, post repair, standardization, or tactical.

**machinist's mate (MM)** • Navy occupational rating that operates and maintains the many engines, compressors, refrigeration units, air-conditioners, gas-operated equipment, and other types of machinery afloat and ashore. In particular, MMs are responsible for a ship's steam propulsion and auxiliary equipment, and the outside (deck) machinery. MMs may also perform duties in the manufacture, storage, and transfer of some industrial gases.

**Mach number** • Ratio of an object's speed to that of sound in air. An aircraft going Mach one is traveling at the speed of sound; Mach two is twice the speed of sound, etc.

**MacNamara's lace** • Fancy curtains and trimmings for barges and gigs, worked from unlaid canvas threads.

**MacNamara lace** • *See:* MacNamara's lace

**Mae West** • *Inf:* Life jacket.

**magazine** • 1. Compartment aboard ship or ashore fitted for the stowage of ammunition. 2. A holder in or on a gun for the loading of cartridges.

**magnetic airborne detector (MAD)** • A device that detects a submerged submarine from low-flying aircraft by sensing the magnetic field of its submerged mass.

**magnetic compass** • A compass using the Earth's magnetic field as its orienting field of reference.

**magnetic dip** • *See:* dip, magnetic

**magnetic flux** • Magnetic lines of force. Magnetic field strength.

**magnetic mine** • An influence mine that functions through sensing the magnetic field of a large steel ship passing overhead.

**magnetic storm** • Worldwide magnetic disturbance that usually starts suddenly and lasts a minimum of several hours. Interferes with electronic communications.

**mailbuoy** • An ancient sailor's joke: supposedly the mid-ocean buoy in which mail is kept for delivery to passing ships.

**Mailbuoy** • Name given to a specific communications satellite for ultrahigh frequency relay.

**mailgram** • Official dispatch transmitted by mail; used in place of electronic communications.

**main battery** • A ship's most important weapon system.

**main body** • The major part, or the most important ships, of a formation or disposition; for example, the aircraft carrier(s) of a carrier strike group.

**main deck** • Uppermost complete deck of a ship; aircraft carriers are a notable exception because the hangar deck is considered to be the main deck even though the flight deck would seem to fit the traditional definition.

**main drain** • Suction line for pumping out engineering spaces.

**main drain system** • A system used for pumping bilges.

**main injection** • An opening in the skin of a ship through which cooling water is delivered to the main condenser and main lube oil cooler by the forward motion of the ship.

**mainmast** • The largest mast on a vessel; usually the second mast aft from the bow of a ship with two or more masts. *See also:* foremast; mizzenmast

**main radio** • *See:* radio central

**maintop** • A top on the mainmast. *See also:* top; foretop; masthead

**main-truck** • The highest part of the mainmast.

**make** • A ship makes headway, makes good a course steered. A line is made fast to something. A lookout makes out a light and reports it. A leaking boat makes water. A man being promoted makes a rate. *See also:* make it so

**make and mend** • British equivalent of "rope yarn Sunday." Any day or part of a day free of work and drills aboard ship. Admiral David Beatty's famous signal to the Grand Fleet at Scapa Flow at the end of World War I ended with this order.

**make it so** • Response by a senior to a junior, telling the latter to carry out some previously specified action.

**make-up feed** • In a closed steam cycle, the water that is needed to replace that lost in the cycle between the boiler and the condenser.

**Mameluke sword** • Cross-hilted type of sword worn by Marine officers.

**man** • To assume a station, as in "Man your gun."

**maneuver** • The movement of a ship or aircraft for a specific purpose. For example, "the destroyer maneuvered into position astern of the oiler in preparation for the upcoming refueling."

**maneuvering board** • A plotting sheet with a polar coordinate grid that can be used to solve a number of relative motion problems.

**maneuvering rudder** • *See:* pilot rudder

**maneuvering ship** • A ship the movements of which are defined relative to a given ship called the reference ship. *See also:* relative motion

**manhelper** • A paintbrush lashed to a long wooden handle.

**manhole** • Round or oval hole cut in a deck, bulkhead, or tank top to provide limited or emergency access. Often placed in watertight doors or hatches. Barely big enough to squeeze through. Fitted with means for closure when appropriate. *See also:* scuttle

**manifest** • A list of all cargo with details as to shippers, consignee, etc.

**manifold** • A fitting with numerous branches that directs and distributes fluids from a large pipe to several smaller pipes.

**manila** • A type of fiber rope. *See also:* abaca

**manned and ready** • Report made to indicate that all assigned hands are present and ready for action.

**manning level** • Number of personnel actually on board, as opposed to allowance or complement. *See also:* complement; allowance

**manning the rail** • An all-hands evolution where the ship's crew line up along the ship's rail to honor a person or occasion.

**man-o'-war** • *See:* man-of-war

**man-of-war** • Fighting ship; armed naval ship. A warship. Most commissioned vessels of the U.S. Navy are men-of-war, but not all; *e.g.*, a hospital ship.

**manrope** • A safety line made up with a series of overhand or figure-eight knots evenly spaced to assist personnel climbing up and down.

**man the rail** • This custom evolved from the centuries old practice of "manning the yards" in sailing ships, in which sailors stood evenly spaced on all the yards and gave three cheers to honor a distinguished person. Today the custom is continued by having Sailors stationed along the rails of a ship, rather than on the yards. Navy ships will often man the rails when entering a port or when returning to the ship's homeport at the end of a deployment.

**mare's nest** • *Inf:* A mess or disarray.

**Marine Corps** • The sea-going soldier corps of the Department of the Navy. Their mission is to be available on short notice for tough combat and police duty worldwide. *Inf:* Leathernecks.

**Marine Corps Institute** • An official training activity charged with the educational development of Marine Corps personnel.

**Marine Expeditionary Brigade, Force, Unit (MEB, MEF, MEU)** • Different echelons of task organizations associated with amphibious assault landings.

**mariners' distance measurements** • cable = 120 fathoms (archaic); fathom = 6 feet; league = 3 nautical miles (archaic); nautical mile = 2,000 yards

**Maritime Prepositioning Groups (MPG)** • A combination of a Maritime Prepositioning Force, Combat Logistics Force and high-speed intra-theater lift. These include Military Sealift Command ships.

**mark** • An exclamation used in taking a reading when the reading must be marked by a specific moment in time, as in celestial observations: "Stand by—Mark! Altitude is 46 degrees, 27.6 minutes." Exact time is noted on the word "Mark." The marked fathoms on a hand lead: "By the mark seven."

**marker ship** • In an amphibious operation, the control ship.

**mark (MK)** • Term used to identify a type of equipment; always followed by a number to indicate the specific equipment, and frequently followed by a MOD (modification) number to indicate the number of modifications that have been made to that type. (*e.g.* "Mark III Mod 2" might be applied to binoculars to indicate that the specific type is the Mark III and it has been modified two different times).

**Mark Twain** • The famous author, whose name was actually Samuel Clemens, chose the pen name "Mark Twain" after hearing the words called out by the leadsmen on river boats.

**marline** • Small stuff (cord), formerly tarred but now usually made of synthetic fiber.

**marlinespike** • Tapered steel tool for separating strands of rope or wire in splicing. *See also:* fid

**marlinespike seamanship** • The art and science of working with rope, line, and related gear.

**marry** • 1. To join, as an LST is married to a pontoon causeway, or two lines such as boat falls laid out side by side and handled together. 2. To set together the unlaid strands of two rope ends when splicing.

**MARS radio system** • Worldwide network of volunteer radio operators who use their facilities to allow deployed servicemembers to communicate with their loved ones back home. The system provides both direct voice communications and the passing of written messages, similar to telegrams, called "MARSgrams."

**MARSgram** • *See:* MARS radio system

**martinet** • A strict disciplinarian; generally

one who is excessively concerned with details of questionable importance.

**Mary Anne** • *Inf:* Floating crane used to salvage aircraft in the water.

**mast** • A vertical spar (pole) used to give height to shipboard components: sails, antennas, etc.

**master-at-arms (MA)** • Navy occupational rating that helps keep law and order aboard ship and at shore stations. MAs report to the executive officer, help maintain discipline, and assist in security matters. They enforce regulations, conduct investigations, take part in correctional and rehabilitative programs, and organize and train Sailors assigned to police duty. In civilian life, they would be detectives and policemen. *See also:* Master-at-Arms (MAA)

**Master-at-Arms (MAA)** • A person assigned the duty of maintaining good order and discipline. Ship's police. Traditionally headed by a chief-master-at-arms (CMAA). There may be special MAAs, such as the ones in charge of the mess decks. In the old Navy, the CMAA had custody of the ship's hand weapons and trained the crew in their use. The master-at-arms rating grew out of this traditional duty. A Sailor can be assigned as an MAA without holding the rating of MA. *See also:* master-at-arms (MA)

**master station** • The governing of two or more synchronized transmitting stations.

**masthead** • Highest point of a mast to which the rigging is attached. Does not include staffs, poles, etc., that might project above that point.

**masthead light** • White light required by Rules of the Road to be shown by a vessel at night.

**material conditions** • State of damage-control security within a ship. Doors, hatches, ports, valves, etc., are designated by the letters W, X, Y, Z to indicate which ones are to be closed (or opened) during different material conditions. For example, if material condition X is set, all fittings labeled "X" would be closed. These designations have retained the old phonetic words (so that Y is called yoke rather than yankee etc.). Condition xray is the least damage-control ready, zebra is the most (set during general quarters), and yankee is in between. Whiskey fittings are those that are closed specifically to counter threats from chemical, biological, and radiation warfare (vents, etc.).

**Maverick** • An air-to-surface guided missile designated AGM-65; homes on infrared emissions from the target for day or night sea warfare and land interdiction missions.

**Mayday** • International distress signal used on voice radio. Derived from the French *M'aidez* (help me).

**meal pennant** • Echo flag hoisted from the port yardarm of a naval vessel at anchor when the crew is at mess. Also called the bean rag or chow rag.

**mean higher high water** • Average height of higher high waters.

**mean lower low water** • The average of lower low water tides for a specific area.

**mean low water** • The average height of all low waters (tides) at a given place.

**mean point of impact** • Geometric center of all the points of impact of the shots of a salvo or of the bombs in pattern bombing, excluding wild shots.

**mean tide level** • The average of the high waters and the low waters.

**mean time** • Time measured by the average rate of the sun's apparent movement.

**mean water level** • The mean surface level

determined by averaging the height of water at equal time intervals.

**measure black, blue, green, white** • Lighting conditions used for night landings on carriers.

**measured mile** • An exact nautical mile delineated by beacons or markers ashore; used in calibrating pit logs and propeller shaft revolutions per minute.

**meatball** • In naval aviation, the meatball (sometimes just called "the ball") is an amber light that appears at the center of a "mirror," which actually is a stack of five lenses designed to aid pilots in making a safe landing. If the aircraft is properly positioned in the glide path, the meatball will be aligned with the horizontal line of green reflected light on either side of the center lens. To be "on the ball" means that the pilot has the meatball in the right place and is on the glide path. *Inf:* The battle efficiency pennant.

**mechanical mule** • *Inf:* A half-ton carrier, designated the M-274, for light infantry weapons and cargo.

**mechano decking** • Portable aluminum decking for a tanker.

**Med** • Common reference used by naval personnel when referring to the Mediterranean Sea.

**Medal of Honor** • The nation's highest decoration, given in nearly all cases for extreme courage under combat conditions. Sometimes mistakenly called the Congressional Medal of Honor. There are three different versions for the different services (Marines and Coast Guard are included in the Navy version), but all three are considered equivalent.

**medic** • Term sometimes used for a hospital corpsman. More appropriate to Army terminology.

**Mediterranean moor** • Mooring a ship with her stern to a seawall and her bow kept from swinging by anchor(s) placed ahead to either side of the bow while maneuvering in. The brow is rigged from fantail to seawall. Called "Med moor" and much used by ships of the U.S. Sixth Fleet in certain ports.

**medium frequencies (MF)** • One of the designations of the radio frequency spectrum; covers the range 300–3,000 kHz.

**meet her** • An order to the steersman to apply sufficient opposite rudder to check or stop a ship's swing.

**megaton (MT)** • A means of expressing the explosive power of a nuclear weapon. One megaton is equal to the explosvie force of 1 million tons of trinitrotoluene explosive (TNT).

**megger** • An instrument used for checking the insulation of electrical cables.

**mentors** • Members who act as counselors and surrogate advisors for younger/newer/subordinate personnel or peers and offer advice and assistance on career development and personal growth matters.

**Mercator chart** • Most commonly used chart for marine navigation. In the form most commonly used, polar areas are greatly exaggerated in size. A major practical advantage of a Mercator projection is that rhumb lines are drawn as straight lines, which is very useful in practical navigation. To construct great circle lines, a different projection must be used. *See also:* Mercator projection

**Mercator projection** • Named for its inventor, a conformal cylindrical map projection in which the surface of a sphere or spherioid, such as Earth, is conceived as developed on a cylinder tangent along the equator. The actual projection is achieved mathematically but is based upon this model. *See also:* Mercator chart

**Merchant Marine** • 1. Commercial ships officially flagged by a nation; may be privately or publicly owned. 2. The personnel of a merchant marine.

**merchant navy** • Term used, somewhat incorrectly, to describe the Merchant Marine.

**merchant ship broadcast system (MERCAST)** • System providing communication with merchant ships.

**Mercury** • Communications relay and strategic airborne command post aircraft. Provides survivable, reliable, and endurable airborne command, control, and communications between the National Command Authority (NCA) and U.S. strategic and non-strategic forces.

**meridians** • Great circles of the Earth that pass through the poles. Used for measuring longitude. *See also:* parallels

**Meritorous Unit Commendation** • Similar to the Navy Unit Citation but awarded for lesser accomplishments. *See also:* Navy Unit Citation; Presidential Unit Citation

**mess** • 1. To eat. 2. A place where people eat. 3. A group of people eating together. The crew's mess is called the general mess.

**message** • Term applied to a specific communication delivered by rapid means (radio, flashing light, etc.). Generally refers to administrative or longer-term subject matter, rather than tactical communications. The latter are more often referred to as "signals" rather than "messages."

**messboy** • Old and obsolete term for wardroom waiter.

**messcook** • Someone who is temporarily assigned to cooking or related food-preparation duties. Someone assigned to such duties permanently would be called a cook or mess management specialist, rather than a messcook.

**mess decks** • Area where the crew dines (messes). In older times, the entire crew generally messed on a single deck that, for the period of the meal, was known as the mess deck. Now the term more accurately refers only to the compartment(s) in which the meals are served.

**messenger** • Light line used to carry across a larger line or hawser. Because it is not practical to heave a heavy line across from ship to ship (or ship to pier), a lighter line with a weight attached to the end is used as a heaving line; then tied to the larger line to serve as a messenger to get the larger line across. Person who carries messages for an OOD or other officers of the watch.

**messenger mail** • *See:* guard mail

**mess gear** • Knives, forks, spoons, etc. The word passed over the ship's general announcing system before meals to inform the crew that it is time to clear the mess decks to allow final preparations for the coming meal.

**mess kit** • Ingenious assemblage of cooking and eating utensils used by troops or members of landing parties. Sometimes used to describe a table setting (knife, fork, etc.).

**messman** • One who serves food to the crew. *Inf:* Bean jockey.

**mess management specialist (MS)** • Rating whose specialties are food preparation and stores inventory management. Renamed culinary specialist.

**mess treasurer** • Person who administers the finances of a mess. It applies to those messes that are self-sufficient, as opposed to those operating under government funding.

**metacenter** • Pertaining to ship stability, the mathematically computed, instantaneous center of the arc generated by the center of buoyancy as it changes when the ship rolls is called the transverse metacenter. That generated when the ship pitches is called the longitudinal metacenter. Location of the appropriate metacenter, with regard to the ship's center of gravity, is a measure of her stability against roll or pitch. For surface ships, the transverse metacenter is the only one of serious concern, unless there has been serious damage adversely affecting the longitudinal metacenter. For a submerged submarine, the entire calculation is different because the center of buoyancy cannot shift, no matter what the submarine's attitude.

**metacentric height** • The distance between the metacenter and the center of gravity of a ship. A measure of stability.

**meta process** • Overarching process used in strategic planning that serves as a guide to other included processes.

**METEM technician** • A meteorological electronic equipment maintenance technician, a term usually referring to a Navy ET who has received special training on meteorological equipment in the METEM school.

**meteorology** • The science that deals with the phenomena of the atmosphere, especially as it pertains to weather and weather conditions.

**MH-53 Sea Dragon** • *See:* Sea Dragon

**micrometer** • A device used for measuring minute distances.

**Mid** • Nickname for midshipman.

**middle line** • *See:* lifeline

**midnight rations** • *See:* midrats

**mid-ocean ridge** • A great median arch or sea-bottom swell extending the length of an ocean basin and roughly paralleling the continental margins. The Mid-Atlantic Mid-Ocean Ridge is a most prominent example.

**midrats** • Food served late at night for those going on or coming off watch. Derived from

the acronym for "Midnight Rations."

**midship guy** • Line between boom heads in a yard-and-stay rig. Also sometimes called a "schooner guy" or a "lazy guy."

**midwatch** • The watch from 000–0400 (midnight–4 A.M.).

**mike** • Phonetic word for the letter M.

**mil** • Unit of angular measurement defined by the Navy as the angle whose tangent is 1/1000 of the radius and equivalent to 3.44 minutes of arc.

**military due process** • Legal procedures under the protections and rights granted military personnel by the Constitution or laws enacted by Congress.

**Military Occupational Specialty (MOS)** • Numerical system used by the Marine Corps and Army to identify special occupational skills of an individual.

**military record** • An individual's overall performance record while a member of the military services of the United States.

**Military Sealift Command (MSC)** • Ocean freight and passenger service operated by the Navy for the Department of Defense. Also includes specially equipped ships for support of ocean, missile, and space research. Formerly known as the Military Sea Transport Service (MSTS).

**military specifications (MILSPECS)** • Guides for determining the quality requirements for materials and equipment used by the military services.

**military standards** • 1. General naval qualifications (knowledge and practical factors) that naval personnel must meet concerning discipline, Uniform Code of Military Justice, ceremonies, regulations, first aid, etc. 2. Document setting engineering and technical limitations to assure uniformity in materials and products.

*See also:* occupational standards

**millibars** • A unit of measure of atmospheric pressure.

**mind your rudder** • A caution to the steersman to steer a more careful course, or to be alert to some special circumstance, such as meeting a current.

**mine** • A submerged explosive charge, designed to explode against or beneath a ship. Automatic mines are self-actuating; controlled mines are fired remotely. Mines may be dropped from the air (aerial), moored, or allowed to drift. Firings may be acoustic, contact, influence (magnetic), or pressure. Sometimes called sea mines to distinguish them from land mines, which are usually antipersonnel mines. Mines are used as antiship or antisubmarine subsurface weapons. The MK56 ASW mine (the oldest still in use) was developed in 1966. Since that time, advances in technology have given way to the development of the MK60 CAPTOR (short for "encapsulated torpedo"), the MK62 and MK63 Quickstrike and the MK67 SLMM (Submarine Launched Mobile Mine). Most mines in today's arsenal are aircraft-delivered to target.

**mine countermeasures** • Procedures for preventing or reducing damage to ships, resulting from mines. Includes channel conditioning, clearance, disposal, hunting, loading, sweeping, watching, and other measures found necessary as a result of increasingly sophisticated mine warfare.

**minefields** • Areas that have been sown with mines. They can be further classified according to their location or purpose. Defensive minefields are planted in one's own waters, or in friendly waters, to prevent intrusion by the enemy. Offensive fields are placed in enemy waters to inflict damage or cause shipping to reroute its track; often placed at choke points carrying heavy ship traffic. They are classed as attrition, nuisance, strategic, sustained attrition, and transitory attrition.

**mine hunting** • The branch of mine countermeasure that determines the positions of individual mines and concentrates countermeasures on these positions; includes locating, clearing, and watching.

**minelayer** • A vessel or aircraft whose mission is to sow mines.

**mineman (MN)** • Navy occupational rating that tests, maintains, repairs, and overhauls mines and their components. MNs are responsible for assembling, handling, issuing, and delivering mines to the planting agent; and for maintaining mine-handling and minelaying equipment.

**mine sterilizer** • A countermeasure device designed to make a mine harmless after a preset number of days.

**minesweeper** • A vessel or aircraft whose mission it is to remove mines. The mines can be enemy mines, or they may be friendly mines no longer needed after the cessation of hostilities. *See also:* minefields

**minesweeping** • Removing or destroying mines to permit safe passage.

**minesweeping boat (MSB)** • Specially constructed boat used for sweeping mines.

**mine tracks** • Tracks fitted on the deck of a minelayer to permit mines to be dropped over the stern.

**mine vessels** • Those vessels designed to plant or sweep mines. Principal types are minelayer, destroyer minelayer, minesweeper, minehunter, and destroyer minesweeper.

**mini boss** • *Inf:* Assistant to the air boss. *See also:* air boss

**minimize** • A condition generally implemented in times of crisis or in conjunction with major operations; where normal high-speed communication traffic is drastically reduced so that high-priority messages will not be delayed.

**minute-guns** • Saluting guns fired at intervals of one minute as an honor to officials entitled to gun salutes; also employed to honor the deceased at a military funeral.

**misfire** • Propellant charge that fails to fire when the trigger has been pulled. For safety reasons, a misfire is treated as a hangfire; *i.e.*, there is the possibility of a delayed detonation until such possibility is ruled out. *See also:* hangfire

**missile defense surface action groups (MDSAG)** • Three *Aegis* ships, either cruisers or destroyers, working together to provide missile defense to a larger entity, such as a Strike Group.

**missile technician (MT)** • Navy occupational rating that performs organizational and intermediate-level maintenance on ballistic-missile weapon systems. MTs operate and maintain their fire-control systems, guidance subsystems, and associated test equipment; as well as missile and launcher/tuber groups and all ancillary equipment. They operate and maintain strategic weapons systems, associated ship/weapon subsystems, and test and handling equipment.

**mission** • The objective or purpose of a military operation or program.

**miss stays** • In tacking, if the head of the ship will not come around through the wind, she is said to miss stays. The result may be to put her in irons, or flat aback; or she may fall off to the original track, gain headway, and try again.

**mizzen** • A fore-and-aft sail set on the mizzenmast. *See also:* aftermast; foremast; mainmast

**mizzenmast** • The mast aft, or next aft, of the mainmast in a ship.

**mizzentop** • A top located on the mizzenmast. *See also:* top; maintop; foretop; masthead

**MK-14** • *See:* torpedo

**MK-26** • *See:* Standard missile system

**MK-37** • *See:* torpedo

**MK-38 gun** • The MK-38 is a 25-mm (one inch diameter) heavy machine gun, effective to 2,700 yards (2,457 meters). Was employed aboard various combatant and auxiliary ships in the Mid-East Force escort operations and during Operations Desert Shield and Desert Storm. The weapons are maintained in a rotatable pool, available for temporary installation on various deploying ships, and permanent installation on certain amphibious and auxiliary ships, patrol craft and Coast Guard cutters. Single barrel, air cooled, semi- and full-automatic, manually trained and elevated machine gun system (MGS) with an unstabilized guidance system, that is manually trained and elevated. Capable of delivering 175 rounds per minute.

**MK-41 Vertical Launching System** • The MK 41 Vertical Launching System (VLS) is the worldwide standard in shipborne missile launching systems. It simultaneously supports multiple warfighting capabilities, including antiair warfare, antisubmarine warfare, ship self-defense, strike warfare, and antisurface warfare. MK 41 is a fixed, vertical, multi-missile storage and firing system that lets Navy vessels launch significant firepower. The capability of VLS to simultaneously prepare one missile in each half of a launcher module allows for fast reaction to multiple threats with concentrated, continuous firepower. *See* *also:* Standard missile system

**MK-45 gun** • A 5-inch, 54-caliber light-weight gun that provides surface combatants accurate naval gunfire against fast, highly maneuverable surface targets, air threats, and shore targets during amphibious operations. Offers significant improvements in reliability and maintainability over the 54-caliber MK-42 gun systems. The MK-45 is controlled by either the MK-86 Gun Fire Control System or the MK-160 Gun Computing System. Effective range is 13 nautical miles (14.9 statute miles) and rate of fire is:16-20 rounds per minute automatic.

**MK-46** • *See:* torpedo; ASROC system

**MK-48** • *See:* torpedo

**MK-50** • *See:* torpedo

**MK-60** • *See:* mine

**MK-62** • *See:* mine

**MK-63** • *See:* mine

**MK-67** • *See:* mine

**MK-75 gun** • A lightweight, rapid-fire three-inch (76 mm) gun, mounted on small combat vessels. Mounted on some Navy frigates and hydrofoils, and on some of the larger Coast Guard cutters. The system is a lightweight, water-cooled, rapid fire, remote-controlled, dual purpose automatic enclosed naval gun. Range is approximately 10 nautical miles (11.5 statute miles, 18.4 km) and the guidance system is remotely controlled. Fires 80 rounds per minute. First deployed in USS *Oliver Hazard Perry* (FFG-7) in 1978.

**MK-116** • *See:* ASROC system

**mock-up** • Model or replica, sometimes life-sized, of a machine, device, battlefield, vessel, etc. Used for planning, design, instruction, or training purposes.

**model basin** • Large tank or basin for testing ship models for speed, power, and general behavior at sea.

**modification (MOD) number** • Part of an equipment identification system used by the Navy to indicate the changes that an individual type of equipment has undergone. It always follows a mark number; *e.g.*, Mark III Mod 2 might be applied to binoculars to indicate that the specific type is the Mark III and has been modified two different times.

**modulator** • That part of radio equipment that alters the amplitude, frequency, or phase of a radio signal in accordance with speech or a signal; or that regulates the length of a pulse.

**mole** • A large, solid-fill, nearshore structure of earth, masonry, or large stone; used as a breakwater or a pier.

**Momsen lung** • A breathing apparatus which permits an individual to breathe normally while escaping from a sunken submarine. It also serves as a gas mask in a submarine and a life preserver on the surface.

**monkey fist** • Weighted knot in the end of a heaving line.

**monocoque** • An aircraft structure in which the stressed outer skin carries either all or a major portion of the torsional and bending stress.

**moor** • 1. To secure a ship alongside a pier using mooring lines. 2. To secure a vessel to a mooring buoy. 3. To anchor a vessel. Although "anchor" is the more specific term and more often used, the more generic term "moor" is technically correct as well. Deck log entries have traditionally used the term "moored as before" to describe a vessel that remains at anchor. 4. To anchor with two anchors and a mooring swivel. To make a regular moor, the ship drops the upstream anchor first, then backs down and drops the second. Then the second anchor chain is paid out while the first is hove in until the ship is centered between the two, for insertion of the mooring swivel. *See also:* flying moor

**mooring** • 1. Securing a ship to a pier, wharf, or mooring buoy. 2. Technically, anchoring with two anchors connected to a single chain by means of a mooring swivel. Commonly used to describe a vessel that is merely anchored (with only one anchor), although in strictest terms, this is an incorrect usage. *See also:* moor; flying moor; Mediterranean moor; mooring swivel

**mooring buoy** • A heavy round buoy anchored with several extremely heavy and strong anchors (usually concrete blocks known as sinkers), and fitted with a swivel and link in the center of the buoy's top surface. Mooring buoys are numbered and marked on harbor charts.

**mooring line** • Line used specifically to secure a ship to a pier.

**mooring staple** • Metal fitting on a ship's side to which a chain may be attached for added security in mooring alongside.

**mooring swivel** • A large swivel fitted into the ground tackle to restrict the ship's swing in her berth. It uses two anchors some distance apart, generally one upstream and one downstream, so that as the current shifts from ebb to flood the ship will alternately ride to each. The mooring swivel has two links to which an anchor chain can be attached. After the two anchors are down, their chains are broken and both shackled to the swivel. Then a single chain is led from the other end of the swivel through one of the hawse pipes and stoppered on deck in the usual manner.

**morning call book** • Book listing persons such as cooks, navigators, watchstanders, etc.) requiring early reveille, their location,

and the time they need to be called.

**morning colors** • The act of hoisting the national flag aft, and the union jack forward at exactly 0800 (8 A.M.) local time. This is done with pride and maximum precision by all ships in port, following exactly the motions of the senior ship present. The "Prep" signal flag is flown at the yardarm for five minutes before morning colors, as a signal that colors is coming. [Note: During the War on Terrorism, the Jack has been replaced by the "Don't Tread on Me" flag.]

**morning order book** • Book in which the executive officer writes instructions for the coming morning's work. *See also:* plan of the day

**morning orders** • Published schedule of activities for the day aboard ship. A part of plan of the day.

**morning watch** • The watch from 0400–0800 (4 AM –8 AM).

**Morse code** • A code using dots and dashes for radio and visual signaling.

**moskee** • *Inf:* An expression of Asiatic origin meaning "okay" or "all right."

**mothball fleet** • *Inf:* Ships that are out of commission, yet maintained in good condition in case they might be needed at some future date.

**motor launch** • Large, sturdily built powerboat used for liberty parties and heavy freight.

**motor torpedo boat** • A large, high-speed boat armed with torpedoes and rapid-fire guns.

**motor tube** • That part of a rocket that contains the propellant charge.

**motor whaleboat** • A small, double-ended, engine-powered ship's boat, sometimes called the lifeboat if held ready for quick lowering.

**mount** • In amphibious warfare, to assemble troops, organize, and prepare for embarkation.

**mount (gun)** • *See:* gun mount

**mounting area** • *See:* area, mounting

**mousetrap** • Ahead-thrown antisubmarine warfare weapon used on small ships. Similar to Hedgehog, but smaller.

**mousing** • Small line strung across a hook to prevent a load from falling off or the shackle pin from being undone.

**movement report center (MRC)** • Both are part of the movement report system, which accounts for all ship and command movements. Sometimes called movement report office (MRO).

**Movement Report System** • System established to collect and make available to certain commands information on the status, location, and movement of flag commands, commissioned fleet units, and ships under operational control of the Navy.

**moving havens** • Restricted areas established to provide a measure of security to submarines and surface ships in transit through areas in which the existing attack restrictions would be inadequate to prevent attack by friendly forces who are on a high war footing with very liberal rules of engagement.

**moving surface ship haven** • A circular haven with a specified radius centered on the estimated position of a ship or the guide of a group of ships.

**Moving Target Indicator (MTI)** • A radar presentation that enables moving targets to be distinguished from stationary ones.

**mud drum** • *See:* water drum

**mushroom anchor** • A large anchor having the general shape of an upside down mush-

room, used on lightships and modern submarines. When housed, it fits snugly into its receptacle under the ship's bottom.

**musician (MU)** • Navy occupational rating that plays in official Navy bands and special groups such as jazz bands, dance bands, and small ensembles. MUs give concerts and provide music for military ceremonies, religious services, parades, receptions, and dances. Each MU is selected for this rating through audition, and must be able to play at least one brass, woodwind, or percussion instrument. Stringed instruments are generally not included.

**mustang** • *Inf:* An officer who has prior enlisted service.

**muster** • Roll call.

**muster out** • Discharge or release from active duty.

**mutiny** • Rebellion against constituted authority aboard ship; illegally taking command away from the commanding officer.

**muzzle bag** • Canvas cover fitted over the muzzle of a gun to shield the bore from water.

# N

**nacelle** • A streamlined structure, housing, or compartment on an aircraft; *i.e.*, the housing for an engine.

**nadir** • That point on the celestial sphere vertically below the observer, or 180° from the zenith. *See also:* zenith

**nan** • Past phonetic word for the letter N

replaced by "november."

**Nancy** • A system of visual communications using a special light visible only by means of special equipment.

**napalm** • A thickener consisting of a mixture of aluminum soaps used in jelling gasoline, as for incendiary bombs and flame throwers.

**Nasty** • *Inf:* Class name given to group of Norwegian-produced, high-speed patrol boats used in the Vietnam War. Derived from the building firm name: Naste.

**national agency check** • Limited review of an individual's background to determine his or her eligibility for a security clearance; usually restricted to a search of police and security records for derogatory material.

**national ensign** • The national flag flown by a warship from the gaff under way, from the flagstaff in port.

**National Geospatial-Intelligence Agency (NGA)** • Center for mapping and cartographic intelligence collection and dissemination. Formerly National Imagery and Mapping Agency (NIMA).

**National Ocean Survey (NOS)** • Formerly the Coast and Geodetic Survey; an office of the government that produces navigational charts and publications.

*Nautical Almanac* • Naval Observatory publication providing astronomical data needed for navigation.

**nautical mile** • Unit of measure frequently used to measure dstances at sea. It is determined by the length of 1 minute of arc of a great circle of the Earth. It's exact measurement is 6,076 feet compared to 5,280 feet of a statute mile, but is frequently used as 2,000 yards by the U.S. Navy.

**nautophone** • Fog horn.

**naval activity** • Unit of the naval establishment under an officer in command or in charge.

**naval advanced logistic support site** • An overseas location used as the primary transshipment point in the theater of operations for logistic support. A naval advanced logistic support site possesses full capabilities for storage, consolidation, and transfer of supplies for support of forward-deployed units (including replacement units) during major contingency and wartime periods. These sites, with port and airfield facilities in close proximity, are located within the theater of operations but not near the main battle areas, and must possess the throughput capacity required to accommodate incoming and outgoing intertheater airlift and sealift. When fully activated, the naval advanced logistic support site should consist of facilities and services provided by the host nation, augmented by support personnel located in the theater of operations, or both.

**naval air facility (NAF)** • Provides operating aid and maintenance facilities to meet special aviation requirements.

**naval air station (NAS)** • Provides operating, testing, overhaul training, and personnel facilities for naval aviation.

**naval alteration (NAVALT)** • Formalized change affecting the military characteristics of a ship.

**naval attaché** • A naval officer attached to an embassy abroad, whose primary responsibility is advising the ambassador on naval matters.

**naval auxiliary air station (NAAS)** • Facility similar to a naval air station, only less extensive. Requires logistic support from its parent air station.

**naval base** • A shore command that provides

administrative and logistic support to operating forces by integrating all naval shore
activities in the assigned area. May have tenant commands residing within its defined
area.

**naval beach group** • Permanently organized
naval command within an amphibious force,
composed of a commander, staff, beachmaster unit, boat unit, and an amphibious construction battalion.

**naval campaign** • An operation or a connected series of operations conducted essentially by naval forces for the purpose of gaining control of the sea.

**naval coastal warfare** • Coastal sea control,
harbor defense, and port security, executed
both in coastal areas outside the United
States in support of national policy and in
the United States as part of this Nation's
defense.

**naval coastal warfare area** • An assigned
geographic area of operations which includes
offshore waters, harbor approaches, harbors,
ports, waterfront facilities, and those internal waters and rivers which provide access to
port facilities.

**naval coastal warfare commander** • An
officer designated to conduct naval coastal
warfare missions within a designated naval
coastal geographic area.

**naval construction force** • The combined
construction units of the Navy, including
mobile construction battalions and amphibious construction battalions.

**naval control of shipping** • Control exercised by naval authorities over movement,
routing, reporting, convoy organization, and
tactical diversion of allied merchant shipping. It does not include the employment or
active protection of such shipping.

**naval district** • A geographically defined

area in which one naval officer, designated
commandant, is the direct representative of
the Secretary of the Navy and the Chief of
Naval Operations. The commandant has the
responsibility for local naval defense and
security, and for the coordination of naval
activities in the area. [Note: Once covering all
parts of the Unted States, as of this writing,
naval districts are no longer being used, with
the sole exception being Naval District One,
covering the Washington D.C. area.]

**naval establishment** • Unofficial term for
the entire Navy, consisting of operating
forces, the Navy Department, and the shore
establishment.

**naval expeditionary warfare** • Military
operations mounted from the sea, usually on
short notice, consisting of forward deployed,
or rapidly deployable, self-sustaining naval
forces tailored to achieve a clearly stated
objective.

**naval flight officer (NFO)** • A naval aviator
who, although not a pilot, performs duties in
an aircraft that are essential to mission
accomplishment. These include radar inter-
cepts, missile control, navigation, intelligence, etc.

**naval forward logistic site** • An overseas
location, with port and airfield facilities nearby, which provides logistic support to naval
forces within the theater of operations during
major contingency and wartime periods.

**naval gunfire spotting team** • The unit of a
shore fire control party that designates targets; controls commencement, cessation,
rate, and types of fire; and spots fire on the
target.

**Naval Institute** • *See:* United States Naval
Institute

**Naval Institute Press** • The book publishing
arm of the United States Naval Institute.

**naval landing party** • Part of a ship's complement organized for military operations ashore. Formerly called a landing force.

**naval mission** • Group of naval personnel who serve in an advisory capacity to assist a friendly foreign power in the administration of its navy.

**naval mobile environmental team** • A team of naval personnel organized, trained, and equipped to support maritime special operations by providing weather, oceanography, mapping, charting, and geodesy support.

**naval port control office** • An authority that coordinates logistic support and harbor services for ships under naval control.

**Naval Postgraduate School** • A school that provides postgraduate education to selected members of the armed forces in a number of disciplines. Originally located in Annapolis, Maryland, but currently located in Monterey, California.

**Naval Reserve** • Qualified naval personnel who are normally in civilian status, but who train to be available for active service in times of war or national crisis.

**Naval Reserve Officers Training Corps (NROTC)** • Program in which students at various colleges and universities take naval training and may be commissioned as officers and ordered to active duty upon graduation.

**naval shipyard** • An industrial activity charged with building, repairing, performing formalized alterations, overhauling, docking, converting, or outfitting of naval vessels.

**naval station** • Naval shore activity with fixed boundaries and a commanding officer; provides fleet or shore activity support. Generally smaller and less complex than a naval base.

**naval stores** • Any articles or commodities used by a naval ship or station, such as equipment; consumable supplies; clothing; petroleum, oils, and lubricants; medical supplies; and ammunition.

**naval support area** • A sea area assigned to those naval ships detailed to support an amphibious operation. *See also:* fire support area

**Naval Surface Weapons Center** • Originally Naval Ordnance Laboratory. Serves as the center for surface weapons development and testing.

**naval tactical data system (NTDS)** • A complex of data inputs, user consoles, converters, adapters, and radio terminals interconnected with high-speed computers. Combat data is collected, processed, and composed into a picture of the overall tactical situation that enables the force commander to make rapid, accurate evaluations and decisions.

**navigation** • The art and science of accurately determining one's position and conducting a ship or aircraft from one position to another. *See also:* celestial navigation; electronic navigation; dead reackoning; piloting

**navigational grid** • A series of straight lines, superimposed over a conformal projection and indicating grid north, used as an aid to navigation. The interval of the grid lines is generally a multiple of 60 or 100 nautical miles.

**navigational light** • A light with fixed characteristics, marked on charts and described fully in light lists, so that passing navigators can use it to fix their positions. Usually on a moored buoy or in some fixed position, as in a lighthouse. Among the typical characteristics are height above sea level, arc of visibility, color, period of repetition, etc. Different types are: alternating—showing color variations; fixed—a steady light; flashing—off more than it is on; occulting—on more than it is off; group flashing—flashing in groups of two or more flashes followed by a period of darkness.

**navigational range** • A pair of lights or day beacons situated on shore, the taller behind the shorter, to mark a line of definite bearing (usually a safe course to steer). When on the line, a navigator reports the range closed; when off the line, the range is open.

**navigation head** • A transshipment point on a waterway where loads are transferred between water carriers and land carriers. A navigation head is similar in function to a railhead or truckhead.

**navigation mode** • In a flight control system, a control mode in which the flight path of an aircraft is automatically maintained by signals from navigation equipment.

**navigation, pressure pattern** • The selection and control of a flight path or track for aircraft by considering the atmospheric pressure pattern in order to take advantage of the most favorable wind conditions.

**Navigation, Seamanship and Shiphandling Training Requirements Document (NSS TRD)** • Identifies the core competencies for SWOs assigned to Navy warships. It outlines a navigation, seamanship and shiphandling training continuum for Surface Warfare Officers, from newly reported ensigns all the way to commanding officers. The TRD is consistent with the specifications and requirements of the Merchant Marine "1995 Convention on Standards of Training, Certification and Watchkeeping for Seafarers." It also conforms to the U.S. Code of Federal Regulations, Chapter 46, which is a list of shipping regulations set by the Department of Homeland Security.

**navigator** • Officer who is head of the navigation department and responsible for the safe navigation of the ship. Can be dual-hat-

ted as the ship's executive officer or some other duty, or may be assigned as the only primary duty.

**navol** • Solution of hydrogen peroxide in water, used as a fuel in the MK 16 torpedo.

**Navy anchor** • Old-fashioned anchor. Anchor with a stock.

**Navy Campus** • An educational program that provides tuition and other assistance for naval personnel to take academic, vocational, or technical courses in their free time.

**Navy cargo handling and port group** • A battalion-sized cargo handling unit composed solely of active duty personnel.

**Navy cargo handling battalion** • A mobile logistic support unit capable of worldwide deployment in its entirety or in specialized detachments. It is organized, trained, and equipped to load and off-load Navy and Marine Corps cargo carried in maritime prepositioning ships and merchant container ships in all environments; also can operate an associated temporary ocean cargo terminal, load and offload Navy and Marine Corps cargo carried in military-controlled aircraft, and operate an associated expeditionary air cargo terminal.

**Navy cargo handling force** • The combined cargo handling units of the Navy, including primarily the Navy cargo handling and port group, the Naval Reserve cargo handling training battalion, and the Naval Reserve cargo handling battalion. These units are part of the operating forces and represent the Navy' capability for open ocean cargo handling.

**Navy College Program (NCP)** • The Navy College Program (NCP) provides opportunities to Sailors to earn college degrees by providing academic credit for Navy training work experience, and off-duty education The NCP mission is to enable Sailors to obtain a college degree while on active duty. While the NCP is primarily geared toward enlisted Sailors, some NCP components are also available to officers.

**Navy counselor (NC)** • Navy occupational rating that offers vocational guidance on an individual and group basis to Navy personnel both aboard ships and at shore facilities, and to civilian personnel considering enlistment in the Navy. NCs assess the interests, aptitudes, abilities, and personalities of individuals to help them make good career decisions.

**Navy Department** • The executive part of the Navy located in Washington, D.C. It differs from the Department of the Navy in that, by long usage, it refers only to the administrative offices at the seat of government.

**Navy Directives System** • Formal system used to preserve and disseminate information, orders, etc.; an "instruction" contains information of a permanent or long-term nature, while "notices" contain short-term information. Presently being changed to an electronic system—Navy Electronic Directives System.

**Navy Electronic Directives System** • *See:* Navy Directives System

**Navy Enlisted Classification (NEC) code** • A system for identifying and designating special skills and knowledge for enlisted personnel. Sailors are assigned both primary and secondary codes. Details are contained in the Manual of Navy Enlisted Classifications.

**Navy Exchange** • A store for naval personnel and their dependents that sells merchandise at a small profit for the benefit of the welfare and recreation fund.

**Navy Hymn** • Hymn also known as "Eternal Father" that is recognized as the hymn of the U.S. Navy.

**Navy junior** • The child of a Navy Sailor.

**Navy Junior Reserve Officer Training Corps (NJROTC)** • High school youth program sponsored by the Navy in which young people may participate in Navy-oriented activities. Uniforms, training equipment, etc., are supplied by the Navy, while the high school provides classrooms, etc. Instructors are retired naval personnel. While there is no follow-on service requirement, cadets (students) may be eligible for advanced rate upon entering the armed forces.

**Navy League of the United States** • A national organization that believes in and works for a strong Navy. A private organization, independent of the Navy, despite its strong ties. Because it is consdered a lobbying organization, active duty personnel may not belong.

**Navy-Marine Corps Intranet (NMCI)** • NMCI is a long-term initiative between the Department of the Navy (DoN) and the private sector to deliver a single integrated and coherent department-wide network for Navy and Marine Corps shore commands. NMCI provides comprehensive, end-to-end information services for data, video and voice communications for DoN military and civilian personnel and delivers global connectivity to make the Navy workforce more efficient, more productive, and better able to support the critical war fighting missions of the Navy and Marine Corps.

**Navy Navigation Satellite System (NAVSAT)** • Navigational system used before the development of GPS. Used the doppler shift from signals transmitted by a satellite to establish position.

**Navy Oceanographic and Meteorological Automatic Device (NOMAD)** • A platform moored at sea to monitor and report weather and oceanographic data automatically.

**Navy Relief Society** • The quasi-official

relief agency operated for the benefit of naval personnel and their dependents. Provides emergency grants and loans to naval personnel in need.

**Navy shower** • A water-saving evolution in which a Sailor attempts to get clean, while using as little water as possible.

**Navy Standard Fuel Oil (NSFO)** • Known in the naval service as black oil, this fuel was once the fleet standard. More refined than bunker crude, less refined than those used in more modern engines.

**Navy time** • Expressed in four digits, 0000–2400, based on a 24-hour day; 1430 ("fourteen-thirty") is 2:30 P.M., 0230 ("oh-two-thirty") is 2:30 A.M., etc.

**Navy Training Management and Planning System (NTMPS)** • The Navy's official repository for training information. NTMPS offers a number of standard manpower, personnel and training reports, as well as an option to develop customized reports, as needed. Subsets of the system are RESTMPS (Reserve Training Management and Planning System) and SURTMPS (Surface Training Management and Planning System.

**Navy Unit Commendation (NUC)** • An honor accorded a naval unit for distinguishing itself in combat or other operations; ranks between the higher Presidential Unit Citation and the lesser Meritorious Unit Commendation. The unit (ship squadron, etc.) is authorized to fly a flag representing the award, and all personnel attached to the unit at the time of the award are authorized to wear a corresponding ribbon on their uniforms for the remainder of their careers.

**Navy yard** • The Washington Navy Yard in Washington, D.C., and the campus of the U.S. Naval Academy are the only naval facilities referred to as yards. Washington is usually called "the Navy Yard" while USNA is just "the

Yard." The term naval shipyard is used to define a repair facility.

**NBC warfare** • Nuclear/Biological/Chemical warfare

**N-codes** • Large Navy staffs often use letter-number codes in prescribing and describing billets on the staff. While these codes can vary, a typical set up might be as follows:

N-1 Personnel
N-2 Intelligence
N-3 Operations
N-4 Logistics
N-5 Strategic Planning
N-6 Communications
N-7 Training
N-8 Requirements and Resources
Subordinate positions obtain their codes by adding digits; for example, N-37 might refer to the staff's antisubmarine officer, and his or her assistant might be N-371. These N-codes parallel those used in other services, where the Army and Marine Corps use G-1, G-2, etc., with similar meanings. Joint or unified staffs usually use J-1, J-2, etc., and Army staffs with a colonel or below as the senior officer use S-1, S-2, etc.

**NCPACE Program** • The Navy College Program for Afloat College Education is a part of the Navy College Program. Academic skills, undergraduate, and graduate courses are available at sea through NCPACE. College courses are provided by regionally accredited colleges and universities, giving Sailors educational opportunities while on sea duty assignments.

**neap range** • Average diurnal range of tide occurring during the first and fourth quarter phases of the moon.

**neap tides** • Those tides occurring near the times of first and last quarter lunar phase; characterized by decreased range in height.

**necking down** • A reduction in diameter, as in a bolt or stud, caused by wear from the vibration of another part.

**negat** • Short for "negative." Used in conjuction with naval signals (visual or radio) as a form of cancellation or saying 'no.' For example, the signal "Bravo Zulu" is naval code for "well done." "Negat bravo zulu" means "not well done" or "poorly done." The negat flag flown above a flaghoist previously flown means that the hoist has been cancelled; i.e., the action previously called for should not be carried out.

**negative** • In any naval message, means no, not granted, do not concur, not approved, etc.

**Neptune** • Mythical god of the sea. Name assigned to P-2 aircraft.

**nest** • Two or more ships moored together, side by side. Onboard boat stowage in which one boat is placed inside, or partially inside, another.

**net** • A group of connected radio stations. A steel mesh that protects ships and harbors from entrance by enemy torpedoes, submarines, and surface craft.

**net-laying ship** • A ship designed for laying and tending submarine or antitorpedo nets.

**nets and booms** • Underwater steel mesh nets and surface floating booms used for harbor defense against submarines, torpedoes, and small surface craft.

**netting** • Same as snaking.

**network-centric warfare** • Strategic concept that involves "flat" rather than vertical linkages among command components. Essentially means that communications and exchanges of data take place among most or all tactical elements without being restricted to flow up and down the chain of command.

Facilitates real-time or near real-time communications and battle space awareness.

**neutral buoyancy** • A submerged submarine has neutral buoyancy, obtained by careful adjustment of water in variable ballast or trim tanks, when her actual weight exactly equals her submerged displacement, so that with screw(s) stopped and planes on zero, her depth changes very slowly. Note that if the water is isothermal and is without differences in salinity, no object can remain indefinitely at the same depth. But if a density layer exists, a submarine can ride on it, with great care. *See also:* balancing; hovering

**neutralization fire** • Gunfire designed to immobilize enemy activity in a specific area.

**night order book** • Official ship's record in which the commanding officer writes his orders to the officers of the deck for the night's activities. The ship's engineer uses a similar book for the engineering OOW.

**night stick** • A short, wooden club carried by personnel on shore patrol duty.

**night vision** • The ability to see well at night. *See also:* dark adaptation

**nimbostratus** • A dark, low, shapeless cloud layer with a mean upper level below 6,500 feet; usually nearly uniform, the typical rain cloud.

**nip** • Sharp bend or turn in a line or wire. *See also:* freshen the nip

**nipples** • The ends of boiler tubes as they enter the tube sheets or headers. Short connectors for screw-thread piping.

**nitrogen gas** • Used for preventing and extinguishing fires in the aviation fuels system aboard ship.

**no bottom** • A leadsman's report indicating that the leadline did not touch bottom.

**no load** • A Sailor who does not pull his or her own weight.

**nomogram** • Any graphic product used to find solutions to complex calculations without having to perform the calculations.

**nonconsumable** • Items requisitioned on an as-needed basis; *i.e.*, specific repair parts and equipment.

**nonjudicial punishment** • Punishment by a commanding officer imposed without trial by court-martial. Specified and limited by the Uniform Code of Military Justice. *See also:* captain's mast; office hours

**nonmilitary vessel category** • Classifications assigned to nonmilitary vessels entering a controlled port in wartime. The four initial classifications are: clean, doubtful, hostile, and suspect.

**nonrated man/nonrated woman** • Enlisted person in the first three paygrades. Not a petty officer.

**nonskid** • An epoxy compound applied to deck surfaces to improve traction.

**nonsparking tools** • Tools made of a metal alloy that, when struck against other objects, will not cause spark of sufficient temperature to ignite fuel vapors.

**non-vortex** • An attempt by mechanical means to stop the swirling motion of a liquid.

**norman pins** • Steel pins located along the after bulwarks of a tug to limit the lateral movement of the towline.

**North Atlantic Current** • A continuation of the Gulf Stream after its juncture with the Labrador Current in the vicinity of the Grand Banks off New England. Movement is generally eastward in an irregular flow, with components that flow northeastward as well as southeastward.

**North Equatorial Current (Atlantic)** • The major westerly flow across the North Atlantic in the trade wind belt, pushed by the northeast trades and fed by southeast currents off the western coast of Africa, providing the source in the Caribbean Sea of the Gulf Stream System. A comparable current in the Pacific provides the source of the Japan Current. A North Equatorial Current also exists in the Indian Ocean.

**Norwegian steam** • *Inf:* Muscle power.

**noseconer** • *See:* coner

**NOTAL** • An acronym for "not all" that is often used as a word in its own right. Means something (a message, for instance) that is meant to be seen by only a select few.

**nothing to the right (left)** • Order given to a helmsman meaning that she or he should not allow the ship to come right (left) of the course because of some danger lying on that side of the course, such as a shoal.

**notice** • 1. A specially numbered announcement or one-time directive. Not permanent, as an instruction is. 2. Notice for getting under way; required material and personnel condition of readiness. *See also:* instruction

**Notices to Airmen (NOTAMS)** • Formalized periodic information concerning any facility or aid relating to air navigation.

**Notice to Mariners** • A publication or electronic communication giving latest changes to navigational charts and other aids to navigation.

**notional ship** • An imaginary, arbitrary ship used in naval logisitics planning.

**not under command** • Said of a ship when she is disabled and uncontrollable through some exceptional circumstance and is unable to maneuver as required by the Rules of the Road. During the day the ship shows two shapes and at night two red 32-point light one vertically above the other. These are called breakdown lights.

**november** • Phonetic word for the letter N.

**no wind position** • Last well-determined position of an aircraft advanced along the heading for the true speed, *i.e.*, assuming the aircraft had maintained constant heading and speed, and the wind had suddenly died. Application of known winds should give a fairly accurate position.

**nuclear yields** • Energy released in the detonation of a nuclear weapon, measured in terms of the kilotons or megatons of TNT required to produce the same energy release. Very low = less than 1 kiloton; Low = 1 kiloton–10 kilotons; Medium = over 10 kilotons–50 kilotons; High = over 50 kilotons–500 kilotons; Very high = over 500 kilotons.

**nugget** • A first-cruise, newly-trained naval aviator; neophyte.

**null** • A symbol in cryptography having no plain text significance. The least signal where intensity varies with orientation antenna; *e.g.*, a radio direction finder (RDF).

**number** • A ship's four-letter identification, flown either as a signal or used as a radio call. Although letters are used, they are referred to as her number; *i.e.*, she "makes her number" means she has hoisted the four-letter identification signal.

**number in grade** • Precedence number assigned to officers; used to determine seniority among officers of the same rank. The lower the number, the more senior the officer.

**1MC** • A ship's general announcing system used to pass the word throughout the ship.

**nun buoy** • Cone-shaped buoy used to mark channels; it is anchored on the right side of the channel, as seen from a ship entering the harbor from seaward. It is even-numbered

and painted red. *See also:* red right returning

**0-1, 2, 3, 4, 5, 6, 7, 8, 9, 10** • *See:* officer paygrades

**oakum** • A material made of old, tarred, hemp rope fiber. Used to caulk seams in wooden decks and boats.

**oarlock** • Device to hold oars when pulling a boat; also called rowlock. *See also:* thole pin

**oars** • Elongated staffs with flat paddles at the ends, used to pull a boat through the water. Command given to the crew of a pulling boat, directing them to stop rowing and stand by with oars in rowlocks, extended horizontally, ready for the next order.

**objective area** • *See:* area, objective

**obligor** • An enlisted Naval Reservist obligated to participate in the Selected Reserve. Derived from "obligate" and pronounced accordingly.

**oblique photograph** • *See:* photograph, oblique

**oboe** • Past phonetic word for the letter O; replaced with "oscar."

**occulting light** • A navigational aid in which the period of light is equal to, or longer than, the period of darkness. *See also:* flashing light

**occupational standards (OCCSTDS)** • Formerly "technical requirements." The formally established skills and knowledge expected of a specific rating. *See also:* military standards

**oceanography** • The exploration and scientific study of the ocean and its phenomena.

**Ocean Shipping Procedures** • A joint manual for the control of merchant shipping during wartime.

**O-club** • *Inf:* Short for officer's club.

**octant** • Navigational instrument used to take celestial sightings. Alternative form of the sextant, providing less of a measuring arc, or one-eighth of a circle, rather than one-sixth.

**office** • *Inf:* The cockpit of a large aircraft.

**office hours** • Marine Corps term for mast, as in captain's mast.

**Office of the Chief of Naval Operations (OPNAV)** • Overall title for the entire Pentagon staff that is under the control of the CNO. The CNO's own personal staff is only a small part of this.

**officer** • 1. Any commissioned or warrant officer of the armed forces. Officers outrank enlisted personnel and are generally selected on the basis of advanced education or experience. 2. The master or any of the mates of a merchant ship. *See also:* commissioned officer; petty officer

**officer's call** • A bugle call, or word passed, for officers to take their stations. Precedes general call for all hands.

**officer candidate** • Person under instruction at an officer candidate school, training to become an officer.

**officer of the deck (OOD)** • Any formally designated service member who, while on watch, is in charge of the ship as the commanding officer's official representative. He or she is responsible for the safe and smooth running of the vessel.

**officer of the watch (OOW)** • An officer on duty in the engineering spaces. Also called the engineering officer of the watch (EOOW).

**officer paygrades** • Standardized levels of military pay for officer personnel in the armed forces. Specific officer paygrades in the Navy correlate to ranks as follows: O-1 is ensign; O-2 is lieutenant (junior grade); O-3 is lieutenant; O-4 is lieutenant commander; O-5 is commander; O-6 is captain; O-7 is rear admiral lower half; O-8 is rear admiral upper half; O-9 is vice admiral; O-10 is admiral. *See also:* paygrade; enlisted paygrades

**officer service record** • Official record of the duties that an officer has performed. Includes qualifications attained, awards, commendations, records of punishment, censures, and periodic evaluation by seniors in the form of fitness reports.

**official visit** • A formal visit of courtesy requiring special honors and ceremonies.

**offshore** • 1. The region seaward of a specified depth, usually the 3- or 5-fathom isobath. 2. Some distance off the shore, as contrasted to inshore. *See also:* offshore wind; offshore breeze

**offshore breeze** • Light wind blowing from land to sea.

**offshore currents** • Nontidal currents outside the surf zone, independent of shoaling or river discharge influence.

**offshore dump** • *See:* floating dump

**offshore wind** • Wind blowing from land to sea.

**offshore winds** • Winds blowing seaward from the land.

**ogive** • The forward, curved section of a projectile, giving it a bullet-like shape.

**oil canning** • The snapping in and out of the hull plating of a ship in heavy seas, accompanied by a characteristic noise. Generally experienced only by small, lightly built ships.

**oiler (AO)** • A tanker specially configured to replenish combatant ships of all types under way at sea. Heavily outfitted with booms and hoses rigged and ready for underway replenishment.

**oil flat** • Oil barge. An oil-carrying yard craft.

**oil king** • Petty officer who receives, transfers, discharges, and tests fuel oil and maintains fuel oil records; also certified to test and treat boiler water and feedwater in a vessel propelled by steam.

**oilskins** • Originally, cotton clothing waterproofed by several coats of linseed oil. Now the term is applied to any wet-weather or waterproof clothing.

**old-fashioned anchor** • The traditional hook anchor. Fitted with a stock, the axis of which is at right angles to both the plane of the flukes and the axis of the shank of the anchor. When the ship tugs at her anchor, the chain drags the stock flat along the bottom, thus causing the flukes to stand upright with the maximum "bite" into the ground. The stockless anchor accomplishes the same thing by a type of hinge built into the flukes.

**old gentleman** • *Inf:* An admiral; corresponds to the term "old man" for the captain of a vessel.

**old man** • *Inf:* Any commanding officer. The corresponding expression for an admiral, though less used, is "old gentleman."

**ombudsman** • A person whose job it is to receive and act on complaints by naval personnel who do not receive satisfaction through normal channels.

**ombudsperson** • Person designated to serve as a direct link to the commanding officer on matters of importance to personnel (and their families) assigned to the command.

**Omega** • A highly accurate subsurface or surface, very low frequency, worldwide radio navigation system using phase differences for positioning. [Obsolete]

**omni-directional** • An antenna capable of sending or receiving radio waves in all directions.

**Omnidirection Range (ODR)** • A navigation system for aircraft based on radio beacons that provide true headings.

**on report** • *See:* report, to place on

**onshore** • Coming from the water toward, or onto, the shore; *e.g.,* onshore winds. On the land; as in onshore repair facility.

**onshore breeze** • A light wind blowing from sea to land.

**onshore winds** • Wind blowing from sea to land.

**on soundings** • Traditionally said of a ship that is near enough to land so that soundings with a deep-sea lead can be taken. Now considered to mean within the 100-fathom curve.

**on the bow** • Said of an object somewhere ahead on one bow or the other. Generally stated more specifically; *e.g.,* on the port bow. The expression "broad on the port bow" means that the object is 45° on the port bow, or the relative bearing is 315°.

**on the double** • Quickly; with speed; as "Man your stations on the double."

**on the line** • 1. Operational aircraft ready for use are said to be on the line. 2. Able to be reached by a communications circuit of some kind. 3. Engines or boilers in use; *e.g.,* boilers 2A and 2B are on the line.

**on the quarter** • Said of an object somewhere astern but not directly astern. Usually stated more specifically; *e.g.,* on the starboard quarter. Broad on the starboard quarter means that the object bears 135° relative.

**on the wind** • Close-hauled.

**open purchase** • Purchase of materials on the open market, instead of by requisition through government channels.

**open source intelligence (OSINT)** • Information of potential intelligence value that is available to the general public.

**open water** • Water with less than one-tenth ice coverage.

**operating forces** • Those forces that directly support military operations.

**operation** • A military action (or the performance of a mission) that may be strategic, operational, tactical, logistical, or training in nature.

**operational** • Capable of operating, as opposed to broken or in need of repair. Usable, as opposed to administrative. For example, a vessel or an aircraft squadron would be considered operational, whereas a training command or accounting office would be considered an administrative activity.

**operational control authority** • *See:* control, operational (OPCON)

**operational control (OPCON)** • Authority over the actual operational employment of a unit; to include such things as combat, deterrence, etc., as opposed to administrative control, which includes such things as logistical support, personnel matters, etc.

**operational immediate** • The second-highest precedence assigned to a naval message. *See also:* immediate; precedence

**operational readiness inspection** • An inspection conducted by a senior authority to determine if a subordinate activity is ready to conduct actual (vice training) operations.

**operational risk management** • A process of assessing potential risk in operations and training.

**operational speed** • *See:* speed, operational

**operations specialist (OS)** • Navy occupational rating that operates radar, navigation, and communications equipment in a ship's combat information center (CIC) or on the bridge. OSs detect and track ships, planes, and missiles. They operate and maintain IFF (identification friend or foe) systems, ECM (electronic countermeasures) equipment, and radiotelephones. OSs also work with search-and-rescue teams.

**opposite number** • Someone carrying out equivalent duties on another watch or ship.

**Ops** • Short for "operations."

**optimum ship routing** • Ship routing technique based on analysis of currents, weather, and wave conditions to reduce transit time and increase safety.

**order** • An order directs that a job be done, not how it should be done. An order differs from a command in that the former does not have to be carried out instantaneously, but the latter is generally executed directly upon receipt. *See also:* command

**orderly** • Messenger or personal attendant, usually for a senior officer.

**order of battle** • The identification, strength, command structure, and disposition of the personnel, units, and equipment of any military force.

**ordinary, in** • Status of a ship not in commission but maintained with a skeleton force. [Obsolete]

**ordinary moor** • Method of mooring with anchors in which the upstream anchor is dropped first.

**ordnance** • Collective term for guns, missiles, torpedoes, bombs, and related equipment.

**originator** • The command by whose authority a message is sent.

**Orion** • Name assigned to the P-3 aircraft; a 10-crew, four-engine turboprop, antisubmarine and maritime surveillance patrol aircraft developed from the commercial Lockheed Electra design. Originally designed as a land-based, long-range, antisubmarine warfare (ASW) patrol aircraft, the P-3C's mission has evolved in the late 1990s and early 21st century to include surveillance of the battlespace, either at sea or over land.

**orlop deck** • Lowest deck of ship with four or more decks. [Obsolete]

**Osborne shackle** • Used in underway replenishment at the end of the first messenger line. It carries a bight of the hose messenger for alongside fueling.

**Oscar** • Phonetic word for the letter O. The dummy used for man overboard drills.

**oscilloscope** • An instrument for producing a visual representation of oscillations or changes in an electric current.

**Osprey** • The V-22 Osprey is a joint service, multi-mission aircraft with vertical take-off and landing (VTOL) capability. It performs VTOL missions as effectively as a conventional helicopter while also having the long-range cruise abilities of a twin turboprop aircraft.

**otter** • A device used in minesweeping that keeps the sweep wire extended laterally.

**outboard** • 1. In the direction away from the center line of the ship. Opposite to inboard. For example, a Sailor standing closer to the lifelines on a ship is outboard of one standing closer to the superstructure. 2. When vessels are nested at a pier, those farther from the pier are outboard of those closer to the

pier. *See also:* inboard

**outchop** • To cross a boundary (chopline) out of an area requiring a change of operational control; for example, "USS *Oriole* will outchop from the Sixth Fleet on 26 October."

**outer bight line** • Line sometimes used in the close-in method of refueling. It extends from the receiving ship to the outboard saddle.

**outhaul** • Any line used to pull out something (move an object away), as when a boat boom is pulled into position perpendicular to the ship. Opposite to inhaul.

**outreach** • Horizontal distance from a mast or king post to the end of a boom.

**overboard** • Over the side.

**overfalls** • Turbulent water surface caused by strong currents flowing over shoals or by conflicting currents.

**overhand knot** • Simplest of all knots; made by passing one end of a line once around its standing part.

**overhaul** • 1. Repair, clean, inspect, adjust. 2. The final phase of firefighting, during which all of the fire is searched out and extinguished. 3. In shiphandling, to overtake. 4. To separate the blocks of a tackle. Opposite of "round in."

**overhead** • Nautical term for ceiling.

**overlay, chart** • *See:* chart overlay

**over leave** • *See:* unauthorized absence

**overseas cap** • Garrison cap or fore-and-aft cap. *Inf:* Pisscutter.

**overt** • In intelligence work, means open and above board. Opposite of covert.

**overtaking vessel** • In the nautical Rules of the Road, a vessel that overhauls another, approaching from more than two points abaft the beam.

**over the hill** • *Inf:* Deserting. To be an unauthorized absentee.

**oxidation** • The process of various elements and compounds combining with oxygen. The corrosion of metals is generally a form of oxidation. Rust on iron is one example.

**P-3** • *See:* Orion

**pack ice** • Offshore ice moving with the wind and current. May be close, open, or drift types; and in the form of fields, floes, or blocks.

**padding** • Words or phrases unrelated to the text of a message, inserted to confuse enemy codebreakers.

**pad eye** • A metal ring welded to a deck or bulkhead; used to connect tow lines, replenishment equipment, etc.

**padre** • *Inf:* Chaplain.

**paint** • To track or detect an object with radar.

**painter** • A line in the bow of a boat for securing to a mother ship. When used under way, the painter is rigged so that it causes the boat to swing out from the side of the ship, thus facilitating its launching.

**pallet** • A portable platform used in handling cargo on forklifts or slings. Palletized cargo is made up to fit the pallets.

**palm and needle** • Sailor's thimble made of leather (which fits over most of the palm) and a large needle; used for sewing heavy canvas or leather.

**pancake ice** • Newly formed ice, appearing as flat, round cakes, usually between 1 and 6 feet in diameter. *See also:* pan ice

**pan ice** • Pieces of generally flat ice varying in diameter from a few yards to several hundred yards, formed by the action of the wind and sea on field ice. *See also:* pancake ice

**panting** • 1. A series of pulsations caused by minor, recurrent explosions in the firebox of a ship's boiler. Usually caused by a shortage of air. 2. When the sides of a ship bulge in and out alternately, due to the changes of pressure caused by pitching.

**pantry** • Place where the officers' food is prepared for serving; may be a part of the wardroom, or the captain's or admiral's mess.

**papa** • Phonetic word for the letter P.

**parachute canopy** • Main supporting surface of a parachute.

**parade** • An area aboard ship where the divisions fall in for muster or inspection. Fair-weather parades are topside, foul-weather parades below. *See also:* all hands parade

**parallax** • The difference in the apparent direction or position of an object when viewed from different points.

**parallel** • *See:* meridian; parallel of latitude

**parallel of latitude** • A circle on the surface of the Earth parallel to the plane of the equator.

**parallel ruler** • A double, connected ruler used on charts to transfer courses and bearings to and from the compass rose. *See also:* protractor; drafting machine; compass rose

**pararaft** • A combination parachute and life raft used by naval aviators.

**paravane** • Torpedo-shaped device towed on either side of a minesweeper to deflect and cut adrift moored mines.

**parbuckle** • Method of raising or lowering a heavy object along an inclined or vertical surface. A bight of line is thrown around a secured fastening at the level to which the object is to be raised, or from which it is to be lowered. The two ends of the line are then passed under the object, brought all the way over, and led back toward the bight. The two ends are then hauled or slackened together to raise or lower the object, the object itself acting as a movable pulley. Parbuckling works best with cylindrical objects, such as a barrel or cask, but any solid object can be handled in this manner.

**parcel** • The act of wrapping a line or splice in strips of canvas or cotton to build up a symmetrical surface for serving. *See also:* serve; worm

**parking harness** • Device fitted over the controls of a parked aircraft to prevent them from being accidentally used.

**parrot** • *Inf:* Identification, Friend or Foe (IFF).

**part** • To break, as to part a line or hawser.

**particulate matter** • Refers to the solid particles of fuel contaminants, such as dirt, grit, or rust.

**party** • Group organized for a special task, such as repair party, working party, recreation party, etc.

**passageway** • Corridor or hall aboard ship.

**pass a line** • 1. Throw or project a line. 2. To carry a line around or to something.

**passdown (file)** • *See:* relief file

**pass down the line book (PDL Book)** • A notebook for a watchstation in which temporary information or instructions are recorded. It is used to make sure successive watches have all needed information.

**passing honors** • Passing honors are rendered by ships and boats when vessels, embarked officials, or embarked officers pass (or are passed) close aboard—600 yards for ships, 400 yards for boats. Such honors are exchanged between ships of the U.S. Navy, between ships of the Navy and the Coast Guard, and between U.S. and most foreign navy ships passing close aboard. "Attention" is sounded, and the hand salute is rendered by all persons in view on deck.

**passive acoustic torpedo** • Torpedo that homes in on sound generated by its target.

**passive sonar** • Sonar that is used to receive sounds generated by a target, as opposed to emanating its own sound that is bounced off the target when the sonar is in active mode.

**pass the word** • Broadcast of information using a general announcing system. To pass information from one individual to another.

**patching** • The plugging in or connecting of required radio equipment; *e.g.*, a specific antenna can be patched to a specific transmitter.

**patent anchor** • *See:* stockless anchor

**patent log** • Device for measuring a ship's speed through the water. *See also:* taffrail log

**patrol vessel** • Small man-of-war used for general escort and patrol duties.

**paulin** • Short for tarpaulin.

**pay** • 1. Monthly salary. 2. To fill the seams of a wooden vessel with pitch or some other substance to prevent leakage. 3. To "pay out" something, like a line, is to feed it outward; to ease it outward or slacken it.

**paygrade** • Level of military pay, from E-1 (recruit) to E-9 (master chief petty officer); from W-1 to W-5 (warrant officer); and from O-1 (ensign) to O-10 (admiral). Paygrades are the same for all armed services though the accompanying ranks will differ. *See also:*

enlisted paygrades; officer paygrades

**paymaster** • General term for any disbursing officer.

**pay off** • To turn the bow away from the wind. Not used as a command, except in the permissive sense: "Let her pay off as she goes."

**pay out** • To slack off or ease out a line.

**pea coat** • The heavy topcoat worn by seafarers in cold weather. Cut short, well above the knees. The coat was originally made of material called pilot cloth, so it is probable that the name was successively pilot cloth coat, pilot coat, P-coat, and finally pea coat. Also called reefer, particularly when worn by officers.

**peak** • Topmost end of the gaff; the ensign is flown from this point while the ship is under way.

**peak tank** • Tank low in the bow or stern (more often the former) of a ship; sometimes designed for carrying potable water. So-called because one end of the tank is at the very bow or stern and therefore comes to a peak.

**peen** • To change the shape of a metal part by striking with a hammer.

**pelican hook** • A quick-release device that is released by pulling a toggle key or pin, or knocking off a bail shackle. The hook has a shape resembling a pelican's beak.

**pelorus** • A gyrocompass repeater used to take bearings.

**pendant** • Length of line or wire, often fitted with an eye or block at one or both ends. One end usually made fast to a mast, yard, spar, etc.

**Penguin** • The AGM-119B Penguin is a helicopter-launched antiship missile developed for use on LAMPS III helicopters and by NATO allies. The Penguin missile is a short-to-medium range inertially guided missile with infrared (IR) terminal homing.

**pennant** • A flag that is longer in the fly than in the hoist, usually tapered to a point. Some pennants terminate in a swallow-tail (two points). Examples are commission and broad command pennants.

**per diem** • Additional money to cover the daily expenses of a person in a travel status or on temporary additional duty.

**perigee** • The point at which a missile trajectory, or a satellite orbit, is nearer the center of the gravitational field of the controlling body or bodies. *See also:* apogee

**period of roll** • Time it takes for a ship to roll from one extremity to the other side and back again. Can be used to determine metacentric height, which is a measure of initial stability.

**peripheral vertical launch system (PVLS)** • A shipboard missile launching system designed to contain the damage sustained by enemy hits by isolating a ship's interior from blast and fragmentation effects. It provides a very high probability of missile availability after an enemy strike and reduces single hit ship losses. It also maximizes crew survivability and provides greater flexibility in ship design.

**periscope** • An optical device of mirrors and prisms used to project one's vision over an obstacle. Most usually a submarine periscope, which allows one to see above the water's surface when the submarine is submerged.

**periscope feather** • The spray formed by the periscope of a submerged submarine moving through the water at moderate to high speed. Can be a problem in combat conditions because the feather is more easily spotted than the periscope itself.

**personnel diary** • A daily record, by name, of all personnel assigned to an activity; recording arrivals, departures, etc.

**personnelman (PN)** • Navy occupational rating responsible for providing enlisted personnel with information and counseling about Navy jobs, opportunities for general education and training, promotion requirements, and rights and benefits. In hardship situations, they also assist enlisted persons' families with legal aid or reassignments. PNs keep records up to date, prepare reports, type letters, and maintain files.

**personnel qualification system** • A formal qualification system in theory, systems, and watch qualifications.

**per standard compass (psc)** • Phrase used in describing a course based upon the standard (magnetic) compass; *e.g.*, steering 090° psc. Today courses are given pgc (per gyro compass) whenever possible. *See also:* standard compass

**peter** • Past phonetic word for the letter P; replaced with papa.

**petty officer** • Paygrades E-4 through E-9. Noncommissioned officer in the grades of master chief, senior chief, chief; first, second, and third class.

**petty officer of the watch** • Senior enlisted assistant to the officer of the deck.

**Phalanx** • A fast-reaction, rapid-fire, 20-millimeter gun system originally designed for close-in missile defense, but updated versions are also capable of engaging littoral threat targets such as high-speed surface craft, small terrorist aircraft, helicopters, and surface mines. Fires special rounds in high volume at a high rate of speed to provide ships with a last-chance defense against threats that have penetrated other fleet defenses. Phalanx automatically detects, tracks, and engages targets using an advanced search and track radar system integrated with a stabilized, forward-looking infra-red (FLIR) detector.

**pharmacist's mate** • *See:* hospital corpsman (HM)

**Phoenix** • Name given to the AIM-54, the Navy's only long-range, air-to-air missile. A highly sophisticated, radar-guided missile that is fired only by the F-14 Tomcat fighter aircraft.

**phonetic alphabet** • A system of words that represents each letter of the alphabet; *e.g.*, alfa, bravo, charlie translates to A, B, C.

**photographer's mate (PH)** • Navy occupational rating that photographs actual and simulated battle operations, as well as documentary and newsworthy events. PHs expose and process light-sensitive negatives and positives; maintain cameras, related equipment, photo files, and records; and perform other photographic services.

**photograph, oblique** • Any photograph taken from an aircraft, except one from directly overhead. May be low (angle between camera axis and horizontal is less than 45°), high (angle greater than 45°), or flat (horizontal).

**pic** • In plaited line, the distance between adjacent crowns.

**picket** • Ship or aircraft stationed away from a formation or in a geographic location for a specific purpose, such as early warning.

**picket boat** • Armed boat that performs sentry, security, and patrol duty.

**picture element (PIXEL)** • A small, individual piece of an overall image.

**pier** • Structure for mooring vessels, which is built out into the water so that ships can come alongside. The seaward end (as opposed to the land end) is the head of the pier. *See also:* dock; wharf

**pier head** • Seaward end of a pier.

**pier head jump** • An immediate departure from a ship as it arrives in port, or a last-minute embarkation as the ship departs; viewed with a mixture of disdain, amusement, and admiration.

**pigboat** • *Inf:* An old-type submarine.

**pigstick** • Small spar at the top of the mainmast from which the commission pennant is flown.

**piling** • Wooden, concrete, or metal poles driven into the river or sea bottom for support or protection of piers or wharves.

**pilot** • 1. An expert on local harbor and channel conditions who advises the commanding officer in moving a ship in or out of port. 2. One who operates an airplane. 3. A book of sailing directions.

**pilot charts** • Charts showing winds, currents, and weather conditions to be expected.

**pilot cloth** • A coarse, heavy, twilled woollen material with a thick nap; used especially for seamen's blue overcoats. *See also:* pea coat

**pilothouse** • A compartment on the bridge centerline housing the main steering controls. In many modern ships, the bridge and pilothouse are virtually the same, whereas older ships frequently had a separate pilothouse and bridge. Also called the wheelhouse.

**piloting** • Navigation involving frequent or continuous determination of position by referring to available geographic points; unlike other forms of navigation, such as dead reckoning, celestial, or electronic, which rely on means other than geographic points to determine position.

**pilot rudder** • A small additional rudder forward of the propeller in a landing craft. Also called a maneuvering rudder.

**Pilot Rules** • A system of collision prevention rules once used in certain waters within the United States; replaced by an overhaul of the Inland Rules. *See also:* International Rules of the Road; Inland Rules of the Road

**ping** • Acoustic pulse signal of an echoranging indicator.

**pinger** • *Inf:* Active sonar. *Inf:* Any acoustic noise maker, such as a submarine distress pinger.

**ping jockey** • *Inf:* Sonarman.

**pinkie** • A landing occurring at first or last light.

**pintle** • Fitting on a rudder that secures it to the hull of a ship by fitting into a gudgeon. The pintles form an axis of rotation for the rudder as it is able to move freely about the pintles.

**pip** • Visual indication of a target on an electronic indicator screen. Also called a blip.

**pipe** • The act of sounding a particular call on the boatswain's pipe.

**pipe down** • An order to be silent or reduce noise, when used alone. In combination with other instructions, it means to use a boatswain's call to signal the commencement of a shipboard activity; for example, pipe down air bedding (bring matresses up on deck), or pipe down chow for the crew, or pipe down sweepers, etc.

**pipe the side** • A ceremony conducted at the brow of a ship in which sideboys are paraded and the boatswain's pipe is blown. *See also:* side honors

**pipe to** • Pass the word and pipe the appropriate call to an evolution, such as pipe to sweepers.

**piping** • 1. Signals sent by means of the boatswain's pipe. Once actual, now ceremonial in function. Boatswains have been in charge of the deck force since the days of sail. Setting sails, heaving lines, and hoisting anchors required a coordinated team effort and boatswains used whistle signals to order the coordinated actions. When visitors were hoisted aboard or over the side, the pipe was used to order "Hoist Away" or "Avast heaving." In time, piping became a naval honor on shore as well as at sea. 2. The thin striping along the cuffs and bib of a Navy jumper.

**pisscutter** • *See:* overseas cap

**piston hank** • *See:* hank

**pitch** • 1. The vertical rise and fall of a ship's bow and stern in a seaway. 2. The angle or bend of a propeller's blades, used to impart motion; *i.e.*, a propeller with zero pitch will not cause a vessel to move through the water. Technically, the axial advance during one revolution of the propeller.

**pit log** • Short for pitometer log.

**pitometer log** • Device for indicating the speed of a ship, and distance run, by measuring the water pressure on a pitot tube projected outside the ship's hull. *See also:* pitot tube

**pitot tube** • Sensing element used to measure static and dynamic pressure for ship or aircraft speed indicators. *See also:* pitometer log

**pit sword** • *See:* rodmeter

**pitting** • Small, deep cavities with sharp edges. May be caused in metal surfaces by high impacts or by oxidation.

**pivot point** • The point about which a ship pivots when turning; on a warship, usually in the vicinity of the bridge.

**pivot ship** • The wing ship in a line of vessels around which a wheeling maneuver is being made.

**plaindress** • A communications term describing a message that contains its address in the heading.

**plain whipping** • A whipping made without using a palm and needle. *See also:* whipping

**plane** • Said of a seaplane or boat when it gains enough speed to ride with most of the forward part of its hull out of the water.

**plane captain** • Person responsible for the material condition of a specifically assigned aircraft.

**plane director** • The person who uses hand signals to direct the movements of taxiing aircraft on an aircraft carrier or ashore.

**plane guard** • A fast ship or helicopter that is positioned near an aircraft carrier during flight operations such that it can quickly recover personnel who have gone into the water as a result of an accident.

**plane handler** • Person who handles aircraft on a carrier fight deck. *Inf:* Plane pusher.

**plane pusher** • *See:* plane handler

**planesman** • Operator responsible for controlling the bow and stern planes of a submarine.

**plank owner** • Traditional term for a person who was assigned to a ship when she was newly commissioned. Custom dictates that plank owners are entitled to a piece of the ship—in the old days, a piece of planking—when the ship is placed out of commission and destroyed.

**plankton** • Small forms of sea life that exist free-floating in the world's oceans; despite their diminutive size, a major source of food in the biological food chain and a vital part of the oceans ecosystem.

**planned position indicator (PPI)** • A radar display in which range is indicated by the distance of a bright spot or "pip" from the center of the screen, and the bearing is indicated by the radial angle of the spot. *See also:* A-scope; B-scope

**planning and overhaul yard** • A shipyard designated as responsible for the design work and maintenance for ships specifically assigned to it. Once called the "home yard."

**plan of the day** • Schedule of the ship's activities for the day, including work, training, meals, recreation, etc. Also called morning orders.

**platform deck** • Partial deck of a ship that does not extend the entire length of the ship.

**platform endorsement** • Part of the Navigation, Seamanship, and Shiphandling Training Requirements Document (NSS TRD) for a specific ship type that formalizes the re-qualification of an Officer of the Deck (OOD) when he or she reports to a new ship. Because different ship types (platforms) behave differently under way, an officer's qualification as OOD on one ship does not make him or her automatically qualified on another. Once earned, the platform endorsement specifies that the OOD is now qualified on the new ship as well as the old.

**plebe** • A first-year midshipman at the U.S. Naval Academy.

**Plimsoll mark** • Mark on a ship's side indicating, by international agreement, how deeply she may be loaded under various expected sea conditions, depending on season and geographical area.

**plot** • 1. A tactical diagram of ship movement (surface plot), aircraft movement (air plot), or submarine movement (underwater plot). 2. Name sometimes given to a tactical and oper-

ational control center aboard ship: air plot, flag plot, etc. 3. To record the courses of ships and aircraft, to diagram movements.

**plotting sheet** • A blank chart, usually on a Mercator projection, showing only the graticule and a compass rose so the plotting sheet can be adapted for specific uses. Often used in celestial navigation position plots.

**plumb** • 1. To measure depth by lowering a weighted line into the fluid being measured. 2. To rig a tackle directly over a hatch.

**pneumatic** • That which is operated or moved by the use of pressurized air.

**Pneumercator** • An instrument for measuring the level and thus the volume of liquid in tanks.

**pod** • 1. Projecting, streamlined container usually located under the wing or fuselage of an aircraft. 2. Group of whales.

**pogey bait** • *Inf:* Candy; soda fountain items.

**point** • 1. A narrow projection of land jutting out into a body of water. 2. A division on older compasses for defining specific directions. Modern compasses use degrees (360 for the complete circle), but older compasses used 32 points, each labeled with a specific name (such as "north", "north by east," "south by southeast," etc. 3. Reference is to a sailing ship's ability to point close to the wind. None can head directly upwind, but some can do better than others. Fore-and-aft-rigged ships or boats can always point higher than square-riggers, but the huge sails that large ships required made the fore-and-aft rig impracticable for them. 4. To move a gun vertically (elevate) as part of the aiming process. *See also:* rain

**point detonating fuze** • An explosives fuze that detonates when the front end of the projectile makes contact with the target.

**pointer** • Person who controls a gun in elevation (range). A team of two, called a pointer and a trainer, aim a manually-controlled shipboard gun by moving it vertically and horizontally respectively. *See also:* trainer

**point oars** • A pulling boat order given when the boat is aground; oarsmen thrust their blades forward and downward at an angle of about 30°. At the command "shove off," the crew pushes together, lifting the boat and forcing it back off the shoal.

**point of intended movement (PIM)** • The planned navigational progress of a ship. This is used as a reference point to ensure that a vessel makes the intended overall progress, even when zig-zag plans, training exercises, emergencies, etc., cause the ship to actually deviate from the track originally laid down. By constant awareness of this theoretical PIM and by making the necessary adjustments to regain this reference whenever feasible, a commanding officer is able to make scheduled rendezvous and arrivals, despite interim distractions or deviations.

**point of tow** • Device on the forefoot of a ship to which paravane wires may be attached. *See also:* shoe

**polar distance** • Angular distance from a celestial pole.

**Polaris** • Missile with model designation UGM-27 (series). Submarine launched, two-stage ballistic missile powered by solid-fuel rocket motors and guided by a self-contained guidance system. It can be launched from surfaced or submerged platforms. No longer in service, replaced by Poseidon and Trident.

**polar lights** • The Aurora Australis and Aurora Borealis of the Southern and Northern Hemispheres, respectively. These celestial light displays, usually associated with sunspot activity or magnetic storms, are seen at night only.

**police** • To inspect and/or clean up.

**pollywog** • *Inf:* Traditional term for a Sailor who has not yet crossed the equator by ship. After crossing and participating in an initiation ceremony, pollywogs become shellbacks.

**pontoon** • 1. Steel boxes 5 by 5 feet, many of which are bolted together to form causeways, barges, etc. 2. Loosely, any watertight structure (box, barrel, etc.) used to float something.

**pontoon barge** • A barge made of pontoons bolted together and propelled by an engine driving an outboard propeller. *See also:* warping tug

**pontoon causeway** • A floating, movable pier made up of pontoons bolted together. Used in amphibious assaults to expedite unloading.

**poop deck** • A partial deck, aft, above the main deck, in wooden men-of-war. *See also:* platform deck; spar deck

**pooped** • Said of a vessel when a following sea breaks over the stern.

**poopy bag** • *Inf:* A lighter-than-air craft; blimp.

**pork chop** • *Inf:* The insignia of the supply corps. Supply officers are sometimes referred to as pork chops or porkchoppers.

**porpoise** • To break the surface of the sea and immediately go under again, as the porpoise does.

**porpoising** • *See:* broach; porpoise

**port** • 1. Seagoing term for left side of a vessel or aircraft, when facing forward. 2. Directional term for left, as opposed to starboard, which generally means right. Although generally assumed to mean right, be aware that there is an orientation factor; in other words, the port bridgewing is on an observer's right if the observer is facing aft. 3. A coastal city accessible to the sea by ships and/or boats. 4. Short for porthole. Roughly equivalent to a window on a ship or boat. *See also:* starboard; port and starboard

**port and starboard** • Port and starboard are shipboard terms for left and right, respectively. It should be noted that these are fixed terms; that is, port is left and starboard is right when the observer is facing forward only. If he or she turns around, the port side of the ship is now on his or her right and vice versa. This means that the port bridge wing is on the left side of the ship when facing forward or viewing the ship from above, and remains the port bridge wing no matter how it is viewed. The terms come from the fact that in old England, the starboard was the steering paddle or rudder, and ships were always steered from the right side on the back of the vessel. Larboard referred to the left side, the side on which the ship was loaded. So how did larboard become port? Shouted over the noise of the wind and the waves, larboard and starboard sounded too much alike. The word port means the opening in the "left" side of the ship, from which cargo was unloaded when in port. Sailors eventually started using the term to refer to that side of the ship. Use of the term "port" was officially adopted by the U.S. Navy by General Order, 18 February 1846.

**port and starboard watch** • A two-section watch.

**portfolio, chart** • A group of charts for a specific geographical area.

**porthole** • Round opening in the side of a ship. Roughly equivalent to a window. The British term is sidelight.

**Poseidon** • Submarine-fired missile with model designation UGM-73A. Successor to Polaris. Poseidon is outfitted with multiple warheads, each of which can be separately targeted. Their range is about 2,900 nautical miles. *See also:* Polaris; Trident

**position** • The location of an object relative to a reference point, or in accordance with recognized coordinates, such as longitude and latitude.

**position angle** • The number of degrees an object seen in the sky is above the horizon. Used by lookouts to describe where an aircraft is in terms of altitude. For example, an aircraft directly overhead would be reported as position angle 90, whereas one close to the horizon would be position angle ten.

**position buoy** • A towing spar used to mark the location of an object towing astern, such as the end of a magnetic sweep cable.

**postal clerk (PC)** • Navy occupational rating that operates a large postal system. PCs collect postage-due mail, prepare customs declarations, collect outgoing mail, cancel stamps, and send the mail on its way. They also perform a variety of recordkeeping and reporting duties, including maintenance of an up-to-date directory service and locator file.

**power of attorney** • An instrument authorizing another to act as one's agent or attorney.

**power standing-wave ratio (PSWR)** • The ratio of the square of the maximum and minimum voltages of a transmission line.

**practical factors** • Items an individual must be able to do, in addition to what he or she must know, to earn an advancement in rating.

**pram** • *See:* scow

**pratique** • Permission granted in a foreign port for a ship to interact with the shore after a certification that she is free of contagious disease. Usually granted by radio.

**pre-action calibration** • Test firing of guns

prior to surface action or exercises. Used to determine arbitrary correction to hit.

**precedence** • The relative order in which messages should be handled. "Flash" messages have the highest precedence (are the most urgent), followed by "Operational Immediate" (often referred to as simply "Immediate)," then "Priority," and the least urgent (lowest precedence) messages are "Routine."

**pre-dreadnought** • A battleship built or designed prior to HMS *Dreadnought*, the first all-big-gun battleship. *See also:* dreadnought

**prep** • One of the many signal flags in a standard Navy flag bag; used, among other things, to presage morning and evening colors by being flown five minutes before the execution of colors.

**Presidential Unit Citation (PUC)** • An honor accorded a naval unit for distinguishing itself in combat or other operations. Of higher degree than the Navy Unit Commendation. The unit (ship, squadron, etc.) is authorized to fly a flag representing the award, and all personnel attached to the unit at the time of the award are authorized to wear a corresponding ribbon on their uniforms for the remainder of their careers.

**pressure** • Force per unit area. The pressure exerted by the weight of Earth's atmosphere is called atmospheric or, if indicated by a barometer, barometric pressure.

**pressure hull** • The cylindrical, pressure-resistant core of a submarine that encloses its operating spaces.

**pressure pattern navigation** • *See:* navigation, pressure pattern

**pressurize** • To compress air or hydraulic fluid to a pressure greater than normal.

**prevailing** • The most frequent or most common, as in prevailing winds.

**preventer** • Any line used for additional safety or security, or to keep something from falling or running free.

**Pri-Fly** • Primary Flight Control station on an aircraft carrier; center for coordinating flight operations.

**primary loop** • The heat transfer medium of naval reactors in highly pressurized water, driven constantly and at high speed between reactor and steam generators by the main coolant pumps in a completely closed loop. This is the primary loop. In the steam generators, heat is transferred to the so-called secondary loop, where steam is generated under less pressure to operate the machinery. *See also:* reactor

**prime meridian** • Meridian from which longitude is measured. Zero degrees longitude. The meridian of the original site of the Royal Observatory at Greenwich, England.

**priming** • The carryover of water with the steam from a boiler. A good watertender will not permit this. *See also:* priming of the tides

**priming of the tides** • This occurs when the tides caused by the sun come shortly before those caused by the moon, resulting in earlier tides than usual. *See also:* lagging of the tides

**prior enlistment or period of service** • Service in any component of the armed forces that culminated in the issuance of a discharge certificate.

**priority** • The second highest precedence assigned to naval messages. *See also:* precedence

**prisoner at large (PAL)** • Person under arrest whose restraint to certain specified limits is morally, rather than physically, enforced.

**privileged vessel** • Obsolete term roughly

equivalent to "stand on vessel" in the modern Rules of the Road. The ship having the right of way and required to hold course and speed. The other ship, the burdened vessel, was required to take avoiding action. *See also:* burdened vessel

**prize** • Vessel captured during wartime and retained for legal prize proceedings, which determine the shares of the value of the vessel for its captors.

**prize master** • Officer placed in command of a captured vessel, with a prize crew, to bring the vessel into port.

**prize money** • Money once paid to members of a crew that had captured an enemy vessel; amount was determined by the value of the vessel and by the crewmember's rank.

***Proceedings*** • Periodical published by the U.S. Naval Institute since 1872 that provides an open forum for the discussion of topics important to national defense.

**proceed time** • Time allowed between day of detachment and the date of reporting to a new duty station, not considering travel time and leave, if any.

**procurement** • The process of obtaining materials and services to support the operation of an activity.

**program torpedo** • Torpedo designed to follow a preplanned course.

**projectile** • The missile fired by a gun; the bullet. Some major types are armor-piercing, fragmenting, and special-purpose.

**projectile flat** • Stowage space for projectiles in a magazine. Also called shell room.

**projectile hoist** • Elevator mechanism for lifting projectiles from their stowage space to guns.

**prolonged blast** • A blast on the ship's whistle of 4 to 6 seconds duration. *See also:* blast; short blast

**promotion board** • *See:* selection board

**propagation** • A transmission of electromagnetic energy.

**propeller guard** • Protective framework along the side of a ship that protects that part of the propeller that projects out from the side of the ship.

**property pass** • Written permission for an enlisted person to take property out of a ship or station.

**proportioner** • A firefighting device that produces foam by mixing a chemical and water.

**protective deck** • An armored deck. In ships fitted with more than one armored deck, the protective deck is the more heavily armored of the two; the other being the splinter deck, fitted above the protective deck.

**protractor** • A transparent plastic semicircle marked in degrees of arc with an attached swinging arm or rule for inscribing bearing and course lines, or transferring them from the compass rose on a chart. Easier to use then the parallel ruler and has the advantage of being easily carried. A three-arm protractor has three swinging arms for finding position with sextant angles between navigational aides, tangents of land, etc., if three or more are in sight.

**prow** • That part of the bow that is above the waterline. Acceptable naval usage, but not favored.

**Prowler** • The EA-6B Prowler provides an umbrella of protection for strike aircraft, ground troops, and ships by jamming enemy radar, electronic data links, and communications. The Prowler is a long-range, all-weather aircraft with advanced electronic countermeasures capability. Manufactured by the Northrop Grumman Systems Corporation, it is a twin-engine, mid-wing configured aircraft that has a side by-side cockpit arrangement. The EA-6B war fighting systems include the ALQ-99 onboard receiver, the ALQ-99 pod-mounted jamming system, the USQ-113 communications jamming system, and the HARM missile. Two significant upgrades now in development are the Improved Capability (ICAP III) and the Multifunctional Information Distribution System (MIDS). The ICAP III, approved for Low Rate Initial Production in June 2003, upgrades the onboard receiving system, providing an accurate threat emitter geo-locator and a selective reactive jamming capability against modern threat systems. The ICAP III upgrade includes new cockpit displays, improved systems connectivity, and improved system reliability. The MIDS upgrade provides the ability to receive and utilize data via the Link 16 tactical data link.

**proword** • A word or phrase in condensed form representing certain frequently used orders and instructions in voice radio communications.

**proximity fuze** • A fuze activated by a self-contained, miniature radar-type device when in close vicinity of a target. Also called variable time fuze. Invented during World War II.

**psychological operations** • Planned psychological activities in peace and war directed at enemy, friendly, and neutral audiences in order to influence attitudes and behavior affecting the achievement of political and military objectives. They include strategic psychological activities, consolidation psychological operations, and battlefield psychological activities.

**psychrometer** • Any device used to measure dry-bulb temperature and wet-bulb temperature.

**public reprimand** • A rare but legal form of punishment given an officer pursuant to the sentence of a general court-martial.

**public works** • Buildings, grounds, utilities, other structures, and land improvements at a naval shore activity.

**pudding** • Chafing gear used to protect, for example, a towline or a spar.

**pull** • Proper nautical term for row. A sailor pulls on an oar.

**pulling boat** • Any boat designed to be propelled by oars. Generally used in reference to a fairly large boat with several oarsmen. The coxswain steers and is in command.

**pulse amplitude modulation (PAM)** • In radar, pulse modulation in which the amplitude of the pulses is varied by the modulating signal.

**pulse code modulation (PCM)** • In radar, a modulation system in which the standard values of a wave are indicated by a series of coded pulses.

**pulse duration modulation (PDM)** • In radar, pulse modulation in which the time duration of the pulses is changed by the modulating signal.

**pulse duration (PD)** • In radar the period of time during which a pulse is present.

**pulse-forming network (PFN)** • In radar, a network that alternately stores and releases energy in an approximately rectangular wave.

**pulse frequency modulation (PFM)** • In radar, pulse modulation in which the modulating voltage varies the repetition rate of a pulse train.

**pulse-jet** • Type of jet engine that uses a flapper valve to alternately compress and eject air. Also called "aerojet."

**pulse length** • The duration, in microseconds, of a radar transmission.

**pulse modulation (PM)** • In radar, a form of modulation in which one of the characteristics of a pulse train is varied.

**pulse oscillator** • A sine-wave oscillator that is turned on and off at specific times. Also known as a ringing oscillator.

**pulse position modulation (PPM)** • In radar, pulse modulation in which the position of the pulses is varied by the modulating voltage.

**pulse repetition frequency (PRF)** • In radar, the rate, in pulses per second at which the pulses occur. Also known as pulse repetition rate (PRR). *See also:* pulse repetition frequency; pulse repetition time

**pulse-repetition rate** • The rate at which recurrent pulses are transmitted, usually expressed in pulses per second.

**pulse repetition rate (PRR)** • *See:* pulse repetition frequency

**pulse repetition time (PRT)** • In radar, the interval between the start of one pulse and the start of the next; the reciprocal of pulse repetition frequency (or pulse repetition rate).

**pulse time modulation** • In radar, the pulse modulation that varies one of the time characteristics of a pulse train, such as pulse duration modulation (PDM).

**pulse width modulation (PWM)** • In radar, pulse modulation in which the duration of the pulses is varied by the modulating voltage.

**pulse width (PW)** • In radar, the duration of time between the leading and trailing edges of a pulse. *See also:* pulse repetition time

**punch out** • Same as bail out; to eject from an aircraft. Refers to the operation of an ejection seat. *Inf:* To leave.

**punt** • Rectangular shallow boat used in painting the ship's side at and above the waterline.

**purchase** • General term for any mechanical arrangement of blocks and line for multiplying force. Blocks can be single, double, or triple, according to how many sheaves they have. After the line is rove around the sheaves and the standing part is made fast to one of the blocks, the entire assemblage is known as a tackle. The tackle is designated according to the number of sheaves in the blocks or the purpose of the tackle. Some of the latter can be quite exotic in derivation, such as gun tackle, luff tackle, and the like. It is useful today to classify the tackle according to its mechanical advantage. Thus, a two-fold purchase, made of two double blocks and four falls (lines between the blocks), has a four-to-one multiplication. A three-fold purchase (two treble blocks, six falls), has a six-to-one advantage. This is the biggest purchase commonly used on board ship. A luff tackle, with one single and one double block, has a three-to-one advantage because of its three falls. A double luff (a triple and a double block, five falls), has a five-to-one advantage. Friction neglected, the rough power advantage of any tackle can be figured by counting the falls.

**pure water** • A term used in nuclear operating machinery to mean water so heavily distilled as to be purer than ordinary distilled water; of quality fit to be used in the primary loop of a nuclear plant.

**Purple-K Powder** • Trade name for an aqueous film-forming foam. It can be used simultaneously with dry chemicals to smother flammable liquid fires. Also called light water.

**purple shirts** • Aviation fuel handlers working on the flight deck of an aircraft carrier; so called because they wear purple shirts for easy identification. *See also:* yellow shirts; blue shirts; green shirts; brown shirts; white shirts; red shirts; grapes

**put away** • Expresses the idea to leave by water, as in "The boat put away from the ship."

**put off** • Same as put away, but usually restricted to putting off from the shore.

**pylon** • A structure or strut that supports an engine pod, external tank, etc., on an aircraft.

**pyrotechnics** • Ammunition, flares, or fireworks used for signaling, illuminating, or marking targets.

**Q-ship** • Disguised man-of-war used for decoying enemy submarines into close gun range.

**quadrant** • 1. A portable device for measuring angles having an arc length of 45° or less (1/8 of a circle). Forerunner of the larger and more accurate sextant. 2. Refers to one quarter of a fuel system on an aircraft carrier. Quadrants are divided into forward port, forward starboard, aft port, and aft starboard. Each quadrant is designed to operate independently of the other, if required.

**quadrantal davit** • A boat davit in which the lower end of the arm is a steel quadrant fitted with gear teeth and the appropriate mechanism for cranking out the arm and lowering the boat.

**quadrantal deviation** • A deflection of the magnetic compass caused by the induced magnetism of the ship's horizontal iron. Cor-

rected by quadrantal spheres. *See also:* Flinders Bar

**quadrantal spheres** • Two iron balls at either side, athwartship, of the binnacle to help compensate for the ship's magnetic effect on the compass.

**quadrature** • Relationship between two celestial bodies when they are 90° apart. They are then said to be in quadrature with each other. When the sun and moon are in quadrature, at first and last quarters of the moon, there is a signficant effect on the tides.

**quarter** • 1. One side or the other of the stern of a ship. To be broad on the quarter means to be 45° away from dead astern, and starboard or port quarter would have to be stated to be more specific. 2. Old term referring to surrendering. To cry for quarter was to ask to have one's surrender accepted. To give quarter meant to accept the other party's surrender. The term comes from the ancient custom of permitting a captured officer to be ransomed at one-fourth of his annual pay, or his estate, if wealthy. *See also:* quarters

**quarterdeck** • Ceremonial area on a ship, kept especially neat and clean. The specific domain of the officer of the deck while in port. Always located near the accommodation ladder or brow—or the principal one if more than one is rigged. In the days of sail, the ship was conned from the quarterdeck.

**quartering sea** • A sea on the quarter. That is, waves are approaching from about 45° on one side of the stern.

**quarterly marks** • Periodic evaluation (quarterly) of enlisted personnel in proficiency in rate, seamanship, mechanical ability, leadership, and conduct.

**quartermaster's notebook** • A log maintained by the quartermaster on watch to provide material for the deck log. It is an official document; entries may be crossed out, but not erased.

**quartermaster of the watch** • Watch station with the responsibilities of assisting the officer of the deck in matters pertaining primarily to navigation.

**quartermaster (QM)** • Navy occupational rating that is responsible for ship safety, skillful navigation, and reliable communications with other vessels and shore stations. In addition, QMs maintain charts, navigational aids, and records for the ship's log. They steer the ship, take radar bearings and ranges, make depth soundings and celestial observations, plot courses, and command small craft. QMs stand watches and assist the navigator and officer of the deck (OOD). QMs also handle the duties that once were the responsibility of signalmen (SM). Originally, the quartermaster was the man assigned to look after troops' quarters. The Army and Marine Corps still use the term with this meaning.

**quarters** • 1. Living spaces aboard ship. 2. Government-owned houses or apartments assigned to naval personnel. 3. An assembly, as quarters for inspection. 4. A gathering on stations, as fire quarters.

**quay** • A solid stone or masonry structure built along the shore of a harbor to which boats and ships make fast, load, unload, etc. *See also:* dock; pier; wharf

**quebec** • Phonetic word for the letter Q.

**queen** • Past phonetic word for the letter Q; replaced with quebec.

**quenching** • The significant drop in underwater sound transmission or reception due to air bubbles trapped in the sonar dome. The roll and pitch of a ship in rough water is a primary cause.

**quick-closing** • Special doors and hatches that can be closed quickly to preserve watertight integrity.

**quick-flashing light** • A navigational light that flashes continuously at least once a second.

# R

**rack** • A framework aboard ship from which depth charges are dropped. *Inf:* Bunk or bed. To rack out means to nap.

**rack time** • Sleep.

**rad** • A unit of measurement of an absorbed dose of radiation equal to 100 ergs of ionization per gram of absorbing material or tissue.

**radar** • Originally an acronym for "radio detection and ranging"; now a term in common use. An instrument or system for determining, by radio echoes, the presence of objects and their range, bearing, and elevation.

**radar balloons (RABALS)** • A method using radar to track a balloon carrying a radar-reflector; used to determine upper-level winds.

**radar countermeasures** • Actions taken to reduce the effectiveness of enemy radar. Many means can be employed, including electronic, such as frequency jamming, and physical, such as chaff and stealth technology.

**radar frequency** • The radio frequency used for the transmission of radar pulses. Different frequencies—hertz or cycles per second—

have diferrent strengths and weaknesses in radar technology. Also, frequency agility—the ability to operate a given radar on multiple frequencies—can make a radar system harder to detect or to employ countermeasures against.

**radar picket** • Ship or aircraft stationed at a distance from a main body to increase radar detection range. Usually placed along a threat axis.

**radar reflector** • Device used to increase radar target signal; used in life rafts and on other vessels that want to be detected by radar.

**radar trapping** • During certain conditions, radar signals can be trapped between layers in the atmosphere and conducted over much greater than normal ranges; the result can be increased detection ranges, or can also be a complete loss of signal.

**radiated noise** • Energy—electronic or sonic—emitted by ships, submarines, and torpedoes that makes them more detectable.

**radio-acoustic range finding** • Determining distance by a combination of radio and sound, radio being used to indicate both the time of transmission and time of reception of a sound wave.

**Radioactivity Detection, Indication, and Computation (RADIAC)** • Term that designates various types of radiological measuring instruments or equipment.

**radio beacon** • An electronic aid to navigation that sends out radio signals for reception by a directional antenna.

**radio central** • Main radio room aboard ship. Also called main radio and radio one.

**radio countermeasures (RCM)** • Actions taken to reduce the effectiveness of enemy radio, such as jamming.

**radio direction finder (RDF)** • A radio receiver with a directional antenna to determine bearings of radio signals.

**radio facility chart** • Information on radio aids to navigation in graphic and tabular form for use by air crews in flight operations.

**radio frequency** • Electromagnetic wave frequencies that lie in the range between 3 kilohertz to about 300 gigahertz; used for radio and television transmissions. Radio frequencies are divided by convention as follows: VLF, below 30 kHz; LF, 30–300 kHz; MF, 300–3,000 kHz; HF, 3–30 mHz; VHF, 30–300 mHz; UHF, 300–3,000 mHz; SHF, 3,000–30,000 mHz; EHF, 30,000–300,000 mHz. *See also:* hertz

**radio frequency spectrum** • Conventional designations for radio portions of the electromagnetic spectrum. VLF (Very Low Frequencies) 10 kHz–30 kHz; LF (Low Frequencies) 30 kHz–300 kHz; MF (Medium Frequencies) 300 kHz–3,000 kHz; HF (High Frequencies) 3 MHz–30 MHz; VHF (Very High Frequencies) 30 MHz–300 MHz; UHF (Ultra High Frequencies) 300 MHz–3,000 MHz; SHF (Super High Frequencies) 3,000 MHz–30,000 MHz; EHF (Extremely High Frequencies - also Extra High Frequencies) 30,000 MHz–300 GHz.

**radio guard** • Ship or station assuming radio communications responsibility for one or more other ships or stations.

**radio one** • *See:* radio central

**radio sextant** • An electronic sextant that receives radio waves emitted by the sun and other celestial bodies, as compared to light waves in standard celestial navigation.

**radiosonde** • Balloon that automatically transmits meteorological information to a weather station.

**Radio Teletype (RATT)** • A communication system in which a radio circuit actuates a

Teletype machine that produces a message in printed form.

**radojet** • Trade name for an air ejector, a device for removing the air from a condenser by means of steam jets.

**radome** • Dome on an aircraft or airship containing radar gear.

**raft kit** • First-aid gear secured to a life raft.

**rail** • 1. An open fence aboard ship to prevent personal injury, made of pipe or other rigid material. Can be used instead of lifelines along the edge of a weather deck, or below in large spaces such as engine rooms, or in front of dangerous equipment. 2. A plank, timber, or piece of metal forming the top of a bulwark. 3. A hand rail, ladder rail, or safety rail associated with ships' ladders.

**rail gun** • A new gun technology that launches projectiles using electromagnetic forces rather than gunpowder.

**rail loading** • Loading of boats that have been lowered partway and are still hanging from their falls, but are at the rail of a ship. After being loaded, they will be lowered the rest of the way to the water.

**rainbow sideboys** • Honorary sideboys who are wearing different-colored jerseys, such as are worn on the flight deck of an aircraft carrier.

**rainmaker** • *Inf:* Coil used to condense steam from the pier. *Inf:* Meteorologist.

**raise** • To come within sight of, as when a lookout raises land when the ship makes landfall. To establish contact on a radio circuit.

**rake** • 1. An angle that stacks, masts, etc., make with the vertical. A raked mast, for example, will usually incline toward the stern (its top closer to the stern than its foot). 2. In naval gunfire target practice, observation of the fall of shot in range; *i.e.*, yards over, yards short. Usually made from a small boat

at the same range as the target, clear of the line of fire, by a raking party. To rake is to make such observations.

**rakish** • 1. Having a pronounced rake to the masts. Probably more for appearance than utility. 2. Smart, speedy appearance. 3. Dashing, jaunty.

**ram** • An underwater ice projection from an iceberg or an ice floe. In the old Navy, an armored projection of the bow below the waterline, intended for use in combat.

**ram air** • Air forced into an air intake or duct by the motion of the intake or duct through the air.

**ram-jet** • Type of jet engine that uses inlet air velocity as its compressor. *See also:* ram air

**rammer** • Part of a gun mechanism that seats the projectile.

**ramp** • Hinged forward section of a landing craft or ship over which its cargo is unloaded when the craft is beached. The after end of an aircraft carrier's flight deck; usually angled downward.

**ramp strike** • When an aircraft attempting to land on an aircraft carrier's flight deck comes in too low and hits the angled ramp rather than the level deck.

**ram tensioner** • A large hydraulic cylinder containing a piston or ram; maintains tension on a highline wire during underway replenishment operations.

**range** • 1. An area designated for a particular purpose, such as a target or degaussing range. 2. The distance an object is from the observer or reference point. 3. An aid to navigation consisting of two or more objects—lights or day beacons—of differing height and lined up with the taller one behind the other on a specified bearing on shore; marked on a chart to indicate a safe course.

4. To lay out anchor chain in even rows.

**range alongside** • To come close aboard of another vessel, without passing lines or otherwise making physical contact.

**range finder** • An instrument to measure range or distance to the target. Can be optical (such as a stereoscopic range finder) or electronic (such as radar).

**rangekeeper** • Instrument that automatically receives and computes information necessary to fire weapons.

**range light** • A second, sometimes optional, white light that, with the masthead light, forms a range that helps other ships determine the course of the vessel fitted with these two lights.

**range marker** • A distance indicator, as on a radar display.

**range strobe** • An electronic range marker on a radar plan position indicator (PPI).

**range tables** • Elements of the trajectories of specific guns and projectiles, compiled in convenient form.

**rank** • 1. Rank represents relative positions of authority within a military organization. Naval officers have ranks such as lieutenant and commander. Enlisted personnel have ranks such as seaman and petty officer, although the term "rate" is more often used in this case. Rank and "paygrade" or "grade" are nearly synonymous. 2. When individuals are in a standard military square or rectangular formation, for parade or inspection, etc., those standing alongside one another are in a rank; those standing in front of or behind one another are said to be in files. 3. Individuals standing in a military formation are sometimes said to be in ranks.

**rapid fire** • Guns fire as rapidly as possible, as fast as they can be reloaded. Aim is on and

shots are hitting, and the objective is to inflict as much damage as possible as quickly as possible. *See also:* slow fire

**rate** • 1. Roughly equivalent to rank, but applied only to enlisted personnel. Not to be confused with rating, which is an occupational specialty, such as boatswain's mate or electronics technician. A rate can be merely an expression of the person's rank, such as "petty officer third class" or it can include the person's rating, such as "boatswain's mate third class." Confusion can be minimized if it is remembered that rating applies only to occupational specialty, while rate involves rank or paygrade. 2. To deserve; *e.g.*, a good Sailor rates a promotion. 3. A chronometer's rate is the number of seconds it gains or loses daily. *See also:* rating

**rate grabber** • One who will do almost anything to get a promotion.

**ratey** • *Inf:* Presumptuous, impertinent.

**rat guard** • A hinged, conical metal shield secured around mooring lines to prevent rats from coming aboard.

**rating** • General grouping of enlisted personnel according to military skills; *e.g.*, boatswain's mate, photographer's mate, etc. Analogous to occupation. Not to be confused with "rate," which indicates rank or paygrade. Ratings are further classified as general ratings, service ratings, and emergency ratings. General ratings are the broad occupational categories, such as gunner's mate, quartermaster, etc. Some general ratings can be further subdivided into service ratings; for example, the gas turbine (GS) rating is subdivided into two service ratings: GSE (electrical) and GSM (mechanical). Emergency ratings are used only in wartime or national emergency as required.

**rating badge** • Insignia of rating and rate worn on the uniform sleeve by petty officers.

**ration** • An allowance of provisions for one person for one day. *See also:* rations

**rations** • Food. May be specialized as in abandon ship, flight, aircraft, emergency, landing party, travel, or leave rations. *See also:* ration

**ratline** • Three-strand, tarred hemp used for snaking. Lines seized to shrouds to form ladders for going aloft.

**rat tail** • Tapered braid that finishes off a stopper.

**rat-tailed stopper** • A braided, tapering stopper used on boat falls and mooring lines.

**Rawin system** • A technique used for the determination of winds aloft by the radar observation of a weather balloon.

**Raymond releasing hook** • Quick-release hook designed for use on boat falls.

**razee** • To cut down the spar deck and associated sides of a sailing man-of-war, thus reducing her freeboard while reducing her draft because of the reduced weight. A wooden warship with the upper deck cut away. To compete with the big frigates of the early U.S. Navy, the British Navy razeed a number of their 74-gun frigates, which were then rated at 44 or 50 guns. Since she could still carry the masts and canvas of the two-decker she had been, such a razee was usually fast, powerful, and heavily built. Only one ship-of-the-line was razeed in the U.S. Navy, USS *Independence*, built in 1814 as a 74. She was razeed to a huge frigate in 1656, and finally broken up in 1914 after an extraordinarily useful career.

**reach rod** • A long handle by which valves can be operated from a distance.

**reactivate** • To restore a preserved ship to service. *Inf:* Demothball.

**reactor** • An apparatus in which nuclear fis-

sion may be sustained in a self-supporting chain reaction. It comprises the fissionable material, a moderator, a reflector to prevent the escape of neutrons, measuring and control elements, and a means for taking off the power produced in the form of heat. The first nuclear reactor onboard ship was installed in USS *Nautilus* and had an effective full power life of about 1,000 hours. Since then, the technology has so improved that some reactors now being built are expected to last the entire useful life of the ship in which installed.

**readiness conditions** • Ships set readiness conditions appropriate to the prevailing circumstances; for example, a ship expecting to go into battle would set readiness condition I (all hands at battle stations, etc.), while a ship in port during peacetime might set the more relaxed readiness condition V. *See also:* condition I; condition II; condition III; condition IV; condition V; condition VI; condition IA; condition IAA; condition IAS; condition IE; condition IM

**ready about** • An order to the crew to be at their stations in preparation for putting a sailing ship about. *See also:* come about

**ready reserve** • A group in which members of the Naval Reserve serve under a statutory military obligation or by written agreement. The Ready Reserve is composed of the Selected Reserve (SELRES) and the Individual Ready Reserve (IRR). Members assigned to full time support positions who serve on extended Active Duty for Special Work (ADSW) or Active Duty for Training (ADT), or who drill for pay are in the SELRES. Members not assigned to a pay billet are in the IRR.

**ready room** • Compartment on carrier where aviators gather for briefings and debriefings, and to stand by for launches.

**ready service ammunition** • Ammunitio

located in close proximity to a gun—rather than stowed in a magazine—and ready for quick use.

**rear admiral** • Rank senior to captain (0-6). Divided into rear admiral lower half (0-7, with one star) and rear admiral upper half (0-8, with two stars).

**rear commodore** • Navy or merchant marine officer designated as convoy commander if the convoy commodore and vice commodore are lost.

**rearming area** • That area where an operation that replenishes the prescribed airborne weapons/stores, ammunition, bombs, and other armament items for aircraft is conducted. This operation may include fuzing and stray voltage checks, as applicable.

**recall** • Order from a ship directing all boats and personnel to return immediately.

**receiving ship (RECSHIP)** • A vessel functioning as a receiving station.

**receiving station (RECSTA)** • An activity designated to receive, process, house, mess, clothe, pay, and transfer transient enlisted personnel. *See also:* receiving ship (RECSHIP)

**reciprocal** • A direction 180° from a given direction. For example, the reciprocal of 090° is 270°, and the reciprocal of 201° is 021°.

**reclama** • A request to superior authority to reconsider its decision or its proposed action.

**recoil system** • System, usually hydraulic, that absorbs the force of the gun as it is driven back in recoil by the force of the firing.

**recruit** • Newly enlisted person, still in basic training.

**Red Cross flag** • The distinctive mark of a hospital ship or a ship temporarily involved in providing medical services.

**red lead** • Anticorrosive priming paint having a distinct reddish appearance; while the name has been retained, modern versions of the paint no longer contain lead. *Inf:* Ketchup.

**red right returning** • An expression used to remind navigators that red buoys are on the right-hand side of the channel when returning to port from seaward. This is true in the U.S. and other nations adhering to the same buoyage system; some nations use a different system that results in green buoys being on the right when returning from sea.

**red shirts** • The firefighters, crash and salvage crews, and ordnance personnel working on the flight deck of an aircraft carrier; so called because they wear red shirts for easy identification. *See also:* yellow shirts; blue shirts; green shirts; brown shirts; white shirts; purple shirts; grapes

**red tide** • A marine phenomenon that turns the sea reddish and kills marine life. Caused by plant-like protozoans called dinoflagellates. Red tide occurs worldwide and can be toxic to humans.

**reducer** • A coupling or fitting connecting pipes or hoses of different sizes.

**reduction gear** • Because turbines operate at very high speeds that are not practical for the necessarily slower speeds of ship propellers, a mechanical gear system is used to convert (reduce) the economical high speed of the turbine to the slower speeds of the propellers.

**reef** • 1. Rock, coral, sand, or any bottom material extending so near the surface of the water that boats or ships cannot pass over it safely. 2. To reef a sail is to reduce its effective area during high wind conditions, by rolling or folding it up and securing it at its reef points. The part of the sail that can be reduced is a reef, as in "take in a reef" or "shake out a reef." In modern yachts it may be rolled around the boom or even taken into a split metal mast with a roller built into the mast's hollow interior. 3. In the days of sail, sometimes applied to mean lowering or taking in a portion of a spar such as topgallant masts, topmasts, and the outer end of a bowsprit.

**reefer** • 2. Fresh-provision cargo ship. 3. Refrigerated compartment. 4. A refrigerator. *See also:* pea coat

**reef knot** • Same as a square knot except that one of the ends is pulled back through the knot. To shake out reefs, the topmen need only pull this end, which immediately releases the knot. Sometimes the term is used as an exact synonym for a square knot, despite the technical difference.

**reeve** • To pass a line or wire through a pulley; nautical past tense is rove.

**reference points (harbor)** • Lettered geographical points on which sortie and entrance plans of a harbor are based.

**reference position** • The announced estimate of navigational position by the officer in tactical command. Usually signaled daily to the formation.

**reference ship** • When determining relative motion among ships, one is designated the reference ship and the other(s) as the maneuvering ship(s). The reference ship appears not to move, while the maneuvering ships move relative to the reference ship. *See also:* relative motion

**reference station** • Tide or current station for which constants, having been determined, are used for comparison of simultaneous observations at other stations.

**refractivity** • The study of how electromagnetic energy is bent (refracted) as it moves through different density layers within the atmosphere.

**refueling** • Loading fuel onto an aircraft or ship.

**regimental combat team** • Part of the task organization of troops for amphibious operations.

**registered matter** • Highly classified matter to which a number is assigned and which is accounted for at prescribed intervals. Documents numbered for administrative convenience only are merely numbered documents, vice registered documents.

**registry, certificate of** • Merchant ship's certificate showing ownership and nationality. *Inf:* Registry.

**regular** • Member of the regular Navy (on full-time active duty), as opposed to reserve components; as in "she is a regular with thirteen years in destroyers and he is a reserve."

**regulation clothing** • Articles of uniform meeting specifications prescribed by uniform regulations and sold at small stores.

**Regulus** • Missile system developed by the Navy in the early days of guided-missile development. Forerunner of modern cruise-missile systems. Never actually employed in combat.

**relative bearing** • The direction of an object relative to the ship's head, expressed in degrees or points.

**relative bearing grease** • A nonexistent item for which new personnel are sometimes sent (all over the ship, of course) as a joke.

**relative motion** • The apparent motion of a ship, aircraft, etc., as compared with that of another. As a simple example, if two vessels are moving on the same course, one at 10 knots and the other at 15, the slower (reference) ship appears to be standing still while the faster (maneuvering) vessel appears to be making 5 knots. If they were on reciprocal courses, their relative motion would be 2!

knots. *See also:* reference ship

**relative plot** • A plot of the successive positions of a ship relative to a reference point, which is usually in motion.

**relief** • Person assigned to assume the duties of another; as in "He is my relief for the midwatch."

**relief file** • Information needed when duties are turned over from the person departing to his or her relief. Also called a passdown or passdown file.

**relieve** • To relieve a person on watch or in a particular billet is to take his or her place.

**relieving tackle** • Tackle to reduce the strain on a piece of equipment, as on a steering engine during heavy weather.

**religious program specialist (RP)** • Navy occupational rating that assists Navy chaplains with administrative and budgetary tasks. RPs serve as custodians of chapel funds, keep religious documents, and maintain contact with religious and community agencies. They also prepare devotional and religious educational materials, set up volunteer programs, operate shipboard libraries, supervise chaplains' offices, and perform administrative, clerical, and secretarial duties. They train personnel in religious programs and publicize religious activities.

**repair officer** • The head of the repair department in a tender or repair ship.

**repair party** • Group of specialists organized to control damage and make repairs throughout the ship.

**repeater** • Flag used to repeat another in a hoist, now called a substitute. *See also:* repeater, gyro

**repeater, gyro** • Remote compass driven by master gyro.

**replenishment group** • Fleet oilers, supply and ammunition ships, and their assigned screen.

**report, to place on** • To record an individual's name for appearance before the commanding officer on a charge of an infraction of rules or regulations under the Uniform Code of Military Justice (UCMJ).

**request mast** • Process by which crew members can submit requests to the commanding officer or executive officer.

**requisition** • Obtaining material utilizing supply documents through the supply system.

**rescue and assistance party** • Group of specially qualified personnel sent off the ship with special equipment to assist in rescue, firefighting, and salvage operations. Formerly called fire and rescue party.

**rescue basket** • Device for lifting an injured or exhausted person out of the water.

**rescue breathing gear** • Face-fitting device that provides oxygen; for use in smoke or gas.

**rescue chamber** • A two-compartment diving bell, transported to the scene of a submarine disaster by a submarine rescue vessel. The bell can make a watertight seal with a submarine's escape hatch and escape trunk, and then be hoisted to the surface with the rescued personnel. *See also:* deep-submerged rescue vehicle

**rescue combat air patrol (RESCAP)** • Air patrols that cover rescue submarines and rescue aircraft. Subdivisions are rescue submarine combat air patrol (SUBCAP) for lifeguard submarines, and rescue aircraft combat air patrol (BIRDCAP) for aircraft on rescue duty.

**reserve buoyancy** • The nonsubmerged watertight volume of a ship. This is of crucial importance to ships engaged in battle, because a damaged ship taking on water will consequently sink deeper using up some of its reserve buoyancy until equilibrium is restored between weight and displacement. Once she sinks entirely beneath the surface, there is no further volume to displace water and she will therefore continue directly to the bottom of the sea.

**reserve cargo handling battalion** • A cargo handling training unit composed of both active duty and reserve personnel.

**reserve fleet** • Group of naval vessels in an inactive status but maintained in case they are needed in an emergency. *Inf:* Mothball fleet.

**Reserve Officer Candidate (ROC) program** • Defunct program for commissioning college students as reserve ensigns; candidates attended officer candidate school during two summer periods scheduled so as not to interfere with college classes.

**reserve salute** • A shrug of the shoulders.

**restrict** • To keep on board. A person may be restricted due to misconduct or illness.

**restricted area** • Ocean area or sea space in which there are special restrictive measures to prevent interference between friendly forces; *e.g.*, submarine havens, danger areas, etc.

**restricted data** • All data concerning the design, manufacture, or use of atomic weapons or the production or use of special nuclear materal. Differs from classified matter in that restricted data specifically refers to nuclear information as defined in the Atomic Energy Act.

**restriction** • Restraint similar to arrest but not involving relief from military duties.

**retirement** • Planned tactical withdrawal, as when a task force retires from an operational area for replenishment. Term used to describe leaving the service at the end of a career with certain continued benefits.

**retraining command** • Activity that confines, and at the same time tries to rehabilitate, persons sentenced by courts-martial to long terms of imprisonment.

**retreat** • Bugle call or word passed that means fall out (disband) from a formation; *e.g.*, retreat from inspection. Bugle call sounded at evening colors.

**reveille** • Word passed to wake the crew in the morning.

**Revenue Service** • Forerunner to the U.S. Coast Guard, charged primarily with intercepting smugglers.

**reverberation** • Sound scattering toward its source. Major types are surface and bottom, from surface and bottom respectively; and volume, from air bubbles or suspended solids in the water.

**reverberation index** • Valuation of the ability of echo-ranging equipment to distinguish target echos from reverberation.

**reverse slope** • Terrain that, because of intervening high ground, can only be reached by high-angle fire. Normally refers to the back side of a hill or mountain.

**reviewing authority** • An officer in the chain of command who reviews the sentence of a court-martial.

**RGM-84** • *See:* Harpoon

**rheostat** • A variable resistor used to regulate the amount of electrical current.

**rhino barge** • A self-propelled lighter made up of pontoons bolted together.

**rhumb line** • A line on the Earth's surface making the same angle with all meridians. Appears as a straight line on a Mercator projection chart and is the standard way of lay ing down a ship's course.

**ride** • A ship at anchor "rides" to its anchor as it swings on the chain attached to the anchor.

**ride the vents** • An expression used in older submarines whose ballast tanks were equipped with flood valves or Kingston valves. The condition of being ready to dive, with flood valves open for entry of water as soon as the main vents are opened to permit trapped air to escape. Modern submarines have ballast tanks open to the sea at the bottom and are always riding the vents while surfaced.

**ridge rope** • The backbone line or wire of a ship's awning.

**riding lights** • Lights required for a ship at anchor, in contrast to running lights. Also called anchor lights.

**rig** • 1. To devise, set up, arrange. 2. An arrangement or convenience. 3. General description of a ship's upper works. 4. A distinctive arrangement of sails (rigging), as in a schooner rig. 5. An arrangement of equipment and machinery, such as an oil rig.

**rig for red** • An order to permit only red lights, providing quick visual adaptation to darkness for those who may have to assume topside watch stations at night.

**rigging** • The ropes, lines, wires, turnbuckles, and other gear supporting and attached to stacks, masts, and topside structures. Standing rigging is more or less permanently fixed, such as the stays which keep a mast in place. Running rigging is adjustable, such as flag halyards or boom hoists.

**right arm rates** • Beginning in 1841 and ending in 1949, certain rates were designated as more crucial than others and were signified by wearing their rating badges on their right arms. During World War II these rates included boatswains mate, turret captain, signalman, gunners mate, fire controlman, quartermaster, mineman, and torpedoman's mate. Other ratings wore their rates on the left sleeve. Today, all ratings wear their ratings on their left arms.

**right-handed** • Twisted from left to right or clockwise. Yarn and rope are usually right-handed.

**righting moment** • The force that tends to right—or move back to an upright position—a vessel that is heeled over. *See also:* stability

**right-laid** • Refers to a lay of line or wire rope in which the strands spiral in a clockwise direction, as one looks along the line. Same as right-handed.

**rig in** • To remove or take in and stow, as a boat boom or accommodation ladder is rigged in when no longer needed.

**rig ship for visitors** • Word passed to all hands to have ship prepared for expected visitors. This involves closing off restricted areas, stationing sentries, providing guides, etc.

**RIM-166** • *See:* rolling airframe missile

**RIM-7** • *See:* Sea Sparrow

**ring** • With reference to an anchor, the heavy ring at the top of the shank to which the hawser or chain is attached.

**ringing oscillator** • *See:* pulse oscillator

**ring knocker** • *Inf:* A Naval Academy graduate.

**rip** • Turbulent water produced by conflicting currents or water flowing over a shoal or irregular bottom. Sometimes called a rip tide. Short for rip current.

**rip current** • Off a beach on which moderate-to-heavy surf is breaking, a rip current is a strong, relatively narrow, seaward-flowing current; caused by the escape of water pushed ashore by the breaking surf. If caught in a rip current, one should swim parallel to the shoreline to get out of it. Sometimes incorrectly called an "undertow." Also called rip tide. *See also:* undertow

**rip tide** • *See:* rip current

**rise and shine** • To get up, go to work, get going. Was originally "rouse and shine," but has evolved into the current term. Although used in civilian life, the term originated in the naval service where it was common practice for sailors to begin shining brightwork soon after getting up in the morning. *See also:* rouse out; show a leg

**riser** • 1. A vertical pipe leading off a larger one; *e.g.,* fire main riser. 2. Lines from a parachute harness to the shrouds.

**roadstead** • Off-shore anchorage, usually characterized by good holding ground and some protection from the sea.

**roaring forties** • Area between 40° and 50° south latitude in which frequent storms, generated by the prevailing westerly winds, are encountered. This area develops very high seas because of an absence of land masses and consequent unlimited fetch.

**rocket ship** • Landing ship used in close support of the landing assault waves during an amphibious landing. Capable of heavy and rapid rocket firing. Abbreviated LSMR for landing ship, medium, rocket.

**rocketsonde** • Rocket sent aloft to register and transmit weather data.

**Rocks and Shoals** • *Inf:* Old naval regulations. *Inf:* Extracts from the Uniform Code of Military Justice periodically read aloud to all hands.

**roddle** • That part of a wire rope clip against which the U-bolt is secured.

**rode** • An anchor line or rope, used instead of a length of chain to anchor a small vessel.

**rodmeter** • That part of a pitometer log that projects from the ship's hull into the water to measure water flow and thus help to determine the vessel's speed. Sometimes called a "pit sword."

**roger** • Used in voice radio to mean "I have received your transmission." Not to be confused with wilco, which means, "I understand and will comply." Past phonetic word for the letter R; replaced with romeo.

**roger dodger** • *Inf:* Affirmative; yes; okay; will do.

**roll** • Side-to-side motion of a ship about its longitudinal axis; caused by wave motion. *See also:* yaw; pitch; heave; list

**roller** • A long, usually nonbreaking wave generated by distant winds; can be a hazard to small craft.

**roller chock** • A chock fitted with rollers to facilitate the passage of a line or wire; the rollers reduce the friction that is found in a normal chock.

**roller path** • A precision-machined, circular roller surface on which the roller bearings of a turret, mount, or director describe a circular path as it rotates. The inclination of a roller path is of paramount importance to proper alignment between gun mounts and fire control directors.

**rolling airframe missile** • The RIM-116A Rolling Airframe Missile (RAM) is a lightweight, quick-reaction, high-firepower, anti-ship weapon system jointly developed by the U.S. and German governments. Designed as an all-weather, low-cost self-defense system against anti-ship missiles, it uses the infrared seeking of the Stinger missile and the warhead, rocket motor, and fuse from the Sidewinder missile. Due to its high-tech radio-to-infrared frequency guidance system, it requires no shipboard support after the missile is launched.

**rolling chock** • *See:* roller chock

**roll in on** • In aviation, the initial maneuver in an attack.

**roll-on/roll-off (RO/RO)** • Method in which a ship's cargo is loaded into vehicles that drive on board ship and remain for the voyage, then drive off at destination. The cargo is not off-loaded from the vehicles during the voyage, but remains in the vehicles.

**romeo** • Phonetic word for the letter R.

**roof** • *Inf:* Flight deck of an aircraft carrier.

**room, log** • *See:* log room

**room to swing a cat** • A very old expression referring to the amount of space required to swing a cat-o'-nine tails when flogging. If there is not room to swing a cat, it means in naval terms that the overhead is very low and there is little space available. *See also:* cat-o'-nine-tails

**root valve** • Valve located where a branch line comes off the main line.

**rope** • 1. Generally, the term "rope" is used to generically describe a kind of material (such as fiber rope and wire rope) with no specific use intended. The term "line" is more often used to describe a specific length of rope that is being used for a specific purpose—such as lifeline, fishing line, or mooring line. One way of thinking about it is that rope is what it is called when it is being manufactured, ordered, stowed, etc., and line is the correct term when it is actually being used to accomplish a task. There are exceptions, however. Manropes and wheel ropes are examples of ropes with specific uses. The expression "know the ropes" comes from the old sailing days when a good sailor had to

know all the specific uses for the many lines/ropes that were used to control the vessel. 2. Strips of metal foil used in radar countermeasures.

**rope yarn Sunday** • Any afternoon, except in a weekend, that is free of ship's work and drills. Traditionally, Wednesday afternoon was designated rope yarn Sunday, to allow the crew time to themselves to repair torn clothing, tar their hair, etc. The term is used today to describe an afternoon off from ship's work.

**rose box** • The strainer at the foot of the suction pipe of a bilge pump.

**rotary current** • A tidal current flowing continually, but changing direction through all compass points during a tidal cycle; covers a huge ocean area. It changes clockwise in the Northern Hemisphere and counterclockwise in the Southern Hemisphere.

**rotating band** • Strip of metal around a projectile for sealing the bore, positioning the rear of the projectile, and imparting rotation. *See also:* bourrelet

**rotor** • 1. The revolving part of a rotating electrical machine. The rotor may be either the field or the armature, depending on the design of the machine. 2. The rotating member of a synchro that consists of one or more coils of wire wound on a laminated core. Depending on the type of synchro, the rotor functions similarly to the primary or secondary winding of a transformer. 3. Several blades mounted coaxially for use on an aircraft; similar to a propeller but generally used for stability or lift functions rather than fo propulsion.

**rotorhead** • *Inf:* A helicopter pilot.

**rough log** • Original handwritten version of the ship's log, recorded at the time of the events being recorded, or nearly so. Incorrect entires may be lined out, but not erased. A smooth log can be prepared from the rough log, but in the case of any legal question, the rough log takes precedence.

**round in** • To bring the blocks of a tackle closer together.

**round line** • Three-stranded, right-handed small stuff, used for fine seizing.

**round to** • To turn a ship into the wind.

**round turn** • 1. To place a loop of line fully around a bitt or bollard to check a strain or weight. 2. An unwanted complete twist in the anchor chains at the hawse when two anchors are in use. 3. *Inf:* To "bring up with a round turn" describes a reprimand.

**rouse in** • To haul in, especially by hand, with maximum speed and force.

**rouse out** • Arouse, break out; *e.g.,* rouse out the duty boat's crew; rouse out the starboard chain. Rouse and shine means to awaken, get up, and turn to. It has been corrupted to "rise and shine."

**route** • To forward a message by a prescribed path and/or method. For example, "route this message to all department heads."

**routine** • The lowest routing precedence assigned to a naval message. *See also:* precedence

**routine deployable** • A strike group so designated is ready to deploy six months before the scheduled deployment date. During this phase, the strike group conducts refresher training to maintain readiness levels.

**routing** • Process of determining the path or method of forwarding a message. Process of directing a ship, formation, or convoy over a considerable distance.

**rove** • *See:* reeve

**rowlock** • *See:* oarlock; thole pin

**royal (sail)** • *See:* sail nomenclature

**rudder** • A flat, vertical surface mounted at the stern of a vessel, below the waterline; hinged by gudgeons and pintles, which allow it to be moved into the flow of passing water when making way. Used to steer a vessel by using the flow of water against its surface to exert a pressure that swings the stern, thereby causing the bow to turn in the opposite direction. Aircraft rudders function similarly to vessel rudders except that they use air flow rather than water flow to steer.

**rudder post** • The after post of the stern frame to which a rudder may be attached. Sometimes called called the sternpost.

**rudder ram** • Part of the hydraulic mechanism for turning a large rudder. The combination of a hydraulic piston and connecting rod make up the rudder ram.

**ruffles and flourishes** • The roll of the drum (ruffles) and short burst of music (flourishes) that is used to honor high-ranking military and civil officials. Usually precedes another piece of music, such as The Admiral's March. The number of ruffles and flourishes for Navy admirals equals the number of stars they wear to denote their rank. *See also:* Admiral's March

**Rules of the Road** • Regulations designed to prevent collisions at sea. *See also:* Inland Rules; International Rules

**run away** • Run a line in as fast as possible by taking hold and running down the deck with it.

**runner** • The term is loosely applied to any line rove through a block. More specifically, a line fastened at one end to a fixed object such as an eyebolt, and rove through a single block; it has an eye on its other end to which a tackle is clapped on.

**running bowline** • Bowline made over the standing part of its own rope so that it form a free-sliding noose.

**running fix** • Geographical position determined by two lines of position obtained by observations at different times. The first line is advanced by dead reckoning.

**running lights** • Required lights carried by a vessel or aircraft under way between sunset and sunrise. *See also:* riding lights

**running line** • Any line used in a nonstatic condition.

**running rigging** • *See:* rigging

**rust** • Ferric oxide, a reddish-brown, scaly or powdery deposit found on the surface of steel and iron as a result of oxidation.

# S

**S-3** • *See:* Viking

**sabot** • A bushing used in firing subcaliber munitions by positioning the projectile or missile in a larger gun barrel or launching tube such that it prevents the escape of gas ahead of the projectile or missile. It falls away as the assembly leaves the muzzle or missile launcher.

**sack** • *Inf:* Bunk, bed. *Inf:* To sack out is to take a nap.

**saddle** • Any device used to support something such as a spar or boom (also called a boom crutch), a boat stowed on deck, or a heavy piece of machinery below decks. A special-shaped saddle is used to support a fuel hose from a span wire when fueling ships under way. *See also:* boat chock; boat skids; span wire

**safety factor** • For heavy lifting operations, a multiple representing extra strength over maximum intended stress. If boat falls that have a breaking load of 9 tons are used to hoist a 3-ton boat, they have a safety factor of 3.

**sagging** • Distortion of a ship's hull caused by waves in a seaway, resulting in the bow and stern being higher than the amidships section; opposite of hogging.

**sail** • 1. A large piece of fabric, traditionally canvas, by which the wind can be used to propel a vessel. 2. The part of a modern submarine extending above the main deck or hull, housing the periscope supports, various retractable masts, and the surface conning station or bridge.

**sail area** • The vertical surfaces of a ship above the waterline on which the wind exerts force. The greater the sail area, the more effect the wind will have upon that vessel. For example, a ship with a lot of sail area, such as a cruiser, will have a more difficult time landing at a pier with an offsetting wind than will one with a much smaller sail area, such as a submarine.

**sail ho** • Lookout report made when another vessel has been sighted.

**sailing** • Today a navigational term meaning to voyage on the sea. Involves selecting courses and finding position. One may sail by Mercator, rhumb line, midlatitude, great circle, or traverse courses.

**Sailing Directions** • Books issued to supplement charts of the world. They contain descriptions of coastlines, harbors, dangers, aids to navigation, applicable Inland Rules of the Road and Pilot Rules, and other data that cannot conveniently be shown on a chart.

**sail locker** • Stowage area for awnings, cots, and related gear aboard ship.

**sail nomenclature (square rigged)** • In a

full-rigged ship, the sails on each mast are, from bottom to top, as follows: On the foremast: foresail or fore course, fore topsail, fore topgallant, fore royal, fore skysail. On the mainmast: mainsail or main course, main topsail, main topgallant, main royal, main skysail. On the mizzenmast: spanker (a fore-and-aft sail with gaff and boom), mizzen topsail, mizzen topgallant, mizzen royal, mizzen skysail. Note that there is no mizzen course; its place is taken by the spanker. Topsail is pronounced "topsul," topgallant is "tuh-gallant," and skysail is "skysul" in the sailor's vocabulary. Royals became common late in the eighteenth century and skysails in the mid-nineteenth century with the tallmasted clippers. At the same time, topsails had become so large that small merchant crews could not handle them well; therefore, they were split into upper and lower topsails. Jibs were rigged between the foremast and the bowsprit. The spritsail was rigged under the bowsprit on a small yard, but was eventually abandoned as a mankiller. Sails rigged outboard of other square sails are called studding sails (often shortened to stuns'l) and are named according to the sail they are outboard of (for example, fore-royal stuns'l).

**sailor** • A person who has spent time at sea and is accustomed to the ways of the sea and ships. Applied to officers as well as enlisted personnel as a term of approbation. In more recent times, often capitalized to signify a member of the U.S. Navy, as opposed to the more generic meaning applied to those who go out on the water for some occupational purpose or recreation.

**Sailor** • *See:* sailor

**Sailor Phone** • The Sailor Phone is a commercial satellite telephone system installed aboard ships for the morale and welfare of the crew. The system can only be used to call out, but is usable worldwide. To utilize the Sailor Phone, the service member purchases an AT&T Global Prepaid Card and uses this card from one of the special phones installed at various locations in the ship.

**Sailor's Creed** • Moral and ethical guidance for all members of the U.S. Navy. The actual creed is: I am a United States Sailor. I will support and defend the Constitution of the United States of America and I will obey the orders of those appointed over me. I represent the fighting spirit of the Navy and those who have gone before me to defend freedom and democracy around the world. I proudly serve my country's Navy combat team with Honor, Courage and commitment. I am committed to excellence and the fair treatment of all.

**sail plane** • *See:* diving plane

**sailplane** • Similar to a submarine bowplane, but located on the submarine's sail. *See also:* bowplane

**salinity** • A measurement of the amount of salts dissolved in sea water.

**sally ship** • Evolution aboard ship during which the crew runs from side to side together, causing the ship to roll slowly. Used to extricate a ship from ice or bottom, or to determine ship's period of roll—a measure of her stability.

**salt and pepper** • *Inf:* Black and white uniform, such as white shirts and blue (black) trousers.

**salt box** • A device used in ship repair facilities to provide the constant electrical load needed to test a ship's service generators.

**salt junk** • *See:* bully beef

**saltwater service system** • A series of pipes that provides saltwater for flushing and fire fighting aboard ship.

**salty** • *Inf:* Nautical; seagoing.

**salute, hand** • A gesture of mutual respect exchanged between military persons or by an individual toward the national ensign. Done by raising the right hand to the cap visor or forehead, palm down, with fingers flat and closed against one another. When exchanged between individuals it should be accompanied by a greeting, such as "Good morning, Sir." Always initiated by the junior and responded to by the senior. In the Navy, left-hand salutes are only permitted under specific circumstances, such as an injured right arm or when blowing a boatswain's whistle during the rendering of honors.

**saluting battery** • Guns used to fire a salute.

**saluting ship (station)** • One designated by the Secretary of the Navy as being capable of rendering such an honor. In general, only major warships and large naval activities are so designated.

**salvage** • To save or rescue material that has been discarded, wrecked, sunk, or damaged.

**salvage group** • In an amphibious operation, a naval task organization designated and equipped to rescue personnel and to salvage equipment and material.

**salvage money** • Money divided by the crew of a ship that has salvaged another and brought it into port to be sold. No longer practiced in the U.S. Navy.

**salvo** • One or more shots fired simultaneously at the same target.

**salvo fire** • Gunfire in which all guns of a battery fire together at regular intervals.

**salvo latch** • Device to prevent the unintentional opening of the breech of a loaded gun until after the gun has been fired.

**Samson post** • Vertical timber on the forward deck of a boat; used in towing and securing. Sometimes used as synonym for king post.

**sandblower** • *Inf:* A short person. *Inf:* Low-level flight, or an aircraft designed for same.

**sand table** • Device for constructing a scale model of an amphibious assault landing beach or some other military objective. Used for training or planning purposes.

**saturated steam** • *See:* superheated steam

**save-all** • 1. Net spread under cargo-handling operations between ship and pier. 2. Any receptacle rigged to catch dripping oil, water, etc.

**scale** • 1. The ratio between the linear dimensions of a chart, map, drawing, and so forth, and the actual dimensions represented. 2. Undesirable deposit, mostly calcium sulfate, that forms in the tubes of boilers.

**scaling hammer** • *See:* chipping hammer

**scarf** • *See:* scarfing

**scarfing** • Adhesively or mechanically locking together two members of the same material—generally a wooden beam or spar—with a long diagonal joint so as to form a single long piece with no sacrifice in strength. The joint is the scarf.

**scarp** • Bank cut into the shore by surf.

**schoolship** • A vessel that has been designated to provide training as its primary mission.

**schooner** • A fore-and-aft rigged sailing vessel, originally and still typically having two masts. The foremast is somewhat shorter than the main, although multimasted schooners were tried for a short time late in the days of sail. *See also:* fore-and-aft sail

**scope** • Number of fathoms of chain out to an anchor or mooring buoy. If at anchor, scope is increased in strong winds for more holding power.

**scour** • The movement of bottom sediments from their resting place by currents or wave motion.

**scouting** • A mission involving search, patrol, tracking, or reconnaissance by a surface ship, submarine, or aircraft.

**scow** • Large, open, flat-bottom utility boat for transporting sand, gravel, mud, etc. Small scows are also called punts or prams, and may be sailed. Large ones are also called barges or lighters, depending on local usage. *Inf:* Any poorly maintained vessel.

**scram** • A nuclear-power term indicating that some difficulty in reactor operation has arisen, causing automatic or deliberate activation of reactor protective features to shut it down. To scram is to lose all reactor power, suddenly necessitating elimination of the difficulty and then carrying on a programmed restart.

**scramble** • Emergency launching of fighter aircraft. In cryptology, to mix at random.

**scrambled eggs** • *Inf:* The gold braid on the visor of a senior officer's cap.

**scramble nets** • Cargo nets rigged over the side for picking up survivors.

**scraper** • Hand tool used to scrape paint and woodwork.

**screamer** • A magnetic device attached to the hull of a target submarine to transmit sound for location of the sub by antisubmarine warfare forces. *Inf:* A derogatory term for a senior who leads by shouting or verbal intimidation.

**screen** • Ships stationed to protect a unit, such as an antisubmarine screen. To examine and evaluate, such as screening applicants.

**screw** • The propeller of a ship. Screws refer to the water in the vicinity of the propellers. "He fell overboard and swam wildly to clear the screws."

**screw current** • Water movement caused by the turning of the propeller.

**screwing** • Dangerous rotary motion of ice floes caused by wind and ice pressure.

**screw the pooch** • *Inf:* To make a serious mistake.

**scudding** • 1. Loose, vapory fragments of low clouds moving rapidly. 2. Driving before a gale. 3. Scudding under bare poles means with all sails down or furled.

**scull** • To propel a boat by working an oar from side to side. To propel oneself in the water by working hands and forearms in a figure-eight motion.

**scullery** • Compartment in a ship where general mess dishwashing is done.

**scupper** • Fittings along the waterways on the weather decks and below to lead water over the side. They resemble small troughs perpendicular to the waterways and downward tending. Scupper pipes through the side of the ship do the same below decks.

**scupper lip** • Extension to prevent scupper discharge from running down the ship's sides.

**scuttle** • Small, quick-closing access hole. To sink a ship deliberately.

**scuttlebutt** • 1. Shipboard drinking fountain. 2. Originally a ship's water barrel (called a butt), which was tapped (scuttled) by the insertion of a spigot from which the crew drew their drinking water. 3. *Inf:* Rumor or gossip.

**sea** • 1. A large body of salt water, smaller than an ocean. 2. Although technically different, sea is often used as a synonym for ocean. 3. Water conditions as caused by wind and weather, as in "heavy seas."

**sea anchor** • Device, usually of wood or canvas or both, streamed by a vessel or boat in heavy weather to hold the bow up to the sea; or by a vessel that cannot anchor to the bottom, yet does not want to drift from a fixed or semi-fixed location. Also called a drogue.

**sea bag** • Canvas bag in which a sailor transports personal gear.

**Sea Basing** • Part of the Seapower 21 concept; pertains to the projection of sovereignty. *See also:* Sea Strike; Sea Shield; Sea Trial; Sea Warrior; Sea Enterprise; FORCEnet; Seapower 21

**seabed** • Bottom of a sea or ocean, beyond the continental shelf.

**Seabee (CB)** • Construction battalions in the Navy have come to be known as Seabees, an obvious derivative from the initials for construction battalion. All naval construction engineers, officers and enlisted, whether they are actually assigned to a battalion or not, are known by this name.

**sea breeze** • Breeze blowing off the sea toward the land. *See also:* land breeze

**sea buoy** • The buoy farthest to sea of those marking a channel or entrance. Sometimes called a departure buoy or farewell buoy.

**sea cabin** • The commanding officer's sleeping quarters, located near the bridge in a major naval ship. It is much higher and smaller than the CO's regular cabin.

**sea cadet** • *See:* United States Naval Sea Cadet Corps

**Sea Cadets** • *See:* United States Naval Sea Cadet Corps

**sea chest** • 1. Sailor's trunk, usually made of wood. 2. Intake between a ship's side and sea valve or seacock.

**seacock** • Valve in the ship's hull that is connected to the sea.

**sea daddy** • *Inf:* An older person who takes a recruit or younger officer in hand and teaches him or her a skill.

**sea dog** • *Inf:* An old sailor.

**seadopod** • Surface barge-mounted capsule maintained at sea bottom pressure to house off-duty divers involved in bottom work so that they do not have to be reacclimatized to bottom conditions before returning to work. Personnel are delivered to the work site by a submersible delivery capsule.

**Sea Dragon** • Designated MH-53E, the Sea Dragon helicopter is used primarily for airborne mine countermeasures (AMCM), with a secondary mission of shipboard delivery.

**Sea Enterprise** • Part of the Seapower 21 concept; pertains to the acquisition of ships, aircraft, etc. *See also:* Sea Strike; Sea Shield; Sea Basing; Sea Trial; Sea Warrior; FORCEnet; Seapower 21

**seafarer** • 1. A sailor or mariner; one who travels by sea. 2. Submarine extremely low frequency (SELF) radio communication system to reach deeply submerged submarines. 3. Name given to a type of antisubmarine warfare blimp.

**sea frontiers** • Essentially defensive command areas that function as operational commands for forces assigned by the Chief of Naval Operations.

**seagoing** • Capable of going to sea. Salty or nautical in nature.

**seagull** • *Inf:* A woman who follows a ship from port to port to be with her man. *Inf:* Chicken served in the general mess.

**Seahawk** • The Seahawk is a twin-engine helicopter, used for antisubmarine warfare, search and rescue, drug interdiction, antiship warfare, cargo lift, and special operations. The Navy's SH-60B Seahawk is an airborne platform based aboard cruisers, destroyers, and frigates. It deploys sonobouys and torpedoes in an antisubmarine role, and extends the range of the ship's radar capabilities. The Navy's SH-60F is carrier-based. The HH-60H, aboard carriers and ashore, is used for search and rescue missions.

**Sea King** • The H-3 is a twin-engine, all-weather helicopter. The SH-3H model is used to detect, classify, track and destroy enemy submarines. It also provides logistical support and a search and rescue capability. The UH-3H model is utility configured for logistical support and search and rescue missions. The VH-3D model supports the Executive Transport Mission.

**Sea Knight** • Medium lift assault helicopter, primarily used to move cargo and troops. The CH-46D Sea Knight helicopter is used by the Navy for shipboard delivery of cargo and personnel. The CH-46E is used by the Marine Corps to provide all-weather, day-or-night assault transport of combat troops, supplies, and equipment. Troop assault is the primary function and the movement of supplies and equipment is secondary. Additional tasks may be assigned, such as combat support, search and rescue, support for forward refueling and rearming points, aeromedic evacuation of casualties from the field and recovery of aircraft and personnel.

**Seal** • Navy special forces teams are known as Seal teams, and individuals who are qualified as members of these teams are known as Seals. The term derives from the acronym SEAL, for Sea, Air, Land.

**Sealab** • An undersea laboratory development program.

**sea ladder** • Metal rungs welded to the ship's side above the waterline. *See also:*

Jacob's ladder

**sea lawyer** • *Inf:* An argumentative person; one who too frequently questions orders and regulations.

**sea legs** • Adaptation to the motion of a vessel in a seaway. To find one's sea legs is to have recovered from seasickness.

**sealift** • The transport of military necessities (ammunition, vehicles, spare parts, etc.) by ship; as opposed to "airlift" in which such items would be transported by aircraft.

**seaman** • Anyone experienced with ships and the sea.

**seaman's eye** • The ability to judge distances and maneuvers at sea. To have a good seaman's eye is the ambition of all professional sailors.

**seaman apprentice (SA)** • Rate to which a person is advanced shortly after completion of recruit training. Paygrade E-2.

**Seaman Recruit (SR)** • Lowest enlisted rating. Paygrade E-1.

**seamanship** • The art or skill of handling a vessel. Skill in using deck equipment, boat handling, and the care and use of line and wire.

**seaman (SN)** • Enlisted person in paygrade E-3 who performs general deck and boat duties.

**Seaman to Admiral (STA-21)** • A commissioning program that keeps participants on active duty at their current enlisted pay grade. This means they receive all the pay, allowances, benefits, and privileges they enjoyed on regular active duty. Participants remain eligible for enlisted advancement while in the program. In addition, Sailors receive up to $10,000 per year to cover tuition, books, and fees.

**seamount** • An isolated mountain structure rising from the bottom of the sea to a point near the surface. One having a flat top is a tablemount.

**sea painter** • Line used for towing a boat alongside a ship under way. Led from the side of the ship to the bow of the boat, where it is secured with a loop and a toggle for quick release.

*Seapower* • Magazine of the Navy League with information supporting the missions of the sea services.

**sea power** • The ability of a nation to use and control the sea, and to prevent an enemy from using it.

**Seapower 21** • A concept of strategy/operations developed to guide the Navy in the twenty-first century; includes the components Sea Strike, Sea Shield, Sea Basing, Sea Trial, Sea Warrior, Sea Enterprise, and FORCEnet.

**search-and-attack unit (SAU)** • Two or more ships or aircraft teamed for coordinated search and attack on submarines.

**searchlight sonar** • Echo-ranging system using a narrow beam pattern for transmission and reception.

**sea return** • Interference on a radar screen caused by reflections from the sea.

**sea room** • Far enough from land for unrestricted maneuvers. Enough room between ships for maneuvering.

**Sea Shield** • Part of the Seapower 21 concept; pertains to the projection of defensive power. *See also:* Sea Strike; Sea Basing; Sea Trial; Sea Warrior; Sea Enterprise; FORCEnet; Seapower 21

**sea slick** • Surface area markedly different in appearance from surrounding water, usually caused by heavy concentrations of plankton.

**Sea-Sparrow** • Designated the RIM-7, this is a variation of the air-to-air (AIM-7) Sparrow missile, adapted for use as a surface-to-air missile on ships.

**Sea Stallion** • The CH-53D Sea Stallion is a medium lift helicopter designed to transport personnel, supplies, and equipment in support of amphibious and shore operations.

**sea state** • Degree of sea roughness.

**sea stores** • Cigarettes and other luxuries sold at sea and abroad, free of federal tax.

**sea story** • *Inf:* A tale of some exciting or interesting experience, real and/or imagined.

**Sea Strike** • Part of the Seapower 21 concept; pertains to the projection of offensive power. *See also:* Sea Shield; Sea Basing; Sea Trial; Sea Warrior; Sea Enterprise; FORCEnet; Seapower 21

**Sea Trial** • Part of the Seapower 21 concept; pertains to experimental work and warfare development. *See also:* Sea Strike; Sea Shield; Sea Basing; Sea Warrior; Sea Enterprise; FORCEnet; Seapower 21

**seaward** • Away from land and toward the open sea.

**Sea Warrior** • Part of the Seapower 21 concept; pertains to training and education. *See also:* Sea Strike; Sea Shield; Sea Basing; Sea Trial; Sea Enterprise; FORCEnet; Seapower 21

**seaway** • A moderate to rough sea.

**seaworthy** • A vessel that is fit for sea. Capable of putting to sea and meeting any usual sea condition.

**Secchi disc** • A white, black, or varicolored disc, usually about a foot in diameter, that measures water transparency.

**secondary conn** • Conning station for use if the main conn—the bridge—is damaged.

**second deck** • First complete deck below the main deck.

**second dog watch** • The watch from 1800 (6 PM) to 2000 (8 PM). Also called the last dog watch. *See also:* dog watch

**secret** • Level of classification that falls between confidential and top secret. Information or material whose disclosure would endanger national security or cause serious injury to the interests or prestige of the United States. *See also:* classified matter

**Secretary of the Navy** • The civilian head of the Navy and Marine Corps. Once a member of the President's cabinet, along with the Secretary of War; the post is now subordinate to the Secretary of Defense, as are the Secretaries of the Army and Air Force.

**section** • 1. Applied to ships or naval aircraft, a tactical subdivision of a division; usually, half of a division in the case of ships, and two aircraft in the case of aircraft. 2. A small group of personnel may be called a section, such as a group assigned to a class for training. Such groups will generally have a section leader, appointed on the basis of seniority or other criteria in some cases.

**secure** • To make fast in a permanent sense, as "Secure the forward hatch for sea." To quit, give up, or knock off, such as "Secure from general quarters."

**seiche** • Periodic wave oscillation—rise and fall of the water's level—whose period varies from a few minutes to nearly a tidal period; found in enclosed bodies of water or superimposed on tide-induced waves in open ocean. Caused by harmonic vibration in response to storm or tidal wave disturbances at sea. Pronounced "say-she."

**seismic sea wave** • An ocean wave of large amplitude, long period, and often very great force; caused by earthquakes, volcanic explosions, and particularly large earth slides under water. Popularly, but inaccurately, called a tidal wave, although there is nothing tidal involved. The Japanese equivalent is *tsunami.*

**seize** • To bind with a small rope.

**seizing** • 1. A wrapping, consisting of several turns of light line or wire, placed around the cut end of a wire rope to prevent the strands of the rope from unraveling. 2. The stopping of motion between two contacting surfaces because of lack of lubrication.

**seizing stuff** • *See:* marline; small stuff

**Selected Reserve (SELRES)** • Reservists who are assigned to full time support positions who serve on extended Active Duty for Special Work (ADSW) or Active Duty for Training (ADT), or who drill for pay are in the SELRES.

**selection board** • Panel of personnel who review records and make recommendations for promotions. Sometimes called a promotion board.

**selector valve** • A valve used to control the flow of fluid to a particular mechanism, as in a hydraulic system.

**self-sustaining** • Said of a nuclear reactor when it is producing enough power to run all associated auxiliaries; hence the load on the ship's auxiliary power equipment, such as diesel engines or battery, has been removed. This phrase is generally used during start-up procedure. *See also:* critical

**semaphore** • Rapid method of short-range visual communications between ships, using hand flags held in specific configurations to represent numbers and letters. Also known as wigwag.

**semi-diurnal** • Having a period of cycle of approximately half of a lunar day, roughly 12.42 hours.

**senior officer present afloat (SOPA)** • When a group of Navy ships is gathered together in a particular locality (such as in a harbor), the senior line officer of the Navy (on active duty and eligible for command at sea) who is present assumes command of the group for administratve and local operational purposes. For example, if several Navy ships are anchored in a foreign harbor together, the senior ship's captain (providing no flag officer is present) would be SOPA, and therefore responsible for the group should some universal decision, such as an emergency sortie, be required. He or she would also take on certain administrative responsibilities, such as initiating colors, setting up guard mail, etc.

**sennet** • *See:* sennit

**sennit** • Braided cordage made from rope yarns or spun yarn, plaited by hand. There are many varieties, such as rounded sennit, square sennit, flat sennit, French sennit, etc. Used for mats, stoppers, manropes, etc., or may be simply ornamental. *See also:* coxcombing; fancy work; MacNamara's lace; square knotting

**sensitivity time control (STC)** • A circuit that varies the gain of a receiver as a function of time to improve the generated picture.

**serve** • Winding on close turns of marline or seizing stuff with a serving mallet; this puts a smooth finish on a line or wire.

**service ammunition** • That used for combat, as distinct from target ammunition.

**service craft** • Naval craft that service other vessels; tugs and fuel barges are examples.

**service force (SERVFOR)** • A naval task organization that performs logistic support of fleet units.

**service life extension program (SLEP)** • A program designed to extend the period of usefulness of service vessels by giving them an extensive overhaul and modernization refit.

**service line** • Logistic support vessels formed in a line to conduct replenishment.

**service medal** • Medal for service in a specific campaign or theater of operations.

**service message** • Brief communications message incidental to the correction, verification, or handling of another message. The exchange of information between stations.

**service number** • Record identification number for military personnel. Previously a unique number, now the individual's social security number is used. *See also:* file number

**service rating** • *See:* rating

**service record** • Collection of official documents recording a military person's conduct, performance of duties, tests, promotions, etc.

**service stripe** • Sleeve marks worn by enlisted personnel to denote length of service. Each stripe denotes four years. *See also:* hash mark

**servicing** • The refilling of an aircraft with consumables such as fuel oil and compressed gases to predetermined levels, pressures, quantities, or weights.

**serving** • Additional protection over parceling, consisting of continuous round turns of small stuff. *See also:* serve

**servoamplifier** • Either AC or DC amplifiers used in servosystems to build up signal strength. These amplifiers usually have relatively flat gain versus frequency response, minimum phase shift, low output impedance, and low noise level.

**servomotor** • An AC or DC motor used in servosystems to move a load to a desired position or at a desired speed. The AC motor is usually used to drive light loads at a constant speed, while the DC motor is used to drive heavy loads at varying speeds.

**servosystem** • An automatic feedback control system that compares a required condition (desired value, position, and so forth) with an actual condition and uses the difference to drive a control device to achieve the required condition.

**set** • 1. The direction of a current—toward which the water is flowing. 2. A ship is set from its intended course by extraneous forces, such as wind and current. 3. To unfurl sails and sheet them home for use, as in "the captain ordered the first mate to set the main sail to take advantage of the wind." 4. To depart on a voyage, as in "the ship set sail for India." *See also:* drift

**set and drift** • The direction (set) and speed (drift) of a current. In navigation, the cumulative offsetting effect (of wind and current) on a ship that causes her to be in a position other than the one deduced (dead reckoned). "Set" is the direction and "drift" is the speed.

**setback** • The force of inertia that tends to move certain fuze parts to the rear as a projectile is fired. Used to arm a fuze.

**set down** • Set to shoreward.

**set taut** • Rake out all the slack. This order is given before "Hoist away."

**set the watch** • To establish the regular routine of watches on a ship or station. Create a watchbill.

**set up** • To remove the slack; to tighten. An order to take in all the slack on running gear before heaving in. Same as "set taut."

**sextant** • Navigational device used to measure the angular distance between two objects, usually between the Earth's horizon and a celestial body. *See also:* octant; radio sextant

**Sexual Assault Victims Intervention (SAVI)** • A Navy program that educates Sailors and civilians about the crime of sexual assault, its consequences, and how to prevent it.

**SH-60** • *See:* Sea Hawk

**shackle** • U-shaped metal fitting, closed at the open end with a pin; used to connect wire and chain, sail and wire, etc. Name given to a cryptographic system used with voice radio communications.

**shadow zone** • Region in which refraction limits effectiveness of echo-ranging sound systems.

**shaft alley** • The space in a ship through which the propeller shafts extend from the engine room to the screws.

**shake a leg** • *Inf:* An admonishment to move faster.

**shakedown** • Period of adjustment, clean-up, and training for a ship after commissioning or a major overhaul. After commissioning or major overhaul, a ship makes a shakedown cruise for this purpose.

**shamal** • North to west prevailing wind in the Persian Gulf.

**shank** • The central shaft of an anchor to which the flukes are attached.

**shape** • Small structure or object of various description, as officially recognized in the Rules of the Road; displayed aloft to inform other vessels of ongoing activities or status, such as fishing, dredging, at anchor, etc. For example, one ball displayed aloft on the forward part of a vessel signifies that that the vessel is at anchor. Sometimes called dayshapes by convention, but not in the Rules of the Road.

**shark chaser** • Small bag of shark-repelling matter usually attached to life jackets.

**she** • By nautical tradition, vessels are often referred to in the feminine gender (she/her).

**shear** • A break in a part caused by an external pressure.

**shears** • Support used in a hoisting rig, consisting of two spars lashed together at the head and set up so as to resemble an inerted V.

**sheave** • The pulley or grooved wheel in a block over which a fall (line or wire) passes. Pronounced "shiv."

**Sheepshank** • A knot used to shorten a length of line

**sheer** • 1. The amount of curvature of a vessel's hull that is caused by more freeboard forward or aft than amidships.

**sheer off** • To steer away from; to bear off.

**sheer plan** • Architectural drawing of a ship showing the vertical sections of the hull at various select points, from amidships to the outer hull as viewed from amidships, superimposed on one drawing.

**sheer strake** • The uppermost strake in a ship's side plating.

**sheet** • A line that controls a sail by regulating the angle at which the sail is set in relation to the wind. *See also:* three sheets to the wind; sheet home

**sheet anchor** • Anchor formerly carried in the waist of a sailing ship. Sometimes the term was used interchangeably with bower, but bower came into more general use with large steel ships that no longer carry an extra anchor in the location of what would have been the waist.

**sheet bend** • *See:* becket bend

**sheet home** • To extend a square sail by hauling on the sheets until the sail is set as flat as possible. A term used most frequently when the sail is first set or when reefs are shaken out.

**shelf** • The area of sea bottom from the point of permanent immersion to the point where the steep descent to great depths occurs. The seaward line is usually regarded as 100 fathoms or 200 meters. *See also:* continental shelf

**shelf ice** • Ice sheet that originates on land and continues out to sea beyond the depths at which it can rest on the sea bottom.

**shell** • 1. Projectile fired from a gun. Originally the word distinguished an explosive projectile from a solid round shot, because the shell was hollow and full of gun powder. Today, shell refers to projectiles from large guns, all of which are loaded with explosive charges. 2. The casing of a block within which the sheave revolves. 3. A light, very narrow pulling boat with oar outriggers and sliding seats, used for competitive rowing (crew).

**shellback** • *Inf:* Traditional term for a Sailor who has crossed the equator by ship. Before crossing and participating in an initiation ceremony, Sailors are considered pollywogs.

**shell room** • Projectile stowage in a ship's magazine, or in the base of a barbette. *See also:* projectile flat

**sheriff** • *Inf:* Master-at-Arms.

**sheriff's badge** • *Inf:* Badge worn by masters-at-arms when on watch. *Inf:* Command insignia worn by line officers.

**shift** • The act of the wind changing direction. *See also:* shift the rudder

**shift colors** • To shift the national ensign from the flagstaff to the gaff upon getting under way, or from the gaff to the flagstaff upon mooring or anchoring. Simultaneously, the jack is removed from the jackstaff upon getting under way or restored to it upon mooring.

**shift the rudder** • Command to the steersman to apply the same amount of rudder in the opposite direction. For example, if the rudder were positioned at *left* 15°, the command to shift the rudder would tell the helmsman to put the rudder over to *right* 15°.

**ship** • 1. Any large vessel, usually sea-going. 2. Although the term has come to generically mean any large vessel, in the days of sail it had a more specific meaning: a vessel with a bowsprit and three masts, entirely square-rigged, except for the jib(s) and the lowest sail on the aftermost mast, or mizzenmast, which was fore-and-aft rigged and called the spanker. In the days of sail, each type of rig had its own name, such as brig, schooner, sloop, snow, brigantine, hermaphrodite brig, bark or barque, barkentine, topsail schooner. Ship was just one of those many types of rigs. 3. To set up, to secure in place; *e.g.*, ship the rudder or ship the oars.

**ship's bell** • When used to denote time, it is struck every 30 minutes, adding a bell at each half hour so that eight bells is reached at the end of a four-hour watch. The process is then begun again at one bell and repeated for the next four-hour watch. In the days before accurate timepieces were prevalent, the crew relied on these bells to know the time and when to relieve the watch. Ships today often continue the practice more for tradition than out of practical necessity. The ship's bell is also used to sound fog signals, as a fire alarm, and as a means of signaling the arrival and departure of the captain, embarked flag officers, and visiting dignitaries. *See:* watch

**ship's company** • Everyone assigned to a ship; sometimes used on shore stations as well; all hands. Does not include riders or passengers.

**ship's husband** • In the old Navy, a widely-used term describing the man in charge of the repair of a particular ship while she was in a shipyard for an overhaul. Similar to the more modern term "ship superintendent."

**Ship's Organization and Regulations Manual** • A directive issued by the type commander and modified by the individual ship, setting up the organization of the ship—watch and emergency bills, chain of command, etc.

**ship's secretary** • Person who assists the executive officer with the ship's correspondence.

**ship's serviceman (SH)** • Navy occupational rating that manages barbershops, tailor shops, uniform stores, laundries, dry-cleaning plants, and cobbler shops. SHs serve as clerks in exchanges, soda fountains, gas stations, warehouses, and commissary stores.

**ship's service store** • The ship's retail store. It carries supplies for health, comfort, morale, and personal cleanliness of the crew.

**Ship Alteration (SHIPALT)** • Formal authorization to make an alteration on specific machinery or parts of particular ship(s) or class of ships.

**ship-a-sea** • To take on water unintentionally.

**shipboard** • Pertaining to a ship, such as shipboard weapons or shipboard closed-circuit TV system.

**ship conversion** • *See:* conversion, ship

**Ship Equipment Configuration Accounting System (SECAS)** • A Navy system used to keep track of the configuration of equipment in the fleet.

**shiphandling** • The art and science of directing the movements of a ship. Applies to maneuvering in formation, in restricted waters, in docking, mooring, etc.

**shipmate** • Person with whom one is serving or has served, most particularly aboard the same ship. A good friend or colleague.

**ship-of-the-line** • A term originating in the days of sail that describes those ships that would be in the main battle line when fleets took part in major engagements. Such vessels were very large by the day's standards, and heavily armed with multiple gunnery decks. The term "line officer" derives from this.

**ship over** • To reenlist.

**ship-over chow** • *Inf:* Any particularly good meal, supposedly served to encourage reenlistment.

**shipping board clamps** • U-shaped fittings, threaded and including an end piece that is secured with two nuts. Used to join wire or make a temporary eye.

**ship rider** • Any person aboard who is not a part of her crew, but who is temporarily assigned to assist with ship inspections or training, etc. The term does not include passengers, who are there for transport purposes only.

**shipshape** • Neat; orderly; as a ship should be.

**shipshape and Bristol fashion** • Neat and clean with all rigging coiled or flemished down; everything in perfect condition, as a ship should be. Implies a condition superior to merely shipshape. Derived from the days when Royal Navy ships were stationed in the port city of Bristol, England.

**ship superintendent** • The person in overall charge of repairs when a ship is in a shipyard for an overhaul or extensive repairs.

**shipworm** • Any of various elongated marine mollusks that resemble worms. They burrow into the bottoms of wooden ships, bottom planking etc., and can be very destructive. Columbus was forced to abandon

the *Santa Maria* because of the depredations of the "teredo," one of the most common such "worms." Poisonous bottom paint and coppering were the best defenses in the days of wooden ships.

**shipyard** • Shipbuilding and repair facility. A naval shipyard is one maintained by the Navy.

**shoal** • Similar to a reef, but more gradual in its rise from the ocean floor.

**shoaling effect** • The change in a wave as it proceeds from deep to shallow water; its length decreases and its height increases.

**shoe** • 1. Fitting on the stem of some vessels from which paravanes are towed. Also called a clump. 2. Generally, a protective device under the keel or bottom of a ship. *See also:* point of tow

**shole** • Flat plate used in damage control to distribute the force at the end of a shore.

**shooter** • A ship providing naval gunfire support. *Inf:* Catapult officer.

**shoot the sun** • Measure the sun's altitude with a sextant to aid in determining a ship or aircraft's position.

**shoran** • An accurate, short-range navigation system often used for aerial surveying and mapping; uses pulse transmissions, transponders, and a receiver.

**shore** • 1. Portable wooden beam used in effecting temporary repairs for damage control. 2. To shore up is to brace up. 3. The land at the edge of the sea. *See also:* shoring

**shore boat** • Civilian-operated harbor passenger boat, sometimes known as a water taxi.

**shore establishment** • Those activities of the Navy not part of the operating forces.

**shore fire-control party** • Specially trained

unit for the control of naval gunfire in support of troops ashore.

**shore leave** • Obsolete term used to describe liberty or short-term absences from the ship. *See also:* leave; liberty

**shore patrol (SP)** • Personnel ashore on police duty. Often made up of personnel from a visiting ship's company, but sometimes organized as a permanently standing force.

**shoring** • 1. Damage control measures using portable beams and other supports to effect temporary repairs to structural members (stanchions, bulkheads, etc.). 2. Process of placing props against cargo to prevent movement in a seaway.

**short-arm inspection** • *Inf:* Medical inspection for venereal disease.

**short blast** • Whistle, horn, or siren blast of about 1 second in duration. *See also:* blast; prolonged blast

**short stay** • Said of an anchor when it has been hove in just short of breaking water. *See also:* up and down; underfoot; heave right up

**short timer** • Person nearing the end of his or her enlistment, service, or tour of duty.

**shot** • A length of anchor chain, usually 15 fathoms.

**shot line** • Light nylon line used in line-throwing gun.

**shoulder board** • Device indicating rank, worn on an officer's overcoat or, with the summer uniform, jacket or coat. Also called shoulder mark.

**shoulder mark** • *See:* shoulder board

**shove off** • Move a boat away from a ship or pier in order to get under way. *Inf:* Depart, leave, go, as in "let's shove off and head over to the Navy Exchange."

**show a leg** • An expression used in rousing out sleeping sailors. Derived from the days when seamen's "wives" were allowed to sleep aboard ship. Women, who put out a stockinged or otherwise obviously female leg for identification, were not required to turn out at first call, although their men were. Nowadays, it simply means wake up, show signs of being awake. *See also:* son of a gun

**Shrike** • Designated AGM-45, an air-to-air missile designed to home in on enemy anti-aircraft radars.

**shroud** • 1. Lines or wires that give athwartships support to a mast. 2. Lines attaching a parachute's canopy to the jumper's harness. 3. The close-fitting casing around a propeller and turbine blades. *See also:* stay

**shuttle** • Device on an airplane catapult that transmits motion to the aircraft.

**sick bay** • Infirmary or first-aid station aboard ship.

**sick call** • 1. A call (and word) passed daily aboard ship for those who require medical attention to report to sick bay. 2. A scheduled time each day at medical facilities when patients may be seen without an appointment.

**side arms** • Weapons that can be worn in holsters; pistols, revolvers, etc.

**sideboys** • An array of personnel lined up evenly along a quarterdeck or some other cermonial area, forming a path through which a dignitary walks in order to be honored. The number of sideboys varies from two to eight—always being an even number—and is determined by the honored person's rank or office. *See also:* rainbow sideboys

**side cleaners** • Crew members detailed to scrub the sides of the ship.

**side honors** • Ceremonial greeting for

important officials as they come aboard ship. May include piping the side, sideboys, the ship's band and guard, and gun salutes.

**side lights** • 1. The red and green, 10-point, port and starboard running lights required of all ships by the Rules of the Road. 2. British term for air ports or portholes.

**side port** • A watertight opening in a ship's side that is used as a doorway.

**sidereal** • Pertaining to the stars.

**sidereal time** • Time measured by the rotation of the Earth, with respect to the stars. Useful in locating stars for navigational use.

**Sidewinder** • The AIM-9 Sidewinder is an all-weather, heat-seeking, air-to-air missile.

**sierra** • Phonetic word for the letter S.

**sight** • An accurately timed, observed altitude of a heavenly body by use of a sextant for navigational purposes. To see for the first time, as to sight a ship on the horizon.

**sight the anchor** • To heave an anchor up far enough to see that it is clear.

**signal** • Short message using one or more letters, characters, flags, visual displays, or special sounds. Any transmitted electrical impulse.

**signal book** • A standard publication governing tactical communications between naval vessels by flaghoist, radio, etc.

**signal bridge** • Area of the navigating bridge (or near it) equipped with flag bags, signal searchlights, and other means of visual communications.

**signaled speed** • *See:* speed, signaled

**signal flags** • Flags used in visual communication. Uniquely colored and patterned flags representing letters, numbers, and specific definitions that can be correlated with codes to convey simple or complex messages.

**signalman (SM)** • Navy occupational rating that once served as lookouts and, using visual signals and voice radios, alerted their ship of possible dangers. They sent and received messages by flag signals or flashing lights. They stood watches on the signal bridge, encoded and decoded messages, honored passing vessels, and maintained signaling equipment. SM rating was absorbed into the quartermaster rating (QM) in 2004.

**signal number** • Old term for officer's precedence number. Replaced by lineal number in the Navy and number in grade in the Marine Corps.

**signal record book (log)** • A record of all visual signals transmitted or received.

**signal-to-noise ratio** • Logarithmic ratio of signal to interfering noise; used to quantify and compare acoustic noise interference.

**silence** • Command given by any member of a weapons crew who observes a serious casualty that requires immediate attention.

**silent running** • Condition of quiet operation in a submarine, for the purpose of denying detection by an enemy listening for noise.

**sill** • Submerged ridge, at relatively shallow depth, separating two ocean basins. The timber or beam at the entrance gate of a drydock over which a vessel must pass when entering or departing a drydock.

**sill depth** • Greatest depth at which there is free horizontal communication between two ocean basins.

**single up** • A command given before unmooring a ship from a wharf or pier. It means to take in the double sections of line between the ship and the pier, leaving her moored by only single strands of line to the bitts, bollards, or cleats. *See also:* double up

**single whip** • A tackle using a single fixed block. No mechanical advantage, but direction of pull may be changed by its use. *See also:* purchase

**sinuating** • Series of curving variations from the base course steered by a ship. *See also:* evasive steering

**siren** • High-pitched, noise-making device used aboard ship when an emergency—collision, grounding, etc.—is imminent.

**sister hooks** • Pair of hooks that fit together to make a closed ring.

**skeg** • Continuation of the keel aft, under the propeller and supporting the rudder post.

**skids, boat** • Fittings on deck designed to hold and support a boat, composed of saddles making up a cradle and gripes to hold the boat down.

**skipper** • *Inf:* Commanding officer, or any captain of a ship or boat.

**skip zone** • Area between ground waves and sky waves in which no radio waves are received.

**skivvy** • *Inf:* Underwear.

**skivvy-waver** • *Inf:* Signalman.

**skyhook** • 1. A large unmanned balloon sent aloft to record meteorological data. 2. System for rescuing personnel from the sea or isolated areas by aircraft.

**skylark** • A distinctly nautical expression meaning to play or have fun; *i.e.*, to have a lark. Derived from the practice of young Sailors laying aloft and sliding down the backstays.

**sky pilot** • *Inf:* Chaplain.

**skysail** • *See:* sail nomenclature

**Skytrain** • The C-9 Skytrain aircraft provides cargo and passenger transportation, as well as forward deployment logistics support.

**sky waves** • Indirect radio waves that travel from the transmitting antenna into the sky, where the ionosphere deflects them back toward the Earth. *See also:* ground waves

**slack** • 1. Ease out a line. 2. The loose part of a line that takes no strain. *See also:* slack water

**slack water** • Period of no tidal motion between flood and ebb.

**SLAM-ER Missile System** • The AGM-84K Standoff Land Attack Missile-Expanded Response (SLAM-ER), an evolutionary upgrade to the combat-proven SLAM, is an air-launched, day/night, adverse-weather, over-the-horizon, precision strike missile. SLAM-ER addresses the Navy's requirements for a precision-guided Standoff Outside of Area Defense (SOAD) weapon. SLAM-ER provides an effective, long range, precision strike option for both pre-planned and target-of-opportunity attack missions against land and maneuvering ship targets.

**sled** • Towed surface gunnery target, smaller and faster than the bulkier target raft.

**sleeve** • Fabric tube towed by an airplane, used as an antiaircraft target.

**slew** • To rotate rapidly, as a gun director slews to get on a new target.

**slice** • An average logistic planning factor used to obtain estimates of requirements for personnel and material. A personnel slice generally consists of the total strength of the stated basic combatant element, plus its proportionate share of all supporting and higher headquarters personnel.

**slings** • Gear for hoisting something aboard; *e.g.*, boat slings.

**slip** • 1. To part from an anchor by unshackling the chain. 2. A narrow stretch of water between two piers. 3. The lost motion in a propeller.

**slipstream** • The stream of air driven backward by a rotating propeller.

**sloop** • A single-masted sailing vessel, rigged fore-and-aft.

**sloop-of-war** • A fully rigged ship mounting her main battery on only a single deck, usually the spar deck, as distinguished from a frigate, which has mounted guns on two decks. Smaller than a frigate, and faster in light airs or moderate breeze. Spar-decked sloops-of-war, developed after the War of 1812, had covered gundecks and sometimes were more powerful than earlier frigates.

**slop chute** • A chute hung over the side for the discharge of garbage. *Inf:* One who is dirty and disorderly in appearance or habits.

**slow fire** • Deliberate gunfire to permit careful adjustment.

**sludge** • Sediment in fuel oil tanks, lube oil sumps, and boiler water drums.

**sluice** • Any channel, especially one for excess water.

**slush** • The preservative substance applied to wire or line for preservation.

**slush down** • To treat standing rigging with a preservative.

**SM-2** • *See:* Standard missile system

**small arms** • Rifles, shotguns, pistols, and carbines.

**small boy** • *Inf:* Frigate or destroyer.

**small craft** • Any less-than-ship-sized vessel.

**small-craft warning** • Red pennant indicating weather conditions unfavorable or dangerous for small-craft operations.

**small stuff** • A general term for any fiber line less than 1-3/4 inches in circumference. *See also:* marline

**smart** • Neat, shipshape, efficient, military, quick.

**SMART program** • SMART (Sailor/Marine American Council on Education Registry Transcript), the primary purpose of which is to assist service members in obtaining college credit for their military experience. SMART will eventually replace the DD 295, the application for evaluation of learning experiences during military service, which is the form currently submitted to colleges by Sailors and Marines.

**Smit towing bracket** • A specially designed deck-mounted device used to connect a tow pendant to the tow.

**smoke-pipe** • Chimney-like device for carrying smoke from below decks to the atmosphere.

**smoker** • Shipboard entertainment, including food, boxing, humorous skits, movies, etc.

**smokestack** • Chimney-like device for carrying smoke from below decks to the atmosphere.

**smoking lamp** • A symbolic term for controlling the use of tobacco. The word is passed that the "smoking lamp is lighted" or "the smoking lamp is out," to tell crewmembers whether or not they may smoke. A lamp aboard old ships, used by men to light their pipes.

**snake eater** • *Inf:* Special forces personnel.

**snake out** • To break out specific items of cargo.

**snaking** • Netting rigged on lifelines, usually between the deck and the footrope, to prevent objects on deck from going overboard.

**snaphook** • *See:* hank

**snatch block** • Single-sheaved block with a

hinged strap that can be quickly opened to take in a line without having to lead the end of the line through the block. A great convenience for line handling.

**sniffer system** • A passive method for finding snorkeling diesel submarines. Now obsolete, it operated similarly to today's smoke detectors, detecting air particles and contaminants emitted from diesel engines.

**snipe** • *Inf:* Engineering department personnel. *See also:* black gang

**snivel** • *Inf:* To avoid a training flight.

**snooper** • A ship or aircraft that is shadowing or observing.

**snorkel** • Device used by a submarine to enable it to draw air from the surface while submerged. To operate submerged with the snorkel showing.

**snorting** • Royal Navy term for submarine snorkeling.

**snow** • A three-masted square-rigger with a lateen sail instead of a spanker mizzenmast. Pronounced to rhyme with "cow." Differs from a ship by having a smaller than usual mizzen stepped closer to the mainmast, with a large lateen sail on it, and perhaps a smaller than usual topsail above. It resembled a large brig with an additional small mast aft. When a full-size mizzen was used, the vessel was no longer a snow, even though she retained the lateen sail. Most Revolutionary War frigates of our Continental Navy were of this latter type; only a few carried a spanker instead of the lateen sail.

**snub** • To reduce firmly, but not absolutely, the payout of a running line; allowing only enough movement so that it will not part. Similar to check, but implies a much stronger resistance to allowing the line to run. *See also:* check; hold

**snug down** • To make preparations to weather a storm at sea.

**solar still** • Survival equipment that distills fresh water by using energy from sunlight.

**solar time** • Time based upon the rotation of Earth relative to the Sun.

**soluble washer** • Device used to delay the arming of a mine after planting.

**sonar** • Underwater sound equipment for submarine detection and navigation. Similar to radar except used underwater.

**sonar chart** • *See:* chart, sonar

**sonar stack** • The assembled electronic components of sonar gear are called the sonar stack.

**sonar technician (ST)** • Navy occupational rating that operates sonar and other oceanographic systems. STs manipulate, control, evaluate, and interpret data for surface and submarine operations. STs coordinate submarine and auxiliary sonar and underwater fire-control interface, operate surface-ship underwater fire-control systems and associated equipment for the solution of antisubmarine warfare problems, and perform organizational and intermediate maintenance on their respective sonar and allied equipment. Service ratings: STG (surface), STS (submarine).

**sonic depth finder** • Device measuring time for a sound signal to reach bottom and return, giving a reading in terms of depth. *See:* Fathometer

**sonobuoy** • A device that when dropped from an aircraft will remain afloat for a time, collecting sonic information for antisubmarine purposes and transmitting that information to the aircraft for evaluation. Can be passive—listening to sounds generated by submarines—or active—sending out sonic signals and receiving their echoes in order to gather ranging information on the target.

**son of a gun** • A child born aboard ship, alongside one of her broadside cannons. The spaces between guns on the broadside were regular berthing spaces, and the term recalls the old days when sailors were sometimes permitted to have their wives live on board. The result of the custom was an occasional birth and, circumstances being as they must have been, the term implied questionable paternity. An old saying was that a true "man-o'-war's man was begotten in the galley and born under a gun."

**soot blower** • Soot removal device using a stream jet to clean the firesides of a boiler while in use.

**sortie** • 1. To depart for a specific purpose; the act of departing. A naval force sorties from a port. 2. A single mission flown by a single aircraft.

**sound** • 1. To measure the depth of water by lowering a measuring device into it. Result is a sounding. 2. To measure the amount of fluid in a tank by lowering a measuring device into it. 3. To blow a bugle call as in "Sound reveille." 4. A long, wide body of water connected to the sea, larger than a strait or channel. 5. A whale "sounds" when it dives.

**sound channel** • A nautical phenomenon at mid-depth that forms a wave guide permitting the transmission of sound over great distances through the sea.

**sound focus (SOCUS)** • A program used to evaluate upper-air parameters, predicting whether sound produced by bombs or naval gunfire may concentrate at some distance away from a target area with sufficient strength as to cause unwanted property damage.

**soundhead** • The container for a transmitting projector and listening hydrophones in an underwater sound system.

**sounding** • Measured or charted depth of water, or the measurement of such depth. *See also:* sound

**sounding, fixing, and ranging (SOFAR)** • An underwater distress signal whose location is determined by measuring its different times of reception at several stations where, by triangulations and time differential calculation, a position can be established.

**sounding lead** • Same as lead line. Pronounced "led."

**sounding machine** • An obsolete system of a heavy weight, a long wire, and a reel for measuring the depth of deep water. Called a deep-sea (dipsy) lead. Replaced by echo sounder or Fathometer.

**sounding patrol** • Crew members who periodically sound the ship's tanks and report the results to the OOD.

**sounding rod** • Long, metal rod used to sound fuel or water tanks (lowered through a special fitting on the tank; functions like the familiar automobile engine dipstick). *See also:* thieving paste

**soundings** • Water of limited depth, as over the continental shelf; a ship is off-soundings when the hand lead can no longer reach the bottom, and on-soundings when it can.

**sound-powered telephones** • Telephones that generate their own power by the sound vibrations of the voice moving in the field of a magnet. A principal means of communication within a ship; does not transmit beyond the wires involved, so it cannot be picked up by enemy listeners; is not dependent upon electricity or any other power source.

**Sound Surveillance System (SOSUS)** • A system of sonar receivers placed on the seafloor and monitored for unusual noises. Generally placed in natural choke points to detect passage of ships, particularly submarines.

**space** • On board naval vessels, compartments (rooms) and large areas inside the ship are often called "spaces," as in "the engineering spaces."

**spademan** • Operator of the rammer on a 5-inch gun.

**span** • 1. Line made fast at both ends with a tackle, line, or fitting made fast to its bight. 2. Wire rope stretched between davit heads, to which lifelines are secured.

**spanker** • *See:* sail nomenclature

**spanner** • A wrench used for tightening couplings on a fire hose.

**span wire** • Steel cable between ships during underway replenishment that supports the fuel hose, or by which cargo is transferred.

**spar** • 1. A long, cylindrical member of wood or metal, tapered at the ends; usually attached to a mast for use as a boom, or for the attachment of equipment such as signal halyards. 2. Sometimes used as a synonym for mast. *See also:* pigstick; boat boom; yardarm

**spar buoy** • A buoy shaped like a spar—long and cylindrical.

**spar deck** • The topmost or weather deck of a wooden sailing ship, from which the sails, rigging, and spars were handled; and where spare spars were stowed, as well as boats, anchors, and other topside gear requiring quick access.

**Sparrow** • Designated the AIM-7, this highly maneuverable radar-guided air-to-air missile can attack enemy aircraft from any direction, in virtually all weather conditions, and has a range of more than 30 nautical miles.

**special court-martial** • The intermediate of the three types of court-martial. The other types are summary (lesser) and general (higher). A special court-martial consists of a military judge, trial counsel (prosecutor), defense counsel, and a minimum of three officers sitting as a panel of court members or jury. An enlisted accused may request a court composed of at least one-third enlisted personnel. An accused, officer or enlisted, may also request trial by judge alone. Regardless of the offenses involved, a special court-martial sentence is limited to no more than six months confinement, forfeiture of two-third's basic pay per month for six months, a bad-conduct discharge (for enlisted personnel), and certain lesser punishments. An officer accused in a special court-martial may not be dismissed from the service or confined.

**special interest vessel (SIV)** • Any vessel identified by U.S. authorities as a potential threat to U.S. security while in U.S. waters.

**special purpose electronic test equipment (SPETE)** • Test equipment that is specifically designed to generate, modify, or measure a range of electronic functions of a specific or peculiar nature on a single system or piece of equipment.

**special sea and anchor detail** • Those personnel assigned duties in connection with getting under way, mooring, or anchoring.

**special sea detail** • Persons assigned duties in connection with getting under way, mooring, and anchoring. They relieve or are relieved by the regular sea detail.

**special services** • Activities involving the welfare and recreation of personnel.

**special services officer** • One who is responsible for recreational activities at a command

**specialty mark** • The design or insiginia part of a petty officer's rating badge that indicates his or her rating.

**special weapons** • Those involving nuclear or atomic energy.

**specific gravity** • The ratio of the weight of a given volume of a substance to the weight of an equal volume of some standard substance, such as water.

**specified command** • A command that has a broad, continuing mission; established and so designated by the President through the Secretary of Defense, with the advice and assistance of the Joint Chiefs of Staff. Normally composed of forces from one service. *See also:* joint command

**speed cones** • Yellow conical shapes, hoisted at the port and starboard yardarms to indicate engine speed to ships astern. No longer used in the U.S. Navy.

**speed error** • An error introduced in a gyro compass by the curved path a ship follows as it traverses the curved surface of the earth.

**speed key** • Special telegraph key used for sending code at a high rate. Also called a bug.

**speed letter** • Priority form of abbreviated correspondence sent by mail. Similar to a radio message in format and treatment, but sent by conventional mail.

**speed light** • Red or white, steady or flashing, light on the mainmast that indicates to other ships in company the speed the ship is making. No longer used in the U.S. Navy.

**speed of advance** • The average speed in knots that a ship must maintain, along an intended track, in order to arrive at its destination at a specified time.

**speed, operational** • The highest speed at which ships will be required to proceed during a particular period or operation.

**speed, signaled** • The speed at which the guide of a group of ships has been ordered to proceed. Others may need to adjust their speeds in order to stay on their assigned stations.

**speed, stationing** • Speed slower than highest operational speed, used for economy reasons when maneuvering or changing stations.

**spider** • Portable magnifying glass on a compass.

**spike a gun** • To make a cannon unusable, usually by hammering a large spike into it. This was a practice most commonly employed when cannons had to be left behind where they might fall into enemy hands.

**spinnaker** • A large, lightweight, triangular sail, set out on a boom when sailing before the wind.

**spin stablilize** • To stabilize a missile in flight by having it rotate around its long axis.

**spit** • Small point of land or a long, narrow shoal; usually sand, extending outward from the shore.

**spit kid** • 1. Spittoon; ashtray. Also spit kit. 2. Derisive term for small, unseaworthy vessel.

**splash line** • In nighttime underwater demolition unit operations, the point off the enemy beach at which swimmers enter the water from rubber boats.

**splice** • To join two ropes—wire or fiber—or two parts of a line by unlaying them and intertwining their strands. Also applies to electrical wires.

**splice the mainbrace** • To have an officially sanctioned drink. Probably derived from a practice in the early days of sail. Braces are the lines attached to a square-rigger's yards by which they may be trimmed to the wind. It appears that the mainbrace in antiquity was the principal fore-and-aft support of a ship's masts, running from an extremely strong fastening at the bow to the tops of her masts and finally to the deck abaft the mizzenmast. Splicing this fundamental line was one of the most difficult chores on board ship, and one on which her safety depended. Thus, it became the custom to reward those who accomplished the task with a drink.

**splinter deck** • A deck fitted with relatively light armor. *See also:* deck; protective deck

**splinter screen** • Light armor around the bridge and/or gun stations in a ship. Designed for protection against bomb and shell fragments. Also called splinter shield.

**split plant operation** • Subdivision of the engineering plant of a ship into two or more independent units for the purposes of damage control. In this configuration, each main engine or turbine is driven by the steam from its own fireroom.

**spoiler board** • Boards lashed across the leading edges of aircraft wings to destroy lift when aircraft are secured in windy weather.

**sponson** • Projecting structure, platform, or short wing on the hull of a ship or aircraft.

**sponsor** • 1. A member of the ship's company (or shore command) designated to assist a newly arriving shipmate, and his or her family, in getting settled into his or her new assignment. 2. By tradition, the woman who christens a ship at its launching.

**spook** • *Inf:* Intelligence personnel.

**spot** • 1. To observe the fall of shot. 2. A gunnery correction to range, deflection, or fuze range. 3. To station aircraft on a carrier's decks. 4. The location of aircraft on deck; *e.g.*, a flight deck spot. 5. To move cargo or cargo-handling gear.

**spotting board** • 1. Miniature flight and hangar decks with aircraft models; used to plan aircraft carrier spotting of aircraft. 2. A

synthetic fall-of-shot trainer used to instruct gunnery spotters.

**spread** • Multiple salvo of torpedoes fired to ensure a hit.

**spring** • 1. To spring a mast or yard is to crack it so that it is unsafe to carry the usual sail thereon. 2. Using a line to impart motion to a ship's head or stern by exerting force on it. For example, going ahead while a spring line is attached to a vessel near the starboard bow will cause the vessel's stern to swing to port. *See also:* spring line; spring velocity

**spring lay** • Rope in which each strand consists partly of wire and partly of tarred hemp or fiber. Combines the attributes—strength, flex, etc.—of both wire and fiber to the same line.

**spring line** • Mooring line tending forward or aft—nearly parallel to the fore-and-aft centerline of the ship—to prevent forward or backward motion of the ship along the pier; makes an acute angle with the side of the ship, which is perpendicular, or nearly so, to the side of the ship.

**spring stay** • *See:* triatic stay

**spring tidal currents** • Tidal currents of increased velocity during the time of spring tides.

**spring tides** • Those tides occurring near the times of new and full moon; characterized by increased angle in height.

**spring velocity** • The average of the maximum flood and ebb velocities at the time of spring tides.

**sprinkling system** • Installed emergency water system for putting out fires and keeping boundaries cool in magazines containing explosives or pyrotechnics.

**spud** • A post or pile used to secure a dredge or scow.

**squadron** • Administrative or tactical organization consisting of two or more divisions of ships or boats. Administrative unit of aircraft; divided into divisions and sections for tactical purposes.

**squall** • Short but intense windstorm, often accompanied by rain or snow.

**square away** • To straighten, make ship-shape, or to get settled in a new job or home. To inform or admonish someone in an abrupt or curt manner.

**square knot** • Simple knot used for bending two lines together or for bending a line to itself.

**square knotting** • Hobby of making belts, watch bands, etc., out of knotted cord. *See also:* sennit; coxcombing

**square-rigger** • A sailing ship, the majority of whose sails are square in shape and rigged generally athwartship, as opposed to one that is fore-and-aft rigged.

**square sail** • Sail cut into an approximate square or rectangular shape and mounted on yards that extend equally on both sides of a mast. The standard sail of a square-rigger. Distinguished from fore-and-aft sail.

**squatting** • When a power-driven vessel proceeds at speed, her stern tends to ride lower in the water than does her bow, due to the bite of the screws; this change in trim is known as squatting.

**squawk box** • *Inf:* Interoffice or interstation voice communication unit; intercom.

**squealer rings** • The rings in the glands of a turbine that have the smallest clearance. Their rubbing is an audible alarm signal for stopping the turbine.

**squib** • Miniature, electrically-fired explosive, used in rockets as an igniter.

**Squid** • Forward-launched ASW weapon developed by the British Navy.

**squid** • *Inf:* Term, usually derogatory, used by persons of other services to describe a Sailor.

**squilgee** • Wooden, rubber-shod deck dryer. Pronounced "squee-gee."

**stability** • Ability of a ship to right itself after being heeled over. *See also:* metacenter; metacentric height

**stability board** • Visual representation, used by damage control personnel as a status board, of liquid loading, location of flooding, effect on list and trim, etc.

**stabilize** • To correct adverse conditions affecting a vessel's stability. To introduce devices or conditions that will improve a projectile's or a missile's ability to stay on course.

**stabilizers** • Retractable fins resembling submarine bowplanes that project from a ship's side below the waterline. Employed to reduce a ship's motion in a seaway.

**stable element** • Gyro mechanism that stabilizes an instrument, such as a gun sight, against the roll and pitch of a ship.

**stack** • A large pipe extending above the main deck to exhaust smoke and gas from furnaces or fireboxes under the boilers. The internal cluster of sonar equipment used by operators when operating the sonar.

**stack cover** • Cover placed over the open end of a smoke stack when the stack is not in use. Also called a watch cap.

**stack wash** • Air turbulence astern of a ship due to stack gases carried aft by the relative wind.

**stadimeter** • Instrument for visually measuring distance to objects of known height by the mechanical solution of a right triangle. Commonly used to measure distance to other ships in formation.

**staff** • Personnel without command function or authority who assist a commander in administration and operation.

**staff codes** • *See:* N-codes

**staff officers** • Those who perform staff functions, such as doctors, chaplains, dentists, civil engineers, supply officers, and medical service officers; as distinguished from line officers.

**stage** • Platform that is designed to be hung over the side of a ship to provide a working area on which personnel can stand to paint, etc.

**staging** • Processing, in a specific area, of troops and/or supplies in preparation for movement.

**stanchion** • Vertical post used for supporting decks; smaller ones are used for supporting lifelines, awnings, etc.

**stand** • Brief period of no change in water level at high or low tide.

**standard commands** • Official words or phrases used in giving orders during important or potentially dangerous activities, such as gunfiring or shiphandling. By their use, rather than just using one's own phrasing, there is far less chance of a misunderstanding. *See also:* standard terminology

**standard compass** • The magnetic compass used by the navigator as a reference or standard. *See also:* gyrocompass; per standard compass

**Standard Missile System** • Standard Missile 2 (SM-2) is a surface-to-air missile defense weapon with both medium and extended range versions available. As an integral part of the Aegis Weapon System aboard *Ticon-*

*deroga*-class cruisers and *Arleigh Burke*-class destroyers, SM-2 can be launched from the MK 41 Vertical Launcher System (VLS) or the MK 26 Guided Missile Launcher System. Its primary mission is fleet area air defense and ship self defense, but it also has a secondary antisurface ship mission. SM-2s use tail controls and a solid fuel rocket motor for propulsion and maneuverability, and the extended range verson has a booster with thrust vector controls. All are guided by inertial navigation and mid-course commands from the Aegis Weapon System and use a semi-active radar or an IR sensor for terminal homing. SM-2 succeeds SM-1 and the Terrier and Tartar missile systems.

**standard rudder** • That amount of rudder in degrees required to cause a ship to turn with a standard tactical diameter.

**Standards of Training, Certification, and Watchkeeping (STCW)** • The Standards of Training, Certification & Watchkeeping (STCW) Convention was drafted in 1978. In it's first version, it had little impact on the US mariner because it really just formalized a system nearly identical to the US system, around the world. It established such things as the requirement for 4 years of experience for a Master 1600 gt license. The big change came in 1995 when the US Coast Guard approached the International Maritime Organization (IMO) and asked them to amend the convention. Significant changes were made to the convention. The STCW 95 amendments did not have to be ratified like the original convention because it was an amendment to an existing convention. The amendments, however, completely re-wrote enforcement related to the Convention, and more importantly created an STCW Code (similar to the USCG licensing regulations) that set stringent standards for mariners to meet. Unlike the original 1978 Convention, the 1995 Amendments required a separate piece of paper to certify that the mariner met the requirements. The STCW Certificate was the result.

**standard tactical diameter** • *See:* tactical diameter

**standard terminology** • Words, terms, and phrases used in official directives to avoid ambiguity or confusion. *See also:* standard commands

**stand at rest** • *See:* at rest

**stand by** • 1. To wait. 2. To substitute for someone who has the day's duty. 3. A substitute. 4. To prepare for or make ready.

**stand from under** • To avoid the wrath of a superior. Literally, to get out and away from danger.

**stand in** • Head in to a harbor, battle, etc.

**standing lights** • Dim red lights throughout the interior of a ship, which enable the crew to move about the ship safely after lights out; red being the color that least impairs night vision.

**standing order** • A permanent or semipermanent order or directive.

**standing part** • That part of a tackle that is made fast. The part on which power is applied is the hauling part. *See also:* purchase

**standing rigging** • That part of a vessel's rigging that provides support and is not normally moved or adjusted when under way.

**standing wave ratio (SWR)** • The ratio of the maximum (voltage, current) to the minimum (voltage, current) points of a transmission line. Indicates the impedance matching quality of the termination of the line.

**stand out** • To depart from port or harbor and take a course to seaward; as in "stand out to sea."

**Starbase-Atlantis** • A youth-oriented program sponsored by the U. S. Navy serving communities by promoting math, science, drug demand reduction, and goal-setting skills. Accomplished through exciting hands-on activities taught by an enthusiastic, caring staff in a safe, stable environment. Exposes children and their teachers to real-world applications of math and science through experiential learning, simulations, experiments in aviation and space-related fields, interaction with Navy personnel, and tours of Navy activities. A dynamic self-esteem building and goal setting program motivates students to set goals and pursue them.

**starboard** • 1. To the right of centerline as you face forward. 2. Directional term for right, as opposed to port, which generally means left. Although generally assumed to mean right, be aware that there is an orientation factor; the starboard bridgewing is on the observer's left if the observer is facing aft. *See also:* port; port and starboard

**star finder** • Mechanical or graphic device for identifying celestial bodies.

**star guage** • Device for accurately measuring the bore diameter of a gun.

**star shell** • Projectile that detonates in the air, releasing an illuminating flare.

**start** • To induce motion, as to start a grounded vessel.

**star tracker** • A light-sensing device properly gimballed and electronically controlled to detect and maintain the line of sight to a star. Functions as an automatic sextant.

**stateroom** • An officer's living space aboard ship. It sometimes serves as the officer's office, as well.

**station** • 1. To assign individuals or a group a specific place to be, such as "station the quarterdeck watch." 2. A post of duty, as a battle station. 3. A specific position in a formation of ships. 4. A naval activity that provides some kind of support. 5. In ship's plans, a section perpendicular to the keel is sometimes called a station.

**stationing speed** • *See:* speed, stationing

**station keeping** • The art and science of keeping a ship in its proper position in a formation.

**stator** • The stationary part of a rotating electrical machine. The stator may be either the field or the armature, depending on the design of the machine. The stationary member of a synchro that consists of a cylindrical structure of slotted laminations on which three Y-connected coils are wound with their axes 120 degrees apart. Depending on the type of synchro, the stator's functions are similar to the primary or secondary windings of a transformer.

**statute mile** • A unit of distance equal to 5,280 feet.

**stay** • Wire or cable supporting a mast in the fore-and-aft direction, such as a backstay (which tends aft) or a forestay (which tends forward). *See also:* backstay; forestay; shroud

**steady** • An order to the helmsman, following that to put the rudder amidships; means to steady the ship on whatever heading she comes to. Useful in evasive submarine maneuvers during depth charging, to minimize rudder action.

**steady as you go** • Order to the helmsman to steer the ship on the course it is heading at the time the order is given.

**steadying line** • *See:* tag line

**steam drum** • *See:* drum, steam

**steam fog** • Fog formed when water vapor is added to air that is much colder than the vapor's source; most commonly, when very cold air drifts across relatively warm water.

**steam generator** • Takes the place of the boiler in a nuclear-powered ship.

**steaming watch** • Engineering watch stood when the main engines are in use and the ship is under way.

**steam lance** • Device for using low-pressure steam on a deck to remove ice, as well as to clean boiler firesides.

**steelworker (SW)** • Navy occupational rating that rigs and operates all special equipment used to move or hoist structural steel, structural shapes, and similar material. SWs erect or dismantle steel bridges, piers, buildings, tanks, towers, and other structures. They place, fit, weld, cut, bolt, and rivet steel shapes, plates, and built-up sections used in the construction of overseas facilities.

**steerageway** • The lowest speed at which a ship can be steered. Because a rudder depends upon the flow of water across its surface to function, it loses its capability at speeds too slow to provide the flow needed.

**steering engine** • The machine that turns the rudder; usually hydraulic with an electric motor. Also called the steering gear. *See also:* ram; rudder

**steering gear** • *See:* steering engine

**steersman** • The individual who steers the ship; same as a helmsman, which is more commonly used in the Navy.

**Steinke hood** • Emergency submarine escape device that consists of a bonnet placed over an individual's head to enclose an air pocket; permits escape from a submarine sunk at moderate depth. It is fitted with a transparent plastic visor for vision.

**stem** • The leading edge of a vessel's bow. The forward end of the keel, extended upward.

**stem band** • A metal band attached to the stem of a wooden boat.

**step** • 1. The act of erecting a mast. 2. The socket or other recess that holds the foot of a mast.

**sterilizer** • Device included in a mine that renders it harmless after a certain period. Required by international law.

**stern** • The aftermost section of a ship.

**stern anchor** • Any anchor carried aft. May be used for a stream anchor. In certain amphibious ships of WWII, the special configuration of which made them ride better stern-to than bow-to, it was the ship's principal anchor. Ship's designed to beach themselves to land troops and equipment (*e.g.*, the WWII LST) needed stern anchors to hold themselves in position and to withdraw off the beach, in a manner similar to kedging. *See also:* kedge

**stern fast** • Stern line used to secure a boat.

**stern hook** • Member of a boat's crew who sands aft and makes the boat's stern secure. *See also:* bow hook

**stern light** • White navigation light that can be seen only from astern to 6 points on either quarter (total of 12 points, or 135 degrees).

**sternpost** • The principal structural member in a vessel's stern; similar to the stem, except at the opposite end of the vessel. The after end of the keel extended upward.

**stern sheets** • Area or seats in the stern of a boat.

**stern tube** • Circular, watertight fitting through which the propeller shaft emerges from the ship. A stern-mounted torpedo tube.

**sternway** • Progress astern; opposite of headway.

**stevedore** • A person who loads and unloads ships' cargo. Generally, the same as longshoreman.

**steward elbow** • Special fitting at the end of a hose, where it enters a fuel trunk during underway fueling.

**stew burner** • *See:* commissaryman

**stick** • *Inf:* Mast.

**stick out** • Pay out, as to pay out the cable on a stem anchor winch.

**stock** • The cross bar of an anchor that prevents the anchor from flipping over once it reaches bottom. Old-fashioned anchors had stocks, but modern ones more often are stockless for more practical stowage and handling.

**stockless anchor** • An anchor without a stock, that can be housed right up into its own hawse and secured merely by putting a stopper on the chain. The old-fashioned anchor was very difficult to secure for sea because of the stock. When larger ships required much heavier anchors, the old-fashioned anchor became impractical. Also called a patent anchor. *See also:* anchor; stock

**stop** • A short line attached to the edge of an awning, boat cover, etc.; used to lash the cover to a support.

**stopper** • Any chain, piece of line, etc., used to prevent movement of a larger chain, line, etc. *See also:* housing chain stopper

**storekeeper (SK)** • Navy occupational rating that functions as the Navy's supply clerks. SKs see that needed supplies, everything from clothing and machine parts to forms and food, are available. SKs have duties as civilian warehousemen, purchasing agents, stock clerks and supervisors, retail sales clerks, store managers, inventory clerks, buyers, parts clerks, bookkeepers, and even forklift operators.

**stores** • Supplies.

**storm** • Meterological disturbance; more specifically, one with winds of 56–65 knots. *See also:* breeze; gale; hurricane

**stove** • Broken in; smashed. Generally used with "in," as "The sea stove in the bulkhead."

**stow** • To put away; to store.

**stowage factor** • Number of cubic feet that cargo will occupy in a vessel.

**straddle** • A salvo in which some of the shots are seen to fall beyond the target and some short of it, or some right and others left. The mean point of impact is thus on or near the target.

**strake** • Continuous line of fore-and-aft planking or plating in a boat or ship that makes up part of the vessel's hull.

**strand** • 1. One of the main subdivisions of a line or wire. 2. To go aground, as in "the boat was stranded on the rocks."

**strap** • A ring of wire or line made by splicing the ends together, used for handling weight, etc. A metal band such as that used to secure lead ballast in the bottoms of ships.

**strategy** • The basic, overall plan by which a naval commander intends to accomplish the assigned mission. Generally pertains to the macro rather than the micro (tactical) view. *See also:* tactics

**stratocumulus** • Low clouds (mean upper level below 6,550 feet) composed of a layer, or patches, of globular masses or rolls.

**stratus** • A low cloud (mean upper level below 6,550 feet) in a uniform layer.

**stray voltage** • An undesired voltage existing between two specified points of a weapon system that produces a detectable flow of current when an electrical measuring device is connected between the two points.

**stream anchor** • An anchor dropped off the stern or quarter to prevent a ship from swinging to a current.

**stress** • A force that produces, or tends to produce, deformation in metal.

**strike** • 1. A combat flight against ground or ship targets. 2. To work for an improvement or promotion in one's job, as in "He is striking for chief." 3. To strike one's colors is to lower the national flag as a signal of surrender. *See also:* striker

**strike below** • Take below decks, as stores are struck below after being brought aboard. Incorrectly used sometimes to describe the action of a person, as in "Strike below and change uniforms."

**striker** • An apprentice or learner. One who aspires to a promotion or to learning the skills of a particular rating.

**stringer** • 1. A longitudinal frame providing strength to a ship's sides. 2. A long timber between piles at the edge of a pier.

**strip ship** • Process of removing superfluous, potentially dangerous material from a ship when war or emergency is imminent. *See also:* clear ship

**strongback** • 1. A damage control bar or beam, shorter than a shore. 2. Padded spar between the davits against which the boat is griped in. 3. A supporting girder for a hatch cover.

**structural bulkhead** • Transverse strengthening bulkhead that forms a watertight boundary.

**strut** • A type of supporting brace. A rigid member or assembly that bears compression loads, tension loads, or both; such as a landing gear transmits the load from the fuselage of the aircraft.

**stud** • The metal piece in a link of anchor

chain that keeps the link from kinking.

**studding boom** • *See:* studding sail

**studding sails** • Extra sails rigged outboard of a square-rigger's regular sails, on light yards called studding booms. Suitable only for light winds. With all studding sails set, a ship would add considerably to her sail area and therefore increase her potential for speed.

**stuffing box** • Device to prevent leakage between a moving and a fixed part in a ship, particularly where a moving part comes out through the hull.

**stuffing tube** • Packed tube that makes a watertight fitting through a bulkhead for a cable or small pipe.

**submarine combat air patrol (SUBCAP)** • A combat air patrol specifically linked to one or more submarines for coordinated operations.

**submarine emergency buoyancy system (SEBS)** • Emergency deballasting system to permit rapid surfacing of a submarine.

**submarine escape lung** • *See:* Steinke hood

**submarine havens** • Sea areas in which no attacks on submarines are permitted, allowing a safe passage for allied submarines in wartime. Submarine havens may be fixed (stationary, as defined by navigational or geographic coordinates) or moving at a specified course and speed.

**submarine marker buoy** • A buoy released from a sunken submarine that floats to the surface and marks the spot for rescue and salvage.

**submarine patrol area** • A stretch of water with specific geographic limits, assigned to a submarine as her area of action. Essentially the same as submarine patrol zones except more permanent in nature and associated with probable focal points of enemy traffic.

**submarine patrol zones** • Restricted sea areas established for the pupose of permitting submarine operations unhampered by the operation of, or possible attack by, friendly forces.

**submariner** • Officer or enlisted person assigned to duty in submarines. The U.S. Navy pronounciation is "submarine-er." The Royal Navy says "sub-mariner," as though "mariner" were a separate word.

**submarine radio rescue buoy** • Device released from a sunken submarine that can rise to the surface and broadcast an emergency signal.

**submarine rescue chamber** • Device similar to a diving bell which can be lowered to a disabled submariine and fitted over an escape hatch, allowing a few people to be brought to the surface at a time. *See also:* deep submergence rescue vehicle

**submarine rocket (SUBROC)** • Submarine-launched rocket-powered depth bomb that can be fired from a submerged torpedo tube. Model designation is UUM-44.

**submarine sanctuaries** • Restricted areas established for the conduct of noncombat submarine or antisubmarine exercises. They may be either stationary or moving, and are normally designated only in rear areas.

**submarine (SS)** • Warship designed for under-the-surface operations. Attack submarines have the primary mission of locating and destroying ships, including other submarines. Fleet ballistic missile (FBM) submarines generally have the primary mission of attacking strategic land targets.

**submarine striking force** • A group of submarines formed for a specific offensive action against an enemy. In modern context, they would probably have missile-launching capabilities.

**submarine tender (AS)** • A ship specially

designed to tend to the needs of submarines; equipped with maintenance shops, repair parts, etc., specifically associated with the equipment found on submarines.

**submerged ordnance recovery device (SORD)** • Surface-manipulated device guided by closed-circuit television for the recovery of sunken ordnance.

**submersible delivery capsule** • Vehicle used in conjunction with a seadpod to transfer divers to and from an underwater work site.

**submersible pump** • Watertight electric pump that can be lowered into a flooded compartment to pump it out.

**submunition** • Smaller weapons carried as a warhead by a missile or projectile and expelled as the carrier approaches its target.

**subordinate** • Someone of lower rank or lesser seniority.

**subsistence allowance** • Money paid in lieu of food furnished. *See also:* commuted rations

**substitute** • Flag used to repeat another flag in a signal hoist; formerly called a repeater.

**subsurface currents** • Currents flowing below the surface. Usually they have different speeds and sets from surface currents.

**sugar** • Past phonetic word for the letter S; replaced with sierra.

**suitcase** • Portable command center for use on the bridge of a surfaced submarine; about the size of a portable typewriter, it is designed to replace several bridge instruments.

**summary court-martial** • The lowest of the three types of court-martial. A summary court-martial provides a simplified procedure for the resolution of charges involving minor

incidents of misconduct. The summary court-martial consists of one officer. The maximum punishment a summary court-martial may impose is considerably less than a special or general court-martial. The accused must consent to be tried by a summary court-martial.

**sump** • A container, compartment, or reservoir used as a drain or receptacle for fluids.

**sundowner** • An extremely strict officer. The term carries a connotation of sadism in the application of the rules. Derived from the ancient regulation that officers and men of a ship in commission must spend the night on board and must, in fact, be back aboard by sundown. A captain who insisted on observance of this regulation after it had outlived its purpose was called a sundowner.

**sun over the yardarm** • *Inf:* An expression meaning that it is time for the first drink (alcoholic beverage).

**superheated steam** • Steam that has been heated beyond the boiling point of water and contains no moisture. Steam that is not superheated is saturated steam.

**superheater** • A unit in a propulsion boiler that dries the steam and raises its temperature for greater efficiency.

**super high frequency (SHF)** • One of the designations of the radio frequency spectrum; covers the range 3,000–30,000 MHz.

**Super Hornet** • The F/A-18E/F Super Hornet is the Navy's newest operational multimission tactical aircraft. It is designed to complement and eventually supplant F/A-18A-D Hornet and F-14 Tomcat carrier-based aircraft. The Super Hornet is highly capable across its full mission spectrum: air superiority, fighter escort, armed reconnaissance aerial refueling, close air support, air defense suppression and day/night conventional and precision strike, including laser, IR and GPS precision-guided munitions. Compared to the original F/A-18 A through D models, the F/A-18E/F has longer range, aerial refueling capability, increased survivability/lethality, and improved carrier suitability. Compared to the F-14 Tomcat, the Super Hornet's cost per flight hour is 40% lower and requires 75% less labor hours per flight hour.

**superstructure** • All structure above the main deck of a ship; may be split or all in one group.

**superstructure deck** • A partial deck above the main deck. *See also:* deck

**Supply Systems Command** • Functional command created in a 1966 Navy Department reorganization that replaced Bureau of Supplies and Accounts (BUSANDA).

**surface effect ship (SES)** • A vehicle designed to move across water or flat earth, supported on a cushion of downward-blasted air.

**surface strike groups (SSG)** • Formerly called surface action groups, these are multiship groups composed of cruisers and destroyers organized for specific surface warfare missions.

**surface-to-air** • Weapons carried aboard ships that are designed to shoot down incoming enemy aircraft and missiles.

**surface warfare** • A career specialty for Sailors involving the manning and operating of surface ships. Naval personnel are Sailors first, then often subdivided into various career specialties such as aviation, submarines, and surface warfare.

**surf forecasting** • Technique of predicting the size and nature of ocean surf along a shoreline. Important for amphibious operations.

**surf line** • *See:* breaker line

**surf zone** • That portion of the littoral where waves are breaking; can be a significant factor in amphibious operations.

**surge** • 1. Deploying a strike group ahead of schedule. 2. To slack off a line by letting it slip slowly around a fitting. 3. Motion of a ship in which it is displaced alternately forward and aft, usually when moored. 4. The horizontal water motion accompanying a seiche.

**surgeable** • A unit that is considered ready and available for rapid deployment in case of unplanned crises.

**surge ready** • The next three-month window, after being emergency surgeable, during which integrated strike group training occurs. It culminates in composite training unit exercises and/or joint task-force exercises.

**survey** • 1. Official procedure that involves removing accountable material from books or records after it is lost or damaged beyond repair. May be a special, formal, or informal survey. 2. To survey an area is to explore and chart it.

**surveying ship (AGS)** • Ship that conducts hydrographic surveys for charting purposes.

**suspect nonmilitary vessel category** • Vessel whose movements are controlled or believed to be controlled by a hostile nation. A vessel known to have visited a port of a hostile nation within a specified period of time, such as within the past 6 months.

**swab** • 1. Nautical term for a mop. 2. *Inf:* A first-year cadet at the U.S. Coast Guard Academy. 3. *Inf:* Sailor.

**swabbie** • *Inf:* Sailor.

**swab jockey** • *Inf:* Deck hand.

**swage** • To make a binding between a fitting and a wire rope by hammering the fitting until its diameter over the wire rope is reduced so that the fitting holds the wire rope tightly.

**swallow** • The larger opening in a block between the sides, through which the fall leads or the line reeves.

**swallow the anchor** • *Inf:* To leave the service or leave the sea.

**swamp** • To fill with water, as a boat may do in heavy seas. The boat may or may not sink as a result.

**swash** • The rush of water up onto the beach following the breaking of a wave. Also called backrush.

**swashplates** • Metal plates in fuel tanks, boiler steam drums, etc., that prevent the surging of liquid when a vessel is in motion; contributes to ship stability.

**sway** • Motion of a ship in which the ship is displaced laterally; distinct from rolling. *See also:* heaving; pitch; roll; surge; yaw

**sweep** • Minesweeping operation. May be either a clearance or exploratory sweep. A rotating radar antenna is said to sweep.

**sweepers** • 1. Word passed for designated personnel to man brooms and sweep the ship clean. 2. Those who sweep down the ship.

**swell** • Wind-generated waves that have advanced into a calmer area and are decreasing in height and gaining a more rounded form. The heave of the sea.

**swept channel** • Area that is kept clear of mines.

**swift boat** • A fast patrol craft (PCF) used for coastal surveillance and riverine interdiction operations, primarily during the Vietnam War.

**swing out** • To swing a boat from its stowed position to its lowering position. Reverse procedure for swing in.

**swing ship** • To steam on various courses to determine a curve of compass error (deviation).

**swivel** • Removable anchor chain link fitted to revolve freely; prevents kinks in a chain. *See also:* mooring swivel

**sword arm** • A device—that resembles a sword blade and contains a pitot tube—that is lowered beneath the hull when the ship is clear of a port or anchorage to measure her speed through the water. *See also:* pitometer log

**synchro** • A small motorlike analog device that operates like a variable transformer and is used primarily for the rapid and accurate transmission of data among equipments and stations.

**synoptic** • In general, pertaining to or affording an overall view. In meteorology, this term has become specialized in referring to the use of meteorological data obtained simultaneously over a wide area for presenting a comprehensive picture of the state of the atmosphere.

**syzygy** • The two opposite points in the orbit of the moon when it is in conjunction with or in opposition to the sun.

# T

**T-2** • *See:* Buckeye

**T-45** • *See:* Goshawk

**tab** • A small, auxiliary airfoil set into the trailing edge of an aircraft control surface and used to trim or move the larger surface. Part of an operation order (OPORD) or operation plan (OPLAN). So named because of the tabs put on the edges of the pages for quicker location.

**tablemount** • *See:* seamount

**tack** • 1. Lower forward corner of a fore-and-aft sail. 2. The direction relative to the wind in which a sailing vessel goes, either on the port or starboard tack, depending on the direction from which the wind strikes the sails. 3. To tack is to come about or change tacks; thus a sailing boat tacks or zigzags upwind. 4. The distance a boat sails on a port or starboard tack is called a tack. 5. To come about by turning the bow through the wind; opposite of wear. 6. A separator, similar to a dash, used in voice radio and visual communications.

**tackle** • An arrangement of line and blocks to gain a mechanical advantage. Pronounced "tay-kul." *See also:* purchase

**tackline** • Short length of line used in a flaghoist to increase the normal distance between flags. Separates two signals on the same hoist, or symbolizes a tack (similar to a dash).

**tactical action officer (TAO)** • The officer in charge of the ship's combat systems; highly qualified individual who has been entrusted with fighting the ship when the commanding officer is indisposed.

**tactical air control group (TACGRU)** • An administrative and tactical force component that provides aircraft control and warning facilities.

**tactical air navigation (TACAN)** • An electronic homing system used by aircraft to find their way back to their aircraft carrier.

**tactical diameter** • The distance gained to the right or left of the original course when a turn of 180° has been completed. When a ship's rudder is put over, the path of the ship inscribes an arc in the water; if continued around to 180° or more, the diameter of the semicircle (or circle) is known as the tactical diameter. To ensure ships turn together (maintain formation) a standard tactical diameter may be defined and the individual ships will define the amount of rudder needed to achieve that diameter as "standard rudder." *See also:* final diameter

**tactical interval** • Specified distance between adjacent ships in formation.

**tactical range recorder** • Equipment used in the evaluation of the visual presentations of ranging echoes from underwater targets.

**tactics** • The employment of units in battle toward accomplishment of the mission. Includes such things as maneuvering, sensor selection, and weapons employment. *See also:* strategy

**taffrail** • The rail around the stern of a ship or boat.

**taffrail log** • Old device that indicated the speed of a ship through the water. It was trailed on a line from the taffrail and consisted of a propeller-like rotator and a recording instrument.

**tag line** • Line used to steady a load being swung in or out. Also called a steadying line.

**tail block** • A block with a tail of rope instead of a hook.

**tailhook** • The hook lowered from the after part of a carrier aircraft that engages the arresting gear upon landing, thus bringing the plane to a stop.

**tailhooker** • *Inf:* A naval aviator qualified to make carrier landings.

**tail on** • Order to lay hold of a line and haul away.

**take an even strain** • *Inf:* Relax; calm down.

**take a strain** • To apply tension on a line, wire, or chain. "Take an even strain" means to relax.

**take a turn** • To pass a line around a cleat or bitt. Usually followed by an order to hold it, check it, or ease it.

**take in** • Command to take aboard a designated mooring line or lines, as in "take in the stern line."

**talker** • A person assigned to pass orders and information to and from his or her station, usually by sound-powered phones.

**tally-ho** • Report made by a fighter pilot when he or she sights an assigned target.

**Talos** • Shipboard antiaircraft missile system. Longest range of the "three Ts" of surface-to-air missiles: Talos, Terrier, and Tartar. Replaced by the Standard Missile System.

**tampion** • *See:* tompion

**tangent latitude error** • An error introduced in a gyro compass by the method used for damping the oscillations of the compass.

**tango** • Phonetic word for the letter T.

**tanker** • 1. A ship that transports fuel to a base or service squadron. An oiler, on the other hand, fuels other ships at sea or an anchorage. 2. An aircraft that refuels planes in the air.

**taps** • Bugle call sounded as last call at night for all hands to turn in, and as a final farewell at funerals.

**tar** • General name for an enlisted Sailor. Derived from the old custom of a Sailor waterproofing his clothing with tar and also putting tar in his hair to prevent it from blowing in the wind and getting caught in the ship's rigging. Sometimes called Jack-tar.

**tar down** • To coat the standing rigging with tar.

**tare** • Past phonetic word for the letter T; replaced with tango.

**tare victor george** • *See:* bravo zulu

**target angle** • 1. The relative bearing upon which another vessel would see your vessel. Useful in determining another vessel's course. For example, if you spot a vessel off your port bow and determine by observation that she has a target angle of 270°, you would know that she will not cross your bow (unless she changes course radically). 2. Relative bearing of the firing ship, from the target, measured from the bow of the target to the right through 360°. *See also:* angle on the bow

**target bearing** • True compass direction of a target from the firing ship.

**target-grid method** • Standard shore bombardment procedure using a specially configured target grid system for determining firing missions and adjustments.

**tarpaulin** • Any flat piece of canvas used for a cover. Often shortened to tarp.

**tarpaulin muster** • Collection of funds aboard ship for some common purpose, such as to assist a shipmate's widow. A tarpaulin was once spread and contributions tossed into it.

**Tartar** • Name for a Navy surface-to-air missile system. Shortest range of the "the Ts" of surface-to-air missiles: Tartar, Terrier, and Talos.

**task element** • Part of a task organization, subordinate to a task group and superior to a task unit. *See also:* task organization

**Task Force Sea Sentry** • A program for refining the science of strategic information management in the U.S. 6th Fleet area of operations. *See also:* Theater Fusion Center

**task organization** • Standard operational organization for the U.S. Navy since World War II. The largest task-oriented entity is the fleet (identified by a single digit, as in 7th Fleet); next largest is the task force (identified by two digits, as in TF 77); next is the task group (identified by two digits, a decimal point, and a third digit [or more if necessary], as in TG 77.1 or TG 77.12); next is the task unit (identified by two digits, a decimal point, a third digit [or more if necessary], another decimal point, and another digit [or digits], as in TU 77.12.1); next is the task element, (formed by adding another decimal and digit[s], as in TE 77.12.1.4).

**tattletale** • A tattletale cord is a bight of six-thread manila hanging from two measured points on a working line (such as a mooring line). When tensioned to its safe working load (SWL), the line will stretch to a certain percentage of its length. When this point is reached, the six thread becomes taut, warning that there is danger of exceeding the line's SWL.

**tattoo** • Bugle call sounded 5 minutes before taps as a signal to prepare to turn in.

**taut** • Tight, without slack. Well-disciplined and efficient, as a taut ship.

**telemetering system** • Measuring, receiving, and transmitting instruments carried by a test missile, together with receiving and recording instruments at a control system; used to evaluate the effectiveness of the missile shot.

**telemetry** • Science involving the taking of measurements and their transmission to detached stations where they can be displayed, interpreted, or recorded.

**telescopic alidade** • A device used with a gyro repeater for taking bearings.

**telltale** • Short pieces of light line attached to edges of sails to indicate the flow of wind. In the old Navy, a compass kept in the captain's cabin to enable him to know the ship's course without having to go out on deck. Was often suspended inverted from the overhead so the captain could see it from his bed.

**temperature** • Measure of the intensity or degree of heat. It is generally expressed in the U.S. Navy in degrees Fahrenheit, a scale in which water freezes at 32 degrees and boils at 212 degrees.

**temporary additional duty (TAD)** • A short assignment away from one's parent command, in addition to regular duties.

**temporary duty (TDY)** • A duty assignment of relatively short duration; often enroute to a permanent duty station.

**tenant command** • A command that is physically located within the jurisdiction of a larger command or base.

**tend** • 1. To take care of, as to tend a diver's air line. 2. An expression of direction, as an anchor chain tends forward.

**tender** • 1. Logistic support and repair ship, such as a destroyer tender (AD). 2. One who serves as a precautionary standby, as the line tender for a diver.

**tend the side** • *See:* attend the side

**terrestrial sphere** • The Earth.

**Terrier** • Medium range surface-to-air missile system. *See also:* Three Ts

**Texaco** • *Inf:* An airborne tanker.

**Texan II** • The T-6A Texan II is one component of the Joint Primary Aircraft Training System (JPATS); along with simulators, computer-aided academics, and a Training Integration Management System (TIMS). This joint program, of which the Air Force acts as the executive service, will replace Navy T-34C and Air Force T-37B aircraft. The program uses commercial-off-the-shelf (COTS) subsystems to the maximum extent possible.

**Theater Fusion Center (TFC)** • Part of Task Force Sea Sentry, the Theater Fusion Center was designed to provide a comprehensive maritime theater picture to joint tacticians at the U.S. European Command and operators at combatant command centers. The TFC is designed to take all the inputs from around the area of responsibility, fuse them, collate them, and send the information back out to the fleet as a product that different watches can use as a comprehensive maritime picture.

*The Bluejacket's Manual* • A guide issued to all Sailors in boot camp for more than 100 years; provides an introduction to the ways of the Navy to new recruits and serves as a reference book for all Sailors throughout their careers. Some editions were titled *The Bluejackets' Manual* (with apostrophe moved to plural form), but the first and latest editions use the singular form.

*The Bluejackets' Manual* • *See: The Bluejacket's Manual*

**the dope** • *Inf:* Information; gossip; news; the word.

**thermal** • Relating to or caused by heat.

**thermocline** • An ocean layer of rapidly changing temperature in comparatively small changes of depth. This layer refracts sound waves, making submarine detection a difficult problem.

**the word** • News, information. *Inf:* The dope.

**The Yard** • Term used to describe the campus of the U.S. Naval Academy. *See also:* Navy Yard

**thief sample** • Sample of oil or water taken from a ship's tank for the purpose of analysis.

**thieving paste** • A chemical coating on a sounding rod.

**thimble** • Metal ring grooved to fit inside a grommet or small eye splice. In the latter case, it will have a grooved outer edge suitable for receiving a specifically sized line.

**thole pin** • Pin fitting into the gunwale of a boat, carrying a rope grommet for use as a rowlock.

**threat axis** • A bearing or general direction in which an attack is deemed most likely. For example, if an enemy aircraft carrier is known to be due north and near the limits of the range of its aircraft, due north would be designated an AAW (antiair warfare) threat axis, and defensive measures—such as stationing of AAW units—could be concentrated in that direction, away from the main body or units that are to be protected. Threat axes can be general or specific (AAW, ASW, etc.).

**three-arm protractor** • An instrument consisting, essentially, of a circle graduated in degrees to which is attached one fixed arm and two arms pivoted at the center, and provided with clamps so they can be set at any angle to the fixed arm within the limits of the instrument. Used to convert angles or bearings to a fixed position.

**threefold purchase** • A tackle containing two three-sheave blocks.

**three sheets to the wind** • *Inf:* Well under the influence of liquor; drunk. The metaphoric reference is to a sailing ship in disarray, with her sheets (lines) flying in the breeze.

**Three Ts** • Three surface-to-air missile systems used by the U.S. Navy. From shortest to longest range, they were the Tartar, Terrier, and Talos. Replaced by the Standard Missile System.

**throttleman** • Person in the engine room who handles the throttles and thus controls the speed of the ship.

**thrums** • Short yarns sewed to canvas to

improve the performance of a collision mat.

**thruster** • A powered propeller or jet, either at the bow or close to the stern, that assists shiphandling by moving the bow or stern laterally.

**thwart** • Plank set athwartships, just below the gunwales in an open boat; acts as a seat and provides support to the sides.

**tidal bore** • Wave created when tidal pressure overcomes river current in a restricted area. The bore moves upstream against the current as the tide comes in.

**tidal current** • Current caused by the rise and fall of tides.

**tidal day** • Period of a complete tidal cycle.

**tidal prism** • Total amount of water that flows in and out of a harbor as a result of tide.

**tidal range** • Total rise or fall from low water to high water, or vice versa.

**tidal wave** • A seismic sea wave.

**tide** • The vertical rise and fall of the ocean level caused by the gravitational forces of the moon and the sun. Bays, rivers, etc., connected to the oceans, are likewise effected. A rising tide is a flood tide; a falling tide is an ebb tide.

**tide race** • A very rapid tidal current in a narrow channel or passage.

*Tide Tables* • Publications giving data, including time and height, on tides at various locations.

**tie downs** • Fittings to secure aircraft on deck.

**tier** • A layer of anchor chain in a chain locker.

**tie-tie** • Cloth straps or strings that tie together, as on a kapok life jacket.

**tiller** • The lever that turns the rudder on a boat; in line with the rudder and extended forward of the rudder post. It has the same function as the helm in a larger vessel.

**Tilly the Toiler** • *See:* crash dolly

**time diagram** • A diagram in which the celestial equator appears as a circle, and celestial meridians and hour circles appear as radial lines; used to facilitate the solution of time problems and others involving arcs of the celestial equator, or angles at the pole, by indicating relations between various quantities involved.

**time orderly** • Messenger whose duty it is to strike the half hour and hour on the ship's bell.

**tin can** • *Inf:* A destroyer.

**tin fish** • *Inf:* A torpedo.

**toe the line** • To behave. Derived from the old sailing navy. The space between each pair of deck planks in a wooden ship was filled with a packing material called oakum, and then sealed with a mixture of pitch and tar. The result, from afar, was a series of parallel lines a half-foot or so apart, running the length of the deck. Once a week, as a rule, the crew was ordered to fall in at quarters— that is, each group of men, into which the crew was divided, would line up in formation. To insure a neat alignment of each row, the men were directed to stand with their toes just touching a particular seam. Another use for these seams was punitive. The youngsters in a ship, ship's boys or student officers, might be required to stand with their toes just touching a designated seam for a length of time as punishment, for some minor infraction of discipline. A tough captain might require the miscreant to stand there, not talking to anyone, in fair weather or foul, for hours at a time. From these two uses of deck seams comes our cautionary word to obstreperous youngsters to "toe the line."

**toggle** • Pin fitted into an eye or ring used to secure gear and to permit quick release.

**Tomahawk** • The Tomahawk Land Attack Missile (TLAM) is a long range, subsonic cruise missile used for land attack warfare, launched from U.S. Navy surface ships and U.S. Navy and Royal Navy submarines. Designed to fly at extremely low altitudes and piloted over an evasive route by several mission tailored guidance systems. The Tomahawk Block II Nuclear variant (TLAM-N) uses an Inertial Navigation System (INS) aided by Terrain Contour Matching (TERCOM) for missile navigation. TLAM-N contains the W80 nuclear warhead. Tomahawk Block III adds Digital Scene Matching Area Correlation (DSMAC) and Global Positioning Satellite System guidance capability. The Tomahawk Block III Conventional variant (TLAM-C) contains a 1,000-lb. class blast/fragmentary warhead, while the submunition variant (TLAM-D) includes a dispenser with combined effect bomblets.

**Tomcat** • The F-14 Tomcat is a supersonic, twin-engine, variable sweep wing, two-place strike fighter manufactured by Grumman Aircraft Corporation. The multiple tasks of navigation, target acquisition, electronic counter measures (ECM), and weapons employment are divided between the pilot and the radar intercept officer (RIO). Primary missions include precision strikes against ground targets, air superiority, and fleet air defense.

**tompion** • A plug that fits into the bore of a gun at the muzzle to keep out dirt and spray. Often mispronounced "tom-kin." *Var:* tampion.

**ton** • A unit of measurement or weight. Units of weight: short ton = 2,000 pounds; long ton = 2,240 pounds; metric ton = 2,205 pounds (1,000 kilograms). Units of volume: measurement ton (ship ton) = 40 cubic feet; register

ton = 100 cubic feet.

**Tongue of the Ocean** • Deep natural basin in the Bahamas running more than 100 miles along the eastern shore of Andros Island. The site of the Atlantic Undersea Test and Evaluation Center (AUTEC).

**tonnage** • A ship's displacement. The gross weight of cargo that a ship is capable of carrying.

**tons-per-inch immersion** • The number of tons necessary to increase a vessel's mean draft by 1 inch.

**Tooker patch** • A hinged, circular, watertight patch; made of wood with a rubber gasket, divided in half to allow it to be passed out through a hole and then opened to its full size. Useful in patching over a damaged porthole.

**top** • A platform on a mast, now obsolete. In sailing ships, this was usually located at the juncture of the lower mast and the topmast; *i.e.*, about one-third of the height of the entire mast. Sharpshooters were detailed to the tops during battle. Consequently, tops are often called fighting tops. [Note: The very top of a mast is called the cap.] *See also:* foretop; maintop; masthead; mizzentop

**topgallant** • *See:* sail nomenclature

**Topgun** • An advanced naval aviation school for fighter pilots.

**top hamper** • General term for superstructure and rigging. Masts, spars, antennas, etc., are known collectively as a ship's top hamper.

**topmen** • In a sailing ship, men working aloft. Sometimes so designated, but the term was indiscriminately applied to anyone while aloft, except recruits and midshipmen sent up for training or punishment.

**top off** • To fill up, as a ship tops off in fuel oil before leaving port.

**topping lift** • A lifting rig consisting of a boom, attached at one end to a mast or kingpost by a gooseneck, that can be worked up and down by a tackle made up of one or more blocks that are connected to the other end of the boom and to a higher point on the mast or post. Thus, a boom may be used as a derrick, to lift objects.

**topsail** • One of the principal sails of a square-rigger. The lowest sail on a mast that can be spread between an upper and lower yard. *See also:* sail nomenclature

**topsail schooner** • Two-masted sailing vessel with essentially a schooner rig except that the fore-and-aft sail on the foremast is not quite so high, leaving room on the mast for two or three yards from which one or two topsails can be carried.

**top secret** • Refers to national security information or material that requires the highest degree of protection. The test for assigning such a classification is whether unauthorized disclosure of the information could reasonably be expected to cause exceptionally grave damage to national security. *See also:* classified matter; confidential; secret

**topside** • Above, in a ship; referring to the deck above, as distinguished from overhead, which refers to the ceiling of a compartment. The topside (or topsides) means the upper deck (or decks); any deck or area that is exposed to the weather is considered topside.

**top up** • To raise a boom with its topping lift.

**torch pot** • A canister that contains chemicals that produce smoke, placed in an exercise torpedo warhead to help locate it after being fired.

**torpedo** • Self-propelled, underwater, explosive weapon designed to be aimed at or to seek a target; and detonated by contact, sound, or magnetic force. Various types are identified by mark and modification numbers. Torpedoes may be launched from submarines, surface ships, helicopters, and fixed-wing aircraft. The three major torpedoes in the Navy inventory are the Mark 48 heavyweight torpedo, the Mark 46 lightweight, and the Mark 50 advanced lightweight. The MK-48 is designed to combat fast, deep-diving, nuclear submarines and high performance surface ships. It is carried by all Navy submarines. The advanced capability version, MK-48 ADCAP, is carried by attack submarines, the *Ohio*-class ballistic missile submarines, and the *Seawolf*-class attack submarines. The MK-48 replaced both the MK-37 and MK-14 torpedoes. The MK-48 has been operational in the U.S. Navy since 1972. The MK-46 torpedo is designed to attack high performance submarines and is presently identified as the NATO standard. The MK-50 is an advanced lightweight torpedo for use against the faster, deeper-diving, and more sophisticated submarines. The MK-50 can be launched from all ASW aircraft and from torpedo tubes aboard surface combatant ships. *Inf:* Fish; tin fish.

**torpedoman's mate (TM)** • Navy occupational rating that maintains underwater explosive missiles, such as torpedoes and rockets, that are launched from surface ships, submarines, and aircraft. TMs also maintain launching systems for underwater explosives. They are responsible for the shipping and storage of all torpedoes and rockets.

**torpedo range** • The distance a torpedo can run with its available fuel supply.

**torpedo retriever** • Fast boat for recovering practice torpedoes.

**torpedo run** • The actual distance a torpedo travels to target.

**torpedo tube shutters** • Movable fairings on the outboard end of submarine torpedo tubes whose closure preserves the streamlined form of the hull.

**torque** • A turning or twisting force, such as that affecting a propeller shaft.

**torque differential receiver (TDR)** • A type of differential synchro that takes two electrical inputs, one to the rotor and one to the stator, and produces a mechanical output. The output is the angular position of the rotor that represents the algebraic sum or difference of the two electrical inputs.

**torque differential transmitter (TDX)** • A type of synchro that is functionally the same as the CDX, except that it is used in torque systems rather than control systems.

**torque receiver (TR)** • A type of synchro that converts the electrical input supplied to its stator back to a mechanical angular output through the movement of its rotor.

**torque synchrosystem** • A synchro system that uses torque synchros to move light loads such as dials, pointers, and other similar devices.

**torsionmeter** • Device for measuring the twist in the propeller shaft from which the horsepower developed by the turbine is calculated.

**toss oars** • An order to raise oars from the rowlocks to a vertical position, with blades fore and aft, and handles resting on the bottom of the boat.

**touch and go** • 1. A near thing. The reference is to a ship barely touching ground, but coming loose immediately and not damaged. In such a case, reporting the incident becomes a matter of ethics and honor. 2. Practice landings on aircraft carriers in which the tail hooks of the aircraft are kept in the up position so that the aircraft can return to the air for another practice run without having to launch again.

**tow** • 1. To pull along through the water. 2. The vessel being towed.

**tow glider** • Antiaircraft gunnery target.

**towing bitts** • Heavy cylindrical castings secured to the deck of a tug near its pivot point; used to secure towing hawsers.

**towing bows** • Beams installed across the caprails on the stern of a tug to keep the towline above deck fittings and personnel.

**towing lights** • Two or three (depending on length) vertical white lights on a vessel to signify that she is towing; required by the Rules of the Road.

**towing machine** • A winch-like device that automatically maintains safe tension on the hawser during towing.

**towing spar** • Wooden device towed astern by ships in formation in low visibility to assist in station keeping. Also called fog buoy.

**towing winch** • Special winch, used by large tugs in towing that compensates for variation in the tension on the towline. *See also:* traction winch

**tracer** • 1. A projectile trailing smoke or showing a light for correction in aim; most usually used in machine-gun ammunition. 2. A message sent to ascertain the reason for nondelivery of a prior message.

**track** • 1. The intended or desired path of travel with respect to the Earth. 2. To follow a target, noting course and speed, as a patrol aircraft tracks a convoy. 3. To mark the progress of a target on a radar scope or plotting board.

**track angle** • Angle between the target course and the reciprocal of the torpedo course, measured from the bow of the target to the right, through 360°, or to port or starboard through 180°. *See also:* angle on the bow; target angle

**track line** • A graphic representation on a chart, plotting sheet, or electronic display of the travel of a ship; with positions, directions, speed, and times indicated.

**traction winch** • A towing machine on a tug that is designed to haul in and pay out using a tractive effort, as opposed to winding the towline on a drum.

**tractor** • 1. An aircraft that tows targets for antiaircraft practice. 2. Small vehicle used on aircraft carriers to move aircraft around. 3. Term referring to landing ships and craft; as the tractor group of a task force moving to the objective area.

**trade winds** • Those generally steady winds from the northeast in the Northern Hemisphere and southeast in the Southern Hemisphere in the lower latitudes. They are caused by the normal flow of air from the poles towards the sun-heated equator, deflected by the rotation of the Earth. Important for commerce in the days of sail.

**trailing edge** • The after edge of an airfoil. The edge over which the airflow normally passes last.

**train** • 1. To move a gun horizontally as part of the aiming process. 2. Service or logistic support ships attached to a fleet. *See also:* point

**trainer** • 1. A piece of equipment or system that is used to simulate real-life conditions for training purposes; for example, a shiphandling trainer allows personnel to practice their conning skills. 2. Person who controls a gun or mount in horizontal movement (deflection or train); a team of two, called "pointer" and "trainer," aim a manually-controlled shipboard gun by moving it vertically and horizontally respectively. *See also:* pointer

**train in and secure** • Put away equipment and cease present exercise.

**training record book** • Part of the Navigation, Seamanship and Shiphandling Training Requirements Document (NSS TRD), gives commanding officers and executive officers a tool to track a surface warfare officer's career qualifications by providing supervisors and leaders a clear picture of their subordinates' professional development with regard to navigation, seamanship and shiphandling experience. The record book includes pages for sea service time, qualifications and facts, and characteristics of the ship on which the officer stood deck watches. It also includes watchstanding records for combat, deck, and engineering departments. The training record book is compatible with Merchant Mariner and federal certifications, so a Navy surface warfare officer can use the record book to more easily pursue civilian and other licenses.

**transceiver** • An electronic device that is capable of both transmitting and receiving signals.

**transducer** • 1. Device for conversion of energy from one form to another; *e.g.,* electrical to mechanical or acoustic. 2. Part of a sonar set that converts sound signals into range information.

**transfer** • 1. Distance gained by a ship at right angles to original course when turning. 2. The movement of personnel from one duty assignment to another.

**transmitter** • A device that sends out a signal, such as a radio transmitter.

**transom** • 1. Planking or steel plates across the stern of a vessel. 2. A settee or sofa aboard ship.

**transponder** • An electronic transmitter that emits a signal when interrogated by another signal.

**transport quartermaster** • *See:* embarkation officer

**transverse frame** • Structural member that extends outward from the keel and upward to the main deck.

**trap** • The wire-arrested landing of an aircraft on the deck of an aircraft carrier.

**trapping** • Atmospheric distortion of radar signals that prevents them from normal travel and from returning an accurate range. *See also:* radar trapping

**traveling lizard** • A short section of line with a thimble at one end, through which passes a small wire cable stretched taut between two fixed structures aboard ship. The lizard can move freely along the wire while firmly gripped by persons needing to make the passage safely from one structure to the other in bad weather.

**triatic stay** • Wire from foremast to after stack or mast of a ship. Also called a spring stay.

**TRICARE system** • TRICARE is the Department of Defense's worldwide health care program for active duty and retired uniformed services members and their families. TRICARE consists of TRICARE Prime, a managed care option; TRICARE Extra, a preferred provider option; and TRICARE Standard, a fee-for-service option. TRICARE For Life is also available for Medicare-eligible beneficiaries age 65 and over.

**trice** • To haul up, as to trice up all bunks, which means to push up all bunks and secure them.

**trice up** • To secure bunks by hauling them up and out of the way. *See also:* heave out and trice up

**trick** • *Inf:* A steersman's watch is known as a trick at the wheel.

**trick wheel** • Steering wheel in the steering engine room or emergency steering station of a ship.

**Trident** • A sea-based strategic system consisting of three-stage, solid propellant, multiwarhead missiles with inertial guidance fired from specially-equipped submarines, and supported by a shore-based support complex. Consequently, the term "Trident" is sometimes used to describe both the missiles and the submarines that carry them.

**trim** • 1. The fore-and-aft inclination of a ship—down by the head or down by the stern. 2. To trim a submarine is to adjust water in the variable ballast tanks, or trim tanks, to establish neutral buoyancy. 3. Shipshape, neat. *See also:* even keel; trim tanks

**trimming system** • The entire system of pipes, valves, pumps, and tanks by which a submarine compensates for expenditure of variable weights so as to maintain neutral buoyancy and stability when submerged. The compensation is done before diving whenever possible and with careful calculation. And when the requisite amounts of water are in the various trimming tanks, the submarine is said to be in diving trim. A trim dive is a dive made for the purpose of checking and correcting the compensation.

**trim tanks** • Variable ballast tanks of a submarine used to maintain neutral buoyancy and stability.

**trip** • To let go, as to trip a pelican hook.

**triplane target** • Towed sonar target used in training ASW ships.

**tropic tides** • Tides occurring semimonthly when the effect of the moon's maximum declination is greatest. At these times there is a tendency for an increase in the diurnal range. The tidal datums pertaining to the tropic tides are designated as tropic higher high water, tropic lower high water, tropic higher low water, and tropic lower low water.

**tropic velocity** • The greater flood or ebb velocity at the time of tropic current, when the moon is near its maximum declination.

**trouble central** • *Inf:* The chaplain's office in a large ship.

**trough** • The hollow between two waves. An elongated area of low atmospheric pressure extending outward from a low center.

**truck** • The highest part of a ship's tallest mast, known as foretruck or main truck, as appropriate. The highest parts of other masts are called caps. *See also:* cap

**true airspeed** • Airspeed corrected for altitude and temperature. *See also:* airspeed

**true bearing** • Direction of an object, relative to true north instead of magnetic north.

**true heading** • Horizontal direction in which an aircraft or ship is heading, relative to true north.

**trunk** • Space aboard ship used for ventilation, maintenance access, etc.

**trunnions** • The major supports of a gun that provide the axis about which the gun rotates in elevation. The tilt of the trunnions introduces range and deflection errors. In days of sail, trunnions were cast integrally with the gun. In more modern guns, they are often part of the gun mount instead of the gun itself.

**try cocks** • Small faucets on the steam drum of a boiler, used to verify the water level if the gauge glass fails.

**tsunami** • *See:* seismic sea wave

**tube sheets** • Oil-fired boilers and nuclear-powered steam generators both operate by transferring heat. The feed water that is to become steam is inside tubes that are surrounded either by fire or by super-heated water at extremely high pressure (the primary loop). At each end, the tubes are meticulously sealed into carefully spaced holes drilled into a large steel plate, which in a nuclear plant, also forms part of the separation between fire (or the primary loop) and the steam side. These are the tube sheets, and they may be of various shapes and sizes.

**tumble** • 1. When a gyroscope (gyrocompass) loses stability it is said to tumble. 2. The act of an automatic releasing hook in opening upon release of the weight.

**tumble home** • The upward curve inward of a ship's side above the waterline; opposite of flare. The result is that the width of the main deck is narrower than the ship's beam at the waterline. Flare was frequently designed into the bow and stern to reduce pitching, but tumble home permitted serving the broadside guns while grappled alongside an enemy, and made hostile boarding more difficult. *See also:* flare

**turbine** • A rotor with many curved blades that is driven by steam or other fluids in order to convert one form of energy into another. Large turbines at electrical power plants generate electricity by converting the flow of rivers, for example. In marine steam propulsion, the turbines convert the steam's heat into rotary motion that is used to drive the ship's propeller. Modern gas turbines aboard ships are modified jet engines and function in a similar manner to steam turbines except that they are driven by the gases created by the burning of fuel without the medium of steam. Turbines aboard ship can be used as electrical generators, as well as a means of propulsion.

**turbo blower** • Also called low-pressure blower. A blower used to complete evacuation of water from submarine ballast tanks after the submarine has been brought to the surface by compressed air and opened to the atmosphere. A far more economical way of completing the surfacing procedure than by using the precious high-pressure air.

**Turk's head** • A specific ornamental design resembling a sultan's turban placed on an oar, rail, spar, etc. for decoration; braided from small line.

**turn** • 1. A tactical maneuver when ships put their rudders over at the same time so that they maintain the same true bearings from one another while changing course. 2. A signal flag used to order turn maneuvers. *See also:* corpen

**turnbuckle** • Metal appliance consisting of a threaded link with a pair of opposite-threaded screws with eyes; capable of being set taut or slacked, and used for setting up standing rigging or other gear. Takes the droop out of rigging.

**turn count masking** • A practice of changing propeller revolutions at random to prevent a listening submarine from estimating the speed of an attacking ship.

**turn in** • 1. Go to bed. 2. Return articles to the issue room.

**turning circle** • Path followed by a ship with constant rudder angle when turning.

**turn of the bilge** • Line on the underside of a vessel's hull, where her sides join her bottom. Some are more clearly defined than others.

**turn out** • 1. To awaken and get up. 2. To order out a working party or other groups, as to turn out the guard.

**turns turtle** • *See:* capsize

**turn to** • Commence working; get to work.

**turn turtle** • *Inf:* Capsize.

**turret** • Said simply, the rotatable, armored enclosure for the heavy guns of a man-of-war. As it evolved, turret became the name

for the entire rotating mechanism inside the armored barbette that supported it, extending far down into the lower levels of the ship where ammunition was supplied from the magazines. Now, the protective shield around smaller guns, such as a 5-inch gun, is sometimes loosely called a turret.

**'tween deck** • Any deck in a ship below the main deck. Generally used in the plural— 'tween decks—to mean inside the ship, between decks.

**twenty-year man (or woman)** • *Inf:* A naval career person who intends to remain in the service for at least 20 years, at which time he or she can draw a pension.

**twilight** • The period before sunrise and after sunset during which light is reflected from the sun. The four kinds, depending on angular distance of the sun below the horizon, are civil at 6°, observational at 10°, nautical at 12°, and astronomical at 18°.

**two-blocked** • Hoisted all the way up. Same as close up.

**two-fold purchase** • A tackle, both blocks of which contain two sheaves.

**type command** • A command which includes all ships of a certain type or types in the fleet; for example, all the cruisers and destroyers in the Pacific Fleet could be grouped into a type command called CRUDESPAC, and the commander of such a group would be COMCRUDESPAC. *See also:* type commander

**type commander** • The officer commanding all ships of a certain type in the fleet; for example, COMCRUDESPAC would be the type commander in charge of all the cruisers and destroyers in the Pacific Fleet. Type commanders are associated more with training, maintenance, and administration than actual operations. The type commander makes sure that the ships under his command are made ready for fleet operations.

**typhoon** • Cyclonic storm originating in the Western Pacific Ocean. Called a hurricane in the Atlantic.

**U.S. Naval Academy (USNA)** • Navy school at Annapolis, Maryland that prepares young people to be officers in the Navy and Marine Corps. Provides them a college education, coupled with specialized professional training. Graduates receive both a baccalaureate degree and a commission.

**U.S. Naval Sea Cadet Corps** • *See:* United States Naval Sea Cadet Corps

**U-bolt** • A U-shaped bolt with threads on each end. The bolt in a wire rope clip.

**UGM-84** • *See:* Harpoon

**UH-1** • *See:* Iroquois

**ultra high frequencies (UHF)** • One of the designations of the radio frequency spectrum; covers the range 300–3,000 MHz.

**Unauthorized Absence (UA)** • The proper all-inclusive term for a naval person absent without authority from the command to which he or she is assigned. Replaces old terms: straggler, absentee, and absent without leave (AWOL).

**unbend** • To untie, loosen, cast adrift.

**uncle** • Past phonetic word for the letter U; replaced by uniform.

**uncover** • To remove one's cap from one's head.

**undercarriage** • Landing gear of an airplane.

**underfoot** • Said of an anchor when it is directly under the ship's bow.

**under hack** • *See:* hack, under

**undertow** • The brief downward and seaward thrust of a collapsing wave top as the wave breaks on a beach. It results from the essentially circular motion of the water within a wave. It can drive swimmers underwater and hold them there. *See also:* rip current

**underwater demolition team (UDT)** • Team of specially trained Sailors who do reconnaissance and demolition work along the beaches just prior to an amphibious assault.

**under way** • Said of a vessel when she is not made fast to the ground in any manner. She may or may not have way on; *i.e.,* she may not be moving, but she is free floating in the sea, or subject to wind, currents, and her own propulsion system. Sometimes seen as two words, but more often used as one in modern naval usage.

**underway replenishment** • Logistical operation in which fuel, food, stores, ammunition, etc., are transferred between ships steaming close aboard on the same course and speed. *See also:* vertical replenishment

**underway replenishment group** • A task group organized to provide logistic replenishment of ships under way by transfer-at-sea methods.

**unified** • Made into a unit or systematically connected. Involving more than one service, as in "because the Army, Navy, Air Force, and Marine Corps are represented in CINCLANT, it is considered a unified command."

**uniform** • Phonetic word for the letter U.

**Uniform Code of Military Justice (UCMJ)** • Judicial code of laws and regulations that govern the armed forces; enacted by Congress as a means of ensuring equal treatment and rights of all personnel in the armed forces of the United States.

**uniform of the day** • Prescribed by the commanding officer or the senior officer present afloat (SOPA). To be worn at all times, except when the working uniform is authorized.

**union jack** • Flag flown at the bow of a ship moored or anchored, consisting of the union of the national flag. Also flown in the boat of a high civil official, and at the yardarm during a general court-martial or court of inquiry.

**unit** • Generic term referring to tactical components at a commander's disposal. It may be a single ship or aircraft, or a group of ships or planes under a single commander.

**United Services Military Apprenticeship Program (USMAP)** • A training system by which active duty service members can earn certification for skills learned through documented work experience—On-The-Job-Training—and related technical instruction.

**United States Armed Forces** • A collective term for the Army, Navy, Air Force, Marines and, in time of war or national emergency, the Coast Guard.

**United States Naval Institute (USNIP)** • A private organization, independent of the Navy despite its strong ties. The Naval Institute is a nonprofit, professional organization that publishes magazines and books, conducts seminars, serves the interests of the Navy and the other armed forces in a number of ways, and provides an open forum for a healthy debate on important topics through its periodicals, *Proceedings* and *Naval History*.

**United States Naval Sea Cadet Corps (USNSCC)** • Youth program co-sponsored by the Navy and the Navy League. Young people participate in Navy-oriented youth activities

including modified boot camp, ship visits, etc.

**United States Naval Ship (USNS)** • A ship that is owned by the U.S. Navy, but not commissioned as part of the Navy. Normally manned with civilian crews and a small contingent of naval personnel; operated by the Defense Department's Military Sealift Command.

**United States Navy Regulations** • General principles for guiding the naval establishment, particularly the duties, responsibilities, and authority of key offices and individuals; issued by the Secretary of the Navy and approved by the President.

**unit of fire** • A unit of measure for ammunition supply, representing a specified number of rounds per weapon.

**Universal Time Constant** • Conceptually, time as determined from the apparent diurnal motion of a fictitious mean sun which moves uniformly along the celestial equator at the average rate of the apparent sun. Actually, Universal Time (UT) is related to the rotation of the earth through its definition in terms of sidereal time. Universal Time at any instant is derived from observations of the diurnal motions of the stars. The time scale determined directly from such observations is slightly dependent on the place of observation; this scale is designated UT0. By removing from UT0 the effect of the variation of the observer's meridian due to the observed motion of the geographic pole, the scale UT1 is established. A scale designated UT2 results from applying to UT1 an adopted formula for the seasonal variation in the rate of the earth's rotation. UT1 and UT2 are independent of the location of the observer. UT1 is the same as Greenwich mean time used in navigation.

**unlay** • To untwist and separate a rope's strands.

**unload through the muzzle** • To fire in a safe direction in order to empty a gun of its charge.

**unship** • To remove from place, in the sense of taking a smaller thing—such as a boat, gun, spare tire, etc.—out of the larger one in which it has been secured.

**up all late bunks** • An order to get up, given to personnel entitled to sleep after reveille.

**up anchor** • The order to weigh anchor and get under way.

**up and down** • Said of an anchor when it is directly under the bow, has broken ground, and is ready to be hoisted (weighed). *See also:* short stay; underfoot

**up behind** • An order to cease hauling and to slack the line quickly.

**upper branch** • That half of a meridian or celestial meridian, from pole to pole, that passes through an observer's position or its zenith.

**upper deck** • The first deck above the main deck.

**uptakes** • Large enclosed passages for exhaust gases, from boilers to the stacks. Also called exhaust trunks.

**upwelling** • A mass of cold, dense seawater that rises up from the depths of the ocean to the surface.

**USOgram** • Many Navy ships can now receive USOgrams, non-emergency e-mail sent through a ship's satellite communications system. You can access the USO web site to read the instructions to download the form for sending USOgrams. The USO charges a $3 fee to cover handling costs. You will need to provide the following information in order to send a USOgram to a service member: Rate, Name, Ship, Department, Workcenter.

**Utilitiesman (UT)** • Navy occupational rat-

ing that plans, supervises, and performs tasks involved in the installation, operation, maintenance, and repair of plumbing, heating, steam, compressed-air systems, fuel-storage and -distribution systems, water-treatment and -distribution systems, air-conditioning and refrigeration equipment, and sewage-collecting and disposal facilities.

**V-22** • *See:* Osprey

**van** • The forward part or group of a formation of ships; opposite of rear. The lead ship in a column would be said to be in the van.

**vang** • *See:* guy

**vaporize** • To change into vapor by heating or spraying.

**vapor lock** • Malfunction of an engine fuel system or pumping system caused by vaporization of the fuel; usually associated with gasoline.

**variable time (VT) fuze** • Fuze that is actuated by the reflection of signals generated by the projectile off of a target when in close proximity. Also called a proximity fuze.

**variation** • Magnetic compass error caused by the difference between the geographic and magnetic poles. Expressed in degrees east or west. Also known as magnetic declination by earth scientists. Daily fluctuation in variation is called diurnal change, which is too small to be significant to navigators, except in polar regions. Over time, the accumulated variation can be significant to navigators and is therefore included on nautical charts (as a specific amount as of a given year and an annual rate of change).

**vector** • A straight line representing both direction and magnitude.

**vector diagram** • A diagram of more than one vector (an arrow representing both direction and speed, the latter by its length) drawn to the same scale and reference direction, and in correct position relative to each other. Useful in solving relative motion problems.

**veer** • 1. To let out or pay out a chain or line. 2. When the wind changes direction clockwise in the Northern Hemisphere, it is said to veer. A veering wind is usually a sign of improving weather in the Northern Hemisphere, worsening weather in the Southern. *See also:* back; haul

**velocimeter** • A device used to measure speed. In oceanography, for example, a sound velocimeter measures the speed of sound in water.

**velocity** • The rate of motion in a particular direction.

**vent** • 1. Valve in a tank or compartment to permit the escape of air when filling it, or when pressure builds up for other reasons. 2. The large valve at the top of a submarine's main ballast tank(s), by which trapped air is released to permit diving. 3. To remove air or other gas or vapor from a system. 4. The touch hole or aperture through which fire was communicated to the powder charge of a muzzle-loading gun.

**venturi** • A tapered portion of a piping system that reduces pressure and increases flow.

**vernal equinox** • One of the two points of intersection of the ecliptic and celestial equator, occupied by the sun when its declination is 0°. The point occupied on or about March 21, when the sun's declination changes from south to north, is called vernal

equinox, March equinox, or first point of Aries. It marks the first day of spring in the Northern Hemisphere. *See also:* autumnal equinox

**vertical launch ASROC (VLA)** • Antisubmarine rocket system launched from a vertical launching system (as opposed to the older deck-mounted box launcher).

**vertical launch system (VLS)** • A modern missile launching system that dispenses with the traditional missile launching rail(s) on older systems. Permits missiles to be virtually launched directly from their magazines. *See also:* MK-41 Vertical Launching System

**vertical replenishment (VERTREP)** • Logistics operation in which helicopters are used in connection with supply ships to resupply the fleet while under way. *See also:* underway replenishment

**Very pistol** • A gun used exclusively to fire pyrotechnics (rescue flares, etc.) into the air as signals. Correct name is actually "Very's Pistol," but it is rarely said that way.

**very high frequency omnidirectional range and tactical air navigation (VORTAC)** • Omnidirectional range station, including tactical air navigation (TACAN), a distance-measuring system.

**very high frequency omnidirectional range (VOR)** • Used principally in air navigation. It provides a magnetic bearing from ground stations. When combined with distance-measuring equipment (DME), this system produces bearing and distance, which establishes a fix.

**very high frequency (VHF)** • One of the designations of the radiofrequency spectrum; covers the range 30–300 MHz.

**very low frequency (VLF)** • One of the designations of the radio frequency spectrum; covers the range 10–30 kHz.

**very well** • Response by a senior to a report by a junior, to acknowledge that he or she as heard the report.

**vessel** • By U.S. statutes, includes every description of craft, ship, or other contrivance used as a means of transportation on water.

**vice admiral** • The rank between admiral and rear admiral. Informally called a "three star admiral" because of the collar device worn by people of this rank.

**vice commodore** • Second in command of a convoy.

**victor** • The phonetic word for the letter V.

**Viking** • The S-3B Viking is an all-weather, carrier-based jet aircraft, providing protection against hostile surface combatants while also functioning as the carrier battle groups' primary overhead/mission tanker. Extremely versatile, the aircraft is equipped for many missions, including day/night surveillance, electronic countermeasures, command/control/communications warfare, and search and rescue (SAR).

**virtual PPI (plan position indicator) reflectosope (VPR)** • A navigational chart fitted to the PPI of a radar for comparing the PPI picture with a chart of the area.

**viscosity** • The internal resistance of a liquid that tends to prevent it from flowing.

**visibility** • The extreme horizontal distance at which prominent objects can be seen and identified by the unaided eye.

**visit and search** • A visit to a private vessel to determine its nationality, character of cargo, nature of employment, etc.

**voice radio** • Electronic communications equipment that transmits the speaker's voice through the air on radio waves to an appropriately tuned receiver.

**voice tube** • Tube running between stations aboard ship; used for simple but effective communication, such as between a bridge wing and the helmsman's station.

**void** • An empty, watertight compartment separating other compartments; aids in the buoyancy of the ship.

**volatility** • Measure of the tendency of a liquid to vaporize; vapor pressure.

**volume reverberation** • *See:* reverberation

**VT fuze** • *See:* proximity fuze

**vulgar establishment** • Average high water interval on days of the new and full moon.

**vulture's row** • *Inf:* Open-air area on the island where spectators often watch flight ops.

**waist** • Amidships portion of a ship.

**wake** • The disturbed water astern of a moving ship.

**wake light** • Dim light at stern, directed down on wake, to assist following ships to keep station.

**wale shore** • Long spar, or shore, used to brace a ship upright in a drydock. Longer and heavier than a regular shore.

**walk back the cat** • Expression meaning to start all over again or to retire to a previously held position and start a process or procedure again.

**Wallis brake** • A wire brake used to maintain a steady load on a wire rope as it is rigged on a drum.

**wall knot** • Knot formed at the end of a line by looping each strand around the one behind it and passing its end through the loop of the strand in front.

**wardroom** • The compartment in which officers gather to eat and lounge aboard ship.

**warfare specialty training** • This is specific training for amphibious warfare, mine warfare, or salvage ships conducted in conjuntion with other basic training.

**warhead** • Forward section of a torpedo or missile that carries the explosive. For training shots, an inert exercise head is fitted.

**warp** • To change the heading of a ship by pulling on lines or chain or both to a pier, dock, or outlying anchor. *See also:* spring

**warping head** • Revolving vertical cylinder for hauling in on lines; part of a windlass.

**warping tug** • A special tug made from pontoon sections and used by an amphibious construction battalion during an amphibious assault. *See also:* pontoon barge

**warping winch** • Winch on the main deck aft, used to warp in the stem when mooring alongside.

**warrant officer** • Officer who is senior to chief petty officer and junior to ensign and above.

**warship** • A vessel that engages directly in combat; as opposed to a service ship, which serves some function that is ancillary to combat operations. Some examples of warships are destroyers, submarines, and aircraft carriers. Examples of service ships are oilers, ammunition ships, and tenders.

**watch** • 1. Duty period, normally 4 hours long. A day's watches taditionally are: evening or first watch, 2000–2400; midwatch, 0000–0400; morning watch, 0400–0800; forenoon watch, 0800–1200; afternoon watch, 1200–1600; first dog watch, 1600–1800; second dog watch, 1800–2000. 2. A buoy is said to watch when it is floating in its proper position and attitude. *See also:* dog watch

**watch and watch** • Period of duty (watch) alternating with an equal period of rest. *See also:* heel and toe

**watch cap** • 1. A Sailor's blue knitted cap. 2. The black band around the top of the stack. 3. Cover for a smokestack, often made of canvas.

**watch-in-watch condition** • A two-section watch situation. In other words, half of all watchstanders are on duty at any given time. Also called port and starboard watches.

**watch officer** • A person assigned to duty in charge of a watch or a portion of it. For example, the officer of the deck (OOD) or the engineering officer of the watch (EOOW).

***Watch Officer's Guide*** • Standard reference work and text book used by deck watchstanders in the Navy.

**watch, quarter, and station bill** • A formal list showing the duties, stations, and billet assignments of all crew members.

**watch station** • A specially designated job or position that must be manned by one or more personnel in order for specific duties to be carried out. For example, when under way, a ship would have personnel assigned to man specific watch stations on the bridge, such as the "quartermaster of the watch" who assists the navigator and keeps the quartermaster's notebook.

**waterborne** • Afloat, or in contact with the water's surface.

**water breaker** • Container for fresh water. Also called water beaker.

**water drum** • *See:* drum, water

**waterline** • 1. The line painted on the hull showing the point to which a ship sinks when properly trimmed. 2. Line of separation along a vessel's hull where the water stops and air begins. *See also:* Plimsoll mark

**waterlogged** • Filled or soaked with water.

**watersides** • In an oil- or coal-fired boiler, fire outside the boiler tubes imparts heat to the feed water inside the tubes, giving rise to the two terms, firesides (outside of the tubes) and watersides (inside of the tubes).

**waterspout** • Essentially a tornado over water.

**water taxi** • Shore boat, available for hire like a taxi.

**watertender** • Person responsible for keeping the level of water in the boilers at the right level.

**watertight closure log** • Official log used to record special openings of watertight closures that are supposed to be closed under the damage control condition in effect.

**watertight door** • A door that is strongly made and fitted with a gasket and dogs, so that when it is closed, it will keep water out.

**watertight integrity** • A ship's degree of resistance to flooding.

**water washing** • A method of cleaning to remove contaminants.

**waterway** • The gutter under the lifelines to carry off deck water through the scuppers.

**waterway bar** • A solid bar used instead of a footline in a lifeline configuration. *See also:* lifeline

**waterwings** • *Inf:* The surface warfare insignia.

**waveguide** • A rectangular, circular, or elliptical metal pipe designed to transport electromagnetic waves through its interior. Particularly useful in radar systems.

**wave height** • Vertical distance between the wave trough and the wave crest. Significant height is the average of the highest third of all waves. Such measurements do not take account of the occasionally encountered rogue wave, which is much higher than any average and causes the greatest danger and damage. Such freak waves are the result of occasional harmonic reinforcement of two or more different wave systems moving in different directions. Because their frequency of occurrence is statistically predictable, prudent seamen can take precautions.

**wavelength** • The distance in the direction of advance between the same phase of successive waves.

**wave off** • The act of a landing signal officer (LSO) or landing signal enlisted (LSE) refusing an approaching aircraft permission to land.

**wave-off** • A call by the LSO directing an aircraft not to land.

**wave period** • Time interval between the passage of two consecutive, identical wave segments.

**way** • 1. A ship's movement through the water, as "the ship has way on." 2. Launching track in a shipbuilding yard. *See also:* under way

**way enough** • In a pulling boat, an order to complete the stroke, then hold the oars in midstroke position awaiting the next command. As the order indicates, there appears to be sufficient way to complete the maneuver intended. The next order may be to "back water," or "boat the oars," or any of a number of combinations possible, depending on the circumstances.

**weapons officer** • Officer in overall charge

of a ship's armament. When guns were the principal weapons, he was called the gunnery officer. Today he or she may have subordinate gunnery, missile, ASW and AAW officers.

**weapon system** • Guns, missile launchers, etc., with all of their supporting sub-systems: target acquisition (radar, etc.), ammuntion supply (magazines, hoists, etc.) and so on.

**wear** • *See:* wear ship

**wear ship** • For a sailing vessel to change tacks (to bring the wind on her other side and thus change her course) she may either pass her bow through the wind, known as tacking, or pass her stern through it, called wearing. Fore-and-afters almost always tack, and square-riggers usually wear, in both cases to avoid stress on rigging from the shock of having sails suddenly catch the wind on the other side. An accidental wear by a fore-and-after is called a jibe.

**weather** • 1. Toward the wind, opposite of lee. 2. To have been exposed to the elements, as a weathered timber. 3. Exposed to the elements, as the weather deck. 4. To pass an obstacle successfully, despite wind and sea setting one down on it, as to weather a cape or storm.

**weathercocks** • Said of a ship that comes up into the wind readily, or must carry a weather helm to stay on course. *See also:* ardent; lee helm

**weather deck** • 1. Topmost deck of a ship. 2. Any deck or portion of a deck exposed to the elements. *See also:* deck

**weather eye** • To keep a weather eye is to be on the alert.

**weaving helm** • A form of zigzag steered by ships. Sinuous course steered by aircraft in which two or more aircraft turn toward each other for mutual support.

**web belt** • Broad, woven, cotton belt that is fitted with eyelets for carrying a canteen, pistol, etc. Worn as a badge of office by sentries, messengers, orderlies, and others. Sometimes called a duty belt.

**weekend warrior** • *Inf:* A member of the naval reserve.

**weigh** • To lift the anchor off the bottom in getting under way.

**well deck** • 1. In amphibious ships that are capable of flooding down their stern areas to allow amphibious craft to enter and depart, that flood-capable area is called the well deck. 2. Part of the weather deck that has some sort of superstructure both forward and aft of it.

**wet dock** • A basin formed, by the construction of barriers with gates, in a harbor of great tidal ranges to prevent ships from being stranded during low tides. Ships enter the basin at high tide, the gates are closed, and the water is retained in the basin when the tide ebbs.

**wet steam** • Steam mixed with free water particles.

**wetting down** • *Inf:* A party traditionally hosted by a newly promoted person to celebrate that promotion.

**whaleboat** • Small double-ended boat—tapered bow shape at stern as well as on the bow. Good in a seaway because it is high at both ends. Favored for lifeboat use.

**wharf** • Structure parallel to the shore line to which vessels can moor. Sometimes called a quay, which is usually a solid masonry structure.

**wheel** • To alter a course in such a manner that all ships in a formation remain in the same relative position. The steering wheel (helm) of a ship or boat is sometimes known as the wheel.

**wheel book** • *Inf:* Small notebook carried by an officer or senior petty officer, in which pertinent information is kept.

**wheelhouse** • *See:* pilothouse

**wheeling maneuver** • When ships are maneuvering together, they "wheel" when they simultaneously turn while maintaining the same relative bearings to one another. *See also:* corpen

**wheel rope** • Lines used to connect a vessel's helm to its rudder.

**whelps** • Projections on the periphery of the wildcat drum that fit the anchor chain and pull it by a sort of gear-tooth action.

**where away** • Answer to a lookout's report of a sighting that acknowledges the report and requests the direction of the sighting.

**whip** • 1. To wrap the end of a line with small stuff. 2. A single line rove through a single block to create a simple lifting tackle.

**whipping** • Binding on the end of a line or wire to prevent unraveling. *See also:* plain whipping

**whiskey** • Phonetic word for the letter W.

**white hat** • *Inf:* Enlisted personnel below the rank of chief petty officer (E-7). *Inf:* Term sometimes used to indicate an enlisted Sailor.

**white shirts** • Squadron plane inspectors, landing signals officers (LSOs), liquid oxygen crews, safety observers, and medical personnel working on the flight deck of an aircraft; so called because of the white shirts they wear for easy identification. *See also:* yellow shirt; blue shirt; green shirt; brown shirt; red shirt; purple shirt; grapes

**wick** • A solid, such as clothing, that has absorbed fuel. JP-5 can easily ignite in this manner, even at a temperature well below its flashpoint.

**wide berth** • At a considerable distance, as "We gave her (the other ship) a wide berth."

**wigwag** • *See:* semaphore

**wilco** • Term, indicating receipt and understanding of a voice radio message. Means "will comply;" not to be confused with roger, which means only "message received."

**wildcat** • That part—the drum—of an anchor windlass that engages and moves the anchor chain. Also called a chain grab. *See also:* whelps

**william** • Past phonetic word for the letter W; replaced by "whiskey."

**William sled** • A two-hulled sled with an expanded metal target on top, used for ship gunnery practice.

**Williamson turn** • Maneuver used to recover a person lost overboard when the person is not visible. When properly executed, the Williamson turn brings the ship back down the reciprocal of the course being steered when the person was lost.

**williwaw** • Violent squall characteristic of mountainous coasts, particularly the Aleutian Islands.

**winch** • An electric, hydraulic, or steam machine aboard ship, used for hauling in lines, as in boat and cargo lifting. Fitted with a horizontal gipsy or a vertical warping head.

**wind** • Moving air, especially a mass of air having a common direction of motion.

**wind bird** • *Inf:* An anemometer.

**windlass** • Machine primarily used for handling an anchor chain with a drum called a wildcat or chain grab fitted with whelps that engage the links. Also fitted with a warping head, a revolving concave vertical cylinder used for hauling in lines.

**windsail** • Canvas wind catchers fitted with canvas tubes to lead fresh air below.

**wind scoop** • Metal scoop fitted into a port to direct air into the ship for ventilation.

**wind ship** • To turn a ship end for end, usually with lines at a pier, although it may be done with prepared anchors and cables. Thomas MacDonough did this with conspicuous success at the Battle of Lake Champlain, thereby achieving victory at a crucial point in the War of 1812. Pronounced to rhyme with "mind." *See also:* spring; warp

**windward** • Toward the direction from which the wind is blowing.

**wing** • 1. Two or more squadrons (groups) of aircraft or airships. 2. The uncovered ends of the bridge on either side of the wheelhouse or pilothouse. 3. The part of a hold to either side of the square of the hatch.

**wingman** • A pilot who flies formation on another; *i.e.*, on another pilot's wing.

**wire drag** • To explore for uncharted shoals or pinnacles with a weighted wire dragged at a fixed depth.

**wiredrawn steam** • A narrow, dangerous, high-velocity steam jet resulting from a small leak or slightly opened valve.

**wire rope** • Rope made of wire strands twisted together, as distinguished from the more common and weaker fiber rope. Sometimes called a cable or wire cable.

**wireways** • Passageways between decks and along the overheads of compartments that contain electrical cables.

**wiring diagram** • A diagram that shows the connections of an equipment or its component devices or parts. It may cover internal or external connections, or both, and contains such detail as is needed to make or trace connections that are involved. *Inf:* A chart showing command relationships.

**wishbone** • V-shaped supporting rods for the upper accommodation ladder platform.

**wolf pack** • Coordinated attack group of two or more submarines.

**woolly-pully** • *Inf:* Marine Corps green uniform sweater.

**work a ship** • To handle a ship by means of engines and other gear; *e.g.*, to work a ship into a slip using engines, rudder, and lines to piers or wharves.

**working party** • Temporary assemblage of persons assigned to a specific job, such as a stores working party whose job it is to bring aboard necessary supplies before getting under way.

**work request** • The formal application, with detailed information, from a ship to a repair activity, asking that specific work be done. *See also:* job order

**world grid** • A grid dividing the world into 1,000-meter (or yard) squares. Used primarily to designate targets for fire missions.

**worm** • To lay marline or other small stuff between the strands of a rope, preparatory to parceling. A memory aid for the proper procedure is "Worm and parcel with the lay. Turn and serve the other way." *See also:* parcel; serve

**xray** • Phonetic word for the letter X.

**yacht ensign** • A modified ensign flown by yachts, whose dip is answered by men-of-war. May be saluted upon arrival aboard or upon departure from the yacht.

**yankee** • Phonetic word for the letter Y.

**yard** • Spar attached at the middle of a mast and running athwartships, used as a support for square sails. *See also:* Navy Yard; The Yard; naval shipyard

**yard and stay** • Cargo moving rig used by a ship alongside a pier or wharf. Two booms are rigged such that one is positioned over the cargo hatch, the other over the side of the ship. Cargo is then maneuvered by tightening and slacking the lines running between the two booms.

**yardarm** • Either end of a yard, referring to the spar. Mounted perpendicularly on a mast to support sails, signal flag halyards, antennas, etc.

**yardarm blinker** • Signal lights, at the ends of yardarms for all-around visbility, that are keyed from the signal bridge to send morsecode messages to all naval ships within visual signalling range.

**yarn** • 1. Fibers twisted together into strands in the construction of line. 2. A story, as to spin a yarn; meaning to tell a story not necessarily true.

**yaw** • 1. Rotary oscillation about a ship's vertical axis in a seaway. 2. Sheering off alternately to port and starboard while at anchor is called yawing. 3. Motion of aircraft similar to that of a ship—that is, rotary oscillation about the vertical axis. *See also:* heaving; pitch; roll; surge; sway

**yawl** • A small sailing craft fitted with two masts, one of which is a tall mast, generally called the main, and the other is a much shorter one abaft of the rudder post, called the jigger. Sails are fore-and-aft rigged. In appearance, very similar to a ketch, except that the aftermost mast of a ketch is forward of the rudder and often larger than that of a yawl.

**yellow shirts** • Plane directors, aircraft handling officers, catapult officers, and arresting gear officers working on the flight deck of an aircraft carrier; so called because they wear yellow shirts for easy identification. *See also:* blue shirts; brown shirts; grapes; green shirts; purple shirts; red shirts; white shirts

**yeoman (YN)** • Navy occupational rating that performs secretarial and clerical work. YNs greet visitors, answer telephone calls, and receive incoming mail. YNs organize files and operate duplicating equipment, and they order and distribute supplies. They write and type business and social letters, notices, directives, forms, and reports. They maintain files and service records.

**Y-gun** • Depth charge launching device used to propel depth charges laterally away from the side of a ship, thus enlarging the size and effectiveness of the pattern. The Y-gun is shaped like the letter Y and can fire depth charges in two directions—either side of the ship—at once. The K-gun can shoot only one depth charge at a time, in a single direction. *See also:* K-gun

**yoke** • The piece fitting across the head of a rudder, to which the ends of the steering lines or rudder rams are attached. The yoke usually has two arms of equal length across the rudder head, or the vertical rudder shaft, and is almost always at right angles to the line of the rudder, though in modern design it need not be. The helm or tiller is of older derivation and is always in line with the rudder, with a single arm. Past phonetic word for the letter Y; replaced with yankee.

# Z

**zebra** • Past phonetic word for the letter Z; replaced with zulu.

**zenith** • That point of the celestial sphere vertically overhead. *See also:* nadir

**zenith distance** • Used in celestial navigation, the arc of a vertical circle between the zenith and a point on the celestial sphere, measured from the zenith through 90°, for bodies above the horizon. This is the same as "coaltitude" with reference to the celestial horizon.

**zerk fitting** • Small plug to which a grease gun can be applied to force lubricating grease into important parts of machinery.

**Zero Dark Thirty** • *Inf:* The wee hours of the morning or very late at night.

**Z-grams** • *Inf:* Special policy messages originated by CNO Admiral Zumwalt.

**zigzag** • Series of relatively short, straight-line variations from the base course; often used as a means to impede an enemy's targeting solution. *See also:* evasive steering

**zinc** • Metal secured to the underwater body of a ship to counter electrolysis.

**zone inspection** • A thorough inspection of a ship conducted by dividing the ship into practical portions. In times past, commanding officers prided themselves on personally inspecting all spaces of their ships at regular intervals, followed by the inspecting party that made notes of discrepancies found. In large, modern ships this is no longer practicable, so it has been replaced with the zone spection, in which a designated officer is responsible for each zone, with an inspection party. Frequently, the captain will join one of the zone inspection parties.

**zone time** • Mean or civil time fixed for zones, generally 15° in width for both land and ocean areas, with some redesignation for convenience.

**zooplankton** • Animal plankton, as distinct from plant plankton.

**zorch** • *Inf:* Aviator talk for zoom, pass through.

**zulu** • Phonetic word for the letter Z.

# About the Authors

Deborah W. Cutler and Thomas J. Cutler are a husband-and-wife team that has long worked together on books, oral histories, magazine articles, lesson plans, and speeches pertaining to naval matters. Tom's name has appeared on many of these products, while Debbie has worked largely behind the scenes until now. Together, they have worked on such titles as *The Bluejacket's Manual, A Sailor's History of the U.S. Navy*, and *Brown Water, Black Berets: Coastal and Riverine Warfare in Vietnam*.

Debbie is a recognized professional in the field of oral history transcription and developmental editing. Besides his writing, Tom is well known throughout the Navy as a teacher and lecturer, having taught at the U.S. Naval Academy for nine years and currently serving as a Fleet Professor with the Naval War College.